Network
Remote Access

AND MOBILE COMPUTING

Network Remote Access

AND MOBILE COMPUTING

Implementing Effective Remote Access to Networks and E-Mail

Edited by Melanie McMullen

 **Miller Freeman Books**

LAN Networking Library
San Francisco

Miller Freeman Inc., 600 Harrison Street, San Francisco, California 94107
Publishers of *LAN Magazine*, The Network Solutions Magazine
A member of the United Newspapers Group

Cover Design: David Hamamoto
Cover Illustration: Rick Eberly
Illustrations: Rick Eberly

ISBN 0-87930-334-4
Library of Congress Card Number 94-78799
Printed in U.S.A.
94   95   96   97   5   4   3   2   1

Contents

SECTION 5: PERSONAL DIGITAL ASSISTANTS

SECTION 6: CASE STUDIES

Introduction

Computer networks are starting to reach far beyond the bounds of a single office building. Network administrators today have to develop dial-in access for an increasing number of remote offices as well as home-based telecommuters. In addition, the network has to accommodate the traveling employee by offering reliable and easy–yet highly secure–access to data that resides anywhere on the enterprise system.

Establishing remote access can be a daunting task. The network administrator has to determine the needs of the faraway users and outfit the network, as well as the users, accordingly. Critical components include asynchronous communications servers, wide area routers, communication lines, modems, remote e-mail applications, and, in some cases, the portable computers themselves.

On the user's side, the mobile platforms constitute an experiment in cross-platform computing. Roving workers often opt for a variety of dissimilar access tools, including laptops, subnotebooks, and other emerging networking gadgets, such as Personal Digital Assistants. These devices, although very different in form and function, should offer users the same seamless access and functionality that someone sitting at a desktop computer physically linked to the LAN would expect.

This type of seamless connectivity can only be achieved by using the right hardware and software tools both on the network and in the field. To help you determine what those tools should be, the editors of LAN Magazine decided to offer this guide to remote access and mobile computing. To save you from hunting around for articles on the topic, we compiled the magazine's best features and case studies on mobile computing over the last few years into one easy reference book. This information should help you understand everything from wide-area routers to communications servers to remote messaging via e-mail. It also includes a section that offers the latest information on how to become truly portable by going wireless.

Mobile madness in computing has officially begun. And with the proper information and toolset, your network and your nomadic users can be ready to discover the promises of anytime, anywhere connectivity.

—*Melanie McMullen*
Editor-in-chief, LAN Magazine

Section 1
Remote Access

According to recent studies by computer industry analysts, more than 4 million people by 1995 will be working at home. These workers will not likely have the patience for any dial-in grief when trying to access the corporate network. But is your network ready for around-the-clock access from users isolated in remote locations?

Before you begin to establish remote access, you need to have a thorough knowledge of the two most common flavors of software that allow for remote communications: remote control and remote node. These basics are explained in "It's a Remote Possibility" and "Hit the Road, Jack."

From there, you can delve into the more complex issues involved in establishing wide-area links that connect to the network via sophisticated dial-up routers. Other stories in this section point out what to consider if you choose to use the common–and cost-effective–point-to-point links, one of the oldest and most reliable methods of interconnectivity for data applications.

It's a Remote Possibility

NOT ONLY CAN YOU PROVIDE REMOTE NETWORK ACCESS, BUT YOU CAN PICK AND CHOOSE BETWEEN METHODS

BY DAVE BRAMBERT

Just suppose for a moment that you are a parent who wants to work part time, yet would like watch the *kinder* at home, too. Or maybe you've got a ton of work to finish but don't feel like being spooked at the office until after midnight. Perhaps you already have hacked a home office out of a basement niche, among the furnace, oily rags, and caustic chemicals. Or maybe you travel a lot and just need to get inventory information or e-mail in between sales calls.

It's likely that you are one of these people–or at least know someone who is. Telecommuting was the buzzword of 1992. Chances are good that it will continue to be a buzzword, too. In fact, some companies are dictating network nodes be nourished at places other than the office.

For example, several Los Angeles-area companies (notably Rockwell) are putting procedures for remote-access computing into corporate policy: the better to remain "green," and, as a side effect, the better to keep the expressways clear. (Before you faint from this altruism, though, keep in mind that tax breaks are a major incentive.)

According to data from Forrester Research (Cambridge, MA), in 1995 4 million people will be working at home. That estimate may be conservative, however, as more and more North Americans are finding it acceptable to work at home.

Telecommuting assumes a few things:
• The telecommuter doesn't mind having home be the workplace, too. A chance bark by the dog could sour a million-dollar deal.
• The telecommuter is not the twitchy, cabin-fever type.
• There is enough time in the day for dial-in grief (i.e., slow response, the modem burns, telephone lines that have been cut by Mr. Terwilliger when he was tilling the garden, etc.)
• The telecommuter is a self-starter who needs little supervision and can stand the lack of human interaction (although one may build a meaningful relationship with, say, the Fuller Brush man).

Of course, telecommuting 100 percent of the time is only one scenario. Many more people need remote access on a part-time basis.

DIFFERENT FLAVORS

Working at the PC and PC network level, you can implement remote access in one of two ways, depending on which applications you (or your users) need or what type of access you require. You can choose from either remote control or remote node.

In remote control, the remote user dials into a PC, which may or may not be on a network. The remote user in effect takes control of the keyboard of the "host" PC. Keystrokes and screen updates are sent back to the remote PC. The remote user may or may not want to log in to the network. It's almost like when the copilot takes over an aircraft–the pilot's wheel moves in unison with the copilot's, even though the pilot may not be at the controls. The remote PC is, in logical terms, at the end of a long wire that repeats commands and screens.

The processing in remote control is done at the host PC, while the remote PC simply reflects the results through screen updates.

Products in this category include:
• Co/Session from Triton Technologies (Iselin, NJ),

- Close-Up from Norton-Lambert (Santa Barbara, CA),
- Carbon Copy from Microcom (Norwood, MA),
- pcAnywhere from Symantec (Cupertino, CA), and
- ReachOut from Ocean Isle Software (Vero Beach, FL).

In remote node, the remote user dials directly into the network. The remote PC attaches to what is really a dial-in router, which in turn is connected to the file server. A login process must take place before anything else can happen. In logical terms, the phone line is a long cord that attaches the remote PC to its network interface card at the host site. The processing is performed at the remote PC or at the network interface card of the node itself; only IPX packets are shipped across the phone lines.
- Products in this category include:
- LANModem from Microtest (Phoenix),
- NetModem from Shiva (Cambridge, MA), and
- GatorLink from Cayman Systems (Cambridge, MA).

There are also some products that incorporate aspects of remote-node and remote-control technologies, providing the best of both worlds.

WHICH IS BEST?

In general, remote control is considered a speedier solution than remote node. Why? Bill Taylor, manager of network products at Multi-Tech, a Mounds View, MN-based firm that offers several solutions for remote networkers, explains: "In a remote-node scenario, you actually have a node on the network that is connected by an async line to the outside world. When you, as a remote user, request something from the file server, the data is broken up into IPX packets. Let's say those packets have a 512-bit data section. Around that data you need a header and a trailer. You then transmit that packet to the node, which strips off the header and footer, re-encapsulates it, sends it over the wire, and your machine treats it as an IPX packet and rebuilds the information. It's very slow compared to sending screens and echoing keystrokes or mouse moves."

However, some situations–e-mail connectivity for a few outside users or remote file copying, for example–dictate the use of remote node.

So which method is best? "We've noticed that people are confused," states a Novell source. One of the key remote-access products is Novell's NetWare Access Server (NAS), a product that offers remote-control capabilities for a Novell LAN. The NAS offers multiuser remote-control ca-

pabilities by slicing the time on the CPU into increments used by several machines at once.

The Novellian says the challenge for vendors is to get the message out about what's best for a given remote-access situation; it's not a one-size-fits-all proposition. "There is almost a religious war out there. What we're seeking to do is help educate the market in a manner that says it's not a battle; [remote control and remote node] are complementary technologies.

"Some players who have gotten some press have one solution or the other and are touting it as the best solution," observes the source. "It's a disservice to the end-user community."

Remote control is best used, "in traditional applications, such as databases, where the workstation element is requesting a large amount of data be brought over and that the processing be done locally. There are thousands of such applications, and they aren't the thing to run in a remote-node arena." For example, you wouldn't want to run a traditional database in remote node, because in such an application, the entire file comes across the network, and records are chosen from that file. In a remote-node situation, it means the entire file must come across the phone lines, then be processed locally at the remote node, a slow prospect indeed.

However, the network vendor acknowledges that things are changing: "The new client-server technology does the processing at the server, and smaller amounts of data are being sent across the wire. It is very well suited for the remote-node situation."

"One of the things we want to do is to allow the common elements of remote control and remote node to be leveraged on a single platform," the source states. "At my desktop, I might be running Procomm and dialing in to an async host such as CompuServe. When I complete that and release that modem, someone else might want to dial in from home." The next release of NAS will support dial-in and dial-out functions, and Novell will continue to enhance that platform. "In the future," the source reveals, "Novell will provide a platform to allow communication for remote control and remote node. Remote control will be an optional feature for the product.

"We're being put in a position to pick one or the other, but the best solution is a combination of the two–sometimes," the source says.

Other considerations come into play when selecting a technology, says Paul Kraska, product marketing manager at Multi-Tech. "If you have a PC at the remote site controlling a PC on the LAN, you've tied up two PC resources," notes Kraska. "With remote node, you don't need a PC. But with remote node comes licensing problems, for example, with .EXE files. And working with a 10,000-record database in dBase, for example, would be almost impossible. Even if you're using a client-server database, you might have a bandit copy of certain records that have been downloaded and changed, and then reloaded later."

One of the points in favor of remote control, says Kraska, is that you don't have to worry about certain licensing restrictions. "Let's say you have 500 salespeople out there with notebook computers," he says. "You need to have 500 different licenses for your sales automation software out there.

Even if you tried to get around the legal part, you wouldn't save yourself any trouble and might be in for more than you bargained for. All of a sudden, it's six months later, and you want to upgrade to the new version. How do you do it? If you do it legally, you buy 500 new versions. Even if it's your own inhouse-developed software, and you don't need to worry about licensing, you still need to upgrade those 500 programs."

As for Multi-Tech, the company has many solutions and has been in the modem business for a while. One of the most intriguing products is the MultiModemLAN, a product that includes a modem, a CPU, and a network interface card–all in one box. This configuration might seem to many observers an eclectic piece of equipment. It hints at remote node by virtue of its direct network connection (without a "host" PC) but offers the speed of remote control.

REMOTE CONTROL ABOUNDS

The market for remote-control software is healthy and still growing. According to Jim Mulholland, director of marketing at Triton Technologies, "The industry ships about 32,000 to 38,000 units of remote control per month, based on our own information and information from market watchers. That's about 400,000 units per year. The growth rate is still very healthy." Mulholland estimates that the industry will grow by 20 percent to 30 percent yearly.

"We at Triton think that number is about 30 percent.

That means next year, 520,000 units will ship; the year after that, about 675,000 units if the growth holds," he says.

Mulholland estimates that Carbon Copy, pcAnywhere, and Co/Session together comprise more than 90 percent of the market, with the first two occupying about 37 percent each, and his company's Co/Session product garnering 18 percent.

Not surprisingly, Mulholland prefers the remote-control method of remote access. Among the disadvantages of remote node, he reiterates the existence of multiple remote copies of the same .EXE files. As for the benefits of remote control, he says, "You can use hardware for remote access one year, then upgrade those and use the others for fax servers, etc. You can't do that with remote-node products. You can go buy a 386 machine for $900 or less to use as a remote-access point. You're also free to switch remote-access applications if you wish because it's a minimal investment–it's software only."

Who are the people interested in strictly remote control? Mulholland says his company sees two types of users: "Power users and novice users. Two markets are remote support and remote access to applications, where everyone can dial into the network."

Mulholland notes that processes are becoming more automatic or user friendly to accommodate novice users. "One of the key things in computing today is memory management," he says. "On your machine, you can use QEMM and similar products, but it's difficult to expect less-experienced users to know how to load things into high memory. If Co/Session 6.1 detects upper memory blocks, it will load itself there. If it can't, it breaks itself into two pieces–data and program–and tries to load one of those into upper memory. The user doesn't need to know any fancy commands–it's done automatically."

Another trend is modem sharing with remote control. "In 1992, you had modem sharing and remote control separate," he notes. "In 1993, you have both. Maybe next year, people will be able to buy things actually called communications systems." As far as dial-in versus dial-out access, Mulholland puts the ratio at 70-to-30 in favor of dial in for 1993.

Mulholland cites support for 800-by-600 dots-per-inch (dpi) graphics, better performance, less memory usage, better speed and ease of use, and more compatibility as his product goals for 1993.

LET'S SHARE

Tom Cross, chairman of Cross Communications in Boulder, CO, makes the claim to fame that his company was the first to offer integrated dial-in and dial-out capabilities. "If I have two networks," Cross states, "I can dial out through the shared modem, go to the destination LAN, and move to another PC. I don't have to worry about where the modem is on either network."

Think of it this way: You're on LAN A, which has a shared modem, and want to get to LAN B, which also has a shared modem. You can now call from anywhere on LAN A to the modem attached to LAN B and get to any machine (as long as you have the rights to do so).

Some systems allow you to see which machines are available from a menu system. CrossConnect, Cross' software, lets you move to different machines on the destination net. So do Co/Session and US Robotics (Skokie, IL) communications products.

Modem sharing is accomplished through support of DOS Interrupt 14, or in some cases, NASI. Interrupt 14, according to Cross, "is like other interrupts. The history is that IBM's customers wanted to put modems on comm servers. They [IBM] came up with this spec that says when you load your communication software, it looks for COM1, COM2, or Interrupt 14. Our software links the modem to the PC, opens a channel, answers Interrupt 14 requests, and can then link to other things."

CrossConnect is one of the few packages that supports Personal NetWare. It also has integrated faxing and, someday, voice and video, too.

NOW THAT'S DIFFERENT

Each application in the remote-control market has its distinguishing features. In the case of Microcom Carbon Copy for Windows, the name points to the application's main distinguishing trait. It is the only (according to company sources) true Windows remote-access application on the market. Other remote-access products, such as Co/Session and Norton-Lambert Close-Up, do Windows but only from the DOS prompt. Carbon Copy actually launches as a Windows application.

There are certain advantages to a Windows application. "It will allow us to help with collaboration because we have a remote clipboard capability," explains Mark Stover, product manager at Microcom. "It's really an enhanced version of Clipboard that allows you to copy from a guest machine and paste it into the other machine's file. For instance, I can have an Excel spreadsheet, cut something, and paste it into a new spreadsheet on the host machine." The remote clipboard works independently of the Windows-for-Workgroups method of clipboard use, and it includes support for Dynamic Data Exchange.

Another unique feature of Carbon Copy for Windows is that it allows both Novell IPX support and async support in one box. Microcom does not separate its LAN package from its workstation package; it's all there. It supports 1024-by-768 dpi graphics with 16 colors, and the next version will offer the same resolution in 256 colors. The elements that are separate are the DOS version and the Windows version.

Similar plans exist at US Robotics, a manufacturer of modems and other communication products. The company's Shared Access line of products includes the Shared Access LAN Modem (a remote-node-type product) and the Shared Access Communications Server 386.

The comm server is particularly interesting. It includes what US Robotics calls Dynamic Access Switching (DAS), which provides the capability to switch automatically between remote control, single-node routing (remote node), and asynchronous dial-up. It also has a built-in 386SX PC, which makes it similar in concept to Multi-Tech's offering. The modem in the product is v.32bis and is based on US Robotics' Courier modem. It will be upgradable to v.Fast when that standard is standard.

"A few solutions are needed," says Gordon Reichard, product manager at US Robotics. "For less than $1,000, a modem-only [plus software] solution might be the right choice. The Shared Access LAN Modem might be the right choice for a slightly larger office, with one to five users gaining access to the network. But with that product plus the comm server, the software will switch dynamically between operations." Even the Shared Access LAN Modem will do double duty, giving users a shared mode when dialing out.

The comm server itself, says Reichard, is designed for an office with 20 users to 30 users on the road. "No software configuration is needed," he notes, saving administrators time on the remote software side. As opposed to the Novell solution, in which multiple users share a CPU chip, "We dedicate a chip to a user," Reichard states. He also cited an advantage to the Shared Access product line's consistent user interface: Users do not require additional training to use another product in the line.

Like other solutions mentioned, Shared Access allows the remote user to see a menu of available PCs on the network. Through the menu, the remote user can choose which PC to control. This feature is particularly handy, notes Reichard, if the remote user is a support person who needs access to individual machines throughout the network.

A NEW ENTRY

A recent entry in the remote-control sweepstakes is ReachOut from Ocean Isle Software. (The company gets its name from the fact that it's in the Florida Keys. The firm manages to put out product even in such trying circumstances.)

What might give the firm an edge is the fact that it employs the original team of developers for remote-control communications–people such as Jim Kendall (Ocean Isle CEO), Ron Chesley, and Doug Fowler, who were responsible for Carbon Copy in the first place. This trio did the original coding of that product and combined their skills to bring out ReachOut.

Although ReachOut is not a Windows application per se–that is, it is not launched as a Windows application–"it is designed specifically with Windows in mind," according to Bob Decker, Ocean Isle's marketing manager. "It's a whole new way of approaching this industry. The previous technology for DOS just did the entire screen [sending the screen over the wire]. But Windows required a new type of functionality. We were the first to send just screen changes and commands back to the remote PC, instead of entire screens." He backs up the claim by noting they demonstrated the product at NetWorld '91 Boston. But Decker even admits that others have picked up the tactic and now offer similar solutions to the problem.

More important to the user, Decker feels, are security and performance. "We have three levels of security. One is user defined, another is defined by the network administrator, and the third is the basic password." The first level, individual security, allows the host PC to have a database of what Ocean Isle calls Viewers (remote call-ins). Each entry has a password, callback phone number, and file access rights. (The middle component, callback phone number, works when someone dials in, makes a positive identification, hangs up, and waits for the host PC to call back.)

The second level of security is user security. It allows the user of the host PC to define security settings that apply to all Viewers that will connect to the host PC. Features such as access rights, printer-redirection access, disable Viewer keyboard, reboot on disconnect, passwords, confirm access, intruder guard, and audit trail are all part of this second level of security.

The third level is supervisor security. This level is the highest and can override any other security at the user or individual level. Supervisor security covers mostly the same items user security does with the addition of the capability to disable the host-user keyboard.

Like other firms, Ocean Isle will complement its remote-control product with a remote-node product called OutLAN. Although the company is less well known than the competition, it is busy building a distribution network and garnering some prestigious customers, such as Lotus and Compaq.

I SHOULD HAVE NODE

On the remote-node side of the equation, a battle for attention rages. Thus far, Shiva and Microtest have raised the most eyebrows. But other companies, such as Cayman Systems, continue to advance the horizon in remote-node computing.

Cayman's product GatorLink is a remote-node product for the Macintosh environment that supports AppleTalk Remote Access (ARA). ARA is a protocol designed for System 7 or later operating systems and is available from Apple (Cupertino, CA).

But on to GatorLink specifics. It is a three-port ARA server for AppleTalk networks. It supports v.32bis speeds, connects directly to Ethernet with a standard 10BaseT connector, and includes management software. After connecting to the GatorLink, users have access to network services like any node on an AppleTalk network.

Vicky Risk, product manager, says "The primary thing that people use GatorLink for is e-mail. Some people also use it for databases. Any network services you get if you are directly connected, you can get through this product. That includes file transfer, e-mail, database services, scheduling, printing, etc."

Since the remote user has access to any services, that

means that if the host network is connected to a TCP/IP net, the remote user can get those services, too. "A real client-server database would be a good application for this product, perhaps a Unix database. As a remote user, you would just log in on a terminal session." That type of application is not uncommon, for example, in an inventory software situation.

Risk says GatorLink is aimed at the Macintosh market, but, "That will be changing. Our direction is to support PPP (Point-to-Point Protocol) as opposed to ARA. With a PPP server, you can support a number of different operating systems and protocols, such as TCP/IP and IPX, and any network operating system. You could in effect have one server for users with different needs."

Those goals will be met, but it is security that tops network administrators' wish lists, Risk insists. "Network administrators are feeling somewhat rushed by their users to provide remote access. Some users are setting up remote access without bothering about security or checking with their network managers. The managers are worried about back-door holes in their security systems–it's a serious concern.

"There are a lot of things that people want, but if you don't satisfy the security requirement, people won't do it. My sense is that it is a make-or-break issue. However, the problem is that administrators are getting pressure from their users," he continues.

"One of the things we're doing about it is access control, limiting access for dial-in users into certain areas of the network, only certain AppleTalk zones." Risk says Security Dynamics, a Boston-area company that manufactures time-sensitive security cards with LEDs, is assisting Cayman with security. The credit card-sized cards have a number that changes regularly and must match the number of the secured device. GatorLink forwards the information to the security device for validation.

Other differentiating features of the product include the lack of a shell at the remote site. Apple supplies the client software; you don't need any additional software from Cayman. Also, the firm uses flash memory in all of its products. Risk adds, "We have a special CPU, a 68302, specifically designed for ISDN and serial AppleTalk, and three mini RISC processors that handle each serial line. Our throughput is good, since we don't have to interrupt a central processor."

CENTRAL EYES

If you are a network administrator considering different strategies for remote access, you may want to centralize if your company is large enough to warrant it. Centralization would simplify support issues.

Cubix, a Carson City, NV-based manufacturer of comm servers, cites several disadvantages to using regular PCs as dial-in hosts:

1. A regular PC with a monitor and a keyboard invites a security breach.

2. Standalone PCs do not have automatic hardware reset upon disconnect. The next dial-in user may view the previous user's session under certain conditions.

3. A PBX with a hunt group or rotary feature may attempt to select a communications processor that is resetting or non-operational.

4. A regular PC with a monitor and keyboard invites a local operator to use it as his or her own and thus remove it from the communications pool.

5. PC-based communication host systems offer limited third-party management tools that do not include watchdog inactivity timers for automatic reset of hung processors. Therefore, a crashed session requires operator intervention to reset the processor.

6. Multiple PCs take up lots of room and often require special power and cooling.

7. Multiple PCs create cabling management problems.

Remember that these are Cubix' ideas on the subject, but even a critical networker would find it hard to argue with any of the seven points.

John Lillywhite, vice president of sales at Cubix, expanded on some of the ideas. "People can now buy remote control and centralize, which is the way Mr. and Ms. MIS like it to be," he says. "It can be managed and administrated centrally.

"My competition is PCs," Lillywhite adds. "We're hitting the Fortune 100 companies who need 1,000 lines. Think of 1,000 PCs piled up and being used as a dial-in solution. We can consolidate a lot of managed PCs into a small space." Cubix manufactures PCs-on-a-card and cabinets intended to meet the needs of dial-in and dial-out networking.

Lillywhite feels that remote node is a remote possibility in such environments. "As we focus on the big guys," he says, "are you going to buy 1,000 copies of Windows, or however many are concurrently dialing in, or will you have centralized access to the file server?"

Lillywhite mentions the number of concurrent users, and his research says really only 10 percent to 15 percent of all remote dial-in users actually dial in concurrently. What that means is if you have 1,000 users, you may need only 100 licenses. "Take the money for the other 900 licenses and buy laptops!" Lillywhite urges.

The automatic reset feature sets Cubix apart from its PC competitors. "What happens if the host PC hangs? What does the PC do? Nothing. It sits there, and it's sick. You have to get your administrator to reset the host machine while you wait. We look at our carrier-detect signal. When it goes away, it tells us that someone hung up. We tie into that signal, and it triggers a cold boot to our card. If you dial into one of our cards, and the software at the server bombs, you hang up, dial back in, and you can start again."

KEEP YOUR DISTANCE

When it comes to remote access of networks, many different methods—and many different price ranges—exist. First, ask what kind of access your users need. Is it just e-mail and file copying? Try remote node, if there are but a few users. Is it your users' desire to run applications remotely? Perhaps remote control is the method of choice. And if you have a lot of users who need remote access, perhaps a call to Cubix or J&L Communications (Chatsworth, CA) is in order.

You can rest easy knowing that a solution for remote access of your network exists today. We couldn't say that two years ago, but such is progress in the LAN industry.

Hit the Road, Jack

JUST WHEN YOU THOUGHT YOU WERE DELIVERING MAXIMUM NETWORK PERFORMANCE, YOUR USERS WANT DIAL-IN ACCESS WITH MINIMAL DECREASE IN SPEED

BY TOM DOLAN

Faced with skyrocketing demand for mobility and productivity, corporate managers are snapping up their notebook PCs and hitting the road. From homes, hotels, and remote branch offices, notebook PCs echo the call of ET. Using pocket-sized superfast V.Blaster modems, hundreds of new users end each business day trying to phone home.

Meanwhile, back at the LAN, systems administrators cringe at the thought of unmanaged, unsupported, and perhaps even ungrateful remote users piling up telephone bills and frustration trying to make their favorite application run from a remote connection. PC application software was not designed for remote access. But what does that matter? Our users–and their managers–want us to do it anyway.

Think of the irony in this situation. For years, the network industry has concentrated on performance. Whether the topic was "Ethernet vs. Token Ring," or "NetWare vs. LAN Manager," or "which file server to use," the issue of pure speed has always been critical. Now these issues are settled. You have installed the LAN of your dreams. The network provides split-second access times with the maximum bandwidth. Now take that scenario and figure out how to run it through a dial-up data connection that offers 2 percent of the data transfer speed.

Sound impossible? For some applications, it may be. But for most, the converging trends of client-server architecture, faster dial-up modems, and cheaper telecommunications services can provide unique opportunities to deliver remote users highly functional access to the network.

At Price Waterhouse, Office of Government Services, creating a remote LAN shell was the perfect solution. "We were looking for something to let remote users look up, search, and pull down WordPerfect files," says Robert Cameron, manager of technical services. "With the remote LAN connection, the users hit <F5> and see the directory, just as if they were on the LAN."

In his installation, Cameron uses Microtest's (Phoenix) LANModem. Remote users run a version of the NetWare shell on their remote PCs. They connect through a dial-up modem into LANModem. "With LANModem, we eliminated the need for extra computers, and we saved physical space," says Cameron.

Cameron's remote users are consultants who work on federal, state, and local government projects. Their remote LAN connection gives them the proper access for their requirements. Security is maintained because "you don't give access to management utilities. Remote-control software makes it too easy to get full access." In addition, he cites the integration of the remote LAN connection with NetWare security. "The LANModem SETUP software uses the same names and groups as the NetWare names."

While planning to add up to 40 users in 1993, Cameron concedes that the users must have the applications' executable files on their remote PCs to achieve good performance. "With the proliferation of notebooks, these people already have the applications."

OPTIONS FOR THE ROAD

Three strategies are commonly used to provide services to remote PC users: application gateways, remote-control software, and remote-node access of the LAN. The application-gateway approach provides a convenient, highly efficient method of transferring data over dial-up connections. Examples of application gateways are Lotus (Cambridge,

MA) cc:Mail Gateway, Lotus Notes, and Microsoft SQL Server. While efficient, these gateways are application-specific, so they won't provide the whole solution.

A second approach is remote-control software. Strictly speaking, remote-control software is a type of application gateway. Keyboard, mouse, and display I/O are sent over a dial-up connection to the remote PC. In effect, the remote user uses his PC to operate the PC that is back on the desk in the office. Remote control is a nice solution for companies that desire two computers for every employee.

A third tactic is the remote-node method. The remote user is given a connection to the host LAN that is functionally identical to the local connection of a desktop user. The remote node offers full application flexibility. In theory, remote-node operation can be identical to local-node operation, except that the remote notebook connects to the network via a modem and telephone line from the road and the local notebook uses a parallel port adapter and LAN cable.

In remote-node access, the PC dials in and becomes a remote node with full network-layer functionality. It operates as if it were the only node on a remote network that was connected to the host network via a single-user router (or, in some cases a MAC-layer bridge). The remote-node PC is truly a one-user WAN. For example, once remotely connected to a NetWare LAN, the user could type SLIST, see the list of available NetWare servers, and proceed to LOGIN. However, unless the installation has been properly planned, you might want to go to lunch while the LOGIN command executes.

OPINIONS FROM THE ROADHOUSE

"Try WHOAMI in a remote node. It takes 20 seconds," says Paul Kraska, product marketing manager at Multi-Tech Systems (Mounds View, MN). He continues, "It takes a very savvy user to use a remote node, but, if you pick the right applications, you save PCs on the LAN side."

Missionaries for remote-node technology sharply contest the simplistic dismissal of their approach. Bill Miller, chief technology officer and vice president of DCA (Alpharetta, GA), argues at a more philosophical level: "It is socially and corporately unacceptable to be out of touch with the network. E-mail and voice-mail connectivity is essential.

"Compare being on the road to being at work. At the office, you run a terminal emulator to IBM host, e-mail, packaged applications, and networked applications. On the road, you want to get back to the network but not have to use the remote version of the application [because it's different from the local version] or get to the IBM host using different access methods and different services. For MIS, separate arrangements for remote access are security, administration, and equipment nightmares."

Proponents of remote-node technology point to its advantages over remote control. The user has only one set of programs to run, and the remote-access application and the local application essentially work in the same way. When using a remote-node application, security and administration will be simpler since the administrator has to support only one configuration set. The user can run Windows without any special considerations. The need for extra remote-access PCs at the LAN is eliminated. And, the user is more likely to have a high-powered notebook that is his or her sole PC.

David Bolles, CEO of Microtest, summarizes the remote-access application difficulty. "Here's the problem with having one e-mail package for the office and a second package for the remote user: Because of the software developer's internal priorities, the remote products always lag behind the development of the new products. So remote users always have second-rate functionality."

ARCHITECTURAL DIFFERENCE

Bernard Harguindeguy, director of product marketing for Novell's NetWare Systems Group (Sunnyvale, CA), points out that the remote-node concept is not new. This technology is becoming feasible because modems are faster and applications are more carefully designed. "We offered the NetWare remote shell many years ago. Then we realized that most of the applications on the market were not of the type that would work well. They were not client-server-like, so the remote-control environment became the next product."

The earliest issues of *LAN Magazine* didn't talk about client-server. They preached the religion of distributed processing. Under distributed-processing architecture, the PC did all the processing while the server managed access to shared data and services. This model relies on fast data transfer between PC and server.

The client-server model provides an intermediate

server where computing, sorting, and analyzing are separated from the process' user interaction component. This division allows high-bandwidth interaction between the file server and the application server and low-bandwidth interaction between the application servers and the user's PC.

PERFORMANCE ISSUES

Accessing the LAN over a dial-up connection presents two implementation problems. First, the LAN PC is usually configured to use shared-file server services as its primary data storage. All data and program files are retrieved from the server on demand. When using Ethernet, files can be retrieved from the server as quickly as they can be from an internal disk drive. However, when the remote LAN user connects with a 9,600-baud modem, the traffic designed to run at 10Mbps slams into a pipe that is one-thousandth the size. Even the best V.42bis modem improves the ratio to only 200 times slower.

To deal with this limitation, remote users must locate program files on their remote PCs. Most remote users already have these files, since it's pretty hard to work on an airplane if you don't have the executables on your notebook's hard drive. If users have these files, then the data transfer-speed problem becomes an application issue.

Short e-mail messages of 500 bytes to 1MB come over in a second or two. For the user, the question becomes: Will those seconds make up for the inconvenience of using one program for local e-mail and another for remote mail? Is the 35 seconds required to download a 20KB spreadsheet from the LAN more frustrating than dealing with fuzzy mouse response and stuttering pull-down menus in a remote-control Windows environment? Such issues cause zealots to line up and shoot trackballs at each other.

A second performance issue for the remote node deals with the use of a LAN protocol over a WAN connection. As Kevin Hynes, a Certified NetWare Instructor and Novell LANAnalyzer instructor, points out, "IPX traffic is sequenced and acknowledged all the time. It causes a major slowdown over a modem because every packet must arrive at its destination and be processed by the application layer before an ACK [acknowledgement] is returned to the sender. In addition, there is header information that could be viewed simply as overhead. IPX can add anywhere from 30 percent to more than 600 percent more traffic over your communication link."

While acknowledging that point, Harguindeguy says IPX has received "an incredible amount of enhancement," including an NLM for asynchronous access. He predicts additional enhancements in 1993.

DCA's Miller favors taking a long-range view of remote-LAN performance. "It's important not to scare people with the bandwidth issue. Remember when the 9,600-baud modems cost a lot? The bandwidth in WANs is [heading] in the right direction, and the number of client-server applications is increasing."

SOME REMOTE GUIDELINES

The issues of remote-node connectivity can be confusing. Modem manufacturers and suppliers of remote-control software present convincing technical arguments against the practice of extending the LAN to a single remote workstation over a slow dial-up connection. Yet, users of remote systems enthusiastically endorse the simplicity, control, and functionality of their remote-access choice.

Technical selections always depend on the twin considerations–the requirements of users, such as which applications they want to run and which tasks they need to perform, and those of applications, such as hardware compatibility and memory requirements. Here are a few guidelines.

Remote node is the choice for remote users who run Windows or GUI applications for word processing, spreadsheets, and mail. The scale tips toward remote control when users have the applications on their remote PCs, and the connection to the host LAN is used to fetch data files of limited size (less than 200KB). SQL-based, client-server applications are ideal for remote-node applications.

Conversely, heavy file access for sorting or searching can be painfully slow when using a remote-node setup. Programs that perform database inquiry by inspecting one record after another won't perform well; they may even time out. Either use remote access, or switch to client-server.

Sometimes straddling the fence is comfortable. Many users will want to use remote node and switch to remote control when necessary. "Our key objective is to let users decide on remote control and remote node. Let them choose based on the application they need to run," says Novell's Harguindeguy. "However, you will soon see the capability to provide the remote node from both Novell and third parties."

SCORING IN OVERTIME WITH SHIVA

NFL Publications Director of Computer Operations Brian Davis uses superlatives to describe the remote-control and remote-node capabilities of his Shiva (Cambridge, MA) LAN Rover. "Our LAN Rover is a breath-taking device that operates flawlessly," he says. Davis supports an Ethernet LAN with 60 Macintosh nodes using Farallon (Alameda, CA) Timbuktu remote-control software as well as remote-LAN access for mail and publishing applications.

Davis uses an Apple PowerBook and LAN Rover to access the LAN. "It's simpler to use e-mail this way. It makes everything as easy as possible for everyone. Going from package to package is too complicated."

NFL Publications is the division of the National Football League that produces game programs, designs team logos, and manages licensed visuals. Davis uses his LAN Rover to beat time zones on critical deliveries. "After 5 p.m., our New York office can connect to our Los Angeles color printers." Output is sent by overnight mail. Five locations in Southern California plus New York connect regularly using LAN Rover.

In addition, Davis has his production vendors dial in to his network to retrieve images, so his four-color photo separations are always on time. The network also provides direct access for the teams. "The LA Raiders use [our network] to send documents through the LAN Rover to the typesetter. It has freed us up tremendously. They can send to our printers without interrupting us."

Davis also supports many major events with onsite connections. At the Superbowl, Davis sets up temporary operations to support the associated football trading cards show. And from a house trailer next to the Rose Bowl, Davis has full access. "We will do a newsletter onsite, and we need to be prepared to have access to databases."

THE PRODUCTS

What features do you need to consider when installing a remote LAN communications server? Check first for support for your network operating system. Does the unit operate with your version of NetWare, AppleTalk, LAN Manager, or other NOS? You may need to support more than

one network protocol, such as IPX, TCP/IP, and ARP. For flexibility, make sure the product offers dial-in as well as shared dial-out service and remote node as well as remote control. Also you need a physical connection to your LAN–Ethernet or Token Ring are the most popular. Review the security features, and understand how compatible these setups will be with your existing system.

Manufacturers implement technical approaches–designed to improve performance–within the LAN protocol service of the modem component. For example, in the LAN driver, software can be smart enough to compress or eliminate unnecessary header information. Called *tokenizing* or *spoofing,* these techniques remove routing information that is not needed in a one-node connection.

From the pricing perspective, several units priced at less than $2,000 offer everything you need for one or two concurrent connections, including LAN hardware, modem, and drivers. For more than $2,000, you can buy units that support eight or more connections. More expensive systems also include single-board processors to provide the "PC" to a remote-control user.

The manufacturers that provide remote LAN products come to the market with devices that reflect their corporate history. Microtest's LANModem and Shiva's NetModem reflect their companies' focuses on the LAN market. They offer single- and multiple-connection products that provide remote LAN services by extending the LAN protocol to the user over the serial line. Current and future units are available with or without an integrated modem.

US Robotics (Skokie, IL) and Multi-Tech have added remote LAN capability to their modem-based communications servers to create integrated remote LAN, remote-control, and shared-modem servers.

US Robotics Comm Server 386 has an interesting feature called *dynamic access switching,* which allows a user to change from remote LAN mode to remote control. In control mode, the user takes advantage of the internal 386 processor.

DCA Remote LAN Node (RLN) extends Ethernet to remote users at the data-link layer. RLN packages the Ethernet frames for remote travel, and with them, any protocol that runs over Ethernet. Eight- or 16-port units provide Ethernet connectivity, so the user can run IPX, NetBIOS, or TCP/IP protocols without changing the configuration at the RLN server. RLN includes a communications processor, an Ethernet card, and software and is installed in a dedicated server.

IT'S YOUR CALL

The demand for remote connectivity will continue to grow. LAN administrators and planners must understand when to apply each approach. Once the appropriate system is installed, the question will not be "Remote control or remote node?" but will be "Who is going to pay the phone bill?"

Guard the Kingdom

YOU NEED TO EXTEND NETWORK OFFERINGS TO REMOTE USERS, BUT AS YOUR KINGDOM GROWS USING ASYNCHRONOUS COMMUNICATION, YOU MUST GUARD ITS RICHES MORE CAREFULLY.

BY PETER STEPHENSON

Telecommuting has become a fact of life for users and network administrators alike. But while providing users the ability to dial in to the network, you also face a heightened security threat: If your users can dial in, so can intruders.

At the local level, physical controls let you know who's using your network. With dial-in connections, you lose those physical controls. However, if you take the proper precautions to safeguard dial-in connections and avoid taking unnecessary risks, dial-in connections won't leave your network more vulnerable.

In essence, expanding the kingdom–whether through bulletin boards, remote e-mail, or asynchronous communications servers–requires you to guard it a bit more closely.

ACCEPTABLE RISK

Before you can accomplish the dual goals of letting in users with minimum effort and reliability while keeping intruders at bay, you must examine your network configuration–What does your network look like and for what purposes do you need to establish dial-in connectivity? More specifically:

• What applications do your users need to access? Are you connecting two facilities?

• How many subnets does your network have? How many servers? How are the subnets interconnected?

• Where does the information reside–on a workgroup server or on a central file server? Does it make sense to isolate critical data or should all data be available to everyone?

Every dial-in communications method carries risks, but not all share the same risks. Examining your network configuration and the purposes of remote connectivity will prevent you from unnecessarily exposing your network–installing remote-control software when all your users really need is remote e-mail, for example.

If you need to isolate information on a network without dial-in access, that need will undoubtedly increase with dial-in; establishing access rights alone might not provide enough security when files are scattered across your volumes. You can attain the next level of security by isolating information, or partitioning–creating separate volumes on your servers for critical or confidential information. However, this approach is not as secure as setting up a separate file server for restricted use.

In most cases a server can be made "invisible" to users without rights to it. You can configure the dial-in gateway to ignore the server's presence unless the caller has specific rights. Legitimate users who become disgruntled or just plain curious (the biggest percentage of unauthorized accesses) don't know the server is there and so don't try to access it. The second best bet, using a separate volume, can have a similar benefit. Both methods, however, force administrators to keep restricted files in their proper locations. If the secure volume or server is designated as the only approved location for such files, that is where they'll probably go. So, apart from providing an operational benefit, creating a separate server offers an administrative tool for keeping everything in its place.

If your risk assessment reveals that you don't want to allow any access from outside to certain files, be aware that such a decision has operational implications. Isolating sensitive files from any outside access will prevent even legitimate users from accessing them from home or on the road. You may decide that such an approach is acceptable, however.

Determining what files you want to allow access to, who you want to be able to access them, and how to partition your network to accommodate those requirements are your first steps toward secure dial-in.

A SENSE OF PURPOSE

Determining acceptable risk, in turn, has to do with how the information on your network is going to be used. Several remote-access methods are available. Some of the simplest, such as remote e-mail connections, can be fairly secure out of the box, without any additional protection measures. Others, such as remote-control access, including (Ocean Isle Software, Vero Beach, FL) and pcAnywhere (Symantec, Cupertino, CA), may require additional security considerations.

You should match your remote-access solutions to the way your organization does business. While for all remote access regardless of method, the hardware technology may be essentially a modem and a communications server, what drives the connection is the application and the business needs of the organization.

At the simplest level, asynchronous connections fall into two categories: fixed and dial-in. *Fixed*, or *nailed, circuits* are dedicated lines that connect two nodes and only two nodes. These circuits are not accessible by outside dial-in since they are full-time connections, open between the end points at all times. Once the connection is made, unless it fails, the circuit is in operation 24 hours a day, seven days a week. By its dedicated nature, the nailed circuit is relatively secure.

Dial-in circuits themselves fall into two categories: dedicated and ad hoc. *Dedicated dial-in circuits* are circuits the organization has designated as point-to-point connections. For example, a distributed database application running between two sites might make a dial-up connection several times a day to exchange and update databases. However, no user is intended to access the servers directly over the dial-up number. The connection is not fixed because the process dials in, updates the information, and hangs up. In contrast, an *ad hoc connection* provides users with random access to network resources.

Several other applications fit into the asynchronous server domain as well. For example, there are mission-crit-

ical applications, such as distributed databases, and workflow applications, such as Lotus Notes and Electronic Document Interchange (EDI) as well as fax gateways that allow users to send and receive faxes from the desktop.

KEEP IT SAFE

What security issues arise on asynchronous circuits? Simply, they fall into three categories: access control, data protection, and protection against rogue code (viruses, Trojan Horses, worms, and so forth). Virtually all security issues boil down to intrusion protection whether the attack is leveled at the data or at the system. Even rogue code attacks may be considered simply a special kind of intrusion. Thus, when protecting network assets, your No. 1 strategy is to protect against intrusion.

Once you've decided what network assets need to be accessed from outside, how data is compartmentalized, and what your general asynchronous requirements are, develop a protection strategy. The protection strategy is based on answers to all those questions.

To begin to devise a strategy, create a simple matrix. The matrix consists of a list of remote-access requirements and a list of approaches to security. One benefit of this technique is that you can simultaneously evaluate the security issues and the connectivity requirements of your system. To use the matrix, simply insert your remote-access requirements along one axis of the matrix and potential security precautions along the other. Then place a check mark in each applicable box. Some remote-access methods may require more than a single precaution and might receive checks in several columns.

Once you have built your matrix and determined what assets, functions, and processes will be carried out remotely as well as the desired methods of protection, you can start thinking about how to implement both the requirements and the protection. Your final planning task is selecting the hardware and software to complete the plan.

WHAT DOES WHAT

Several techniques are available for protecting an asynchronous system. They fall into two broad categories: administrative controls and technological solutions. If you would employ an administrative control technique on the LAN directly, you should usually employ the same technique as a baseline for remote access.

As discussed earlier, administrative controls include the partitioning of volumes and establishing separate file servers. Such controls would also include establishing passwords and password requirements, such as length and number of attempts before lockout.

While in most cases, any controls that you establish for the network as a whole should be applied to the system once remote access is added, there are some exceptions. For example, if you have a five-character password requirement on the LAN, according to the rule, you should have at least the same requirement on the network with asynchronous access capabilities. But in some cases, you will want more stringent controls for remote access.

In the case of connections that are not intended for human use, such as interprocess connections, distributed databases, and unattended file transfers, you will want significantly more protection. For such communications, you might want to increase the password length from five characters or seven characters to 10 characters or 15 characters.

Why? Baseline administrative controls implemented on the network might not be practical for dial-in application. For example, three failed password attempts might result in a lockout for users. But if the same lockout guidelines were employed for dial-in access, an entire process could be shut down by an intruder attempting to break the password. Increasing the password length beyond that which is practical for people (remembering and typing a 15-character password is inconvenient for users) is an excellent way for processes to communicate securely even though the lockout provision has been disabled. Processes have no trouble remembering and typing long random passwords, but they are extremely difficult to discover by intruders. Traditional password-guessing techniques become essentially useless in the face of long random passwords.

Other administrative techniques are dedicated file servers for sensitive information, dedicated volumes, dedicated communication servers, and nailed communication circuits. Other administrative controls include encryption, extended passwords (either more characters or multilevel), and isolated subnets. For e-mail systems, applications such as Lotus cc:Mail which requires off-line mail readers for remote access also limit direct on-line user interaction over dial-up links.

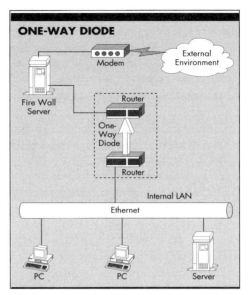

FIGURE 1: A one-way diode is a type of fire wall that provides a high level of security since it allows communication in only one direction.

TECHNOLOGICAL CONTROLS

Once you've exhausted administrative controls, you may need to throw some technology at the problem of access control. Depending on your requirements are, you might consider several solutions from the hardware/software protection category.

General-purpose asynchronous communications servers do not usually provide any access control. You will probably have to add capabilities to achieve protection. However, some specialized servers do provide access control. For example, CentrumRemote from Centrum Communications (San Jose, CA) offers passwords and dial-back capability. Many modems and communications packages also offer dial-back support. Adding dial-back modems or other dial-back products such as TraqNet from LeeMah Datacomm Security (Hayward, CA) can enhance general-purpose asynchronous communications servers for reliable security.

Dial-back systems provide a simple, relatively low-cost way to secure a dial-up link between processes or within applications. Using a dial-back system, remote users call the system they want to dial into and authenticate themselves to it. The system hangs up and calls the user back. Thus the user must not only know the proper information for authentication to occur, he or she must also be in the correct location. In this way, dial-back systems create the illusion of a nailed circuit. Should an intruder manage to discover an interprocess password, attempts to defeat the dial-back system would be futile.

For road warriors who cannot be at the same phone for each call, dial back can be difficult. Solutions such as LeeMah's InfoKey system or InfoCards help make dial-back access control useful even when the system cannot actually dial the caller back. InfoKey is a device used on the remote end to establish an encrypted dialogue with the LeeMah TraqNet device on the network. The dialogue is based on passcodes and hardware-embedded serial numbers. Unless the dialogue progresses successfully, TraqNet will not allow the network and the remote PC to connect, much less communicate.

LeeMah's InfoCard and Cambridge, MA-based Security Dynamics' SecurID are personal tokens that create dynamic passcodes used in place of passwords. The passcodes are created in the card based on such constants as serial numbers and PIN numbers. The card-generated passcode must match the code generated at the host or network end, otherwise the connection will not be made. Since some variable, such as time of day, is included in the passcode-generation algorithm, the passcodes, unlike fixed passwords, are almost impossible to guess.

An important addition to the dial-in tool kit is data encryption. Of course, passwords should always be encrypted, but, especially if cellular modems are in use, all data should be considered for encryption during transmission. And digital signatures are useful authentication methods because they may be applied to an entire message or to single packet. Once you identify a message or groups of packets as authentically yours, a digital signature system appends your signature to the packet. Once the packet arrives at its destination, the software looks back to make sure the signature it carries matches the original.

HIGH-RISK ACCESS

Interprocess communication, access to dedicated applications such as e-mail, and access to dedicated servers such as fax servers may be fairly easy to protect using the methods discussed thus far. Direct access to the network using remote-control or remote-node software is a different matter entirely.

If the majority of applications running on the network are graphical or Windows-based, you will probably want to use remote-node access methods to connect your road warriors. Remote-node software sets up the remote PC as a node on the network using the asynchronous link as a means of moving the transport protocol, such as IPX/SPX for NetWare, packets. The remote user gets a similar response to what he or she would get if connected to the network locally.

Certainly, LAN disk access will feel a bit slower and data searches and loading applications will also be lower performance due to the relatively low asynch speed, but Windows screen redraws, mouse/cursor movement, and the appearance of characters on the screen as the user types will feel nearly normal. As a node, the remote PC acts as it would if connected locally. The remote node executes functions using that machine's memory.

Remote-control software, on the other hand, executes the application's program in the memory of a gateway machine on the local network and ships screen and keyboard information back and forth over the remote connection. The two PCs (gateway and remote) must stay in synch, and the remote PC's response time is limited. The result is poor performance and a jerky display. However, on text-based applications with little need for complex screen redraws, remote control can be a good bet.

What about the security issues using these two types of dial-in, ad hoc access? Anyone who knows the phone number of the modem can attempt access, and finding the phone number of a modem requires little effort. Applications called "war dialers" are a favorite tool of dial-in crackers. Sophisticated war dialers, such as Toneloc (a shareware program found on underground BBSs), can tell the difference between a modem, fax, and PBX.

Crackers use war dialers to locate modems and PBXs as a prelude to attempting an intrusion. The war dialer can be set up to dial all the numbers in a particular group using a number mask. That means that a cracker could attempt to call all the numbers in an area code, a single exchange, or some subset. The dialing is usually done late at night when most numbers will be unmanned.

The war dialer dials a number. If it answers or keeps ringing, the program hangs up and moves on to the next. If, however, the dialer encounters a tone, it records the phone number and the type of tone in a database for later investigation by the intruder. War dialers don't dial numbers in any particular order, so they are very hard to trace.

The net result is that hiding your modem phone number by not listing it is of virtually no use in protecting your system from intrusion. Both remote-control and remote-node programs offer some basic system protections.

Traditionally, remote-control programs have offered the least protection since theoretically all you need to gain access is another copy of the program. However, most remote-control program developers will make agreements with corporate customers to create specially serialized versions. The remote software won't connect (handshake) successfully with the LAN gateway software unless they are of the same serial number group; only company-owned copies can connect.

Remote-node software is somewhat more secure. When the remote node attempts to log in, it will be treated as if it were a local node. The usual network ID and password will be required. Remote node uses a gateway similar to those used for remote control, except that remote-control gateways are actually executing the network application. Remote-node gateways are true gateways in the sense that they provide a communications connection only. Thus remote-node gateways can often be set up with fire walls that prevent access to the gateway until proper authentication has occurred.

USING FIRE WALLS

Using fire walls offers the greatest security for dial-in access. In a building, a fire wall separates portions of the building to prevent the fire from spreading. If a fire starts in one part of the building, it cannot spread past the fire wall and so is contained to a manageable area.

Network fire walls perform the same function. Equipped with "fire doors" that permit legitimate users to pass between portions of the network, these fire walls stop the spread of an intrusion before it can reach the network. Fire walls are among the few techniques for protecting a network with Internet connections.

The key to an effective fire wall is the presence of a gap between internal and external worlds. The gap can't be bridged unless proper authentication occurs. The gap, then, should be very robust. An ID and password don't constitute such a gap since they are, at best, a lock on a door to the network. Unlocking the door gets you into the network. A fire wall must be a solid barrier. Breaking down the barrier gets you nowhere since no bridge has been placed across the gap. Breaking down the barrier does little more than drop you into the gap between worlds.

Typical fire walls consist of hardware similar to bridges or routers that contain two interface cards. One card communicates with the outside world while the other communicates with the local network. The cards could both be NICs or could be a combination of a NIC and an asynch card. Software or firmware prevents the two cards from communicating until authentication requirements have been satisfied. Routing tables and sophisticated filters can add to security by limiting the type of remote connection allowed. Attempts to break down the fire wall do not result in a connection between the two hardware components and, therefore, do not provide access to the network.

A special kind of fire wall is a *one-way diode*, essentially a pair of routers that allow communication in one direction only–from the local network to the outside. No communication is allowed from outside in (see Figure 1). This approach is suited only to situations where, either, dial-out is the only requirement, or applications can reside on an application server outside the diode.

A good example of diode use is connection to the Internet. Suppose an organization wants Internet access to exchange mail and access Internet resources but does not want any user on the Internet to be able to access the internal network. The diode would be placed between the internal network and the Internet node. Users on the internal network could connect out to the node to collect mail and access Internet resources, but Internet users could not get beyond the node. The internal network is protected, but full Internet functionality from the local organization perspective is available.

In high-risk environments, adding dial-back, token, or InfoKey protection to provide true authentication will enhance fire walls. All authentication provides identification, but identification is not, necessarily, authentication. Nowhere is this concept more important than on dial-up circuits.

Identification can be spoofed. Password guessing and other masquerading techniques allow an intruder to pretend to be a legitimate user and gain access to the network. Authentication, however, provides positive identification by adding additional identification requirements beyond ID and password. Personal tokens, dial-back, and InfoKeys require that in addition to ID or PIN number–information the user knows, a random, token-generated passcode–something the user possesses in the form of an InfoKey, for example–or fixed location (the dial-back) be available.

The familiar ATM card issued by most banks provides an example of authentication. Without both the PIN (something you know) and the card itself (something you possess) you can't use the automatic teller machine to get money out of your account.

THE BOTTOM LINE

Protecting an asynchronous circuit can be a bit more complex than meets the eye. The key to good protection is the astute mix of business requirements, administrative security on the LAN, and access controls appropriate to the needs of the organization.

Generally speaking, do not allow too much or unnecessary access from outside. A good approach is to establish access rights based on the user's need to know. Simply being the boss does not, for example, imply universal need to know. Set common need-to-know, general-access rights at a level that protects information but does not unnecessarily restrict general, authorized users. From there, add protection in proper proportion as the sensitivity of the assets being protected increases.

Use fire walls where appropriate to protect easily accessed systems from uncontrolled connections. Add positive authentication for access to especially sensitive assets or to where a free run of the network could be the result–as with Internet access.

Finally, wherever possible, consolidate access gateways into modem pools or multiport communications servers and, wherever possible, audit all incoming and outgoing connections. A good audit trail can help you discover security holes and will also help recreate an intrusion to analyze it and recover from damage.

Today's protection technologies coupled with administrative controls within network operating systems can make external access safe. However, you must analyze your requirements thoroughly and apply the appropriate measures. If you do those two things, you can use the electronic highways that are making our world a single electronic village with minimal risk to your organization's valuable data.

The Route To Linking WANs

LEARN HOW TO AVOID PROBLEMS IN NETWARE ROUTER DESIGN AS YOU ADD WIDE-AREA LINKS TO YOUR NETWORK.

BY HOWARD MARKS

In Networking 101, a you learned the difference between a bridge and a router. Bridges connect Ethernet to Ethernet or Token Ring to Token Ring: They work at the data-link layer of the OSI model. Routers are smarter. They work at the network layer–OSI layer 3–so they don't just blindly forward packets. Routers look inside the network MAC-layer packet for a destination address from a network layer. Routers, unlike bridges, are responsible for knowing the route that a data packet should take to get from network No. 1 to network No. 34.

One of NetWare's strengths has long been its ability to link several separate local area networks through its built-in routing functions. Most large NetWare networks are really a collection of interdependent LANs linked by NetWare routers. NetWare's built-in routing is simple to install and best of all it comes free with every copy of NetWare.

Welcome to Networking 202, where you learn that as great as a routable network-layer protocol can be, it's not perfect–especially if you're including wide-area links. Transmission rates suffer significantly under such circumstances. In this test drive, I look at several products that offer solutions to some of the difficulties in routing the NetWare Core Protocol (NCP), particularly over WAN links. The Newport LAN2LAN Mega and Eicon Router for NetWare are combination hardware and software solutions to link NetWare routers to phone lines or X.25 networks. Novell's MultiProtocol Router is a platform for these connections or a local router that connects the home-office worker to the corporate network.

WHY IS IT SO HARD?

NetWare's protocols were originally designed for use on relatively small local area networks of workstations and file servers with limited memory and processing power. The NetWare protocols were therefore designed to be small, fast, and not too demanding on the workstation's processor. Some of these design decisions, while advantageous for LANs, become problematic as the network grows, especially if wide-area links are included.

The first problem is that Novell's NCP is an request? inquire/response or "ping-pong" protocol. When a NetWare workstation requests a large data transfer, like a file read or program load, from a NetWare file server, NCP sends a single data packet to the workstation and waits for a response before sending the next data packet. On a LAN, this protocol is very efficient; only lost packets need be retransmitted and only minimal workstation memory is needed to store a single packet.

However, as you expand the network by adding WAN links, the latency caused by the distance between the file server and a workstation renders this protocol significantly less efficient. Data travels through a cable at a fixed velocity so just as it takes you five hours to fly from New York to Los Angeles, longer if you go through O'Hare, it takes a certain amount time for your data to go from point A to point B, and longer if there's a stop.

As a basic design requirement on an Ethernet network, the first bit of each packet must reach the most distant station before the transmitting station sends the last bit. At most, this would take 10 microseconds to 15 microseconds. On a New York-to-Los Angeles WAN link, this transmission would take at least a thousand times longer–15 milliseconds to 50 milliseconds depending on the propagation delay of the telephone company's switching equipment.

A line with 15 milliseconds of latency can carry only 33 data packets and their acknowledgments per second, even if the phone line's speed capacity is unlimited. If each packet is a 1KB Ethernet packet, a T-1 line will be transmitting data only 6 percent of the time. Of course each NCP session has its own outstanding acknowledgment window so each user can send 33 packets per second.

This ping-pong protocol made NetWare all but unusable over satellite links. After all, getting data from New York to Boston, about 200 miles overland, through a satellite means sending it 24,000 miles to the satellite and 24,000 miles down from the bird for total latency of about half a second.

To add insult to injury, NetWare only sends a 512B IPX packet just in case one of the networks on the path cannot handle larger packets. The maximum data transfer rate for a single workstation with 512B packets and the NCP protocol is just 16KBps or 133Kbps.

Novell has addressed these problems by introducing two enhancements to the NetWare protocols. The most significant of these, the erroneously named "burst-mode IPX," actually modifies the workstation-to-file server NCP protocol to allow up to 64KB to be sent with a single acknowledgment. Using burst-mode IPX, WAN performance can improve 2 percent to 500 percent.

To use burst mode, you load the packet-burst NetWare loadable module (NLM) in a NetWare 3.11 file server and use the BNETX shell at each workstation. The NLM and BNETX shell are available on CompuServe as part of the packet signature NetWare security enhancement. (Note that the first release of the BNETX shells, version 3.26, didn't work reliably with Microsoft Windows. Version 3.31 is supposed to fix these problems.)

Large-packet IPX, formerly available only within the NetWare MultiProtocol Router but now available within the packet-burst version 2.0 NLM, allows routers to negotiate the largest packet size that all routers and networks in the path can handle. Then the system will send packets using this largest packet size rather than the default of 512B. If all networks in the path are wide-area links or Token Rings, packet size can increase to 4KB.

Large-packet IPX reduces the packet header and trailer overhead, and more importantly the effect of packet propagation delay through each router, to improve workstation performance.

Using standard IPX- and NetWare-based routers, you can expect a performance loss of 30 percent to 50 percent for each router your data crosses between workstation and file server. Using large-packet IPX and burst mode, this degradation will be as low as 20 percent. High-performance RISC-based and multiprotocol routers from Cisco (Mountain View, CA) and Wellfleet (Bedford, MA) can reduce this performance loss even further.

LIVING WITHIN MEANS

The biggest problem you're going to face isn't installing the routers or the performance loss crossing routers but tuning your application to live with the limited bandwidth of affordable telephone lines. Even simple acts like logging in to your file server can transfer hundreds of kilobytes of data across your wide area network.

Several types of lines are available for LAN-to-LAN connections. Standard leased lines are pretty much universally available for a fixed monthly charge at data rates of 56Kbps and 1.544Mbps (the T-1 line). Fractional T-1 service is available in some areas at data rates of 128Kbps, 384Kbps, and 512Kbps. Often local telephone companies will force you to purchase a full T-1 line to the long distance carrier's point of presence at the central office. In most areas, 56Kbps services are also available as a Switched (that is dial-up) service, at rates just slightly higher than those for voice lines; in other areas, Switched 56Kbps service is significantly more expensive.

In addition to using point-to-point and dial-up links, you can also take advantage of packet-switched networks using the X.25 protocol especially in international networks where point-to-point leased lines are prohibitively expensive if available at all. Unfortunately X.25 networks add a large and unpredictable amount of latency as packets can make several stops at intermediate points on their way from point A to point B.

Much of the delay is caused by the error checking that takes place at each intermediate node on an X.25 network. Frame relay, a new WAN technology, is available from WillTel and will soon be available from the major long distance carriers and X.25 vendors. Frame-relay networks take advantage of the high reliability of modern digital phone lines by error-checking only once a packet has arrived at its final destination. If an error is detected, the packet must be re-sent from the origin. Because the error rate is usually low, frame relay reduces the latency added by X.25.

SOME SOLUTIONS

The products in the following test drives each address some aspect of solving the problem of connecting multiple LANs. You should note that all of the products reviewed will perform better in a faster PC. Routers should be 486- or 486SX-based machines.

Since NetWare routers don't do any floating point math, a 33MHz 486SX is just as good as a 33MHz 486DX. Heavily used local LAN-to-LAN routers will get a performance boost by using a high-speed bus—either EISA or MicroChannel. Since even the ISA bus is fast enough to keep up with a T-1 line, routers serving a remote link need not be the more expensive EISA machines.

Additionally, the following tips will help you maximize WAN performance:
• Put all programs remote users will need on local hard disks or local servers. Loading programs across a low-speed link is intolerably slow.
• Keep all search paths limited to local drives and servers.
• Attach, as opposed to logging in, to remote servers to avoid running the remote login script. A remote login script may cause files to be loaded across the WAN and reset paths to the remote server.
• Convert dBase and other traditional DOS applications to use database servers. Client-server applications require 10 times to 1,000 times less data be transferred.
• Use low-speed lines, up to 56Kbps, for file transfers, electronic mail exchange, remote administration and other noninteractive applications.
• Use data compression where available.
• For multiple sites, look into frame relay as a less expensive alternative to private lines.
• Use high-speed lines–256Kbps and faster–for multiple real-time database access stations. Client-server technology will allow use of 56Kbps to 128Kbps lines.
• Use large-packet transfer when available.
• Use burst mode except with slow lines and small packet sizes.

BIG RED ROUTER

Novell NetWare MultiProtocol Router

NetWare system administrators won't be surprised by anything in the NetWare MultiProtocol Router's big red box. They'll find a copy of NetWare Runtime, a special one-user version of NetWare 3.11 and an assortment of tools and NLMs to help manage the network. The most significant of these additional programs are the NLMs needed for routing the AppleTalk, TCP/IP, and OSI protocol stacks. These NLMs are generally available only as parts of the NetWare for the Macintosh and NetWare FTAM (file transfer access method) products at extra cost.

The NetWare MultiProtocol Router (NetWare MPR) is closely integrated with Novell's WAN Links products Link/X.25 and Link/PPP. Like the Eicon Router for NetWare and Newport LAN²LAN Mega, Novell's WAN Links products are made up of a high-speed synchronous communications card, which Novell OEMs from Newport for the Link/PPP, and NetWare drivers for the card. Most of the protocol enhancements and management utilities are in the NetWare MPR, which is required to run WAN Links.

Installing and using a NetWare MPR is just a little different from installing a typical NetWare file server. Once you've performed the typical NetWare installation loading the public and system files through the INSTALL NLM, you load the NetWare MPR as a product option, which requires loading the BTRIEVE NLM. Rather than have you enter LOAD and BIND commands into the file server's AUTOEXEC.NCF file, as you would for a typical file server installation, the NetWare MPR comes with the INETCFG installation program, which uses the familiar NetWare menu user interface to allow you to configure LAN and WAN interface cards.

The INETCFG utility stores its configuration information in a Btrieve database and, through the INITIALIZE SYSTEM command you add to your AUTOEXEC.NCF, loads the drivers for each card and binds the appropriate protocols. When you load INETCFG, you first use the LAN and WAN Board Parameters menu to add drivers for each LAN or WAN card in your router. You can then select a driver and enter the card configuration. You have to enter the card configuration parameters just as you'd type them if you were entering the load command for the driver. If Novell is going to go as far as making you use this utility to set up your cards, it should work the way the JUMPERS utility does, letting you choose values for interrupt and other parameters from a list.

When you get to the list of LAN cards and press INSERT you'll get a list of the LAN drivers that are in the SYS.SYS-

TEM directory. While this list makes life simpler if you're using a LAN card that's supported with the set of drivers that come with the NetWare runtime package, it makes things more difficult if you use cards, such as the Intel EtherExpress 16s or SMC Elite 16s (as I do), with drivers provided by the card manufacturer. To set up a third-party driver, put the driver diskette in the server drive, type LOAD A:DRIVER, bind IPX to the driver, log in as supervisor from a workstation, copy the driver from the workstation to the SYS.SYSTEM directory, unload the driver, and then run IN-ETCFG.

One advantage of this method of router configuration is that a single LAN card can be configured as multiple virtual LAN cards each using a different packet type. This features allows you to route AppleTalk traffic in ETHER-NET_SNAP packets and NetWare traffic in Ethernet_802.3 packets through a single NE2000 card.

After you set up the cards, you can select which protocols the router should forward and configure the parameters for each protocol. The NetWare MultiProtocol Router includes version 2 of the PBURST NLM which now includes the large-packet IPX enhancements. Additional enhancements include a Reliable parameter, which causes the NetWare MPR to filter out repetitive SAP and Routing Information Protocol (RIP) packets. In a large network with wide-area links, this repetition can eat into the available bandwidth. If you load the optional SAHANDLE NLM, you can also configure a router to not pass SAP packets at all.

SAP filtering makes managing a large internetwork easier by allowing you to segment it into separate regions. That way users in New York don't see file servers and print servers in Los Angeles. Using the SAHANDLE NLM you can configure the router to filter specific types of SAPs and pass others. The only downside to SAP filtering is that, since the NetWare shell will attach only to a file server known at the default server, logging in to a server that is really part of another region is a multistep process.

TCP/IP AND APPLETALK

The TCP/IP protocol stack can be configured as an end node or router on the network. You can configure the TCP/IP routing functions to use static routing tables you've built, or to use the IP RIP, with or without "Poison Reverse" to create dynamic tables. You can also configure parameters as the cost of each link, and since RIP only

crosses links that cost 15 or less, you can filter RIPS by setting link costs.

If you're using the Multiprotocol Router to carry traffic across a TCP/IP backbone, the NetWare MultiProtocol Router will tunnel, or encapsulate, IPX packets within TCP/IP packets.

The AppleTalk router supports both Phase 1 and Phase 2 of the AppleTalk protocol stack and can perform transition routing. The NetWare MPR also comes with the AT-CON program, an AppleTalk diagnostic utility.

The documentation for the NetWare MPR is more of the same bland Novell speak. It would be much better with a few screen shots and clearer demarcation of which functions apply only to WAN Links.

The NetWare MultiProtocol Router is ideal for midsize networks that don't need the performance of an enterprise router like a Cisco or Wellfleet. At $995 it's significantly less expensive and gives you the opportunity to integrate other NLM-based services like managed hubs.

MEGA SIMPLICITY
Newport System's LAN²LAN Mega

Larry Stevenson and the folks at Newport Systems Solutions are old hands at making NetWare networks talk across wide-area links and their current LAN²LAN Mega shows that experience has paid off. Of the products reviewed, this product was the simplest to install and configure.

The LAN²LAN Mega, like the Eicon Router for NetWare, is primarily a high-speed synchronous serial interface card, Newport's network interface card (WNIC), which Novell has resold on an OEM basis for the past few years, and drivers that make the WNIC card look like a LAN card to NetWare. LAN²LAN Mega comes with drivers for NetWare 2.x-based servers, NetWare 3.x-based servers, as well as LAN²PC Mega, a driver for workstation IPX.

LAN²PC is a good tool to keep in your bag of tricks for WAN application design. With a typical remote router solution, a field office with a single PC would need to install a second PC to be a dedicated router to connect to the WAN. The worst offender I've seen is IBM's Data Interpretation System (DIS), which requires three 386-based PS/2s at the remote site to support a single user. With LAN²PC, that single PC can connect to the file server through services like Switched 56Kbps DDS (AT&T's Digital Data

Phone Service). You'll have to dial manually as Newport doesn't support any of the proprietary dialing protocols for DSUs (data service units).

A WNIC uses 64K of memory, either upper memory blocks (UMBs) or extended memory, which can be shared by multiple WNICs, an interrupt and a block of eight I/O ports. WNIC cards are available for both the ISA and MicroChannel buses. On the ISA card, the base I/O address is set using a three-position DIP switch; the memory address and interrupt are software controlled.

For users whose pockets aren't quite deep enough for T-1 lines, linking offices using Newport's data compression module is a big help. The data compression module plugs into the WNIC as a daughter board and compresses all data sent across the wide-area link. While the actual throughput of the line varies with the type of data being transferred, bitmapped graphics can be compressed more than executable programs can be, for example. The LAN2LAN Mega's data compression module averages about a 4-to-1 compression ratio on typical LAN data.

The data compression option makes 56Kbps lines at least usable for some more interactive applications. Unfortunately the processor in the data compression module isn't fast enough to keep up with a full T-1 line. In fact, Newport doesn't recommend using it on lines that are faster than 128Kbps.

Another performance-boosting feature is load balancing. The LAN2LAN Mega will automatically route packets to multiple ports on the same card in a round robin fashion sending one packet through each port in turn, which makes two low-speed links look like one faster link. If you have a T-1 line connecting just two sites and you're using part of that line for LAN traffic, you can get better performance using two logical lines rather than one.

If you choose not to use data compression, you can plug a two-port expansion unit into the same daughter board socket on the WNIC increasing the number of ports on the WNIC to four. Since a WNIC has only one daughter board socket you can have two ports with compression or four without.

Newport continues to use security PALs (programmable array logic chips) on the WNIC cards. LAN2LAN Mega looks for a card with the primary PAL, if you want to use the cards you got from Novell, you'll need to get a new PAL or use them as secondary cards.

LAN2LAN Mega supports line speeds from 1200bps to E-1 speed (the European equivalent of T-1, or 2.048Mbps). A single WNIC card can handle an aggregate 2.048Mbps across all its ports. Newport supports X.25 and point-to-point links. Newport has promised frame-relay support in a future version.

For many LAN installers, the hardest part of hooking up a remote LAN link is dealing with the phone lines and telecommunications equipment. Selecting a DSU, dealing with the phone company, and configuring the DSU for the bridge or router are uncommon tasks for a typical CNE. The LAN2LAN Mega manual includes setup information and switch settings for some of the more common DSUs. In general, the LAN2LAN Mega documentation is clear and includes a useful flow chart to direct you to the right page for your installation.

Installing the LAN2LAN Mega for NetWare 3.x requires setting up a NetWare file server, an existing server, or one that's been set up with NetWare runtime or the Novell MultiProtocol Router, running the INSTALL program from a workstation and adding the appropriate LOAD and BIND commands into the server's AUTOEXEC.NCF file. Installing it on a NetWare 2.x-based router running the INSTALL program and linking the right driver in ROUTEGEN.

The LAN2LAN Mega is managed through the SURVEYOR program. With SURVEYOR you can check the status of a router and read statistics including compression ration, packets and data transmitted, and packet breakdowns by protocol. A packet generator/exerciser and WNIC diagnostic programs are also included. The LAN2LAN Mega is the most straightforward WAN link for NetWare. It doesn't have fancy Windows-based management; it just gets the job done.

YOU CAN WITH EICON
The Eicon Router for NetWare

The Eicon Router for NetWare goes a step beyond the other products in this roundup. Where Newport's LAN2LAN and Novell's WAN Links are designed to be used in pairs with a LAN2LAN or WAN Links machine at each end of the link and are therefore best for the small WAN made up primarily of NetWare LANs, the Eicon Router for NetWare can also connect to an enterprise router such as a Cisco or Wellfleet.

For large WANs, enterprise routers present several significant advantages. They can handle more ports per router, higher aggregate data rates, load balancing across multiple wide-area links, and provide more sophisticated control over protocol implementation than PC-based routers can. Enterprise routers' biggest advantage is that they can route Systems Network Architecture SNA data along with LAN traffic replacing IBM front-end processors and other more expensive communications controllers. With the Eicon Router for NetWare, you can use a 16-port Cisco AGS+ at corporate headquarters connected to 56Kbps lines leading to the Eicon Router that runs on PCs in each field office.

Like the LAN²LAN Mega, the Eicon Router for NetWare is primarily a high-speed synchronous serial WAN interface card. In this case, the EiconCard HSI (high-speed interface) and a set of drivers make the wide-area-interface card look like a LAN card to NetWare. Eicon's 68000-based HSI card has 1MB of memory and can handle data rates to E-1 speeds. Rather than use an add-in hardware compression module, Eicon uses the 68000 on the HSI for data compression. This method seems to work as well as the Newport hardware compression.

The Router for NetWare can support data rates to E-1 speeds using High-Level Data-Link Control (HDLC) on point-to-point links and 384Kbps over X.25 or frame-relay networks. The EiconCard HSI supports V.24, V.35 or X.21/V.11 hardware interfaces to DSUs and modems.

The EiconCard HSI requires an interrupt, 64K of memory, and a bank of I/O addresses. The interrupt and I/O addresses are set through the Eicon configuration program. Eicon has similar cards available for MicroChannel.

The Eicon Router for NetWare adds a nice Windows-based Router Manager's Console to the basic card and driver combination. The Router Manager's Console runs under Windows 3.x and allows a network manager to view the status of all the Eicon NetWare or OS/2 routers on his or her network. The console displays a list of routers in your network along with their up time and current status. The program periodically polls the routers and collects statistics about how much data has been transmitted, how many packets have been routed, and port throughput. If you double click on a router, you can view the data from the last poll and cumulative data since the router was started.

You can even zoom in to look at a single port on an EiconCard in a router's statistics or to view particular connections between routers. If you look at a specific connection, you can get important information like the actual data compression and the breakdown of packets routed by protocol.

To install the Router for NetWare for version 2.x, you need to link the appropriate drivers into the router software with ROUTEGEN, expand and run the Eicon configuration lc utility. To install the Router for NetWare NLM for NetWare 3.x, install NetWare Runtime or a NetWare Multi-Protocol Router and run the Eicon installation and configuration programs from a workstation connected to the server, then add several LOAD and BIND commands to the AUTOEXEC.NCF file.

The configuration program gives you very detailed control of the card and protocol settings for the router but I had trouble navigating the configuration program's windows, which require that you go to a parameter and press <F4> to get to the next screen. I had to fumble a bit to get to the window I wanted even though I had the screen shot from the manual on my desk. Installing the Router for NetWare NLM took a few tries.

Once the Router for NetWare was installed, the only problem I had was the third Eicon NLM loading before the second one finished initializing the EiconCard. If this happened, the third NLM for the Router for NetWare would fail to load and I'd have to load it manually. Once all the NLMs loaded, the Router for NetWare NLM hummed right along. It performed respectably in my tests, even at 56KKpbs.

Eicon's Router for NetWare would be a good choice for small WANs or as satellite routers for small field offices. Its frame-relay support and Windows-management console make it the most sophisticated of the internal WAN routers for NetWare.

BRIDGING AND ROUTING
Newport LAN²LAN MPR

Recently, I looked at a beta test version of Newport LAN²LAN MultiProtocol Router (MPR), which should be available by now. Unlike the other products discussed here, the Newport LAN²LAN MPR doesn't run under the NetWare operating system or rely on NetWare's IPX routing functions. Instead, LAN²LAN MPR is a 32-bit 386 program that loads from DOS and takes over the PC. Like

NetWare-based routers, LAN2LAN MPR routes both IPX and IP traffic, but unlike the NetWare MPR, LAN2LAN MPR doesn't yet route AppleTalk or OSI protocols. The good news is that like $10,000 to $30,000 bridging routers from Cisco and Wellfleet, the LAN2LAN MPR acts as a MAC-layer bridge for data packets that use protocols other than IPX and IP.

If you use NetBIOS- or NetBEUI-based software such as Windows for Workgroups (WFW), you can't create a single workgroup that has users on different Ethernets connected by NetWare routers. A user on one side of the router will not be able to share resources with a user on the other side because the NetBEUI packets used by WFW aren't forwarded by the NetWare-based routers. If you used a 386 PC running LAN2LAN MPR to connect those two Ethernet segments, it could bridge the NetBEUI packets and the two workstations could share each other's resources.

The down side of MAC-layer bridging is that it sends many more packets across the link, thereby using valuable bandwidth. Routing better isolates traffic to the proper network segment than bridging does, but using routing exclusively means forfeiting the use of protocols such as NetBEUI and Digital Equipment's Local Area Transport (LAT), which use a single address space and can't be routed.

You can use a LAN2LAN MPR to link two Ethernet segments locally. And with the same WNIC cards that are used in the LAN2LAN Mega, you can link them over telephone lines from 1,200bps to 2.048Mbps and X.25 packet-switched networks. Newport is working on support for frame relay.

The LAN2LAN MPR can currently be used only with Ethernet networks. But it does use spanning tree protocols to determine the path a packet should take and to prevent packets from being retransmitted ad infinitum around a loop. You can configure the MAC-layer bridging to exclude packets from a set of workstations or to include specific protocol types and control all the usual spanning tree parameters. MAC-layer bridging can also be selected on a port-by-port basis so local networks will be bridged and remote links won't be clogged with NetBIOS traffic.

The LAN2LAN MPR reduces overhead by suppressing NetWare RIP and SAP messages, which are merely rebroadcasts of information already sent across the link. At the far end, the LAN2LAN MPR generates SAPs and RIPs to keep the other routers from removing a server from their server list because they haven't heard from it in three hours.

Installing the LAN2LAN MPR is simple. You configure the LAN and WNIC cards and run the INSTMPR program. After that, you set the machine's AUTOEXEC.BAT to load MPR. The router PC must use either SMC Elite 16 or Eagle NE2000 Ethernet cards. LAN2LAN MPR includes a SNMP MIB 1- and MIB 2-compliant agent, so a router running LAN2LAN MPR can be controlled by any SNMP management console, such as those made by Hewlett-Packard (Palo Alto, CA) and Sun Microsystems (Billerica, MA). LAN2LAN also includes Newport's SURVEYOR diagnostic and a traffic-generation program.

A Phone Call Away

REMOTE OFFICES ARE NO LONGER DISENFRANCHISED FROM
CORPORATE NETWORK RESOURCES, THANKS TO A FLURRY OF LOW-COST,
SIMPLIFIED ROUTERS.

BY CHRISTINE STREHLO

A router's merit was once judged by the number of protocols it routed. In the late 1980s, users needed efficient solutions for interconnecting many disparate LANs within the enterprise to keep up with the frenzy of downsizing applications and moving away from legacy systems. After a brief fling with LAN bridging, more efficient multiprotocol routing became the order of the day.

Investment in multiprotocol technology paid off for companies such as Cisco Systems (Mountain View, CA) and Wellfleet Communications (Bedford, MA), two leaders in the high-end router market. Faced with numerous competitors employing varying degrees of bridging and routing technologies, today's multiprotocol routers are the result of years of extensive investment in software and hardware development.

But along with the ability to route a multitude of LAN protocols has come increased configuration and management concerns, as well as a very high price tag. In fact, cost and maintenance issues have profoundly shaped the router market. While many large organizations installed LANs in remote-office sites, few had the courage to install a router in a faraway office–the cost alone of leased or dial-up synchronous phone lines prohibited the growth of routing at remote sites.

Instead, remote LANs were outfitted with e-mail applications, such as Lotus Development's cc:Mail, that offered remote-connection capabilities. The popularity of laptops and notebooks also led to widespread demand for remote-user connectivity products for individual users.

Neither of these alternatives, however, provided groups of users in remote offices with what they really need: complete and free access to network resources, including, but not limited to, the productivity applications that keep the corporate machine running. For example, cc:Mail remote users don't have access to other applications on file servers, nor can they spool to a fax server on the LAN. Thus, users located away from the corporate network experience a certain level of disenfranchisement.

A MARKET FOR LOW-COST ROUTERS

Clearly, the market for complex multiprotocol routing is limited to the corporate center where management expertise lives. The remote office, which characteristically lacks a knowledgeable network administrator, is another market altogether. Pricing for high-end multiprotocol routers starts at about $8,000.

Although this price range is acceptable to users at some sites, when an organization starts thinking in terms of connecting several hundred remote sales offices, cost issues can overshadow other motivations for connecting remote sites.

Router manufacturers, such as Cisco, acknowledge the importance of cost issues. According to Cisco Director of Product Marketing (Platforms) Brent Bilger, one of Cisco's larger customers once told the company, "We aren't going to roll out the next stage of our networking plan because your price point is wrong." But instead of switching vendors, as Bilger feared they would, the client decided to wait a year and half for the release of Cisco's low-cost routers designed for remote offices with fewer users. Now, says Bilger, the client is rolling out the next phase of its enterprise connectivity strategy.

Clearly, low-cost routing seems to be an answer for many larger corporations. Basically, remote-office routers

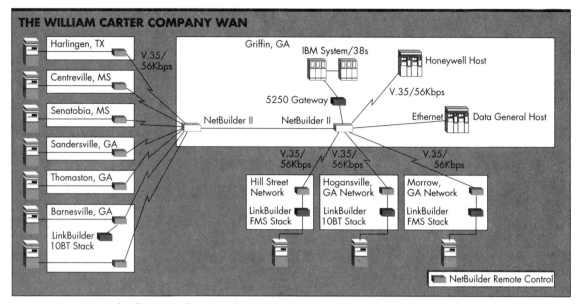

A WAN FOR ALL SEASONS: The William Carter Co. has augmented a terminal-based manufacturing system with remote-office routing. 3Com NetBuilder routers at each remote site connect workstations and terminals to the Griffin center's two NetBuilder II central routers.

are designed to make much simpler decisions than are routers located at the central site. As a product class, remote-office routers are generally configured as the far end of a point-to-point connection with the central network perhaps located in the corporation's headquarters. Prices generally fall in the $3,000 to $5,000 range. (On the low end, Eicon Technology, Lachine, Quebec, has a $995 router that connects remote sites to central sites via X.25 networks).

Thus, the remote router need only decide if data packets generated at the remote office are destined for local workstations or workstations situated somewhere on the WAN. If they have a local destination, the router ignores them. If they are destined for the WAN, the router forwards them over a leased or dial-up telecommunications connection to a central network router.

Most products in this category forward a wide variety of routable protocols and can also forward nonroutable protocols, such as LAT, by encapsulating the nonroutable protocol in a routable one. Thus legacy applications running on IBM and Digital Equipment platforms are fully accessible to remote users.

Early in 1993, several router manufacturers set their sights squarely on the low-price, low-maintenance segment of the router market. Several major players have released

simpler low-cost routers designed to directly connect branch offices of large organizations to the enterprise WAN.

3Com (Santa Clara, CA), Cisco Systems, Wellfleet, Proteon (Westboro, MA), Advanced Computer Communications (ACC, Cupertino, CA), and Telebit (Sunnyvale, CA) are just a few vendors that have released or announced remote-office router products, while Novell has a software solution that can be incorporated into existing NetWare servers. The rest of the industry is not far behind in introducing or releasing remote-office routers.

Some vendors are simply scaling down available products, adding new capabilities, and reducing prices. For example, in March, Telebit introduced a small-footprint model of its NetBlazer 40, a $4,599 dial-in router designed for remote access.

In December of 1992, 3Com made a big splash unveiling its Boundary Routing System Architecture and its explanation of the remote-office market. In March of 1993, 3Com followed this preparatory positioning statement with software additions to its NetBuilder line of bridge/routers for remote-office use. In June, Cisco Systems unveiled four remote-office routers as well as router-management software that provides automated internetwork administration.

According to Martin Palka, an analyst with Dataquest in San Jose, CA, worldwide unit sales for the remote-office router market were 8,612 in 1992, a figure he predicts will grow to 82,245 in 1997. Those figures translate to a 75-percent compound annual growth rate from 1993 to 1997. Palka characterizes the growth rate as the result of the chronic downsizing of mission-critical applications in the enterprise.

COST ISSUES DEFINE THE MARKET

Manufacturers going after the remote-office router market agree that performance is no longer an issue because today's competitive router products forward traffic at wire speeds. Likewise, router makers are claiming not that their products simplify routing on the network overall, but that they simplify the task of maintaining routing capabilities at the remote office and minimize the cost of providing full corporate LAN access to these offices.

Thus the critical issue concerning remote-office routing is cost, an issue driven home by the cost of the connecting line: Even in an area already well serviced by T-1, a company could spend as much as $11,000 a month for a single T-1 connection from a remote site to the central office. Slower lines are less expensive, but the limited bandwidth must be used efficiently. Thus, remote-office routers are also characterized by bandwidth-saving features.

According to Palka, Dataquest defines remote-access routers as low-end multiprotocol products that accommodate less-expensive asynchronous dial-up telephony connections, such as 9.6Kbps to 64Kbps lines, excluding the very expensive T-1/E-1 lines, which allow transmission at 1.54Mbps.

Another cost factor is the capital investment in hardware and software. The attraction of inexpensive routers is quite strong. "Every time prices drop on these products, another crew of people throws the hat into the ring and says, 'Okay, now I can buy these things,'" according to Jay Batson, an analyst with Forrester Research in Cambridge, MA. "These are new customers or old customers who haven't networked certain locations because the capital cost of investment wasn't justified for that location. They say, 'Now I can put this router into a 12-person office,' and later, 'Now I can put this router into an eight-person office.'"

However, the cost of remote routing is more acutely felt by the LAN administrator at the central location, since that person is charged with the additional management duties. Compounding this pressure is the fact that remote-office routers are intended to be installed in volume. Every regional sales office, bank branch, retail outlet, and manufacturing site in the country is a candidate for remote-access routing, regardless of the hardware and software running in the home office, according to manufacturers of these devices.

One feature common to remote-office routers is the ability to configure the remote router from a central management point. To add or delete addresses or update router-table information, the network administrator can make the necessary changes at the console of the central router, located at headquarters. The updates are sent along the wire to the remote site automatically.

How does this arrangement differ from central router management? Users, vendors, and analysts concede that centralized management is a tremendous timesaver. A company installing full-performance routers at 50 remote sites faced a huge planning and implementation chore, even with the help of configuration and management utilities that enabled the user to preconfigure the box before carting it to the remote site.

"Even so," says 3Com's Joe Furgurson, "you have to go in on the weekends and hope you do everything right, because if you don't, you have to roll back and reconfigure." Furgurson is the product line manager for 3Com's Net-Builder remote-router products.

COST-SAVINGS DEFINE PRODUCTS

While manufacturers of remote-office routers adhere to Dataquest's description of the market, vendors are working hard to differentiate themselves from the pack. For example, from 3Com's point of view, remote-office routing is best suited to topologies in which a remote LAN has a single point of entry–one phone line connecting the remote site to the central site. This configuration ensures all routing decisions performed at the remote site are reduced to a yes-or-no condition–to forward or not. 3Com's Net-Builder is restricted to this one-line configuration for that specific purpose.

From the point of view of 3Com's competitors, however, 3Com has oversimplified the idea. To some, 3Com's products are "smart bridges" that rely on filters and utilities to reduce network broadcast traffic. True remote-office routing, they insist, must include an alternate path so the re-mote router can also determine the most efficient path to the central site.

According to Wellfleet Director of Access Products and Protocols David Yates, true routing is characterized by the ability to choose an alternate path to the end point and is essential for remote offices for the same reasons that rout-ing is essential for the central network. Broadcast traffic must be handled efficiently if the connection itself is to re-main cost-effective.

"Why have bridges gone out of fashion?" Yates asks. "Because they are pretty dumb devices that are easy to configure but have a lot more broadcast overhead. Broad-cast storms were a reality for bridge users. If not, fewer users would have converted from bridges to routers."

OPTIMIZING BANDWIDTH

Predictably, 3Com's Furgurson disagrees, citing several features that enable 3Com's NetBuilder line to fully ad-dress the issue of bandwidth optimization without requir-ing that a remote site establish redundant telecommunica-tion connections and thus increase cost. Indeed, bandwidth optimization features define the merits of a remote-office router. Serious competitors, including 3Com, Cisco, Well-fleet, Proteon, and ACC, recognize a handful of mandatory bandwidth-optimization features and have handled them in subtly different ways.

One such feature is data compression using nonpropri-etary protocols such as PPP. For example, 3Com's Net-Builder PPP support enables the remote routers to signifi-cantly optimize bandwidth. According to Furgurson, text-based traffic can achieve four-time compression under PPP, while spreadsheet data may achieve two-time com-pression.

"That can have a huge impact if your line is only 64Kbps, which is one 180th the bandwidth of an Ethernet line," says Furgurson. "The goal is effective throughput on an expensive resource. Data compression gives two to three times more throughput for the WAN link, and that's really important when you're spending $500, $1,500, or $2,000 a month for a 64Kbps WAN link."

Filtering is also a feature routinely offered by 3Com, Wellfleet, ACC and other vendors. 3Com is currently fo-cusing on filtering NetWare Service Advertising Protocol traffic and Routing Information Protocol traffic. An auto-matic filter-configuration utility is also planned for early 1994.

ACC's Nile remote router includes a feature called ex-press queuing, designed to provide "predictable response time" for session-oriented users. "Without express queuing, a file transfer will dominate the LAN port," Bauer says. "We set aside a sliver of bandwidth so that file-transfer per-formance doesn't suffer noticeably, response time doesn't degrade, and data compression shoves more traffic through. While we are squeezing more data into this small pipe, we also don't want to sacrifice the performance of traffic through that small pipe."

DIAL OPTIONS

Dial technology enables the remote site to use the con-nection only when traffic exists for it and to give fine-grain control over when that connection is open. A connection would automatically be established as needed.

Two facilities are already available from 3Com: band-width on demand and dial backup. Bandwidth on demand kicks in the dial connection when the primary WAN con-nection is very busy with WAN traffic; dial backup kicks in when the initial connection is down and when a failure oc-curs on the telecommunications end.

Scheduled dial is also available in 3Com's NetBuilder line, enabling the user to declare the periods the dial con-nection can be open. And dial on demand for IP and IPX packets is also available, greatly minimizing the connec-tion time for those particular protocols, Furgurson adds.

Kurt Bauer, ACC marketing manager, cites indepen-dent studies indicating that 75 percent to 80 percent of all costs for the life of a LAN are associated with wide-area ex-penses. "That's where the notion of bandwidth optimiza-tion was born," he says. "It also involves making the avail-able services as flexible as possible. That goes beyond multiprotocol routing, frame relay, and X.25."

Bauer adds, "end-user demand for bandwidth contin-ues to increase, and we will experience this higher de-mand into the foreseeable future. While cost per bit con-tinues to decline, bandwidth will never be free. People need to really manage the cost of the network [as well as the operation]."

EASING MANAGEMENT

3Com's Furgurson says that central management capabilities fall squarely in the realm of the cost-saving features that define remote-office routers. "[Remote-office routing] requires only that you make configuration changes at the central site, which transmits these changes to the remote sites.

"This [configuring at the central site] can affect by a factor of five or 10 the number of routers you have to reconfigure, decreasing your risk and decreasing the amount of time required to achieve a software change on the network. From both an ongoing management perspective and from an initial installation standpoint, this approach is very low cost, which is appealing to customers," Furgurson says.

Again, the major players in this market offer centralized, automated management and configuration of remote routers, with variations. Cisco has long been offering centralized router management of its multiprotocol routers and is offering a software utility called Autoinstall for its remote-office line.

Using Autoinstall, the administrator simply assigns an address to the central router to which the remote router is connected. A configuration file at the central site that equates to that remote LAN is downloaded to the remote site.

Cisco also offers a utility called Autoinstall Manager, which reduces the repetition involved in configuring multiple routers. Instead of configuring several routers by hand, the administrator can enlist Autoinstall Manager to automate the task.

Says Bilger, "Autoinstall Manager asks, 'What router does it look like?' and you say, 'It looks just like that other router I already installed.' It will bring up that configuration, letting you change addresses if you need to or other small details and save it.

"You might be able to get it [configuration] down to an hour using Autoinstall and 10 minutes using Autoinstall Manager," Bilger adds. "You still have to know what you are doing. You are creating a network–assigning addresses, making decisions. Once you've made those decisions, though, the process is relatively simple."

Wellfleet's management facility, called Site Manager, fa-

cilitates software upgrades to remote routers as well. The remote sites can also be managed using SNMP.

Remote-office routing "really cuts the cord," says 3Com's Furgurson, "because no matter how many protocols you have running at the remote site, and no matter how involved the setup of those protocols, the setup of the remote box–the box over which you have the least control or the least access–remains the same."

THE SHAPE OF THINGS

Even as manufacturers stuff cost-cutting features into their remote-router products, most remote offices do not have the economic justification to lease high-bandwidth lines. As those remote offices grow, bandwidth demand will surely increase.

Alternatives such as frame relay and X.25, then, are important to explore. According to Dataquest's Batson, frame relay can provide the fail-safe qualities of redundant connections to the central office.

While X.25 provides error checking and line redundancy over leased lines, overhead is associated with the service. Says Batson, "It's slow. Each node [on the X.25 network] really doesn't need to do as much error checking as it does now."

Instead, Batson believes, frame relay support in remote-office routers is probably more valuable in the long run. Frame relay checks for errors at the end points of a mesh of leased lines, instead of at the midpoints, significantly cutting overhead.

"It's a way to rely on someone else's network to provide fault tolerance and redundancy, and all you have to do is buy one line between you and them. It's being marketed heavily as an inexpensive method–$75 a month for a frame relay 56Kbps line," says Batson.

While each vendor has taken a different approach to product features and configurations, vendors seem to know at least viscerally that they need to keep prices at commodity levels and continue to improve the ease-of-use and management features of their products. If they can do that, they can play in a market that seems to be wide open.

PPP: Getting to the Point

YOU MAY NOT NEED HIGHER-LEVEL TECHNOLOGICAL SOLUTIONS FOR CONNECTIVITY. IN MANY CASES, A SIMPLE POINT-TO-POINT PROTOCOL WILL GET THE JOB DONE.

BY GARY KESSLER

All you really need is whatever it takes to get the job done. For example, if you commute to work three miles each way, a Volkswagen Bug or even a bicycle would suffice. No need for a full-featured luxury car; that type of transportation would be overkill. So it is with host connections to the Internet. If all you have are a few sites, connecting to the Internet via leased or dial-up lines using some relatively simple protocol may be preferable to wide-area technologies, such as X.25, Fiber Distributed Data Interface (FDDI), Switched Multimegabit Data Service (SMDS), frame relay, and Asynchronous Transfer Mode (ATM).

Of course, these technologies have their applications, but point-to-point links between LANs, hosts, terminals, and routers can provide sufficient physical connectivity in many application environments. In addition, many regional and commercial network services provide access to the Internet, and point-to-point links provide an efficient way to access the local provider.

Still, until the last several years, surprisingly few hosts were connected to the Internet with simple point-to-point serial links even though point-to-point communication is among the oldest methods of interconnectivity for data applications. Furthermore, nearly every computer today supports simple point-to-point communication.

WHY NOT?

One reason for the small number of point-to-point IP links has been the lack of an encapsulation protocol that was accepted as either a de facto or Internet standard on which products can be developed, even though several such schemes exist for the transmission of IP datagrams over nearly every type of LAN, MAN, and WAN.

To address this need, the Internet community has adopted two schemes for the transmission of IP datagrams over serial point-to-point lines, called the Serial Line Interface Protocol (SLIP) and the Point-to-Point Protocol (PPP). Although both were developed for the Internet protocols and were designed with IP in mind, SLIP is pretty much limited for use with IP while PPP may be used for other Network-Layer protocols.

SLIP

While not an official Internet standard, SLIP is a widely used protocol and comes with Berkeley Unix, Digital Equipment's Ultrix, Sun Microsystems' Unix, and some TCP/IP implementations for PC-based systems.

Defined in Request for Comments (RFC) 1055, SLIP is designed for host-to-host, host-to-router, router-to-router, or workstation-to-host communications over asynchronous or synchronous, leased or dial-up, serial lines. It is designed to operate at speeds from 1,200bps to 19.2Kbps but can be used at higher speeds.

SLIP is one of the simplest protocols ever invented. Most common SLIP implementations accept IP datagrams up to 1,006 bytes in length. The datagrams are transmitted byte by byte down the serial line, preceded by a special character called ESCape (octal 333, decimal 219; not to be confused with the ASCII ESCAPE character) and followed by a special character called END (octal 300, decimal 192).

If a data byte within the IP datagram has the same value as the END character, it is replaced with the two-byte sequence ESC and octal 334 (decimal 220); a byte with the same value as ESC is replaced with the two-byte sequence ESC and octal 335 (decimal 221).

TABLE 1: POINT-TO-POINT (PPP) REQUESTS FOR COMMENT	
RFC No.	Title
1220	PPP Extensions for Bridging; May 1991
1331	Point-to-Point Protocol (PPP); May 1992
1332	PPP Internet Protocol Control Protocol (IPCP); May 1992
1333	PPP Link-Quality Monitoring; May 1992
1334	PPP Authentication Protocols; October 1992
1376	PPP DECnet Phase IV Control Protocol (DNCP); November 1992
1377	PPP OSI Network-Layer Control Protocol (OSINLCP); November 1992
1378	PPP AppleTalk Control Protocol (ATCP); November 1992

SLIP is simple to implement and works well in many environments. Its simplicity, however, leaves it with a number of deficiencies including:

• **Addressing**. SLIP does not provide any mechanism for hosts to communicate addressing information with each other; thus both computers in a SLIP connection must know each other's IP addresses for routing purposes.

• **Protocol identification**. SLIP has no protocol-type field and, therefore, only a single protocol may be used over a SLIP connection.

For example, if two hosts running both TCP/IP and OSI are connected over a SLIP connection, the multiple protocols cannot share one SLIP line. As an aside, although SLIP was designed for use with IP, SLIP frames do not have to contain an IP datagram; any higher-layer protocol information can be carried by SLIP. The restriction is that only a single Network-Layer protocol may be used over a single SLIP line.

• **Error correction and detection**. SLIP provides no error-correction or error-detection mechanism. This deficiency is potentially expensive, in a protocol sense, for several reasons. First, SLIP will be used primarily over low-speed lines, so transmission time is an important consideration. Second, while IP will, in fact, detect bit errors, such errors are far more efficiently detected and corrected at lower protocol layers than at higher layers.

Clearly, some form of error correction at the Physical Layer would add to the efficiency of the communication. Furthermore, some applications may ignore the TCP and IP checksums, assuming instead that the network has detected damaged packets before handing them up to higher layers.

• **Compression**. SLIP provides no mechanism for packet compression. Such a mechanism could provide significant

performance improvements, particularly since SLIP is associated with low-speed lines.

PPP

The Point-to-Point Protocol, specified in RFC 1331, is a proposed Internet standard. A large body of work related to PPP has been written within the Internet community, and Table 1 lists current PPP-related RFCs. Paper copies of RFCs are available through SRI at (415) 859-6387; you can also send e-mail to mail-server@nisc.sri.com.

PPP was designed to define a standard encapsulation protocol for the transport of different Network-Layer protocols (including, but not limited to, IP) across serial, point-to-point links. PPP also describes mechanisms for network-protocol multiplexing, link configuration, link-quality testing, authentication, header compression, error detection, and link-option negotiation.

PPP has three main functional components:

1. A method for encapsulating datagrams over serial links, based on the ISO High-level Data-Link Control (HDLC) protocol.

2. A Link-Control Protocol (LCP) for establishing, configuring, authenticating, and testing the data-link connection.

3. A family of Network-Control Protocols (NCPs) for establishing and configuring different Network-Layer protocols.

Figure 1 shows the components of the PPP protocol stack. At the Physical Layer, PPP is designed to work over any asynchronous or synchronous, dedicated or dial-up, full-duplex bit-serial circuit. It can employ any common serial-communications protocol, including EIA-232-E (formerly RS-232-C), EIA-422, EIA-423, EIA-530, and CCITT V.24 and V.35. PPP does not place any particular restric-

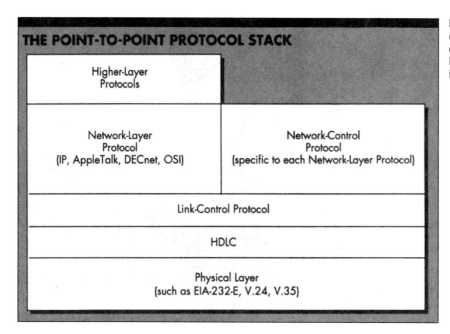

Figure 1. Shown are the components of the PPP protocol stack. For communications to be established, the Physical Layer and HDLC Data-Link Layer must first be operational.

tion on the type of signaling, type of transmission speed, or use of modem-control signals.

The PPP Data-Link Layer is based on the concepts, terminology, and frame structure of HDLC. HDLC may be used in both the synchronous and asynchronous communications environments. A description of the specific PPP frame format follows.

The two PPP hosts use the LCP to establish, configure, and terminate the data-link connection. LCP procedures have been defined to allow agreement on the encapsulation format options, handle varying limits on packet size, authenticate the identity of the hosts, determine when a link is functioning properly and when it has failed, detect a looped-back link, and identify other common configuration problems. LCP information is carried in the PPP/HDLC frame.

In essence, two parallel protocol stacks reside on top of the LCP. Network-Layer protocol packets, containing higher-layer information, are used to exchange user information; NCP packets are used to control the Network-Layer protocol connections.

Point-to-point links may exacerbate the problems associated with a given Network-Layer protocol. Assignment and management of IP addresses, for example, a problem in any LAN or MAN environment, is particularly difficult over dial-up lines. Network-Layer protocol problems are handled by a family of NCPs that manage the specific needs of their particular Network-Layer protocol.

PPP FRAME FORMAT

As Figure 2 shows, the fields of the PPP frame are:
• Flag—bit pattern 01111110 (hexadecimal 7E), used to indicate the beginning and end of the frame.
• Address—an all-ones (hex FF) octet, specifying the HDLC All-Station address; PPP does not assign individual station addresses.
• Control—in HDLC, this field indicates the frame type and contains any associated sequence numbers; in PPP, only HDLC Unnumbered Information (hex 03) frames are used.
• Protocol field—a two-octet field specific to PPP and used to identify the protocol encapsulated in the Information field. To comply with HDLC's rules for an extended Address field, the first octet must end with a 0 (it must be even) and the second octet must end with a 1 (it must be odd).
Table 2 lists some of the protocols currently supported by PPP. Note that protocol field values in the "0---" to "3---" range identify Network-Layer protocols, and values in the "8--" to "B--" range identify the associated NCP. Values in the "4--" to "7--" range are used for those protocols with

TABLE 2: FIELD VALUES FOR THE POINT-TO-POINT PROTOCOL
Value (in hex) Protocol Name

Value (in hex)	Protocol Name
0021	Internet Protocol
0023	OSI Network Layer
0025	Xerox NS IDP
0027	DECnet Phase IV
0029	AppleTalk
002B	Novell IPX
002D	Van Jacobson Compressed TCP/IP
002F	Van Jacobson Uncompressed TCP/IP
0031	Bridging PDU
0033	Stream Protocol (ST-II)
0035	Banyan VINES
0201	802.1D Hello Packets
8021	Internet Protocol Control Protocol
8023	OSI Network Layer Control Protocol
8025	Xerox NS IDP Control Protocol
8027	DECnet Phase IV Control Protocol
8029	AppleTalk Control Protocol
802B	Novel IPX Control Protocol
8031	Bridging NCP
8033	Steam Protocol Control Protocol
8035	Banyan VINES Control Protocol
C021	Link Control Protocol
C023	Password Authentication Protocol
C025	Link Quality Report
C223	Challenge Handshake Authentication Protocol

low-volume traffic which have no associated NCP, and values in the "C--" to "F--" range identify datagrams used in the LCP.

• Information field–contains a datagram from the protocol identified in the Protocol field. The default maximum size of this field is 1,500 octets, although larger sizes may be supported.

• Frame Check Sequence (FCS)–contains the remainder from a cyclic redundancy check to detect bit errors. This field is usually 16 bits in length but may be extended (for example, to 32 bits) by mutual agreement between the end users.

PPP LCP PACKETS

All LCP packets have the same general format (see Figure 3). The one-octet Code field identifies the type of packet; all LCP packet types are listed in Table 3. The one-octet Identifier field is a number chosen at random used to associate requests and replies. Any packet sent in response to a request must contain the same Identifier-field value as the request. The two-octet Length field indicates the length of the entire LCP packet, in octets. Any additional information, such as data or configuration options, follows the Length field.

LCP packets are classified into one of three types according to function. The first type is *Link-Configuration packets*, used to establish and configure a PPP link. Following are the types of Link Configuration packets and their functions:

• Configure-Request–sent by a PPP host wishing to open an LCP connection; a single LCP connection must be established before any Network-Layer protocol communication can take place.

A series of Configuration Options, such as the maximum packet size, asynchronous control characters, type of authentication protocol, link-quality monitoring reporting period, and compression type, may also be encoded in the Options field following the Length field. A PPP host re-

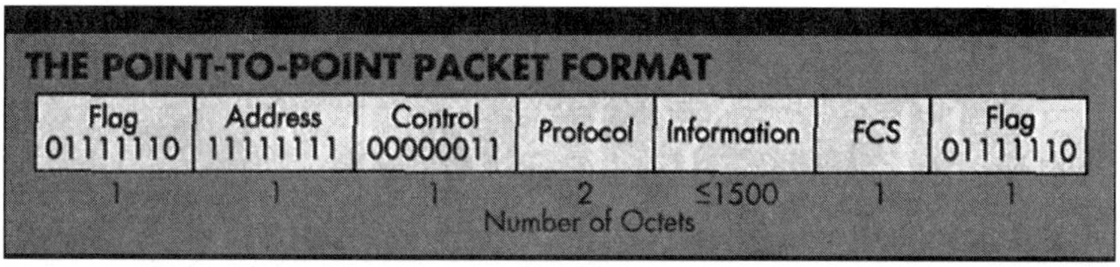

THE POINT-TO-POINT PACKET FORMAT

Flag 01111110	Address 11111111	Control 00000011	Protocol	Information	FCS	Flag 01111110
1	1	1	2	≤1500	1	1

Number of Octets

Figure 2. PPP frame fields include: Flag, which indicates the beginning and end of a frame; Address, which specifies the HDLC All-Station address; and Control, which indicates frame type.

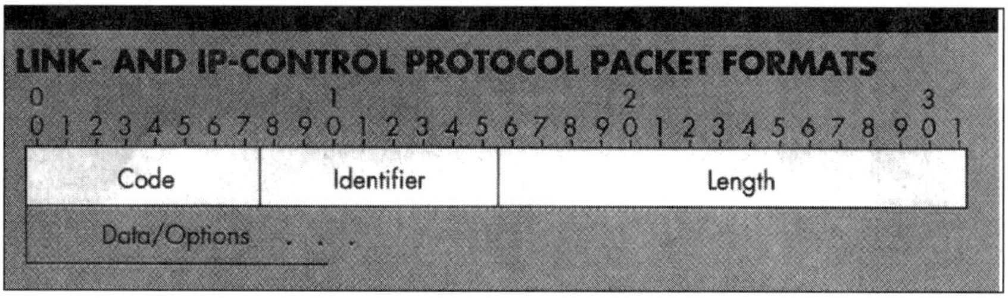

LINK- AND IP-CONTROL PROTOCOL PACKET FORMATS

```
  0                   1                   2                   3
  0 1 2 3 4 5 6 7 8 9 0 1 2 3 4 5 6 7 8 9 0 1 2 3 4 5 6 7 8 9 0 1
```

Code	Identifier	Length
Data/Options . . .		

Figure 3. LCP packets share the same general format.

ceiving this packet must respond with one of three Configure reply packets:

• Configure-Ack–sent when every Configuration Option received in a Configure-Request is acceptable. This reply indicates successful establishment of the LCP connection.

• Configure-Nak–sent when every element of the received Configuration Options is recognizable but some are not acceptable to the receiver. This packet will list the unacceptable Configuration Options from the original Configure-Request, along with option values that are acceptable to this host, in the Options field. The originating side may elect to send a new Configure-Request with new Configuration Option values, or the two sides may negotiate the value for a specific option.

• Configure-Reject–sent when one or more Configuration Options received in a Configure-Request are not recognizable or not acceptable for negotiation (as configured by a network manager). This packet lists the unacceptable options in the Options field. The originating side should send a new Configure-Request that does not contain any of the options listed in the Configure-Reject.

The second type of LCP packets are *Link-Termination packets*, used to terminate a PPP link. A PPP host wishing to close an LCP connection sends a Terminate-Request packet and the other host will respond with a Terminate-Ack packet. Any desired data may be exchanged in the Data field of these packets.

The third type of LCP packets are *Link-Maintenance packets*, used to manage and debug a link. Types of Link-Maintenance packets are:

• Code-Reject–sent if a PPP host receives a packet with an unknown Code-field value. A copy of the rejected LCP packet will be carried in the Data field.

• Protocol-Reject–sent if a PPP host receives a PPP frame with an unknown Protocol-field value; this response could occur if the sending host is attempting to use a protocol not supported by this host and will usually occur during attempts to configure the new protocol. The Data field carries a copy of the rejected frame's Protocol and Information fields.

• Echo-Request and Echo-Reply–provide a loopback mechanism as an aid in debugging, performance testing, link-quality determination, and other functions. During initial LCP configuration, each PPP host may choose a self-identifying 32-bit Magic-Number; the host chooses the value at random using some unique seed such as the time of day, a network address, or the machine's serial number. The Echo packets and the Magic-Number can be used to detect Data-Link Layer loopbacks; as long as the Magic-Number in incoming packets is different than this station's Magic-Number, the station can be sure that the data link is operating properly.

• Discard-Request–may be used in exercising the local-to-remote direction of the data link, as an aid in debugging, performance testing, and other functions. The receiver automatically discards this packet.

PPP OPERATIONAL PHASES

To establish communication over a point-to-point link, connections are established one layer at a time, starting at the bottom of the protocol architecture, as Figure 1 shows.

Figure 4. PPP operations begin and end with the Link-Dead Phase, which represents an unreceptive Physical Layer. Once an external event indicates that the Physical Layer is ready for communications, the link is up and PPP moves to the next phase.

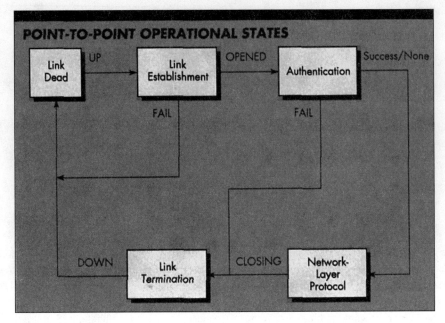

Figure 4. PPP operations begin and end with the Link-Dead Phase, which represents an unreceptive Physical Layer. Once an external event indicates that the Physical Layer is ready for communications, the link is up and PPP moves to the next phase.

First, the Physical Layer and HDLC Data-Link Layer must be operational. Next, LCP packets are exchanged to configure and authenticate the link. NCP procedures will be used to establish Network-Layer connections for one or more Network-Layer protocols. The link remains operational until LCP or NCP procedures are used to terminate the PPP link, or it otherwise fails.

Figure 4 shows the PPP phases of operation. They are:
• **Link-Dead phase.** This phase is the initial and the final phase of PPP operations, representing the Physical Layer not ready for communication. When an external event, such as an RS-232 control lead signal, indicates that the Physical Layer is ready, the link is up, and PPP moves to the Link-Establishment phase. In a dial-up environment, the link will usually return to this phase automatically after disconnection of the modem; in the leased-line scenario, this phase will typically be long enough only to detect the presence of the device on the line.
• **Link-Establishment phase.** The PPP connection is established through the exchange of LCP Configure packets, as previously described; any other packets will be ignored. During link establishment, LCP configuration options are determined and/or negotiated. Note that only LCP-specific options are configured during this phase and that any Network Layer-specific options are handled by the appropri-

ate NCP. This phase is successfully completed and the LCP link opened after the exchange of a Configure-Request and its corresponding Configure-Ack. If configuration fails for any reason, PPP returns to the Link-Dead phase.
• **Authentication phase.** In some communications environments, users may want to require a peer PPP host to authenticate itself before allowing the establishment of a Network-Layer connection. This phase is optional; if a PPP implementation requires use of some specific authentication procedures, then the use of that authentication protocol must be negotiated during the Link-Establishment phase.

RFC 1331, the base PPP document, does not describe specific PPP-authentication protocols (RFC 1334 discusses that subject). If the authentication procedures are successful (or if no such procedures are implemented), PPP moves to the Network-Layer Protocol phase; if authentication is unsuccessful, PPP moves to the Link-Termination phase.

Authentication procedures, if used, should be initiated as soon as possible after the link is established. In addition, link-quality determination may also occur simultaneously, which provides a given PPP implementation with the opportunity to determine whether the quality of the physical connection is adequate for the desired Network-Layer protocols. Link-quality monitoring is a configurable LCP option and is the subject of RFC 1333. Link-quality determination procedures should not add excessive delay to the authentication process.

• **Network-Layer Protocol phase.** Each Network-Layer protocol, such as IP or DECnet, must be separately configured by the appropriate NCP. Each NCP connection may be opened and closed at any time. After an NCP connection has been opened, PPP will transport the corresponding Network-Layer protocol packets. However, PPP hosts will throw out any packets received if they do not have corresponding NCP connections. During this phase, PPP link traffic may consist of any combination of LCP, NCP, and Network-Layer protocol packets.

• **Termination phase.** PPP may terminate the link at any time. This termination will typically occur at the request of the user for such purposes as maintenance or reconfiguration but may also occur due to loss of carrier, authentication failure, inadequate link quality, or the expiration of an idle-period timer. One PPP host sending an LCP Terminate-Request packet and the other responding with a Terminate-Ack signifies link termination. PPP informs the Network-Layer protocols of this event, and PPP returns to the Link-Dead phase. Note that the closing of the link by LCP is sufficient to terminate all NCP connections, while the termination of all NCP connections will not terminate the PPP link.

NCP OPERATION

Each Network-Layer protocol must have its own NCP and may establish and terminate connections in any appropriate fashion at any time during the Network-Layer Protocol phase. For each Network-Layer protocol, a different control procedure exists; the first NCP that was specified, naturally, was for IP and is called the Internet Protocol Control Protocol (IPCP), although subsequent NCPs have been written for AppleTalk, DECnet, and the OSI Network-Layer protocol.

As an example of one set of control procedures, consider IPCP (described in RFC 1332). The Information field of PPP frames carries IPCP packets with a Protocol-field value of hex 8021. These packets have the same format as LCP packets, although IPCP only uses packet types one through seven (see Table 3).

The originating PPP host initiates an IP connection by sending an IPCP Configure-Request packet, which may in-

TABLE 3: LINK-CONTROL PROTOCOL PACKET TYPES

Type	Packet Name
1	Configure-Request
2	Configure-Ack
3	Configure-Nak
4	Configure-Reject
5	Terminate-Request
6	Terminate-Ack
7	Code-Reject
8	Protocol-Reject
9	Echo-Request
10	Echo-Reply
11	Discard-Request
12	RESERVED

clude such IP-specific options as the local IP address and an indication of the compression protocol to be employed. The destination host will either agree with the options, disagree with the options, or begin a negotiation process.

As an aside, compression can provide a significant improvement in performance on slow serial lines, particularly for interactive traffic. The only compression protocol currently supported by the IPCP is the Van Jacobson TCP/IP header-compression method, described in RFC 1144, which can reduce the size of TCP/IP headers to as few as three octets.

Once the IPCP connection has been successfully established, the two PPP hosts can exchange IP datagrams. The Information field of PPP frames carries the IP datagrams, where the Protocol field has a value 0021. After IP data exchange is concluded, the hosts can close the IPCP connection by exchanging IPCP Terminate packets.

CONCLUSION

More and more sites are accessing the Internet and other TCP/IP hosts and networks via the use of serial point-to-point connections. While SLIP has been, and continues to be, widely used, PPP is gaining use because of its additional features and flexibility and is expected to be an official Internet standard in 1994. In addition, PPP will not be limited to just traditional dial-up or leased lines: The PPP working group has already started defining PPP procedures over X.25, Integrated Services Digital Network (ISDN), Synchronous Optical Network (SONET), frame relay, and extended-configuration options.

Section 2
E-mail and Messaging

The most basic form of network-based interaction, electronic mail, has matured way beyond its initial incarnation. The e-mail applications available today allow users located on the LAN–and connecting on the run–to forward basic text-based messages as well as elaborate electronic forms, spreadsheets, voice, video, and graphics.

Application developers are now tailoring their e-mail products to the needs of the nomad. "How Far Can You Go" looks at several of these remote mail applications and their disparate methods of connecting to the enterprise e-mail system. The user on the go isn't constrained by location or platform, either. With the help of cellular communications and other wireless services, network users can send messages whenever and wherever using any number of portable computing devices.

But a good enterprise e-mail system needs more than innovative user applications and connections. An efficient mail configuration requires sophisticated directory services and a stable underlying store-and-forward system; "Mail Masonry" explains the challenges found in establishing such a system. Once all of these pieces are in place, your network e-mail will then be ready to go the distance.

How Far Can You Go?

REMOTE E-MAIL ALTERNATIVES MAY NOT PREPARE YOU FOR A LUNAR LANDING, BUT THEY CAN HELP YOU FEEL LIKE YOU'RE IN CLOSER TOUCH WHILE ON THE ROAD.

BY REBECCA J. CAMPBELL

A well-dressed man squats down under the awning outside a windowless convention hall. He unfolds his laptop computer and digs a wireless modem out of his case. Within minutes he completes his e-mail transfer and repacks his equipment, returning to the convention.

Scenes like this one are now commonplace as remote communication technology develops. An increasing number of companies must grapple with the available technology, trying to accomplish many different levels of connectivity for those on the road and in remote offices. The only people that seem satisfied with the current technology are the ones with simple messaging needs.

There are two basic types of remote e-mail users: those who are stationary in remote offices and those on the move. Each has different types of needs, and vendors are beginning to realize that a modem and phone line don't begin to fulfill e-mail requirements for either user.

Kitty Weldon, data communication specialist for The Yankee Group (Boston), breaks down the different types of remote users into telecommuters, business travelers, remote branch offices (measured in number of offices, not users), and nomads. Nomads are folks continually on the road, such as salespeople, in contrast to the occasional traveling businessperson.

Analysts seem unable to agree on the potential marketplace numbers, and the numbers vary wildly. Even so, vendors are beginning to recognize the profitability of catering to the remote marketplace as shown by the new and improved products introduced within the past year for both remote offices and travelers.

REMOTE ANSWERS

One of the most recent developments for branch offices is an answering machine for e-mail. In February 1994, Calculus (Deerfield Beach, FL) introduced OutPost. OutPost consists of a piece of hardware that sits between your external modem and PC on the remote site and software at both the remote and home office. A light and a beep alert the remote site when mail is received, eliminating the need for constant polling. OutPost running at the remote site would be like a workstation at the main office running an e-mail TSR notification program.

Another helpful aid comes from Baranof Software (Brighton, MA) and is called MailCheck. MailCheck is a remote post office checker for the central mail administrator. Periodic polling reveals any downed post offices or those having problems and provides reports and alerts to the system administrator.

REMOTELY USABLE

At the top of the priority list for most companies looking for remote connectivity is ease of use for the uninitiated and technophobic. After all, people shouldn't have to learn the technology behind their tools. Lotus Development's (Cambridge, MA) recent introduction of cc:Mail Mobile for Windows made great strides in the right direction with several important features.

The first was Lotus' implementation of icons to represent different sites. Dialing sequences can be set up for connecting from an office, hotel, or home in any city or country. Although a wide range of icons are provided, users, including beginners, can easily customize and add icons.

Another key feature of cc:Mail Mobile for Windows is its variety of connectivity options. Users may select and prioritize their method of connection. Options include modem, wireless, NetWare, TCP/IP, X.25, Integrated Services Digital Network (ISDN), PBX, or direct (see Figure 1.) With these options, users don't have to learn a new program when they travel. A docking option keeps the mail and BBS features in sync. Although cc:Mail Mobile for Windows is not the only e-mail program with these features, cc:Mail is one of the better sellers.

REMOTE SERVICES

Value-added public-access networks such as AT&T EasyLink Services (Parsippany, NJ), MCI Telecommunications (Washington, D.C.), and CompuServe Information Service (Columbus, OH) also provide connectivity links between both the main office and travelers and the main office and stationary remote locations. Since these services provide both an 800 number and local telephone access numbers, they are quite attractive to those watching their long distance budget, and they can also ease calling hassles. If you've ever tried to get the correct tonal timing for dialing an access number, access code, and telephone number through a modem on different types of telephone exchanges, you'll understand why dialing a hassle-free local number is so attractive.

Value-added networks provide a particularly cost-effective link between offices on different continents. In addition, the diverse telephone systems, equipment, and dialing sequences required in Europe and Asia to complete long distance calls to the United States are often described as nightmarish by international travelers. Being able to make local calls to value-added networks in other countries is a more attractive option.

The Yankee Group projects that approximately 10 percent of the remote branch offices will be using value-added services by 1997. Companies such as CompuServe and MCI are working hard to stay current with user needs by adding services such as cc:Mail Hubs, Lotus Notes servers, and mail interchangeability with all the major public value-added networks.

Value-added networks are quite aware that their value diminishes if the public perceives that privacy violation is a possibility and have set forth very clear position statements about the security of e-mail transmissions. Even so, some companies consider their data too sensitive to entrust to public-access networks.

"If our e-mail resides on our equipment, we know ex-

actly who has access," states Bob Jacobson, technical contributor at Hewlett-Packard Labs. "Some of our data is just too competitive-sensitive to even think about using a public-access network."

BREAKING THE RULES

The topic of remote e-mail rarely surfaces without mention of rules-based processing. Rules are user-definable settings whereby the conditions under which e-mail messages will be downloaded are determined. Some e-mail programs have rather crude rules processing, while others offer quite flexible and sophisticated rules processing.

At the most basic level, rules allow the user to determine if a message is downloaded by designating a size limitation, subject header keywords, or sender in a configuration file before dialing the host file server. At a more complex level, programs such as BeyondMail (Beyond, Burlington, MA) offer sophisticated rules-based processing features set at the host system and the remote computer.

BeyondMail can even be set to automatically forward mail to other users or to return messages prepared ahead of time to the sender. These features are valuable for users on the road. While cc:Mail Mobile for Windows does offer sophisticated rules-based processing, the rules are interpreted at the remote end, necessitating a download of message headers for questionable e-mail.

So why don't more people use sophisticated e-mail such as Beyond? "BeyondMail has some of the features that come closest to meeting our needs," says John Dubiel, manager of planning and technology at Boston Edison, "but with more than 1,400 users on our messaging system, we cannot consider switching vendors. The conversion and retraining costs would be too great."

BeyondMail's fortunes may change with stronger marketing in the future because of its February acquisition by Banyan Systems (Westboro, MA). Under the terms of the agreement, Banyan acquired the outstanding stock and assumed certain liabilities. A large part of the costs was attributed to the purchase of research and development.

REMOTE FILTERS

Some companies with a particularly active e-mail community have a need for both occasional and regular human intervention to prevent their travelers from downloading unnecessary messages while on the road.

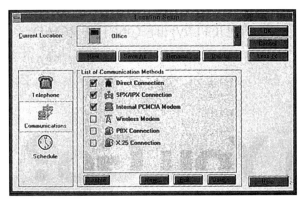

Figure 1. cc:Mail's Mobile for Windows allows users to select up to eight communication methods per location.

Some top executives operate their electronic correspondence just like they do their paper systems–through administrative assistants. With some people receiving upwards of 40 messages per day, Jacobson has been charged with the task of designing mobile connectivity systems for traveling professionals at HP Labs that can be easily filtered by humans. He's still looking.

One type of message the traveler does not need to see is the e-mail "bomb." E-mail bombs are bad enough in the office but are particularly annoying to those on the go. E-mail bombs are messages blasted to a large group of people, or even to the entire company, but of interest or concern to only a few. Messages of complaints, advertising, and politicking are best left either unsent or for a company BBS. "I had a great idea for a new add-on for e-mail–a hormone filter," quips Boston Edison's Dubiel. "For some reason, people lose it when they are writing."

WIRELESS REMOTE

Only within the past year have most of the major e-mail vendors, such as Lotus (cc:Mail) and Microsoft (Microsoft Mail), released remote versions of their programs that included wireless capabilities.

While wireless connectivity is still in its infancy, many companies and industry analysts perceive this market to have extremely high growth potential. "The question is when rather than if," states Roberta Wiggins, director of Wireless Mobile Communications, the Yankee Group. Wiggins estimates that at the end of 1993, there were only 990,000 users of wireless products but says that number will explode to 9.9 million users by the year 2000, a tenfold increase.

There's no doubt that wireless modem technology has

a long way to go before it can be considered a consumer commodity. Wiggins doesn't expect that change to happen for another three years to five years. As of this writing, wireless modems weigh about 12 ounces and cost upward of $750. Reliability of wireless networks and longer message lengths present additional concerns to customers. Speed and transmission rates are possible limiting factors in making wireless a single-source remote platform.

Another aspect of wireless e-mail is that compatible software and hardware must be running at the file server as well as on the remote PC. RAM Mobile Data is one company expecting to break that barrier in 1994, enabling dial-up links to both public networks and the home-office LAN without the need for a special setup on the file server side.

Once again, security issues figure in the wireless picture as they can with public-access networks. Potential wireless customers also voice some concern over saturation and peak usage. Cellular callers experienced long waiting periods before calls went through during recent natural disasters. Since radio communications are not running near their maximum capacity, officials were able to reliably turn to networks such as RAM. RAM and Ardis cover major metropolitan areas, and company spokespeople point out that heavy usage can be handled by subdividing cells and adding towers.

NOT REMOTELY SATISFIED

But what are companies really looking for in remote e-mail? That's just it: E-mail provides only a portion of the data required to keep people apprised of events on the home front. Companies have diverse information requirements, but a common thread is the need to be able to pull data from different sources. Many companies want to tightly integrate their e-mail and database applications.

In February 1994, RAM and Oracle (Redwood Shores, CA) teamed up to announce a "cooperative effort" to develop products that will make wireless access to Oracle databases a reality. Although no specific product or date was announced, the agreement is at least an acknowledgement that vendors are beginning to recognize user requirements.

Group discussions are often cited as a "must" for remote travelers and offices. All locations need to be kept in the information loop. Access to a wide variety of databases is also a requirement, which is why a lot of companies are standardizing on or actively exploring Lotus Notes.

Unfortunately, Lotus Notes and cc:Mail (one of the two most popular e-mail programs around) are not integrated as well as they might be. When you pull information from a Lotus Notes database into cc:Mail, the Dynamic Data Exchange links and graphical information are lost because the file is translated into a plain ASCII text file, according to Jacobson. This loss of information is unfortunate because more companies are deploying Lotus Notes on a wide scale and need to pass information from Notes' databases to executives on the road.

For those in branch offices (as well as those with multiple servers), the replication feature of Lotus Notes is considered especially attractive. Keeping all sites in sync is a matter of establishing a telephone connection between locations. "The challenge is to allow the traveling professional to access his data on his laptop as if he were at a stationary workstation," says Jacobson.

Few e-mail programs also offer an integrated BBS program, a feature that Microsoft Mail users lack but that cc:Mail users have. Encouraging users to make use of a BBS system can help to eliminate some (but not all) of those pesky e-mail bombs that seem to occur in many companies. But the biggest advantage of an integrated BBS is a platform for discussion that all users can access. Lotus' recent introduction of its new cc:Mail Mobile for Windows helped make the BBS messages, as well as regular e-mail messages, as accessible from the road as they are locally.

A REMOTE LONGING

The people who are designing remote platform infrastructures for their companies want and need it all: ease of use, reliability, security, interchangeability, and integration. In short, they need to duplicate the desktop environment at the remote PC. Simple messaging, and even document attachment, is here, but vendors need to provide much more to satisfy remote needs. E-mail is generally only the transportation vehicle for more complex data transfers to those in the field.

The technology available today provides some tools but lacks the flexibility and refinement truly needed. Although good products have been introduced in the past year, further development will need to take place. Analysts and users predict a three- to five-year wait for fully functional deployment.

Boston Edison's Dubiel sums up the goals of most companies seeking remote solutions: "We are trying to work smarter and eliminate the information float."

Mobile Messaging

WITH DIGITAL CELLULAR TECHNOLOGY ON THE HORIZON AND A BEVY OF PDAS COMING TO MARKET, YOUR MESSAGES MAY SOON BEGIN ARRIVING VIA AIRMAIL.

BY CHERYL KRIVDA

It's been that kind of day. Customers have stretched your support staff to the limit, you sent off that department budget that the boss couldn't live without for another moment, and that queue of urgent e-mail messages has stretched into an invisible PC otherworld.

Seeking relief, you scoop up your palmtop, push past the demands of your employees, and walk out into daylight. In minutes, you are seated at your favorite watering hole, sipping a little brew, and . . . productively responding to the electronic correspondence awaiting you.

Sound good? Howard Case thinks so. Case, vice president of messaging for RAM Mobile Data (New York), thinks that the possibilities offered by wireless messaging technologies are not only good for productivity but also an efficient way to keep in touch. "The prospect of picking myself up from my office and going to an outdoor cafe for an espresso, but still being in touch and being able to catch up on some e-mail, is a very liberating experience," he explains.

Wireless messaging, made possible by a variety of miniature computing devices that use radio frequency (RF) or cellular technology to communicate with packet-switched, circuit-switched, or cellular data networks, is a relatively immature market. But Case isn't the only one who sees benefits to this emerging, untethered approach to business. Analysts say that wireless messaging is poised for what may be an incredible takeoff.

Although the 1992 installed base of two-way messaging users numbered only 500,000, The Yankee Group (Boston) expects the numbers to grow to 7 million by the year 2000. Revenues for wireless messaging network services, which totalled a mere $210 million for 1992, are expected to rocket to $2.9 billion by the year 2000.

BLAME IT ON THE MAIL

This enormous growth will be attributed to the entrenched base of 20 million current e-mail users, according to Roberta Wiggins, associate director of wireless mobile communications for The Yankee Group. Approximately 12 percent of those users have potential mobile messaging requirements, meaning wireless messaging technologies could help these mobile users stay connected with their critical e-mail networks.

Although the possible user nodes for wireless messaging are still a moving target both literally and statistically, even conservative analyst estimates suggest that the numbers could be staggering. Including portable computers, Personal Digital Assistants (PDAs), and pagers, a total of 20 million to 25 million users is not an unrealistic expectation for potential wireless messaging users by the end of the decade, says Eric Zimits, an analyst for the San Francisco-based research firm Volpe, Welty, and Company.

For now, wireless messaging comprises only a small fraction of the total wireless communications market. But consider the context: wireless data services will grow from being a $145 million business in 1992 to an $895 million bonanza by the year 2000, according to Datacomm Research Company (Wilmette, IL). This growth means that wireless will be responsible for nearly 10 percent of the projected $10 billion total data-communications market.

A FIELD OF DREAMS

Popular applications for wireless messaging technology include vertical applications such as field service, where users require access to the company information base, and field sales, where users can communicate with decision makers about quotes and deliverables.

But industry watchers view wireless messaging as a technology that could serve innumerable applications needing the benefits of fast, efficient information transmission. With the development of such applications comes the expansion of the traditional definition of "messaging." The term that once meant person-to-person communication on the order of "Meeting at 1 p.m." now means more.

"Messaging" now covers a wider scope, including the field-service rep who receives his day's sales call stops on an alphanumeric pager, the salesperson who negotiates a customer's product discount with the sales manager, and a visiting nurse who receives a patient's medical history on a palmtop computer prior to the visit.

And as e-mail becomes more entrenched as a critical corporate application, more and more professionals want to stay in touch, even while they are physically distant from the network. Wireless messaging technologies have made these applications–and many others–a reasonably priced reality.

AFTERNOON DELIGHT

The annual growth rates of 20 to 25 percent in wireless messaging and paging stem from users' need to stay in touch without being tethered physically to their offices, explains Steve Spiro, director of customer-owned paging for Motorola's Paging Products Group (Boynton Beach, FL). "It's an issue of productivity and customer delight," he explains.

Wireless messaging users can enhance their productivity by quickly responding to messages, requests, and problems. Customers who need to reach the wireless user are delighted to give up games of telephone tag, he says.

The most elementary wireless messaging technology is one-way messaging, which uses paging applications to send information to a user's pager. Given the burgeoning promise of two-way wireless messaging, however, few analysts consider one-way messaging an enduring technology in the wireless messaging arena.

Like a snowball rolling down the mountainside, two-way wireless messaging has increasing momentum and size on its side. Born of pager technology, some of the first two-way wireless messaging applications used alphanumeric pagers that let users send phone numbers and brief messages. Although pagers are still a player for those who

opt not to make the investment in the more expensive notebooks, subnotebooks, and palmtop and laptop devices, these sophisticated computers represent the vision that wireless messaging is pursuing.

PICK A PACKET

Transmission media for wireless messaging is limited to two choices, with a third on the way. Packet-switched RF networks such as those offered by Ardis (Lincolnshire, IL) and RAM Mobile Data enable users who pay for the service to communicate within regions.

Ardis, formed in April 1990 from a partnership between IBM and Motorola, inherited the infrastructure already in place from both companies, which was deployed in some 400 major metropolitan areas. With some 70 companies as clients and approximately 32,000 end users on the network, Ardis has a decided advantage in the marketplace.

Yet RAM Mobile Data, created by a partnership between BellSouth and RAM Broadcasting, has been picking up speed as well. Now in approximately 100 major markets, RAM has heavily publicized its offerings, educating the market about the availability of the packet-switched wireless messaging market.

The technologies of both vendors are similar, using Ericsson GE Mobile Communications (Totowa, NJ) hardware products and RF-enabled modems. Both vendors charge by the packet, which encourages users to send small messages or bursty traffic rather than large files.

Cellular circuit-switched products use the nation's analog cellular network, which is better suited for lengthy transmissions such as file transfer. As with voice, cellular data-transmission charges are based on the amount of time the network is used by the sender, although some carriers offer packaged services that can transcend the time/money equation.

Both of these wireless-network options establish connectivity using specially designed modems, which have either RF or cellular capabilities built-in. These modems, compared with an ice cream sandwich in size, are expected to shrink to the dimensions of a credit card as PCMCIA technologies become more prevalent.

SELLING CELLULAR

On the horizon is Cellular Digital Packet Data (CDPD),

THE MOBILE PROFESSIONAL MARKET

Users (in Millions)

	'91	'92	'93	'94	'95	'96	'97	'98
Cellular Subscribers	7.6	10.5	13.5	16.5	20.0	24.0	28.0	32.0
PCs	0.0	0.0	0.1	0.5	1.0	1.5	2.1	2.6
Paging Subscribers	11.5	13.2	15.2	17.2	19.2	22.0	24.0	26.0
Mobile Data	0.25	0.50	1.2	2.1	3.0	4.3	5.7	7.4
Mobile Computers*	0.0	0.0	0.023	0.075	0.255	0.795	1.515	2.595
PDAs	0.0	0.0	0.002	0.022	0.094	0.289	0.889	1.749

* Portable computers with integrated wireless communications capability.
Source: The Yankee Group, 1993

Figure 1. Count on 1995 as the watershed year for wireless messaging, when trends in each technology collectively push wireless messaging to the communications forefront.

a carrier service that intends to fill idle voice time on cellular systems with packets of digital data transmissions. CDPD offers the ubiquity of cellular service as well as transmission speeds of 19.2Kbps, which can be four times faster than existing wireless networks.

The two key players in CDPD are Ameritech Cellular, a spinoff of the Chicago-area RBOC, and McCaw Cellular Communications (Kirkland, WA)

Both vendors are part of an eight-member consortium supporting CDPD development. The consortium is composed of GTE Mobilnet (Atlanta) and all of the RBOCs except BellSouth, which is interested in the success of RAM Mobile Data, and US West (Denver), which pulled out after reported disagreements with the other carriers. The consortium is working to establish an open specification for transmitting data packets.

Yet no one is really sure what CDPD will cost or how users will react to the carriers' newest network. The carriers are betting that CDPD will help enable and expand wireless messaging technologies; The Yankee Group's Wiggins agrees. Because cellular already has nationwide coverage and the advantage of people who are familiar with the technology, many prospective users may see CDPD as an add-on to their current cellular voice services, she says.

The carriers have said little or nothing, however, about the hardware devices required to use CDPD, Wiggins notes. "For carriers to implement and create nationwide connectivity, billing, and support requires cooperation among carriers that they haven't had before," Wiggins says.

ANYWHERE, BUT NOT EVERYWHERE

Cost is a compelling factor for end users trying to determine which technologies and vendors to use. Gone is the perceived need to select one vendor; some users feel that bringing multiple vendors in for different applications buys them leverage.

But using multiple vendors requires heretofore unseen interconnectivity. "The lack of standards is blatant" in wireless messaging now, Wiggins explains. "Vendors are trying to promote their own solutions, but they're still coming from [their own] position, with their own standard."

The lack of standards is compounded by the fact that CDPD may not be available nationwide for years. Ira Brodsky, president of Datacomm, watches the CDPD market closely. "To provide certain types of wide-area services for the general business traveler, it is not good enough to provide service in 50 percent of his locations. It has to be 100 percent." CDPD is not even promised for all major cities, and until it is, "I see this evolving somewhat more slowly than some of the people more directly involved with CDPD would care to admit publicly," Brodsky says.

How quickly CDPD carriers can bring their services to market may depend to some degree on how quickly they see wireless messaging taking off. Every successful packet-switched and cellular circuit-switched installation translates into lost revenues for the CDPD carriers, which forces them to keep delivery plans on the fast track.

TAKING STOCK IN WIRELESS

But waiting for CDPD–or any other future wireless messaging technology–may not be in the best interests of users who could enhance productivity with currently available products. Some users who have an eye toward future technical enhancements are gaining benefits with today's wireless messaging technology. Stephen Schoenfeld, managing director of Lehman Brothers (New York), uses a RAM Mobile Data application that allows message exchange between himself and brokers on the floor of the stock exchange. He communicates this way in numerous cities across the country, saving time and effort on what would normally be endless games of telephone tag.

Currently the application is only used for e-mail messages, not orders or executions, but Schoenfeld says that usage will change. In the future, he would like the product to handle the complete range of stock transactions and provide access to news services and other information sources. He also would like to move from the current palmtop computer to pen-based computing. The palmtop is "too small and very hard to type the messages. And I'd like to see the modem put into a PCMCIA card," Schoenfeld says.

But after using the wireless technology for six months, Schoenfeld says he is happy with it. In the financial-services industry, he adds, constant contact with clients and colleagues is a must, and wireless messaging helps him achieve that kind of communication.

Schoenfeld is part of the white-collar work force that is only now beginning to embrace the wireless messaging technology. Unlike field-based blue-collar workers who may have been previously unexposed to computers, white-collar workers have the advantage of being familiar with PCs and laptops.

Companies that bring wireless messaging into blue-collar environments can cost-justify the technology based on the fact that each employee saves 20 minutes to 60 minutes per day in time not spent looking for or using a telephone. Rob Euler, vice president of business develop-

ment for Ardis, estimates that 3 million field-service and logistics workers are potential wireless messaging users.

In contrast, white-collar environments can cost-justify wireless messaging because it extends critical corporate applications outside company walls, making employees more productive and empowered by information. Euler says that the white-collar market includes 2 million potential users.

Two other groups moving toward wireless messaging are those interested in a mobile office and those who want personal computing in a wireless platform. For these users who want the desktop extended to the field, Euler says, the office applications must be modified for the wireless paradigm.

"There is a lot of work to be done to make those solutions a reality and to capture the 10 or 14 million potential users in that category," Euler says. Vendors such as WordPerfect, AT&T, Novell, and Lotus have expressed interest in going wireless, but he adds that the hardware vendors need to get more involved in producing devices that work with RF equipment.

Another issue, he says, is that the wireless industry still requires unique APIs for individual network vendors, which makes application-software interoperability difficult. "One of the things we are working on is industry-standard APIs that take away the unique interface to either Ardis, RAM, or eventually CDPD. Then the jobs necessary to make applications wireless capable could be reduced to basic application work," Euler says.

But is the market ready for a standards group that could get the major players on track? "No, and I would just as soon not use that approach," Euler insists. "It is a little early in the life of this technology to have a standard by committee. I think we can achieve a standard by putting products in the marketplace that work and getting a lot of people to use them," he says.

While Euler and others dislike the idea of standards, some prospective buyers feel uncomfortable with the idea of buying products that may not protect their investment. Denise Anderson, principal with analyst firm Sequoia Telecom Associates (Redwood City, CA), advises buyers to evaluate the current benefits of wireless messaging and ignore what may come. After evaluating the site's needs, consider how wireless messaging could improve productivity and efficiency. Then forget vendor promises.

"What good is waiting to bet on [what might come] if there is an immediate need," she asks, where a site can "recoup benefits or savings or improve service to their customer? If you have a driving need, go for what is on the market now. If you wait for the next thing to come, by the time it comes, someone will already be talking about the one after that."

CULTURE SHOCK

Implementing new technology such as wireless messaging is not strictly a technical exercise. As with the introduction of all technological change, corresponding corporate cultural changes may be required.

"You need baseline policies on how these technologies are going to be employed. Who is going to use them? Do you know who is going to benefit? Where does the productivity come from?" asks analyst Zimits.

On the bright side, he notes, many companies already considered issues involved with wireless messaging when they incorporated e-mail systems in the 1980s. "It is a matter of extending that concept of electronic mail outside the office, and that's probably not the greatest hurdle in the world," he says.

While some wireless messaging users resent their employers' ability to track their whereabouts, most new users are field-service personnel or salespeople who can benefit by having access to corporate information off-site. "If they can get their jobs done faster and make more money for themselves or their companies, they clearly see the benefits very quickly," Motorola's Spiro explains. "If you can delight your customers by responding quickly, that's worth it."

Even those companies that introduce wireless messaging to employees who have no previous computer experience generally report good results. Ardis' Euler notes that Otis Elevator gave its technicians a hand-held computer to record repairs, service calls, and parts used.

"There was a set of emotional and organizational issues that Otis had to deal with to put this into their hands," Euler recalls. But 60 days later, the technicians refused to go back to their old system. They enjoyed having access to the information that enabled them to tell a customer when a part would arrive or what day they would return to complete a job. "They are just so much more empowered, and they derive a lot of personal satisfaction out of it," he says.

JUST LIKE WIRE?

Despite its advantages, wireless messaging technologies do not offer an exact replica of the wired alternative. Those who expect to perform file transfers, print services, and manipulation of large images on a wireless network will be disappointed, at least for a while. But technical advances are arriving, almost weekly.

At the June 1993 Electronic Messaging Association trade show in Atlanta, Ericsson GE introduced the Mobidem AT, a wireless modem that uses the standard (circuit-switched) Hayes AT command set. The use of the AT command set means that Mobidem users can use applications designed for circuit-switched modems with only minor adjustments to their communications scripts.

The manufacturer of Mobidem says that the use of the AT command set will short-circuit the universal API issue now troubling the wireless messaging industry. Bill Frezza, director of marketing and business development for the hardware manufacturer, says that vendors who have been panting to enter the wireless messaging market can more easily wireless-enable their products when APIs are not an issue.

Already vendors such as Lotus Development (Cambridge, MA) and AT&T EasyLink Services (Parsippany, NJ) have jumped on the wireless bandwagon. Both partners of Ericsson, the two companies announced wireless access to their cc:mail and EasyLink products, respectively. RadioMail, a San Mateo, CA-based wireless messaging vendor, recently announced a wireless service that delivers, among other things, breaking news and financial information to wireless users.

Another vendor playing in the wireless messaging ballgame is Intel (Santa Clara, CA), which announced that it would begin selling Ericsson-based wireless modems bundled with popular communications packages, all through its retail channels. When the new distribution strategy begins later this year, it will mark the first time that Intel or Ericsson has sold wireless products using a retail strategy.

PICKING PARTNERS

One issue that has not been widely addressed by most vendors is how users will support their wireless messaging systems. Chuck Napier, manager of new business development for GTE Mobilnet, warns that the diversity between traditional computer vendors and radio vendors may complicate wireless messaging support.

"It is a problem, but it's a short-term problem," he says. LAN providers are unaccustomed to the demands of the radio environment, and wireless carriers know little about computers and protocols. A merger of the technologies may be needed, so customers can have one point of contact for their wireless messaging systems.

Vendors seem to intuitively know that such combined expertise is needed, judging by the number of industry partnerships that have been formed and are continuing to develop. The existing BellSouth/RAM Broadcasting, IBM/Motorola, and Ericsson/ Lotus/AT&T EasyLink/Ardis partnerships were matched in June by an announcement that Motorola's Paging and Wireless Data Group (Schaumberg, IL) plans to work with more than 20 leading wireless messaging vendors to establish common, worldwide standards for a family of PCMCIA-format intelligent modems. Motorola announced plans to develop such products.

Even so, the number of new-product announcements hitting the market each week, as well as the fear, uncertainty, and doubt being created by some players who have no products, may be retarding the development of the market.

In fact, several vendors who asked to remain anonymous voiced anger and frustration with other vendors who announce future directions without any specific product plans. Such announcements, they say, are designed to keep their names in the press but really serve to encourage potential buyers to wait for the next generation of technology. "A lot of people have been frozen into confusion," agrees Ericsson's Frezza.

SWELL TECHNOLOGY

But the future, as seen through the eyes of those who are shaping it, is tempting indeed. The anticipated growth of Personal Communications Service (PCS) is expected to expand the wireless messaging market horizontally. Until now, the only way for the market to grow has been vertically. With the advent of PCS devices in smaller form factors and at more affordable prices, the boundaries of wireless messaging services will swell the ranks of providers, customers, and equipment. "What we are seeing now in the marketplace [in terms of] the current service providers

and the current users is really just the tip of the iceberg," agrees GTE's Napier.

One trend that will accelerate horizontal growth is the increasing willingness of applications vendors to go wireless. At press time, two major e-mail providers were preparing to deliver product versions that can operate with wireless networks. And with Intel beginning to distribute wireless modems through retail channels later this year, the wireless market will grow through sheer consumer awareness.

What may not improve dramatically in the near future is the speed at which wireless messaging applications run. Large file transfers and high-bandwidth applications, such as multimedia presentations, are still best suited for traditional wired technologies. Although interested users have voiced a preference for wireless messaging that operates at wired speeds, vendors and analysts alike say that may be a pipe dream for now.

Wiggins reports that The Yankee Group expects 1995 to be the watershed year for wireless messaging. In that year, she says, digitization of the cellular network, the growth of PCS devices, and the widespread availability of PDAs should combine to push wireless messaging into the forefront of the communications business (see Figure 1).

As vendors begin to address performance needs, they will need to consider the best means of filtering and forwarding messages. "You want an agent that sits on your LAN and [determines what] is appropriate to send out wirelessly and what is best left to send over a wire," explains Ericsson's Frezza. He suggests that such agents should allow user-definable parameters that specify which message types should be forwarded wirelessly.

PLANES, TRAINS, BUSES, AND AUTOMOBILES

Avis Hits the Airwaves

Avis uses wireless messaging to simplify travelers' car rentals. Grace Dieterich, systems manager for the Garden City, NY-based company, reports that Avis passenger buses at 16 major airports are now equipped with Motorola 9100 mobile data terminals, which have built-in computers, displays, keyboards, and radios.

When travelers board the Avis pickup bus, the bus driver types their customer information into the terminal. The information is transmitted across the Ardis network to the Avis network in New York using a multichannel X.25 link.

The Avis system processes the information and sends it back through the network. The system instructs a local printer to print a rental agreement, selects a car from those available based on the customer's preferences, and determines the location of each car in the lot. The display lists the travelers' names and car locations in an order that enables the driver to efficiently drop each passenger at the waiting car.

The first Avis wireless messaging system was installed on a test basis at LaGuardia Airport in the spring of 1992. The service was rolled out to other airports a few months later and was very successful, allowing customers to more quickly get their cars from Avis. In a matter of months, the number of people using the system has doubled, meaning that now more than a quarter million customers use the service. In addition, Avis management is pleased with the product because it enables more efficient customer service without significant increases in staff.

Like many new users, the bus drivers were initially leery of the terminals, but now they love using them. "They like it particularly because they are [no longer] getting garbled radio messages in a congested airport area," Dieterich says.

Avis is exploring further uses of the technology in airports where buses are not used or common busing prevents the company from installing the product. Dieterich says she is also considering using wireless messaging for field sales people who need access to the Avis network. "Once you see how well it works in one application, you become very curious to see how else you might utilize it," she explains.

Mail Masonry

AN INTEROPERABLE, MULTIVENDOR MESSAGING INFRASTRUCTURE CAN PROVIDE A STURDY FOUNDATION FOR GLOBAL DIRECTORY SERVICES AND APPLICATIONS.

BY NINA BURNS

Building a corporate messaging system is like building a house. First you want a solid foundation and frame. Then you want services, such as electrical and plumbing. Finally, you want the finishing, which is, after all, what really attracts buyers–the curb appeal. But if the foundation is not sound and the services are not reliable, then no matter how nice the finishing, you will have unhappy buyers.

Messaging is the same way. If you install an unreliable foundation (the underlying store-and-forward transport), and the services (such as management and directory services) are unreliable or incomplete, then no matter how nice the user interface is, you will have unhappy customers and an unreliable system.

Just as the general contractor hires subcontractors and specialists to provide expertise in each of the components of the house, the systems integrator or the information technology department are becoming the general contractors for messaging. They must purchase each of the components from the supplier that will provide the best value, all the while mixing and matching services and applications to meet business requirements (see Figure 1).

Over time, most applications will be mail enabled, and new groupware and workflow applications will take advantage of a stable, underlying store-and-forward system as widespread as the telephone system. But until products fitting this new model are widely available (and keep in mind that software development can have a long transition period), users will have to deal with a mix of different systems and use creativity to integrate them on the network.

ONE IS THE LONELIEST

Except in the case of products that supported Novell Message Handling System (MHS), the accepted model, until recently, was to purchase a complete e-mail system from the same vendor. Products such as Lotus cc:Mail, Microsoft Mail, and most others supplied proprietary transports, directory services (or address books), and a user interface.

This setup locked users into one vendor, limited the users' ability to build mail-enabled applications, provided little or no interoperability among disparate e-mail system, and provided no transition to open systems.

To compound this problem, today most user organizations are faced with integrating a variety of proprietary e-mail systems on numerous host- and LAN-based systems. Users are dissatisfied with cross-platform performance. Interoperability, functionality, and management are costly and inefficient. The most commonly voiced complaints can be divided into functional and operational issues.

Functional problems include:

• Everyone is not connected or does not have access to e-mail.

• Addressing and naming conventions differ across e-mail systems and other applications.

• Cross-system functionality is not consistent.

• Attachments are not always usable or available to the recipient.

• Privacy and security need to be addressed before outside organizations can have access to the network.

• No global synchronized directory exists.

• Users need to have multiple mailboxes and IDs.

• Users have no single source of mail; instead, they have e-mail, fax mail, voice mail, and pager messages, none of which are integrated.

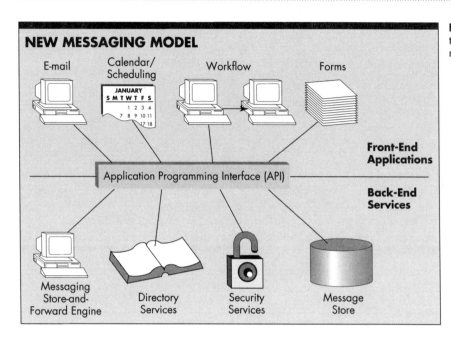

NEW MESSAGING MODEL

E-mail

Calendar/Scheduling

JANUARY
S M T W T F S
1 2 3 4
7 8 9 10 11
17 18

Workflow

Forms

Application Programming Interface (API)

Front-End Applications

Back-End Services

Messaging Store-and-Forward Engine

Directory Services

Security Services

Message Store

Figure 1: Stable messaging infrastructure enables the emergence of a whole new generation of applications.

• Using various e-mail systems within the company creates too much disparity in functionality.

Operational malfunctions include:

• Current systems are unpredictable, unreliable, and inconsistent.

• Manual processes–especially directory synchronization, gateways, and management–are slow and unreliable.

• Company management doesn't know what corporate e-mail should cost, therefore they don't plan the budget appropriately.

• Users don't know who to call for support and service.

• There are no service-level agreements, so the users don't know what to expect.

• Network-management tools and applications are not available.

• No published policy and use guidelines for cross-platform systems exist.

SHARE AND SHARE ALIKE

Given the challenge of answering these complaints, most companies recognize the need to establish a global electronic messaging network to link departments, business units, and divisions with each other and customers, suppliers, and trading partners. Companies have many reasons for investing in a utility that will serve applications and users.

A global messaging infrastructure can enable the transition into distributed computing and decentralization and can offer support for cross-organizational applications and teams. Global messaging also improves efficiency and reduces costs. In particular, it can streamline the business by allowing companies to perform fewer manual processes. This automation can reduce material costs and duplication of efforts, especially if the company standardizes.

Enterprise mail allows corporations to share information more efficiently and to build effective information channels across organizations. The e-mail infrastructure can become the vehicle for reengineering processes.

Enterprise mail offers speed in communication, allowing management to communicate quickly on timely topics such as technology and corporate changes. Mail also allows companies to reduce response times to customers and other market forces.

WE DELIVER

A corporate messaging system is a good business value for companies. Quantifiable cost benefits include savings in paper, employee time, and phone expenses. Other savings include fewer fax messages and reduced courier-service expenses. A messaging system also paves the way for less-expensive application development.

TABLE 1—POINT-TO-POINT GATEWAY, PROS AND CONS

PROS	CONS
Good solution for limited number of systems (two or three)	Quickly unmanageable
Low barriers to entry	Many vendors to coordinate
Quickly implemented	Directory synchronization
Widely available	Performance limitations
Relatively inexpensive	Version control
Can be used to isolate mail systems from others	Availability in all environments
Good workgroup solution	Poor scalability
Excellent interoperability	

TABLE 2—SWITCH TECHNOLOGY, PROS AND CONS

PROS	CONS
Can be transparent	Locked into one vendor
Lower barriers to entry than backbone	New, as yet unproven in very large environments
Scalable compared to gateways	
Lower cost compared to backbone	Not as scalable as backbone
Often preserves native functionality user interface, and so forth	
Interoperability	
Reduces management overhead compared to point-to-point gateways	
Reduces the number of vendors	

Figure 2 shows the cost of delivering a two-page letter via e-mail, the U.S. Postal Service, facsimile, and a courier service. Labor costs, supplies and communications charges (for fax and e-mail) are included in the analysis. E-mail costs also include e-mail hardware and software, support, and maintenance costs. Fax costs do not include the price of fax machines and maintenance.

If you extend the analysis in Figure 2, you can see that converting just 20 percent of your correspondence to e-mail easily pays for acquisition and maintenance costs of the e-mail system (see Figure 3).

GETTING IN THE FLOW

Keep in mind that this analysis takes into account only e-mail as an application using the infrastructure. In fact, the real return on investment comes from the line-of-business applications, such as workflow automation applications (including purchase-order processing, sales-force automation, customer-inquiry systems, and manufacturing processes) that will use the messaging infrastructure.

The following examples are taken from actual cases where the value of e-mail was measured by its benefit to the company:

• Made more customer contact for less money spent on advertising.

• Eliminated the need to hire new order-processing operators and increased the sales volume by automating ordering systems. This setup proved to be much faster than people taking orders over the phone.

• Reduced risk associated with out-of-date legal information.

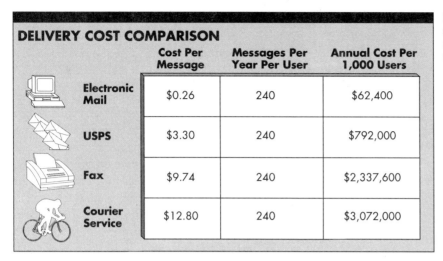

DELIVERY COST COMPARISON	Cost Per Message	Messages Per Year Per User	Annual Cost Per 1,000 Users
Electronic Mail	$0.26	240	$62,400
USPS	$3.30	240	$792,000
Fax	$9.74	240	$2,337,600
Courier Service	$12.80	240	$3,072,000

Figure 2: Electronic delivery is significantly cheaper than conventional methods, and the savings are easy to compare.

• Increased the number of loans processed daily.

• Increased the productivity of a sales force by improving the success rate of sales calls because account information was readily available and up to date.

• Decreased the cost of goods by reducing the number of errors and returns due to incomplete or out-of-date information.

• Improved customer satisfaction and reduced inquiry costs by decreasing the turn-around time on customer-service inquiries.

The key to building a reliable, stable, multivendor messaging infrastructure that also addresses complaints about current systems in interoperability at three levels: transport, directory services, and applications. The best approach to an open-systems transition is to develop a plan and a phased integration and transition for each of the three levels.

TRANSPORT

Just as with networking, the first standardization is taking place in the lower layers. A number of techniques are available for integrating disparate mail systems into a cohesive, companywide infrastructure.

One strategy is to dictate one e-mail platform across the company. This arrangement reduces the complexity–and thereby the operational costs–and it enhances interoperability between various client platforms, such as DOS, Macintosh, Windows, and Unix. This strategy thus lends itself to easy-to-manage operations and growth.

However, this arrangement extracts a large price. It reduces your options for software since few vendors provide clients for all platforms. It also locks you into one vendor, who may be able to service your current needs but who offers no guarantee to meet your long-term needs. This plan also reduces future application diversity, because single providers don't usually support multiple APIs. It also assumes that users will hand in current and legacy systems for new systems, often neither feasible nor cost-effective.

Other alternatives allow you to interconnect current systems and transition to standards over time. Matching integration techniques to your environment is critical to an efficient and cost-effective solution. Three common architectures available for integration are point-to-point gateways, message switches, and backbones.

POINT-TO-POINT GATEWAYS

Gateways translate messages from one system to another. They map user names in one system to those in another to ensure delivery, and they translate the format of the envelope and message between systems. One gateway is needed between each two different mail systems you want to interconnect. For example, if you have four e-mail systems to connect, you need six gateways to connect each one to the other; for five e-mail systems, you need 10 gateways.

This architecture quickly becomes unmanageable as the environment gets too complex, usually as soon as you have more than two or three systems. However, for interconnecting just one or two other systems or for low-vol-

TABLE 3—BACKBONE, PROS AND CONS	
PROS	**CONS**
Reduces number of gateways	Often difficult to implement
Easier to manage than multiple gateways	Requires good planning and management practices
Can be based on open standards	
Greater redundancy and fault tolerance	Higher barriers to entry
Better leverage	Probably overkill for fewer than four or more systems
Scalability	
Interoperability	Directory synchronization
Flexibility	Can be lowest common denominator
Supports integration into other services such as directory, EDI, voice-mail, and fax	Can be very expensive
Standardized method for handling attachments	

ume systems, point-to-point gateways are cost-effective, provide good message integrity between systems, and are readily available (see Table 1).

Gateways from proprietary e-mail systems, such as cc:Mail, WordPerfect Office, and Microsoft Mail, are available to just about every other system, including PROFS, Simple Mail Transport Protocol (SMTP), Novell MHS, SNADS, X.400, and public e-mail services such as MCI Mail, AT&T Mail, and SprintMail. Likewise, gateways are available from Novell MHS to all these other mail systems.

MESSAGE SWITCHES

A relatively new approach to integrating diverse messaging systems is message switches. These switches typically interconnect a number of e-mail systems. Connections are made using native protocols, and translation takes place only when needed. These switches usually provide message exchange, directory services, and some management capabilities beyond what is generally available in gateways (see Table 2).

Alisa Systems, Banyan, Computer Data Systems, Digital Equipment, Novell, SoftSwitch, Wingra, and WorldTalk all provide message-switching products and services.

BACKBONES

An e-mail backbone provides a common set of protocols for interconnecting diverse e-mail systems. Typically, gateways are used between the proprietary e-mail systems and the backbone protocol. In this setup, one gateway is needed for every e-mail system. Several mature backbone technologies are available to choose from. The most common ones are SNADS, SMTP, X.400, Novell MHS, and proprietary transports such as cc:Mail and Microsoft Mail. Your choice will depend upon your current environment, network architecture, and future plans for moving to open systems (see Table 3).

DIRECTORY SERVICES

A variety of directory services have been deployed that meet specific application requirements such as e-mail, network name services, and human resources. However, these application-specific directories are not typically designed to act as corporate or global directories that service multiple applications and supply access to all users.

Each system has its own naming conventions and address schemes; therefore, when interconnecting a variety of e-mail systems, directory integration is a large consideration. The goal is to have the ability to add a user just once, and then that user becomes visible in all the requisite directories. Furthermore, you want to allow access to the directory by users on a variety of platforms and from within current applications.

Current e-mail directory-integration products integrate the stored directory information from a variety of diverse

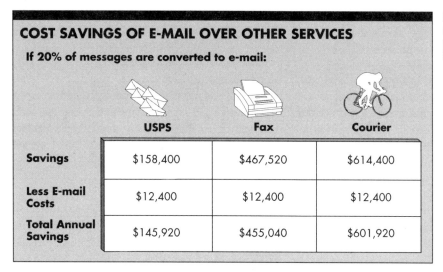

COST SAVINGS OF E-MAIL OVER OTHER SERVICES

If 20% of messages are converted to e-mail:

	USPS	Fax	Courier
Savings	$158,400	$467,520	$614,400
Less E-mail Costs	$12,400	$12,400	$12,400
Total Annual Savings	$145,920	$455,040	$601,920

Figure 3: Delivery cost savings are easy to determine and alone can justify your entire messaging infrastructure. Other benefits are free.

mail systems, including SMTP, PROFS, cc:Mail, Microsoft Mail for PCs, and X.400. These solutions typically maintain duplicates of all the names stored in different address books or directory services across the network and give each entry an "alias" name. A user sees only the directory entry in the native format of his or her application. With this arrangement, users remain shielded from the complexities of a variety of unfamiliar directory formats.

However, few commercial products have been available, and those that do exist are available only on limited platforms.

The trick is to integrate e-mail and other directories scattered throughout your organization into a single, corporate-level directory service that reflects all the information stored in the disparate systems. This directory must have the ability to update and manage all directories in a consistent manner. You really have only two choices for accomplishing this synchronization and management. Either construct a corporate directory-services backbone (often based on X.500 or X.500-like directory services), or integrate diverse directory services through a switch or through gateways.

Most users have had to create their own directory integration, including update and synchronization capabilities, using tools supplied by a variety of vendors. This undertaking is complex, especially as the directory becomes a critical corporate asset. It requires flexibility, management facilities, and security commensurate with the critical na-

ture of the information stored. However, new directory integration products are entering the market, and industry-standard APIs, X.500 solutions, and published APIs are helping. Alisa Systems, Banyan, Computer Data Systems, Digital Equipment, Hewlett-Packard, Novell, Retix, SoftSwitch, and WorldTalk all provide directory-service and integration products.

APPLICATIONS

Once the interconnected messaging infrastructure is complete, it can be used not only for interpersonal messaging (messages sent from user to user) but also for applications that generate e-mail messages destined for users or other applications (mail-enabled applications). The availability of published APIs is critical to this model, because messaging services will be used by a wide range of different applications.

APIs define the boundary between the message transport and directory services and applications (see Figure 1). Consequently, the establishment of industry-standard APIs stimulates the widespread commercial deployment of messaging technology and applications. APIs provide easy access to the transport and directory services of the messaging infrastructure for a variety of applications.

Published APIs can be used by the applications provided by a single vendor, by applications provided by any other vendor or third-party developer, and by custom applications developed by end users. This availability allows the applications to be developed separately from the underlying message transport technology. So, over time, a greater number of applications will emerge to provide a range of functionality and creativity which could not be achieved through the efforts of a single vendor or supplier. It also means that if the underlying transport and directory services change over time, the applications do not need to change, because the APIs will remain constant. This structure will facilitate a much smoother transition to standards.

Standardization on a few APIs is likely to promote an unprecedented growth in the messaging industry. Novell Standard Message Format (SMF), Microsoft MAPI, Apple Open Collaboration Environment (AOCE), X.400 API Association (XAPIA), Common Messaging Calls (CMC), and Vendor-Independent Messaging (VIM) are likely to be the most commonly supported.

BETTER DAYS

The good news is that suppliers are splitting along the infrastructure and application line. This division means more choices for users and better applications supplied at a faster rate. More messaging-integration products are becoming available, and new X.400 products are improving functionality and performance and bringing prices down. new groupware and workflow applications are emerging, and users have access to a variety of APIs for custom development.

The bad news is that there are still a lot of APIs to choose from. And the splitting of the application from the infrastructure will take time. Directory-services and integration products, a critical component to the new model, are lagging way behind the messaging integration products.

Furthermore, a variety of critical issues still need to be solved within user organizations. Users quickly find out that as soon as you begin to contemplate a corporate directory to service applications and users, you need to address a number of technically and politically challenging issues, not the least of which are corporate naming conventions and management architectures. The key to success is planning, carefully scrutinizing vendor solutions, and being realistic about what is available today and how you will implement a transition over time.

The True Cost of E-Mail Ownership

COMPANIES STRUGGLE WITH BUILDING A FINANCIAL CASE FOR E-MAIL. HERE'S HOW TO SHOW THE FINANCIAL ANALYSTS THAT YOU'VE BUILT A COST-EFFECTIVE SYSTEM.

BY NINA BURNS

E-mail has arrived. E-mail is an accepted way for businesses to exchange correspondence, deliver documents, and distribute scientific research. E-mail helps people avoid telephone tag, decrease travel expenses, and share gossip. E-mail serves to create workgroups of people in different locations, even across international boundaries.

Business people, engineers, scientists, public figures, and students use e-mail. Bill Clinton is the first U.S. President to have a public e-mail account. Countries are organizing national e-mail systems, corporations are implementing private e-mail systems, and utility companies are creating e-mail subscription services. And regulatory agencies are trying to keep pace with this new form of communication.

E-mail systems are developing to include compound documents, faxes, personal paging systems, telex, images, and video. The basic store-and-forward electronic messaging technology, which enables one person to send a message at his leisure and the recipient to gather the message at her convenience, is here to stay.

Despite e-mail's utility, corporations struggle with building a financial case for messaging. E-mail isn't an electronic novelty anymore. But for e-mail to be perceived as a serious communications tool, it must be treated as any other mature business technology.

To build the financial case for e-mail, network planners must delve into some of the most difficult issues in business and accounting, including the meaning of value. Network planners must struggle with how value is measured. Is value defined as saved paper, saved time, lower computing costs, or increased employee productivity? If an e-mail system allows managers to track the amount of time spent on jobs that were not formerly monitored, then how do planners build a financial case for e-mail?

Planners must analyze some of the accounting issues relevant to distributed technology, such as what happens when logical networks are constructed. For example, if one computer houses a piece of software used by five different cost centers, how do you allocate the cost of the maintenance, disaster recovery, storage and backup, and depreciation?

WHY CALCULATE THE COST?

For private corporations and even countries, the issue is not whether to have an e-mail system but how to provide the most cost-effective system. Consequently, companies need a method to find the cost of ownership for technical and business reasons.

Planners should perform a cost analysis for technical reasons, such as:
• to understand their cost basis for e-mail and evaluate alternative ways to provide services;
• to decide the long-term cost-effectiveness of an e-mail backbone;
• to make technology and architectural choices; and
• to decide how or when voice mail, fax, telex, personal pager, video, and e-mail should be merged.

Planners should also perform a cost analysis for business reasons, including:
• to determine the business value of e-mail to the company;
• to set internal charge-back prices so the computer department can recoup costs;
• to gain corporate funding for messaging projects;

TABLE 1: THE COST BASIS FOR E-MAIL

ACQUISITION	COSTS
E-mail and integration software	Fixed
E-mail and integration hardware	Fixed
Disaster-recovery software and hardware	Fixed
Uninterruptible power supplies	Fixed
Documentation	Fixed
PERSONNEL	
For design	Recurring
For installation	Recurring
For backup	Recurring
For management and administration	Recurring
OPERATIONS	
Data-center storage-space overhead	Recurring
Backup systems purchased	Fixed
Storage cabinets purchased	Fixed
Leased phone lines	Recurring
Security systems purchased	Fixed
Software-support contracts	Recurring

• to calculate return on investment;

• to establish profit margins; and

• to decide whether to enter the messaging-service industry.

For many years, e-mail implementers fought for acceptance within the corporate environment, but in the past three to five years, e-mail systems have become a serious part of the information technology environment. Many technologies have merged, including PC and LAN-based e-mail systems, voice mail, personal pagers, wireless transmission, fax, and telex. When technology advances so quickly, it's easy to get into trouble financially. Aside from the legal and regulatory issues, any profit-making company will want to understand how far it should take a technology and what the bottom line will be. To do so, the planners must analyze the technology from a variety of standpoints.

FINANCIAL ANALYSIS

At first, you might think financial analysis is difficult because investment in technology often yields an intangible product. You can't physically touch messages. But financial accounting tools are used to track other intangibles, such as worldwide currency exchanges and components in the process of being manufactured. Why

does financial analysis of technology seem so difficult? Performing a financial analysis of the technology won't be as much of an issue for companies putting in their first system as it will be for companies who have already invested in a technology. In the past, fewer options existed for selecting a system. If you had IBM mainframes or Digital Equipment VAXs, only one or two companies could deliver an e-mail system to meet your requirements. Price wasn't the factor; finding the system that would run on your computers was the challenge.

Many more e-mail systems are available today, and usually several are installed within one company. When these systems were installed, most companies did not envision that they were building a corporatewide e-mail system. Consequently, the planners did not anticipate or account for the direct and hidden costs of integrating the multiple diverse systems in an attempt to build a corporatewide e-mail infrastructure.

In addition, most e-mail systems in place today were purchased for technical reasons and later examined for cost. Companies are now conducting retroactive cost-based analysis and cost justifications. E-mail spread throughout the organization in a variety of ways, without the participation of the finance department and usually without cost analysis or justification.

FINANCIAL MANAGEMENT

Technologies are described as mature when they stabilize and gain popularity. For example, the telephone system is a mature technology. With the exception of voice mail, the accounting and cost justification of telephone systems has not changed over the past several years.

The opposite is true for e-mail. Distributed e-mail is an emerging technology; it is changing rapidly, with little historical base to draw on, and has few tools for measurement and management. The first time a company tries to account for e-mail, it typically applies traditional methods.

Network planners need to rethink the accounting methods for e-mail. Should you expense the system in one year or depreciate it over five years? Should you charge as a service or as a product, or as a combination of both? At what point is gathering accounting information so labor intensive that it increases the price of providing the system? Since most software does not provide the utilities necessary to bill the customer for usage, companies must

TABLE 2: THE COST COMPONENTS FOR E-MAIL SYSTEMS	
ITEM	UNIT OF MEASURE
EQUIPMENT	
Server and backup hardware	Dollars depreciated over years
Assorted cabling	Dollars depreciated over years
Phone lines	Recurring cost: leased equipment in dollars per month
Uninterruptible power supply	Dollars per month per power units
Cabinets	Dollars depreciated over years
Facility	Capital expense: dollars depreciated over years
Server software	One-time cost in dollars
Licensing fees	One-time cost in dollars
Additional e-mail software	One-time cost in dollars
Backup software	One-time cost in dollars or hourly cost for in-house development
Gateways	One-time cost in dollars
STAFFING	
In-house support	One-time cost in dollars or hourly cost for in-house development
Software development	One-time cost in dollar is commissioned outside company or hourly cost for in-house development
SUPPORT AND MAINTENANCE	
Help-desk support	One-time cost in dollars or hourly cost for in-house development
Client software installation and maintenance	One-time cost in dollars or hourly cost for in-house development
Network installation and troubleshooting	One-time cost in dollars or hourly cost for in-house development
Management coordination	One-time cost in dollars or hourly cost for in-house development
Nightshift backup and monitoring	One-time cost in dollars or hourly cost for in-house development

build additional systems on top of their off-the-shelf e-mail systems so they can satisfy the finance and accounting departments.

THE IMPACT OF CHANGE

Computer technology changes more in one year than the basic financial accounting models have changed over the past few decades. Technologists are accustomed to rapid change, but financial analysts often see the subject of their analysis change, while the financial accounting models remain constant.

Most companies have just begun to feel comfortable accounting for centralized data processing, only to watch the newest technology become completely distributed. The corporate finance and accounting departments react accordingly, but just as distributed cost accounting was refined within specific departments or cost centers, the decentralized systems began to sprawl across departments and international divisions.

In financial terms, centralized mainframe-based systems could be depreciated over seven to 10 years, but decentralized hardware has changed so rapidly that many companies depreciate it over only three to five years. Divide a couple of million dollars of equipment by five years instead of 10 years, and this depreciation method has a significant impact on the bottom line.

In technical terms, technology migrated not only from a centralized to a decentralized architecture but also from a physically networked system to a logically networked system. If several departments at different levels use a single computer within a given day, how do you allocate the cost of that machine?

MAPPING TO BUSINESS

The financial analyst considers profits with acceptable loss or risk boundaries. For the technologist, performance with acceptable nonperformance or risk boundaries is important. How do you make the analysis make sense to people who measure benefits based on different goals?

To build the financial case for e-mail, you must look at

TABLE 3: COST ANALYSIS

Item	Total Cost	Annual Depreciated Cost
Hardware inventory	$123,000	40,959
Misc comm costs	8,975	2,992
Software inventory	57,000	19,000
Maintenance contracts	28,346	9,449
Personnel costs	347,700	120,000
(e.g. ongoing maintenance only)		
Total cost*	$565,021	$192,440

*Includes development and first-year maintenance costs.

the financial goals within the corporation. Corporate America is embroiled in an age-old struggle to answer the question, "Are we making money?" The finance department's job is to find out, "Are we making money?" and "If so, where, how, and how can we make more there again?"

The e-mail department can be viewed as any other profit-making organization within the company; however, the nontechnical population of the company does not understand the role of the e-mail department if messaging's financial advantages aren't well described.

CREATE THE ARGUMENT FOR E-MAIL

The newest advances in e-mail could make messaging a profit-making division. This messaging-services department could protect the company from unauthorized access to the e-mail system, create a system that will scale elegantly with an increased number of users, help enter a new market at the right time, create competitive-edge technology, save millions in paper costs, and eliminate time delays in processing orders.

Once armed with the financial arguments to describe ideas, the technology manager is at a distinct and quantifiable advantage when voicing recommendations. Cost justification, break-even analysis, and profit potential are three basic arguments for e-mail.

THE PHILOSOPHY OF FINANCE

Like e-mail and networking, finance has its own jargon. Just as the protocols used on the network represent a fundamental communications concept, your organization's accounting methodology is the basic concept of business. These methods tell how the company feels about the econ-

omy, about the utility of any investment, and–most importantly–about the long-term outlook of your e-mail project.

The finance and accounting departments are on a quest to find out how much everything costs, how much money the company makes on the investments, and how to maximize the best investments while minimizing the least profitable ones. For this reason, you should examine the concept of cost justification.

The words "cost justification" show a bias. Finance makes a subtle and very important distinction: In financial terms, calculating the cost of anything implies a certain number of negative financial consequences, such as overhead, labor costs, and no return on investment. If you talk to any financial analyst or corporate executive about the cost justification of a system, they assume it's unprofitable.

The key is to create a more positive mindset. You need to overlay a business structure on a financial model that allows management to see the e-mail systems as product lines or services that will improve the profitability of the company.

THE COST BASIS

Because e-mail systems were the first widely used decentralized computer systems, adequate tools to track and troubleshoot problems, let alone sophisticated accounting structures, don't exist. Implementers of e-mail systems blaze the trail for other decentralized or groupware systems.

Until more sophisticated monitoring and troubleshooting tools evolve, the human effort required to support e-mail will remain the most expensive system item, and accounting structures will be custom modifications.

The *cost basis* is the amount of money the company spends to design, install, and maintain the e-mail system. (The definition of any financial term can be implemented slightly differently from company to company; these differences are described below as accounting methods.)

Table 1 shows the general cost basis for e-mail, including acquisition, personnel, and operations costs. In each of these categories, the costs are distinguished as fixed and recurring. The *fixed-cost basis* is the sum of all one-time costs that add value for more than one year, while the *recurring costs* are incurred either annually or hourly as modifications are made or outside service contracts negotiated.

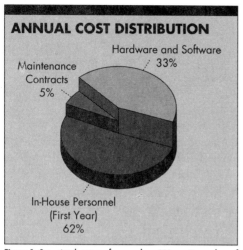

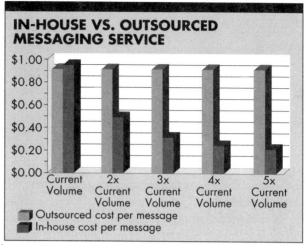

Figure 1: Operational costs can far exceed acquisition costs—and are often hidden.
Figure 2: The benefits of outsourcing all or part of your e-mail system versus its cost need to be analyzed.

E-MAIL'S FINANCIAL COMPONENTS

Table 2 shows an e-mail system's cost components, including equipment, personnel, and support, as well as its most common units of cost measurement. Once you have the basic pieces of the system, you can itemize them so you can get the cost basis of the e-mail system in financial terms.

An e-mail system supporting 4,000 users, with a mix of MS-DOS, Macintosh, and Unix workstations, and with post-office servers and gateways costs $565,021 with an annual depreciated cost of $192,440 (see Table 3). The system uses a Simple Mail Transport Protocol (SMTP) backbone with external connectivity through a public-service provider. The analysis does not include public e-mail access and usage costs of $35,000 annually, nor does it include charges for fax service. Software development, installation, and ongoing maintenance are included in personnel costs.

The first-year cost for this 4,000-user system is only $141 per user. The annual, fully depreciated cost for each user is $48 per year. As Figure 1 illustrates, at 62 percent, the total cost for support, service, and development significantly outweighs systems cost, at 33 percent.

BUILD VS. BUY

The following example compares the cost of an in-house e-mail system to the cost of the average bidder for public e-mail services.

First, the job is put out for bid with the service providers, and the least-expensive response is selected. In this case, the public-service providers bid an average of 76 cents per message, including all communications costs for initial traffic of 76,000 messages per month (current volume). In the cost analysis, add to this amount the in-house support fees (15 cents) to maintain consistency, which returns the 91-cent figure. The in-house message fee is based on an internal budget of $1 million to develop and support an X.400 backbone, including all support, hardware and software, communications lines, and maintenance.

Based on previous message-volume history, e-mail-enabled traffic and additional e-mail users could potentially double or even triple the volume of messages over the next few years. For this reason, the in-house budget is compared to the outsourced solution at several volume levels (see Figure 2).

Figure 2 indicates that outsourcing the e-mail system to a public-service provider often makes sense initially, but the metrics change over time as the volume increases and the technology changes. Many companies, in their immediate quest for lower costs, fail to recognize this economy of scale.

Figure 5 shows the advantage of an economy of scale that an in-house system usually provides over a straight per-message fee offered by public-service providers, even though most service providers offer breakpoints on mes-

TABLE 4: PROFIT RATIOS

Gross profit margin	$\dfrac{\text{Gross profit}}{\text{Number of e-mail users}}$
Operating profit margin	$\dfrac{\text{EBIT (earnings before interest and taxes)}}{\text{Number of e-mail users}}$
Net profit margin	$\dfrac{\text{Net income}}{\text{Number of e-mail users}}$
Return on investment	$\dfrac{\text{Net income}}{\text{Total sales}}$

sage volume. You can use this graph to determine whether the breakpoint represents real cost savings over the cost of in-house systems.

In outsourced systems, many of the intangibles are add-on features that each end-user company must negotiate in a service contract. When these factors are summed and quantified, the result is often referred to as the *fully loaded cost* of producing a system. If these numbers are kept separate from the initial cost estimate, they are referred to as the *fixed cost* of doing business.

Even if the goal is to outsource a portion of the messaging, the fully loaded cost of the system must be calculated for providing the system in-house and via a service provider. The company that ignores these issues will get a mighty big surprise the first year the maintenance and add-on bill is presented by the outsourcing firm.

APPLYING PROFIT RATIOS

Profitability ratios, such as gross profit margin, operating profit margin, and net profit margin, measure the earning power of a company or project. In this case, the profitability ratios are for the e-mail system. These financial ratios provide powerful tools for describing the e-mail system in terms of profitability rather than having to justify the system. The key to using ratios is understanding that they are most effective when used to compare things.

To meaningfully compare these ratios, you must find comparable numerator and denominator figures for the companies or services you wish to compare. In these examples, the number of users is the common denominator. Where the financial ratios generally use "sales," we will use "customers on the system" or "e-mail users."

Table 4 shows some profit rations applicable to e-mail systems. Using the cost basis for the system described here (not including outsourcing all or part of the system), we

can perform some useful financial analysis to determine the return on investment, pricing structures, and profitability.

Using the annual cost in Table 3, we can deploy an e-mail system for 4,000 users at the annual costs of:

Software = $19,000
Hardware = $43,951
Maintenance = $9,449
Operations = $120,000
Total Annual Cost = $192,440

If we charge an annual fee of $100 per user, our gross profit is $400,000, and our net income is $207,560. (Net income is calculated by subtracting total costs from gross profit.) Extending the analysis, we can apply the ratios as shown in Table 5: return on investment = 52%, net profit = $52 per user.

You can use the ratios to determine what to charge for your e-mail service. Consider the customers' price sensitivity to determine how much they're willing to spend up front on a product or service and how much they're willing spend to support the product or service over time.

In economics, price sensitivity is called *the elasticity of demand*, or the change in volume of sales expected as prices increase or decrease. To make more money on this investment, we could charge less for the basic e-mail services, and then sell additional services, such as directory services, fax services, or paper mail delivery services.

Changing pricing metrics, pricing units, or depreciation methods has a direct impact on the return on investment. For example, changing your depreciation from three years to five years would significantly improve profit margins without increasing prices because it drives down the annual cost and therefore increases net income. But be careful; most companies are primarily interested in encouraging employees to use e-mail and want to remove barriers and operate at close to break-even.

MARKETING AND PRICING E-MAIL

One goal of quantifying what you've spent is to compare that number with other services and products that provide the same level of service. When you compare your e-mail system to other systems, you can make informed decisions about whether to make changes or to outsource some or all of the system and about the impact of management structures and architectural designs. The techni-

TABLE 5: SAMPLE PROFIT MARGINS ON AN E-MAIL SYSTEM

Gross profit margin	=	$\dfrac{\text{Gross profit (\$400,000)}}{\text{Number of e-mail users (4,000)}}$	=	$100 per user
Net profit margin	=	$\dfrac{\text{Net income (\$207,560)}}{\text{Number of e-mail users (4,000)}}$	=	$52 per user
Return on investment	=	$\dfrac{\text{Net income (\$207,560)}}{\text{Total sales (\$400,000)}}$	=	52%

cal benefits of using the system are one quantifiable crite-rion. Pricing is another. Even when two systems have the same features, a system's pricing has a direct impact on how you can compare them.

The messaging service providers take advantage of pricing structures. For example, one company will quote e-mail pricing in 1,000 character units, the next will quote pricing in terms of the time necessary to transmit the mes-sage, and a third will price its service based on type of message and features used within that message (for ex-ample, one message addressed with six carbon copies and one fax). The trick is to make sure that you're comparing apples to apples.

QUANTIFYING VALUE

Expressing the value of e-mail to the company in ex-actly the terms company executives understand is critical, particularly because distributed processing is new, e-mail is newly recognized as a communications tool, and elec-tronic value must always be compared to some quantifi-able unit, such as decreased costs, that the corporate man-agement is used to handling. For example, you can measure decreased costs in saved paper, saved employee time, saved phone expenses, fewer fax machines, reduced courier-service expenses, reduced labor costs vs. alterna-tive delivery methods, and less-expensive custom applica-tions. The following examples of business value are taken from actual cases where the e-mail's value was measured by its benefit to the company. In these cases, e-mail:

• made more customer contact for less money on advertis-ing;

• eliminated the need to hire new order-processing opera-tors and increased sales volume by automating ordering systems, which are faster than operators taking orders over the phone;

• reduced risk associated with out-of-date legal information;

• increased the number of loans processed daily;

• increased the productivity of the sales force by improving the success rate of sales calls because account information was readily available and up to date;

• decreased the cost of goods by reducing errors and re-turns because of incomplete or out-of-date information; and

• improved customer satisfaction and reduced inquiry costs by decreasing turn-around time on customer-service inquiries.

APPROACHES TO BUSINESS VALUE

You can use one of three basic financial approaches to analyze the value of e-mail to the business: profit maxi-mization, break-even analysis, or cost minimization. The goal is to present the argument in terms that speak to up-per management and the financial analysts. The approach you take depends on your goal and the organization's view of e-mail. Profit maximization is a good approach if you need to prove the value of e-mail to the company. If e-mail is already accepted, then break-even or cost-minimization models are more commonly used.

A profit-maximization analysis proves that e-mail will help the company reap the greatest benefits. This type of analysis is usually applied to a product. The goal is to prove that e-mail systems have a direct impact on the bot-tom line by increasing sales.

A break-even analysis is usually applied to e-mail when a company is convinced of its value but cannot di-rectly apply the system to any profit-making product or service. The goal of this analysis is to find the lowest charge at which the system can be provided to each person to recover the cost of implementing it. For example, if the system costs $150,000 per year to create and maintain and there are 600 customers, you can divide $150,000 by 600 and find it costs $250 per year. You can then divide $250

TABLE 6: QUANTIFYING WHAT YOU HAVE

$$\frac{\text{Total number of bytes}}{\text{Total messages}} = \text{Average message size}$$

$$\frac{\text{Total number of bytes}}{\text{Average message size}} = \text{Average number of messages}$$

$$\text{Total number of failed messages} \times 100 = \text{Average error rate}$$

by 12 months and get a monthly cost of $20 for each customer. You can then compare this cost to the costs of other communications services, such as the phone system, and "sell" them in-house just as you would any other electronic service.

A company may do a break-even analysis to provide in-house e-mail services to executives or between international divisions of a company. The system may be given at cost to the clients to help sell a service or product, but the e-mail system is not considered a product or service itself.

Cost minimization is used when e-mail is already endorsed by a company. In that case, the decision revolves around how to provide the system in the most cost-effective way. The system costs do not have to be tied to any profit-making division; rather the goal of this analysis is to find the least-expensive way to provide service. The process usually includes putting the system specifications out for bid, then comparing the bids based on some additional intangible factors, such as quality of service, dependability of the service provider, or financial strength of the service provider.

You can take advantage of store-and-forward technology to create quantifiable statistics on system performance. These statistics can be used as the basic units of compari-

son for financial analysis. For example, to calculate the average message size, divide the total number of bytes by the number of total messages. To calculate average number of messages, divide the total number of bytes by the average message size. And to calculate the average error rate, multiply the total number of failed messages by 100.

Units of measure can be in terms of materials, for example the equivalent amount of paper, or they can be in terms of time, such as the amount of time saved by sending something via e-mail vs. paper mail. The most useful units of measure can be easily converted to time and materials, depending on the analysis you are asked to prepare. The advantage is that you can also use these measures to evaluate your staff's technical efficiency and your system's scalability.

GO FORTH AND ANALYZE

Changing the mind-set of users and managers from one in which they justify costs to one in which profit potential or value is realized creates a whole new opportunity for electronic messaging within the enterprise.

Cost-justifying e-mail is not a demanding exercise, but to build a business case for a corporate messaging system that management views as strategic, you need to thoroughly consider the hard vs. soft dollar savings, fixed and recurring costs, hidden and operational costs, the hardware and software acquisition costs and staffing and training costs. You also need a methodology and tools to prove the value and profit opportunity to your business. Given the tools, you can discover the best way to make a business argument for a distributed system, including a contribution to corporate efficiency, increased revenues, better corporate communication, and monetary savings.

E-Mail on a Budget

SMALLER COMPANIES, WITHOUT GREAT RESOURCES FOR MANAGING E-MAIL, CAN STILL REAP THE BENEFITS OF SUCH SYSTEMS–IF THEY SET UP THEIR E-MAIL CORRECTLY.

BY PETER STEPHENSON

E-mail systems can be confusing and complex. The maze of addressing and naming schemes is enough to make your eyes cross. Big corporations spend large amounts of money to ensure that their employees can communicate from wherever they might be. Mail administrators work full time to synchronize new directories, add new links and gateways, and manage systems already in place.

But for small businesses, without such resources, does administering e-mail represent too much cost and effort? Not if it's done right.

Even really small companies–mine, for instance, with just two of us–can get a lot of e-mail power for a little money. I travel abroad as a consultant and lecturer and can think of very few places where I can't access my e-mail or where people just about anywhere else can't get a message to me. And the startup cost for my e-mail system is less than $5,000 (not including PCs to run the software).

Like many small business owners, I have neither the time to manage a complex mail system myself nor the budget to hire someone to do so. My e-mail solution is low cost, low maintenance. Yours can be, too, if you understand some e-mail basics. You won't need the level of technical detail you would if you were implementing a larger system, so let's begin with the premise that simpler is better, at least for now.

Following that premise, the suite of products I use in my system comes, directly or indirectly, from cc:Mail (cc:Mail, a division of Lotus, Cambridge, MA). It is simply the most straightforward PC-based system with which I have worked. The examples in this article discuss the implementation of cc:Mail.

E-MAIL 101

When you begin an e-mail implementation, you'll probably find you have to dig for the information you need. The high priests of e-mail seem either unwilling or unable to share their expertise. They assume you know all about Message Handling System (MHS) naming and addressing conventions, how mail gateways work, or how to make public mail connections. Don't count on the manuals for much, either. You'll be as disappointed as I was.

Some general explanations are in order. Beginning at the beginning: What is e-mail? It can best be described as a *store-and-forward* technology. E-mail systems don't exchange mail between people directly any more than the postal service picks up your mail and takes it directly to your neighbor. The postal service takes all letters to a post office, sorts them, and distributes them. It may distribute them to your neighbor (because you live in the same neighborhood and use the same post office), or it may send them to another post office for delivery in that neighborhood.

Occasionally, like a letter that you mail, an e-mail message may have to go to more than one post office. For example, if you send a letter from Upper Elbow, IA, to Lahaina, Maui, HI, the letter may make several stops. Its first stop may be at a post office in Cedar Rapids. From Cedar Rapids it might go to a "gateway" post office in San Francisco. Then it would cross the Pacific to a post office in Honolulu. Finally, it would go to the neighborhood post office in Lahaina.

At each stop, the letter has been stored (in an outbound queue at the receiving post office) and forwarded to the next post office until the recipient in Lahaina collects his or her letter. If the recipient has delivery service, the letter will show up in his or her mailbox.

Otherwise, the person will have to go to the Lahaina post office to collect the mail. E-mail works in exactly the same way, making intermediary stops until it is forwarded to the final destination. If you don't collect your e-mail, one way or another, you won't receive it. As a remote user, not calling for your mail is like leaving your letters at the post office.

MAPPING THE TERRITORY

Let's examine how to use public e-mail services by looking at the territory you want to cover.

For example, I travel the world so I need a service that covers the world and connects to my private system. One such service–the Internet–provides this capability, but in many cases, it's awkward to use directly. When I'm in China, I can access the Internet. More importantly, people I work with can access the Internet. But not everyone does. So, for me, the Internet is necessary but not sufficient as a public carrier.

Within the United States, another large system serves most of my colleagues who do not use the Internet. That service, also available in many other countries, is MCI Mail.

MCI Mail is the most economical public mail service, with the possible exception of the Internet. Best of all, MCI Mail connects directly to the Internet, so I can have a network that spans the globe for pennies a day. All I have to do is to connect MCI Mail and my private e-mail system. Outside of my internal associates, nearly everyone with whom I work can access either the Internet or MCI Mail. Outside associates and clients can use either of those services or buy a copy of cc:Mail Remote and dial in to our cc:Mail system.

Some of my associates have their own cc:Mail post offices. We have made the connection to them directly (sort of like being in Upper Elbow and connecting to Cedar Rapids), and this large private network joins the public ones.

With these tools, I can send mail nearly anywhere in the world and the cost is relatively low because I am connecting to other, far grander resources. The tail (my little post office) is really wagging the dog (the network of private and public mail systems to which we attach).

Many of your associates, customers, suppliers, and others can connect to you through gateways. One of you will have to pay for periodic phone charges as your two systems exchange messages, but that's not a big expense. Finally, for those recipients who cannot for whatever reason use e-mail, your system should provide a couple of ways to generate faxes or printed mail directly. Figure 1 shows a high-level diagram of our system.

Although I'll discuss the components of this system in greater detail, note that the local cc:Mail post office is little more than a few directories that reside on your network's file server. For small systems, you don't need to invest in a separate server for the post office. Also, the router, which cc:Mail uses to call a gateway, does not require a lot of computing or storage power. It can be an old 286 with a 30MB or 40MB hard drive.

Modems should be at least 9,600bps, so long distance connection times are as short as possible. Beyond that basic advice, there is nothing magical about this system. Figure 2 shows the worldwide connections represented by the "Associate's cc:Mail Post Offices" cloud in Figure 1. Note the store-and-forward nature of the system shown in Figure 2. With the exception of link 2, Malaysia (which requested this arrangement), the system is a series of hops from one post office to the next. Link 1 from Hong Kong is a remote user. I've shown the sporadic connections as lightning bolts, whereas the remaining connections operate on a scheduled basis. I'll discuss scheduled connections (called *polling*) later.

Both figures represent a minimal investment by our company to set up and maintain a system (shown in Figure 2 as "HQ"). That system covers a lot of territory–probably more territory than most of you require–and offers reliable communications with a potentially huge number of users worldwide.

STARTING THE PROCESS

Your first step on the road to implementing your own e-mail system is to sketch the paths you'll need in the system. Those paths will look a lot like Figure 2. You'll also want to draw a diagram that resembles Figure 1, a high-level overview, while Figure 2 shows a plan for a specific path. On your path plan, show all the direct links you'll need to other cc:Mail post offices and permanent remote users (such as our Hong Kong user). You'll have two basic

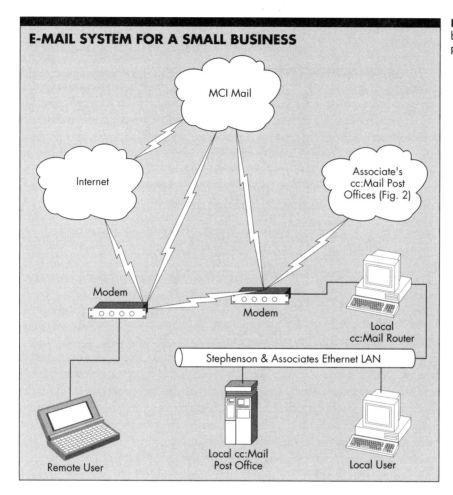

E-MAIL SYSTEM FOR A SMALL BUSINESS

MCI Mail

Internet

Associate's cc:Mail Post Offices (Fig. 2)

Modem

Modem

Local cc:Mail Router

Stephenson & Associates Ethernet LAN

Local cc:Mail Post Office

Remote User

Local User

Figure 1: This diagram shows a small business e-mail system using public and private mail networks.

kinds of cc:Mail links: post office-to-post office and remote-to-post office links.

Next, consider your local users. Local users are those connected directly to your internal LAN. You'll need to know the number of local users and what kinds of computers they use. cc:Mail easily supports DOS, OS/2, Unix, and Macintosh machines–the desktop computers most used in small businesses.

Finally, consider your requirements for connection to outside public networks such as MCI Mail. Those requirements will impose on you additional configuration and software purchase requirements. These connections are by no means limited to MCI Mail. You can connect directly to the Internet; to AT&T services, such as AT&T Mail; and to many other public systems. The mechanism is pretty much the same no matter which system you choose. Remember that I'm restricting this discussion to cc:Mail and associated routers and gateways. Other e-mail products such as DaVinci Systems' (Raleigh, NC) eMail and Microsoft Mail (Microsoft, Redmond, WA) have similar support.

Once you've designed your system, you must determine which and how many products you will purchase.

The central hub of your e-mail system is the main post office. In thinking about your home post office and any other post offices you plan to implement, you may, for example, decide that your Cleveland headquarters needs a post office and your West Coast office in San Francisco needs one, too. For this configuration, you need two platform packs from cc:Mail. These packs can be DOS, Windows, OS/2, Unix, or Macintosh.

cc:Mail comes in two configurations: platform packs for a single local user–the administrator–and multiple remote users and user packs for multiple local and remote users. Simply put, *local* means users who will access the post office directly from the LAN on which it is located. All others–those who must dial in, for example–are *remote* users.

If you have no local users except the administrator (which is a rare occurrence), you don't need any user packs. User licenses come in 10, 25, and 100 users. Allow for a few more users than you have on the network. With that planning ,you can expand or do some fancy routing tricks without having to buy more user packs.

Decide whether you'll need a copy of cc:Mail Router. If your remote users are a few traveling staffers with laptops who will dial in to your post office from the road, you won't need cc:Mail Router. The cc:Mail Dialin program that comes with the platform pack should suffice. If you are connecting to other post offices or dissimilar systems, you'll need cc:Mail Router.

cc:Mail Router can handle most of the intersystem connections you're likely to make. In some cases you'll need special link software to go with cc:Mail Router.

Finally, you need to select which external connections requiring cc:Mail Router you want to set up and order the appropriate link products. Here, we'll just consider the link to MCI Mail.

To connect to MCI Mail, you'll need a Remote Electronic Mail System (REMS) account, which is a Mail account for connection to your company's e-mail system. All users within your company share the same MCI Mail account; however, their mail is routed to and from them as it is on their home system. This process sounds complicated but MCI Mail transparently handles all the difficult work. To get your MCI Mail REMS account, call (800) 444-6245 or (202) 833-8484. Your account should be set up within a couple days.

Finally, for connecting several cc:Mail post offices in remote locations, you will need a platform pack with enough user packs to cover all users at each location, a PC to act as a router–a 286 will do, and a copy of cc:Mail Router for each location. You will also need a modem, preferably 9,600bps minimum, at each location.

Once you have assembled the pieces, a plan to use them, and accounts on any public e-mail service, you can start setting up your system. The first step is setting up the post offices.

BUILDING A POST OFFICE

With advance planning, building a cc:Mail post office is an easy project. But before you put in the first installation disk, consider user naming conventions and the name of your post office. You'll want to follow a few rules regarding naming conventions to make your life easier. The alternative is to create complicated addresses manually.

The first rule is to avoid creating a name of a person or a post office that is longer than eight characters. cc:Mail truncates names under certain circumstances, which isn't a problem until you start using those names in other systems, such as MCI Mail or the Internet. Sometimes one or more of the systems can become confused because of duplicate names and deliver your message to the dead letter office.

Names in cc:Mail can follow several conventions to which cc:Mail can adjust to meet various naming requirements. The most common naming convention, the one people use in conversation, to send paper mail or memos, is first and last names (Peter Stephenson). cc:Mail likes that designation just fine, but a more convenient location might be last name, first name (Stephenson, Peter). Imagine trying to locate a mail user in a large directory using the first name, last name convention when you don't know the first name.

The convention that most of the e-mail world seems to like best is first initial, middle initial, last name with no spaces or periods (prstephenson). A useful variation on that is the elimination of the middle initial (pstephenson). Finally, that name would appear in many systems truncated to eight characters (pstephen).

For post office names, the easiest convention is to name your headquarters' post office after your company and any branch post offices (the sales office in Upper Elbow) as a derivative of that name which clearly describes its location. For example, you might name the main post office mycorp and the Upper Elbow sales office mycorpue. Notice that I used names of eight or fewer characters.

If you are connecting to a system that truncates post office (also called workgroup) names to eight characters, a nine-character name such as mycorp-ue could be the Upper Elbow office in Iowa or the Upper Sandusky office in Ohio, since both would be truncated to mycorp-u. That

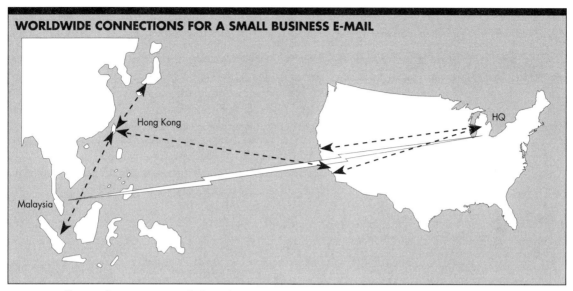

Figure 2: Pictured here is Stephenson & Associates' Worldwide cc:Mail connections.

type of naming problem drives e-mail systems nuts. The results are also pretty tough on network mail system administrators. E-mail systems thrive on uniqueness. In fact, if allowed only one hard-and-fast rule, I would make it: Ensure that each user name and each post office name is unique within your system.

Remote users will use their individual copies of cc:Mail Remote. Remote users may also set up local post offices, which they will use in the same fashion whether they are talking to users on their local LAN or on a remote one. cc:Mail Router takes care of the post office-to-post office connection automatically.

SETTING UP THE ROUTER

This task is the first that you may find a bit tricky. The actual installation is pretty straightforward. However, setting up the polling sequences is where a little extra care will help ensure success.

Let's start with a description of the polling process. *Polling* describes how your cc:Mail post office connects to other systems, which could be other cc:Mail post offices or external systems such as MCI Mail. If you are connecting other cc:Mail post offices, all you'll need is the router. If you are connecting to dissimilar systems, you'll need gateway software.

Polling other cc:Mail post offices can take one of two forms. You can poll other post offices on the same LAN or you can poll remote post offices using a modem and a dial-out connection. Most small businesses won't have multiple post offices on the same LAN so I'll concentrate on setting up a dial-out system. Remember that the post offices on both ends should have cc:Mail Router. However, for small post offices that only receive incoming polls, the Dialin program that comes with your platform pack will work. You can use Dialin only on the receiving end.

Once you install Router, configure it using the RTADMIN program. A word about paths: If you followed the installation instructions, when you set up your platform pack you created three directories: \CCMAIL (with the cc:Mail programs in it), \CCDATA (this is the actual post office), and \CCADMIN (the administrator tools). When you set up cc:Mail Router, create a directory on the same volume called \CCROUTE. The manual in its current incarnation is for the older gateway program, and it suggests \CCGATE. Because the new terminology is "router," I suggest the \CCROUTE directory name.

\CCDATA is the actual post office. A post office is nothing more than a collection of files, which usually contain messages. Depending on the type of e-mail system you use, a file may exist for each message received and each message sent.

Some systems use separate subdirectories for in-baskets and out-baskets. cc:Mail uses a single directory, \CC-DATA, which contains all the message files and the databases and indexes that make them work with the cc:Mail executables. Those executables simply move messages in and out of the appropriate files in \CCDATA as requested by users, other post offices, or gateways. So when cc:Mail asks for your post office or your post office's address, it wants to know the path to \CCDATA. We keep our post office in F:\CCDATA, so that's the path I usually tell the program.

When a cc:Mail post office needs to know the address of a remote cc:Mail post office polled by dial up, the remote address is the phone number that must be called to reach it. Thus, if I want to poll a cc:Mail post office in Upper Elbow, I will show that post office's phone number as the address when I set up the user directory for the platform pack. (Gateways always use a special addressing convention. I'll discuss the MCI convention a bit later.)

Setting up the user directory is very important to the polling process. Remember that users are either local or remote. A remote user cannot also be a local user; remote users cannot access the post office from the LAN on which it is located. However, local users can have both local and remote access. So if you have users who travel and require both local and remote access, they should be classified as local. Users who dial in exclusively from a standalone remote location are remote users with their address being the post office name.

The second piece of the addressing issue involves remote post offices and gateways. Remote post offices must be shown by name in your user directory. The name of the post office is shown, it is designated as a post office, and its address is the location of its \CCDATA directory if it is on the same LAN or of its dial-up phone number if it must be polled by modem.

All users for whom the remote post office is "home" must have their addresses shown as the remote post office. Even if the remote post office polls you instead of you polling it, the same entries must be made in the user directory.

For example, my home post office is called SandA-Net. Let's suppose that I poll (or am polled by) my office in Upper Elbow. That post office is called SandA-UE. In my SandA-Net user directory I must show SandA-UE as a post office. Now, if I have a user at the Upper Elbow office

named Jerry Jones (probably Jones, Jerry in the directory), his entry on my SandA-Net user directory is Jones, Jerry. His location is remote, and his address is SandA-UE.

Remember that if the SandA-UE post office is not shown in the SandA-Net user directory, the system won't be able to find Jerry if I send him a message. The generic definition of an address is a user name at a location. You must have both to have a valid address.

The first thing you'll do when you get into the RTADMIN program is set the intervals between various events that the router controls. Be careful because you can potentially add lots of charges to your long distance bill. First, the number of retries refers to the number of times the router will try a number that is busy, doesn't answer, or, for whatever reason, doesn't connect when called. The retry interval is the interval between those retries.

You can set up polling in one of two ways. One is Auto, the other is scheduled. If you set a poll to Auto, it will dial out at the interval designated by the Auto setting on the menu. If you set your router to poll Upper Elbow at auto interval and that interval (always in minutes) is 60, your phone bill will include a phone call to Upper Elbow every hour of every day (unless you limit the number of days in your configuration). That frequency may be way too expensive for the results. So here's a strategy that has worked well for me.

First, I set the Auto interval to about 240 (every 4 hours). Next I set the router to poll every remote post office that I call once a day (or in one case every other day) at around 4 a.m. (scheduled polling). I set the minimum priority as Low and the minimum number of messages at 0. With these settings, whether I have messages to send or not, I check in daily (usually) with each remote post office during the least-expensive time of day to call.

I need to take urgent messages into account. So I set each remote post office as an additional entry on my router's schedule. That entry is set to Auto. But to make sure that the call doesn't go out every four hours whether I need to poll or not, I set the minimum priority at Urgent and the minimum number of messages at 1. If I need to send an urgent message, I can mark it as such and it will go out at the next scheduled Auto poll. If I have no urgent messages, the Auto poll time will pass without a call going out. Urgent messages go; the rest wait for 4 a.m. If, however, I have an urgent message to go, any other messages to that remote post office that are waiting in the queue will go as well.

One last piece of advice. Don't set the number of retries too high. I've found that when a remote system is down (the most common reason for a failed connection) calling back 50 times only serves to increase your phone bill (some carriers start billing after the third ring or so–that is usually less time than the system takes to decide it can't connect so you get billed for a nonconnected call). I set the retry at 1. Don't worry though. If the call is not completed, the router will try again at the next auto polling time.

The rule of thumb is to balance the auto interval, the retry interval, and the number of retries to get the call connected without spending a lot of money. In my settings, the retry interval is 5 minutes; auto is 240 minutes; and retries is 1.

I set my MCI Mail gateway to poll at the auto interval seven days a week. Since that call is a toll-free call, frequent polling collects the mail regularly and doesn't raise my phone bill.

THE LINK TO MCI MAIL

Configuring cc:Mail Link to MCI Mail can be the most difficult and confusing part of setting up your system. But this description should ease a lot of the pain you might otherwise experience if you tried to perform this process without a little coaching.

cc:Mail MCI Mail Link is a pretty good program; however, it has some very serious drawbacks that can catch you unprepared. First, the manual is almost useless. cc:Mail says the manual is being rewritten, but the company is remarketing a third-party program that simply lacks the professionalism and quality of a genuine cc:Mail product.

Another potential difficulty is that you must call the product's developer, Computer Mail Services (Southfield, MI), to get an activation code, a throwback to the Neanderthal days of copy protection. The trouble is the product that will be shipped to you from cc:Mail or your dealer is likely to be an older release, so if you don't do things just right, you're likely to find yourself in a lot of trouble. Also, be very careful to enter all the information required for your activation code in precisely the following order or you'll have to reinstall cc:Mail Link.

Before you begin installing Link, call cc:Mail support at (415) 966-4900 and get your ID number. You'll need it for tech support. As soon as you get to tech support, tell them you need the update file for Link. You'll get that file off the cc:Mail bulletin board at (415) 691-0401, but you'll need the file's password. The file is called CCX110.ZIP.

Once you have the zip file, make sure you have made your account arrangements with MCI. You need a REMS account, and you should have an Off Net Registration (ONR) account for each person who will use MCI Mail. With the ONR account you'll never have to worry about complicated addressing since MCI Mail handles all the tough stuff in the background.

Name your new MCI account and your users, too. I suggest you name the REMS account something that describes your company; when people want to send you e-mail they will need to know who you are. I used SandA (as in "Stephenson and Associates"). Remember the eight-character rule. Give your users descriptive names following generally accepted naming conventions whenever possible (such as first initial last name with no spaces). Truncate the name to eight characters.

If you're adding to an existing e-mail system, you'll probably want to grandfather existing names where you can. That method is fine, but be aware that the system will do some truncating.

The cost of the ONR accounts adds $10 per person per year to the annual REMS fee of $100. That's a small price to pay for the ease of use that ONR provides in addressing schemes. If you decide to save the $10, realize that your mail administrator will have to use some pretty fancy addressing as will people trying to reach your users from outside MCI Mail (for example, from the Internet).

Once your MCI work is complete, you'll have a name and an account number for your REMS account and a user name for each ONR account attached to it. You need the REMS name and number so write it down and keep it in a safe place. The Link to MCI Mail has a handy worksheet in the front to record all this information.

Next, configure cc:Mail Link. During the configuration you'll need your REMS account number, serial number of the software, and some other stuff. Follow the directions to the letter. Once the configuration program has created the personal key, a unique code based on the information you've entered up to this point, call Computer Mail Services (using the number in the front of the manual) and get your activation code. Enter the activation code and exit the administrator program. You should perform a quick test to make sure that the program works. Run MCILINK.EXE to make sure that the program runs and dials MCI Mail. You probably won't have any messages, but at least you'll know you've set up the Link correctly.

For the upgrade, first exit MCI Link and return to the DOS prompt. Next make sure you're in the \CCROUTE\MCI-MAIL\PUBLIC subdirectory. You'll find only two Hayes modem files in the subdirectory, if your release of MCI Link is the one that needs upgrading (release 1.0). Those files will be HAYES12.SPL and HAYES24.SPL. If you also have a HAYESU96.SPL and lots of other modem script files, you have the newer release and you don't have to upgrade. You can also determine which release you have according to the actions you took to get your activation code. If the ADMIN program never created a personal key when you did your original configuration, you have the new release. If that is the case, you're finished installing the Link.

Let's assume that you have the older release and have to upgrade. You'll need to make a few file name changes. Rename all the *.SPL files (the modem scripts) to *.SP1. Next, change the *.DAT files to *.DTA. Unzip the CCX110.ZIP file and copy its contents to the \CCROUTE\MCIMAIL\PUBLIC subdirectory. Overwrite the executable files in the subdirectory. You have completed the upgrade and should run a quick test.

Run MCIADMIN again. Go into the communications menu and make sure you have the correct modem selected. I use a Hayes V Series Ultra 96, which is not supported directly by release 1.0 but is supported by release 1.1, so we have to select it from the new list. Exit the ADMIN program and run MCI Link. It should execute and call MCI Mail. Again, you probably won't have any messages yet, but if it can connect, it will probably work fine.

Finally, let's explore some special rules for ensuring that you can send and receive messages via MCI Mail to and from the Internet (or CompuServe, among other system). That setup is fairly tricky and not very well documented.

SETTING UP ALIASES

The key to sending and receiving successfully from a remote e-mail system is the correct use of aliases. An alias is a way of associating the user name on one system with a different name for the same user on your system. Since messages are inbound and outbound, you may need two aliases. If you are starting from scratch, keep things simple by using the same user names on all systems for each user. However, this naming system is often not practical.

If we assume the worst and use aliases, you will need an alias for every use you expect to contact via your REMS account. That includes users of MCI Mail, the Internet, CompuServe, and any other systems you access via MCI Mail. The only exception is when you answer an incoming message directly using "reply to message" in cc:Mail. When you do so, the complete address of the sender is preserved.

If you plan on continued communication with that remote user, you should write down his or her exact address from the incoming message address lines so you can enter correctly in your user directory as an alias. Remote users whom you wish to contact should be included in your user directory with their full remote addresses. Setting up the user directory is a job for the mail administrator. Once setup is complete, it is transparent to users; they only see the remote user's name and a description of who he or she is.

You add outbound aliases to the address field in your post office in the same way you add new users using the ADMIN program in \CCADMIN.

First, the correct address entry format for any remote user you expect to contact via MCI Mail is:

MCIMAIL -{NAME: Real Name | EMS: Remote system : MBX: Account name or number}

The format is extremely important. A single space lies between MCIMAIL and -{. No space exists on either side of the curly brackets ({ or }). One space on each side of the pipe (|) exists. There is a space after the colon (:) following the field name (NAME, EMS, and MBX) but none before. The field names must be uppercase. Here are some of the possible contents of the fields:

NAME: The remote user's real name: Peter Stephenson, Jerry Jones, and so forth.

EMS: The remote mail system name: MCI Mail for remote users on MCI MAIL, Internet for remote users on the Internet, Compuserve for remote users on CompuServe, and so forth.

MBX: The remote user's mailbox or account name/number: 613-7331 (my MCI Mail account; you would put the remote user's MCI Mail account here) for MCI Mail (don't use MCI Mail user names since they may not be unique), prsteph@mcimail.com (my Internet address) for the Internet (another example is ghupp@cc-mail.com for Ginny Hupp, cc:Mail's MCI Mail guru), and so forth.

Here are two actual examples. The first is my account at MCI Mail, the second is Ginny Hupp's Internet account:

MCIMAIL -{NAME: Peter Stephenson | EMS: MCI Mail | MBX: 613-7331}

MCIMAIL -{NAME: Ginny Hupp | EMS: Internet | MBX: ghupp@ccmail.com}

Both are working addresses. I can't speak for Ginny, of course, but I'll be happy to respond to your test messages.

Note that we had to place the addresses on three lines because of space limitations. You can put most addresses on a single line.

In addition, a list of third-party products for use with cc:Mail is available by calling cc:Mail; you can also download it from the cc:Mail bulletin board.

If you implement this system, you'll find that world, quite literally, is at your PC keyboard. There is almost no place you can't reach by e-mail with this approach. You can add to this system any time with extra gateways and options, such as group calendaring, to make it even more useful.

Multimedia Mail

NEW MULTIMEDIA MESSAGING STANDARDS AND INNOVATIONS MEAN MORE POWER AND BETTER INTEROPERABILITY FOR ENTERPRISE E-MAIL.

BY NED FREED

Multimedia mail is rapidly becoming a fact of networking life. Workstation users are no longer satisfied with sending simple, plain-text messages. Now they want to send word processing files, spreadsheets, and other data files as e-mail messages. And they don't want to go through the hassle of manually encoding and decoding to reduce information to the plain ASCII text required by yesterday's mail systems.

Demand is also increasing for network applications that can support digital audio and video messages. In the best of all possible e-mail worlds, a user should be able to exchange multimedia business presentations that would be the envy of Cecil B. deMille, complete with PostScript text, video with accompanying audio, lots of fancy graphics, and spreadsheets.

If you are dealing with a single computing platform, such as PC or Macintosh, then you can always shop around for a platform-specific e-mail system sophisticated enough to meet your multimedia needs. But very few sites rely on only one computing technology and one set of network protocols. In today's world, you have to interconnect different workstations with different audio and display capabilities running different operating systems. This complexity requires a standards-based e-mail system. You need a common language to bring down this electronic tower of Babel. You need a protocol that provides a common thread, allowing you to exchange multimedia messages across disparate platforms.

YOURS AND MIME

The Multipurpose Internet Mail Extensions (MIME) standard was developed by the Internet Engineering Task Force (IETF) to address just this need. MIME was specifically created as a format for multipart/multimedia messages on the Internet, but it is rapidly gaining acceptance for use in enterprise networks. A number of vendors, including Frontier Technologies (Mequon, WI), Innosoft (West Covina, CA), and Z-Code Software (San Rafael, CA), among others, have incorporated MIME support into their commercial e-mail systems. Users of their products can exchange multimedia messages with those on LAN and WAN infrastructures as well as across the Internet. And since MIME is an open standard, different MIME-capable e-mail packages can be installed to support different e-mail environments at any point in the network.

The advantages offered by MIME are virtually endless. Corporate users have already discovered that MIME is the perfect vehicle to ship binary files around the network. Consider, for example, that you have just finished your quarterly sales report, and you want to submit it to the vice president of sales and marketing. Rather than generating a printout with the appropriate spreadsheets and pie charts, you can format the document as a MIME message and send it electronically. The graphics files, spreadsheets, text, and even the PostScript formatting all remain intact and identifiable with a MIME-capable e-mail system.

MIME brings new muscle to e-mail, and it marks the beginning of a new age in electronic communication. Once MIME-capable e-mail systems become commonplace, other new technologies can emerge. These include active mail, which uses e-mail messages to initiate applications such as interactive electronic forms, and Electronic Data Interchange (EDI), which allows users to utilize e-mail for business transactions.

The advent of multimedia mail brings, of course, a range of new headaches as well. E-mail security becomes a bigger and more serious issue than ever before. Network administrators also have to start thinking seriously about how they want to enable multimedia mail for their users and what impact lots of large multimedia messages will have on their networks.

But before taking a look at the future possibilities and problems presented by multimedia mail, let's consider the state of the MIME standard and explore the multimedia options currently available to network administrators.

THE BIRTH OF MIME

The MIME standard has been proliferating steadily since it was first issued as a Request for Comment (RFC) by the IETF in June 1992. MIME has been approved as two draft standards by the IETF: RFC 1521 and RFC 1522. Virtually all vendors interested in e-mail are beginning to embrace these new standards.

What exactly does MIME offer to the network user? MIME provides a standardized way to define multipart/ multimedia messages, so different types of formatted message data can be sent across any computer network, including the Internet, without losing structure or formatting information. For example, MIME makes it possible to send PostScript images, binary files, audio messages, and digital video across IP-based networks either as standalone messages or as individual parts of a multipart message. For example, a user can send a video message with accompanying audio and a plain text transcript.

Since MIME was designed to be an Internet standard, it has to support all sorts of message types as they pass through the transports and gateways that make up the links of the Internet. So MIME was written as an extension to RFC 822, the current Internet e-mail message format standard. RFC 822 specifies that Internet mail messages use the ASCII character set. And like all RFC 822 messages, the content of MIME messages can be limited to relatively short lines of seven-bit ASCII. Nontext data, then, has to be converted to ASCII characters of seven-bit bytes before they can be transmitted over the network. This conversion is usually done automatically.

If all types of mail messages–text, PostScript, audio, and video–are reduced to the same kind of seven-bit ASCII data, the mail system has to have a way to determine what kind of message format is being sent or received. The MIME standard uses RFC 822-style headers to describe different message types and different multimedia body parts, so the mail system can properly interpret each part of the e-mail message and assemble and present the pieces correctly.

The MIME specification defines four different header fields:
• A MIME-Version header, which labels a message as MIME-conformant. This header allows different MIME-aware mail user agents to process the message appropriately.
• A Content-Type header field, which is used to specify the data types within the message. Within the Content-Type header are various fields used to describe different message types and subtypes. There is a "text" type, a "multipart" type (for multiple parts in a single message), an "application" type (for data shared between applications, such as a spreadsheet), a "message" type (for encapsulated mail messages), an "image" type, an "audio" type, and a "video" type.
• A Content-Transfer-Encoding header field, which can be used to specify the encoding used to get the message through a given message transport, such as the Internet.
• Two optional header fields, a Content-ID and a Content-Description header, which serve to label and identify the data in the message.

MIME DELIVERS

MIME was really designed to be an information delivery mechanism. Specifically, it is a standardized way to identify different types of messages using headers to label and describe different message types and different parts of a multipart/multimedia e-mail message. Although this labeling sounds simple enough, the framework created by MIME opens up an entire realm of new possibilities for e-mail.

For example, IETF committees are currently working on specifications for multinational character sets. With such character definitions in place, e-mail correspondents will be able to exchange mail in Swedish, Korean, Japanese, Vietnamese, Russian, or other languages using much broader character repetoires than ASCII provides. And since each of these definitions is defined within the MIME framework, they are encompassed by the MIME standard and can be specified using MIME headers.

Figure 1. Unlike conventional e-mail agents, a MIME User Agent (UA) includes a parser, which identifies message components, and a dispatcher, which forwards those components to the appropriate display device.

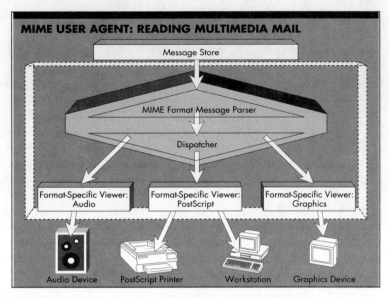

Another group is working with MIME to create a set of definitions for e-mail audio types that would be compatible with most phone messaging systems. These definitions would create a set of compressed audio types that would be ideal for applications such as voice mail, where audio fidelity is not a major issue. Once these definitions are in place, we will see e-mail systems emerge that are capable of interfacing with voice mail systems, sending and receiving e-mail as voice mail.

Remote printing is another potential application. For example, an additional image subtype based on the TIFF specification has been developed, enabling users to send e-mail messages to remote printers, including fax machines.

Another specification for vector graphics is being developed to allow users to transmit critical drawings, such as schematics and blueprints, as e-mail. Another group is working on rich text and related formats specifically for the Windows environment. And other groups are developing MIME definitions for proprietary document formats, such as WordPerfect. The possibilities seem to be nearly endless.

AN EXTENSIBLE USER AGENT

No matter what specific support definitions emerge, MIME's power is in its ability to support different types of e-mail transmissions across disparate computing platforms. Some of the MIME-capable e-mail products starting to emerge, such as Innosoft's PMDF e-Mail Interconnect 4.3 and Z-Code Software's Z-Mail 3.0, are using MIME as a canonical or intermediary format to handle message conversion. In these systems, a message can be received by a MIME e-mail system in any format, converted to a MIME message, then reconverted to any other e-mail format. For example, an incoming cc:Mail message is converted to MIME, then reconverted from MIME to DEC's Message Router format for receipt without losing data. Since MIME is capable of dealing with any kind of electronic message, MIME is an ideal intermediate format for gateways.

Some MIME-capable e-mail systems can also be configured to convert the actual contents of MIME messages. For example, the Conversion Channel in PMDF can tell the difference between spreadsheets, graphics, files, and word processing documents sent as e-mail using the MIME headers. The Conversion Channel can then call on a conversion library, such as Digital's Compound Document Architecture (CDA) Converter Library, to automatically translate messages to a different format. For example, an incoming Lotus 1-2-3 spreadsheet could be automatically translated into a Microsoft Excel spreadsheet.

The real cornerstone of any MIME-based mail system is the MIME-capable mail user agent (MIME UA). In fact, the MIME standard describes how mail user agents identify different message types, so the user's mail interface

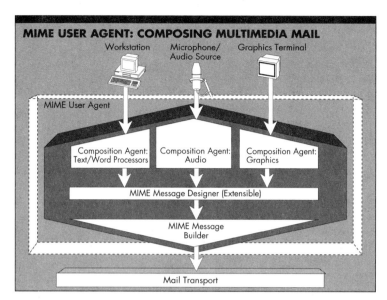

Figure 2. To create MIME messages, the Message Designer calls various composition agents to build a multimedia message.

can properly display the data for the user. A MIME UA can handle complex multipart messages, regardless of the mail transport agent, computer operating system, or network operating system. The trick, however, is finding a MIME-compatible user agent that is not only MIME-aware (able to interpret incoming MIME messages) but also MIME-capable (able to create as well as read MIME e-mail messages).

A MIME UA differs from a conventional mail user agent. Where most mail agents have a simple viewer to display text e-mail messages, the MIME UA has a MIME parser and a dispatcher (see Figure 1). To display a multipart/multimedia message, the MIME UA first passes the message through a parser, which identifies the different components of the message from the header information. The UA's dispatcher then accesses a specific viewer for each message type, specifying output as a graphic, text, PostScript, and so forth. MIME capabilities can also be added to an existing e-mail user agent, or you can install a new user agent that has MIME support built-in.

The MIME UA offers the user real advantages because it means his or her MIME-compatible e-mail package can be extended easily. For example, to support new image formats, the user can purchase new viewer software and then tell the MIME UA how and when to call it; you don't have to buy a new user agent, as would be the case with a conventional e-mail system. Furthermore, add-on viewers can

be provided by virtually any vendor. So as your needs change and expand, your multimedia e-mail support can change and expand as well.

IF YOU BUILD IT

To create MIME-compatible e-mail messages, the MIME UA uses a MIME Message Builder, which communicates with the mail transport system and a Message Designer to assemble the parts of the MIME message (see Figure 2). The Message Builder uses different composition agents called by the MIME Message Designer. The idea is that you tell the Designer what you want to build, and it, in turn, calls the various available composition agents to build a MIME e-mail message. For example, to create audio messages, the composition agent may provide an interface to a microphone, or to create graphic messages the composition agent may interface to a graphics terminal. And since the Message Designer is extensible, you can add composition agents to support almost anything–MacPaint, Microsoft Word, Lotus 1-2-3.

When shopping for a MIME e-mail system, remember that creating a user agent that can compose MIME messages is much more difficult than creating a MIME-aware user agent that can simply read MIME messages. Ultimately, if you are building really complicated, interactive messages, you will stretch the capabilities of any MIME user agent. No MIME Message Design Tool will be able to

Figure 3. By creating a MIME-capable e-mail enclave, you can add a multi-media interface to your existing e-mail system.

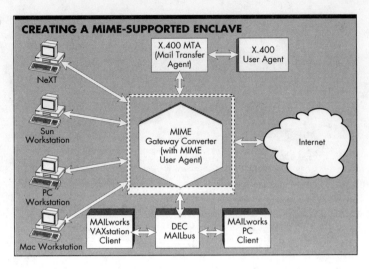

write programs for you, and this kind of message is really a kind of program. However, the MIME UA model does work as a simple programming language and lets you compose simple multimedia messages, making it something akin to a fifth-generation programming language.

ADDING MIME SUPPORT

If you already have an existing proprietary, multimedia-capable, e-mail system such as NeXTMail, Microsoft Mail, cc:Mail, or QuickMail, then you can add MIME support to your system using an enclave approach (see Figure 3). The universal problem with proprietary multimedia mail packages is message format compatibility. If you are using Microsoft Mail, for example, and you need to send multimedia messages over the Internet, there is no guarantee the recipient is using the same sort of system with the same e-mail software or viewing capabilites. And even if they have the same system, the Internet mail infrastructure won't be able to support the binary structure of Microsoft Mail attachments. Without the MIME infrastructure to package the message, that message can no longer be either transportable or decipherable.

The solution is to create an e-mail enclave by installing a MIME-capable e-mail gateway between the local workstations and the WAN or Internet mail transport. The MIME gateway would be responsible for converting all e-mail messages to and from MIME. The MIME e-mail gateway can act as a repository of all knowledge about the e-mail system. For example, if you are supporting cc:Mail

users, then the gateway knows how to handle incoming MIME messages to make them compatible with cc:Mail.

The enclave design offers some real advantages. Since the gateway acts as the repository of all local e-mail knowledge, it can also be configured to act as an e-mail converter system. Converter libraries can be installed on the gateway to handle conversion of both message formatting and content. If you have a user registered with the gateway who prefers to receive text as Microsoft Word files, for example, the gateway can be programmed with that information, and incoming text messages are automatically converted from their original format, say Word-Perfect, to Microsoft Word before they are forwarded to that registered user. Similarly, incoming Lotus 1-2-3 spreadsheets can be received as MIME messages by the gateway, then converted to Microsoft Excel before they are forwarded.

The enclave concept is finding its way into many computer networks as an interim solution, but it may also offer advantages for the long term. It has the advantage of looking to the past, allowing the user to leverage the software and file formats already installed on the network. It also looks to the future, allowing the user to more easily extend the e-mail infrastructure as new formats proliferate. Just as the MIME user agent is extensible to support different multimedia viewers, a MIME-capable e-mail gateway can be set up with conversion libraries to make it extensible to support multiple proprietary formats. A network no longer has to offer universal coverage of all known e-mail formats. As the world of e-mail becomes more complex, this modular approach allows the administrator to specify filters for incoming messages, so those messages can be read easily by local users.

For the enclave premise to be practical, it has to be tied to a directory of information where user preferences can be registered and stored. There are two logical models to register user preferences: You can either give everyone free choice with regard to e-mail formats, or you can provide preference templates that limit the selection to specific formats.

If you run the network at a small high-tech company with 25 employees, then per-user selectability makes sense, since each user has specific technical needs and preferences that should be addressed. If you have a company with 200,000 employees, then the preferences available for word processing software will be limited, and the cookie-cutter approach offered by templates is clearly more practical and cost-effective.

The use of preference templates allows you to limit the choice of e-mail conversion formats to reflect available computing resources. For example, if the accounting department is all PC-based and only uses WordPerfect, then you can direct them to register for e-mail services using WordPerfect templates for PC services only. So by using templates, you can limit the users' e-mail format choices to a specific set of conversion parameters.

Some software products currently available, such as MAILbus Conversion Manager from Digital Equipment, allow the system administrator to create specific e-mail templates for different groups of users. Unfortunately, such approaches are complex and difficult to use with large user populations. Most likely, user preferences will eventually be registered in the X.500 directory.

Developed as a part of OSI, X.500 was designed to handle large applications with decentralized directories that reside on servers scattered throughout the network. These directory servers periodically exchange information about their users to keep directory information current. The advantage of using X.500 services as a basis for creating e-mail registration templates is that X.500 is a network standard, which means it is platform-independent and, like MIME, extensible. MIME-capable channels can be added to X.500 directory services easily, so when a user browses the e-mail directory for an address, the user not only gets

an e-mail address for the recipient but also could receive a GIF or TIFF picture as a MIME message as well.

No matter which model you choose when creating your e-mail system, adopting MIME as the messaging format allows the system to become extensible, so it can embrace virtually any new format or mail system. MIME's modular architecture makes it relatively easy to add new e-mail channels and format conversion channels without having to migrate to an entirely new e-mail platform. And the MIME architecture paves the way for other e-mail possibilities as well.

INTERACTIVE MULTIMEDIA E-MAIL

One of the challenges with MIME is that multimedia messages become quite large, and not all users will have the computing power needed to read every part of a MIME message. What if you are a PC user who receives a MIME message consisting of plain text, spreadsheets, audio, and video parts? Unless you have the right hardware and software, you won't be able to view the audio and video segments; but the text and spreadsheet body parts may be meaningful to you. Rather than trying to break the message apart yourself, you could use a client-server e-mail approach and access only those parts of the message you want.

The Interactive Mail Access Protocol (IMAP), as specified in RFC 1176, is designed to support just this kind of client-server e-mail environment. The concept behind IMAP is that large messages should be handled by powerful server systems, and clients should have to run only lightweight e-mail agents to access those message parts they can handle. So smaller workstation systems, such as PCs, don't have to process unnecessary e-mail and large blocks of data that are meaningless to them.

Compared to the MIME user agent model, IMAP offers a more primitive method for users to filter their own MIME messages. Since IMAP lets users preview a message's structure before they receive it, and since MIME messages are clearly described by MIME headers, users can simply access the header information, then determine which parts of the message they want to receive. This option is particularly valuable for users who access e-mail from multiple locations. For example, if the IMAP server is configured to send multimedia messages to the Sun workstation in your office, but you are accessing e-mail from your laptop at home, you can manually filter the message beforehand, access the text messages you can read on the laptop, and save the multimedia portions for review on the Sun in the office.

ACTIVE MAIL

Now that MIME offers the ability to send binary files in a uniform fashion around local and wide area networks and the Internet, new possibilities, such as enabled or active mail, become available. Enabled mail implements additional processing at different stages in the e-mail process. The enabled mail model becomes clearer if you visualize it as three distinct processes: delivery time, the point at which e-mail reaches the recipient's delivery system; receipt time, the point at which e-mail crosses the threshold into the delivery system; and activation time, the point at which the recipient actually reads the message. Proprietary e-mail systems that support enabled mail have their own scripting languages to create specified computational processes that are executed when the mail message is received.

Enabled mail brings in the concept of active mail. Traditionally, e-mail, including multimedia mail, has been passive–messages are received and displayed by the recipient. With *active mail*, a message can contain a program that can be executed when the recipient reads it. Of course, the potential offered by active mail could be a godsend to some users, providing an easy way to handle bug fixes or provide remote activation of everyday computing services, such as system backup. It could also prove to be a nightmare, giving malevolent outsiders another means to attack your computer system.

MAIL FRAUD

Clearly, some specific issues have to be addressed to make active mail workable. First is the security issue. A means has to be defined to read any active mail message without doing potential harm to a user's system. For example, if you open an anonymous active mail message, you don't want to trigger a bad reaction, such as erasing your hard drive or sending vital files across the Internet.

Work is currently under way to define e-mail languages that would support safe active mail transactions. Put simply, these mail languages would remove any features that could do potential harm to a computer system and replace those functions with new primitives that allow only limited operations on public files. By replacing general-language primitives with safe primitives, the active mail environment can be rendered safe for general applications.

A number of proprietary e-mail programming languages have evolved, as well as one or two more general languages. Safe-TCL was jointly developed by Nathaniel Borenstein of Bellcore (Morristown, NJ) and Marhsall Rose of Dover Beach Consulting (Mountain View, CA) as a base language with the syntax to support many enabled mail primitives. The authors say that Safe-TCL is sufficiently secure, with safe primitives that are powerful enough to support most active mail applications. Safe-TCL also has the added advantages of being extensible and portable, so it can support a variety of functions on multiple mail platforms.

Once a universal e-mail language has been defined, MIME messages can be incorporated into active mail via a relatively simple process. Binary files for applications can be sent along with execution instructions written in active mail. As a simple example, consider an interactive birthday card delivered in something akin to Safe-TCL and MIME. When opened, the active mail language instructs the computer to activate the audio and video readers on the recipient's workstation and then automatically accesses the audio and video MIME messages enclosed to show the sender singing "Happy Birthday."

ELECTRONIC DATA INTERCHANGE

Another e-mail technology that can take advantage of MIME is EDI. EDI is actually much further along in the development process than enabled mail. Defined by both the ANSI EDIFACT and OSI X.12 standards, EDI provides a standardized way to set up electronic forms. Many companies are exploring EDI applications to support computerized purchase orders, employee review forms, insurance claim forms, and other applications where a user can effectively fill in blanks on an electronic form.

EDI itself doesn't define the actual appearance of the form but rather the meaning associated with each field in the form, such as which field is a part number and which field is a unit price. Once the information is entered, it is sent to a central location for processing. The information is usually transferred as a batch process, and it can be sent to a local EDI server, or it can be sent to a remote location as e-mail.

MIME becomes an important part of the EDI infrastructure, since with a MIME-capable e-mail gateway, EDI-formatted information can pass unscathed through the e-mail infrastructure. MIME recognizes EDI data just as it handles any other kind of specially formatted information.

GET THE MESSAGE

With all these potentialities, multimedia mail is at the forefront of a whole new way of thinking about electronic messaging. Today's MIME-compatible e-mail systems offer users a range of new applications for e-mail. And the beauty of MIME is that it is an industry standard; it's extensible and modular and can be retrofitted to most existing e-mail infrastructures. MIME is an enabling technology that can be used as a basis for a whole host of exciting new applications. Once multimedia messaging becomes commonplace, the possibilities for extensive e-mail applications seem almost infinite.

MIME-CAPABLE
E-mail Systems

The following products currently support the Multipurpose Internet Mail Extensions (MIME) standard. Note that other MIME-ready e-mail systems are being developed, so this list is not comprehensive.

Frontier Technologies
10201 N. Port Washington Rd.
Mequon, WI 53092
(414) 241-4555
Super-TCP/NFS for Windows

Developed for the PC platform, specifically Microsoft Windows, Super-TCP/NFS includes a MIME-capable e-mail handler as part of its e-mail support. The same e-mail package includes support for SMTP, POP 2, and POP 3, and has distribution lists, address books, and automatic forwarding.

Hewlett-Packard
19310 Pruneridge Ave.
Cupertino, CA 95014
(800) 752-0900
MPower

MPower is a suite of collaborative multimedia tools for Unix (specifically HP-UX) developed to run on HP Series 700 workstations, Series 800 multiuser systems, and X terminals. Included is the MPower mailer that uses the Unix *sendmail* command and includes support for MIME.

Innosoft International
1050 East Garvey Ave. S.
West Covina, CA 91793
(800) 552-5444
PMDF e-Mail Interconnect V4.3

Developed to run on the Digital OpenVMS and OSF/1 platforms, PMDF was the first commercial e-mail distribution and routing system to incorporate MIME. Building on the MIME-capable PMDF user agent, PMDF has e-mail channels to interconnect a wide range of messaging systems, including cc:Mail, All-in-One, VMSMail, SMTP, and Novell's MHS. Support packages are also available to connect to Digital's Message Router and X.400 systems and to provide e-mail-to-fax services.

International Messaging Associates
1389 Mitchell Ave., Suite 102
South San Francisco, CA 94080
(415) 871-4045
Internet Exchange for cc:Mail

IMA's Internet Exchange for cc:Mail is a cc:Mail-to-SMTP/ MIME Internet mail gateway that runs under Windows 3.1. It was specifically developed to provide a standards-based multimedia connection between cc:Mail and SMTP, giving e-mail users a means to exchange multimedia messages with the Internet.

Z-Code Software
4340 Redwood Hwy., Suite B-50
San Rafael, CA 94903
(415) 499-8649
Z-Mail 3.0

Z-Mail 3.0 is a Unix-based e-mail system that includes full MIME support. MIME messages can be passed through both SMTP and X.400 transport protocols and gateways. In its current release, Z-Mail also supports Motive 1.2 and has added features, such as directory services

Strange Bedfellows

WHILE THE MAC IS USER-FRIENDLY, E-MAIL SYSTEMS–AND THE X.400 STANDARD IN PARTICULAR–CAN BE HARD TO WORK WITH. HERE'S HOW TO PAIR AN UNLIKELY DUO.

BY JOEL SNYDER

The memo from management seems strange. "Macs on X.400 by next month." You know what a Mac is. But what's X.400?

X.400 is the common name for a set of standards for e-mail, by far the most popular network application; look on any PC, any Macintosh, any workstation, and you're likely to find e-mail.

Scratch the surface of this cybernetic paradise, though, and you'll find its seamier underside: incompatible systems, strange addresses, obscure incantations, *ad hoc* gateways, and unsupported transports.

E-mail grew on different networks, from different products, using different growth paths. Because of e-mail's spontaneous growth, getting a message from one side of the office to the other can seem like a minor miracle. To solve this problem, companies around the world are building backbones to process, route, and deliver the new lifeblood of many organizations: e-mail. (See Figures 1 and 2.)

X.400 e-mail is also referred to as MHS (Message Handling System), MOTIS (Message Oriented Text Interchange System), and IPM (Inter Personal Messaging). ITU-T Recommendation X.400 (formerly CCITT Recommendation X.400) is actually just one of a set of more than two dozen international standards that describes how to build interoperable e-mail systems. More than 1,000 pages in the X.400 series handle everything from protocols to testing to how you link your X.400 e-mail system to the telex network.

Although the first usable X.400 standards were published in 1984, software that links X.400 with personal computer e-mail systems has just started to become available. Between 1992 and 1993, no fewer than 11 companies introduced almost 30 new products designed around X.400 e-mail.

X.400 has become most popular in Western Europe. In North America, X.400 is overshadowed by the Simple Mail Transfer Protocol (SMTP), the TCP/IP-based e-mail system used in the Internet.

MAIL THE X.400 WAY

Revised in 1988, the current X.400 model of an e-mail system is based on a distributed client-server model. A user gains access to the e-mail system via a User Agent (UA). The UA is responsible for helping users compose, send, receive, and manage their e-mail. It connects to a big cloud generically called a Message Transfer System (MTS), responsible for transferring e-mail messages (see Figure 3). E-mail messages get shoveled into and out of the MTS by the UA. If the MTS does its job, the messages pop out on the other side for someone to read.

An MTS is made up of lots of smaller pieces: Message Transfer Agents (MTAs) and Message Stores (MSs). MTAs are the individual systems that run the e-mail backbone. MTAs handle routing of messages, format conversion, generation of receipts, and management of the e-mail backbone.

MSs, new in the most recent (1988) X.400 standards, sit between a particular UA and the rest of the MTS. An MS provides secure, continuously available storage. For example, if your UA ran on a Macintosh, you'd probably want an MS to receive and hold mail for you. That way, if your Mac was turned off, your mail wouldn't get bounced back to the sender. Also, by storing your e-mail on the MS, you could read your mail when you're in someone else's office or on the road.

A UA is one way of getting e-mail into and out of an X.400 backbone. Another is via Access Units (AUs). AUs are used as gateways to other systems when the connection to the X.400 backbone isn't a single person running UA software. Some AUs are delivery oriented. For example, a fax AU could be plugged into an X.400 network to let users send mail to recipients who have only fax machines. X.400 also has a physical delivery AU that lets an X.400 be connected to the real post office (remember back before e-mail's existence?) Most important are gateway AUs, which connect non-X.400 e-mail systems to X.400 backbones.

The X.400 standards define 93 different options, attributes, and characteristics that can be selected for a particular X.400 message. These options range from the simple expansion of distribution lists upon message delivery to complex attributes such as authentication information guaranteeing that once you read a message, you can't claim you didn't see it (or, in X.400 terms, *nonrepudiation of delivery*). X.40 is more feature-rich than micro-based e-mail systems.

To do the dirty work of shuttling e-mail around the world, X.400 defines a set of high-level protocols that transfer messages between UAs, AUs, MSs, and MTAs. X.400 is usually run over an ISO-based network, but that's not the only way to go. In the TCP/IP world, RFC 1006 describes how X.400 can be run over TCP. Several X.400 vendors–including Apple–have added TCP/IP compatibility so you can retain your investment in TCP/IP networking.

X.400 also allows for no network link. For example, many X.400 products use a shared file system (such as NetWare or NFS) to communicate between a UA and an MTA. That approach is proprietary, but it reduces the requirement for either an ISO or TCP/IP stack. Files are stuffed into the MTA's system; the MTA periodically checks for messages, eliminating the need for memory and CPU hogging network software.

The X.400 protocols have the imaginative names P1, P2, P3, and P7. Pay attention, because there's no easy way to remember them. P1, or the *message transfer protocol,* is the protocol that an MTA uses to talk to another MTA or to an AU, such as a gateway. P3, the *submission and delivery protocol,* is what a UA uses to talk to an MTA, while P7, the

message store access protocol, is what a UA uses to talk to an MS. P2, the *interpersonal message protocol,* is a sort of pseudo-protocol; it describes the format of the e-mail carried in each of the other protocols. P2 is the end-to-end X.400 protocol, while P1, P3, and P7 are point-to-point protocols.

E-mail goes hand in hand with directory services, which is why X.400 is often mentioned in the same breath as X.500. The X.500 directory standards (also a family of documents) are used several places in X.400 as a place to keep user-friendly names, distribution lists, and capabilities of UAs. X.400 also has a very strong security and authentication model, and X.500 is one place where public keys used in the encryption and signing of X.400 messages can be stored.

Lots of OSI books discuss X.400 briefly, but one of the few in-depth discussions is Cemil Betanov's *Introduction to X.400* [Artech House, (800) 225-9977]. Betanov discusses both 1984 and 1988 X.400 with breadth and depth. If you are going to dive into the world of X.400, Betanov can help you navigate the shark-infested waters.

MORE THAN ONE WAY TO MIX

The client-server and distributed nature of X.400 networks means Macintosh computers can be integrated into the world of X.400 in several ways: using pure X.400, a split X.400 UA, or an X.400 gateway.

In a pure X.400 world, Macintosh users would use a native X.400-based UA. The X.400 agent communicates over a network to an X.400 MTA using the P3 protocol or to an X.400 MTS using the P7 protocol. This approach has some significant advantages. Because the Macintosh-to-X.400 link is standardized, different users could have different UAs to meet different needs, yet all would connect to the same MTA. Or, the MTA could be changed out, upgraded, expanded, or replaced without affecting end users.

Unfortunately, no "pure" X.400 world for the Macintosh exists right now. Both Isocor (Los Angeles) and Enterprise Solutions Limited (Westlake Village, CA) have announced intentions to market pure X.400 UAs for the Macintosh. Neither has begun shipping software, although both predict 1994 availability.

Even if a real X.400 UA were available for the Macintosh, purists might insist that it run over an ISO network. That capability is unlikely to be in the first releases of these products. Because most X.400 MTA software is designed to run on Unix systems, TCP/IP will be a much more common transport. Macintosh users shouldn't care much: Apple's TCP/IP Connection and OSI Connection are both easy to install and manage.

SPLITTING X.400

Many companies believe the effort of running a full X.400 UA on a personal computer isn't worth the benefit. As Audrey Augur, a product manager at Digital Equipment, says, "That's like giving a V8 engine to someone who only goes 10 miles per hour." One popular approach to X.400 e-mail splits the UA into two parts: one on the personal computer and one on a server system.

This split would seem to invite chaos, defeating the gains of a standardized e-mail system. That's almost the case. Vendors agreed that the two parts of an X.400 UA can communicate via a standardized API. And then they went out and defined lots of them. X/Open's API is aimed straight at X.400. Microsoft's Mail API (MAPI), Lotus' Vendor Independent Messaging (VIM), and Apple's Open Collaborative Environment (AOCE) all give different models that show how a UA can be put together across a network. They're not specific to X.400 but are general solutions for the problem of splitting e-mail UAs into client and server pieces.

Digital's TeamLinks software is the only Macintosh product that splits an X.400 UA. TeamLinks Mail is half of an X.400 UA. The other half resides on a minicomputer running either OpenVMS or OSF/1. The two pieces "talk" using either Digital's DECnet protocol family or AppleTalk. TeamLinks is a family of applications that run on Macintosh, MS-DOS (Windows), OpenVMS, and several Unix-flavored operating systems. TeamLinks is actually a suite of groupware applications. A conferencing system, document routing, and e-mail are the main elements.

TeamLinks brings X.400 features to the Macintosh (and to Windows) but only in conjunction with Digital's Mailworks server. TeamLinks offers a subset of X.400 attributes, among them: messages characteristics, such as importance, sensitivity, and priority; dates, such as reply-by date and expiration date; notification, including delivery (basic/full) and receipt (basic/full); other options, such as reply requested, keep copy, alternate recipient, no conversions, and return content.

Digital intends to replace the MAPI-like interface internal to TeamLinks with one conforming to AOCE in the next release of TeamLinks for Macintosh. Standard interfaces mean you will be able to buy the halves of your X.400 UA from different vendors and mix and match to your heart's content. The operative word here is "will"; that level of interoperability is still a few years down the road.

TeamLinks handles X.400 addresses in a user-friendly way. Addressing in the X.400 world is always a sore point, particularly with TCP/IP users accustomed to short and easy-to-remember addresses, such as "president@whitehouse.gov." X.400 user addresses, called O/R names (originator/recipient names), have highly structured fields that get verbose fast. An equivalent X.400 address for Bill Clinton would probably look something like: C = "US," ADMD = "ATTMAIL," PRMD = "USGOV," O = "WHITEHOUSE," OU = "PRESIDENT," S = "Clinton." TeamLinks helps to deal with this electronic mess by including an address book function that reduces addresses of any type to user-selected nicknames, such as "The Prez."

TeamLinks also allows off-line operation, a valuable feature for anyone who travels a lot. I was able to go on the road with a PowerBook, compose messages, and then connect using ARA (AppleTalk Remote Access) over a modem to send the queued messages and receive new mail. TeamLinks lets the user store mail locally on a Macintosh disk or leave it in a file cabinet on the server.

CLEARING A PATH

The Wollongong Group's (Palo Alto, CA) PathWay Messaging is a hybrid of X.400 and proprietary technologies. The PathWay Messaging approach to X.400 connectivity is similar to Digital's: Split the UA between a personal computer (PC, Mac, or workstation running X/Motif) and a server. PathWay Messaging uses vendor-proprietary extensions to standard TCP/IP e-mail protocols to bridge the two parts of the UA. In PathWay Messaging, the client part is called PathWay Messenger, and the server is called PathWay Messaging Services. Because the Wollongong Group has extended the TCP/IP connection, many X.400 features such as receipt notification, expiration time, importance, and sensitivity are available to PathWay Messaging users.

The PathWay Messaging Services server, which runs on several different Unix platforms, includes a full X.400 MTA. The PathWay Messaging combination of client and

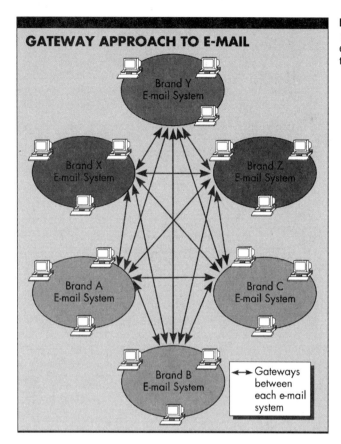

GATEWAY APPROACH TO E-MAIL

Brand Y E-mail System

Brand X E-mail System

Brand Z E-mail System

Brand A E-mail System

Brand C E-mail System

Brand B E-mail System

← Gateways between each e-mail system

Figure 1: A gateway approach to e-mail is not scalable. The number of gateways required is a function of the number of e-mail environments, and is equal to n(n-1)/2, where *n* equals the number of e-mail environments.

server brings X.400 features to the Macintosh platform by building on a familiar TCP/IP mail environment.

GATEWAYS R US

Existing Macintosh e-mail networks have another alternative: a gateway between the existing e-mail system and an X.400 network. For example, suppose your task is to connect an existing QuickMail for Macintosh network to X.400. Worldtalk (Los Gatos, CA) offers a software product that runs on the QuickMail server to transmit QuickMail messages to the Worldtalk 400Server, a full X.400 MTA that runs HP 9000 Unix and SCO Unix (Intel) computers. Retix (Santa Monica, CA), the king of X.400, also offers a compatible solution: QuickMail to any one of its OS/2, MS-DOS, or Unix platform X.400 MTAs. Isocor, StarNine and InterCon can also make the QuickMail-to-X.400 connection.

Most gateway products are intimately tied to a particular server, Worldtalk, for example, sells gateways that work only with its own server software. Isocor and Retix take the same approach, while StarNine and InterCon work only with the Apple X.400 server. That's not as strange as it seems. Remember that an e-mail gateway into an X.400 network must appear to the network to be a full MTA itself–it has to talk the P1 protocol to some other MTA. An X.400 MTA is not something that fits into an init on a 1MB MacPlus running the mailserver software.

The most popular Macintosh mail packages are all well covered when it comes to connections to X.400. Microsoft Mail, Lotus (Cambridge, MA), cc:Mail, and CE Software's (West Des Moines, IA) QuickMail all have several paths into X.400 networks. Lotus cc:Mail Router X.400 and Microsoft Enterprise Messaging Server were both announced several months ago, but product availability schedules have stretched out into 1994.

In TCP/IP-dominated environments, Macintosh users may be using SMTP, Post Office Protocol (POP), and Inter-

Figure 2: In a backbone architecture, messages are translated from the native e-mail system's format into a standard format, such as X.400, then translated into the recipient e-mail system's format for delivery.

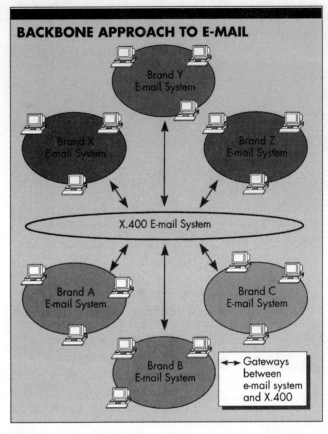

active Mail Access Protocol (IMAP) protocols to build an e-mail system. Because most X.400 MTAs run on Unix platforms, the best way to link TCP/IP-based mail systems into X.400 is at the X.400 MTA itself. Most X.400 MTA manufacturers have SMTP gateways available. Pure SMTP users can connect directly to that system. POP and IMAP users can't throw away their POP/IMAP server system just yet: No X.400 MTA offers POP and IMAP as alternatives to the X.400 P7 protocol.

APPLE'S ENTRY

Macintosh managers uneasy about diving into a Unix-based X.400 gateway should investigate Apple's own X.400 solution, MacX.400. Not only does MacX.400 work entirely in the Macintosh hardware and software environment, but a solution based on MacX.400 and a third-party gateway can be thousands of dollars less than competing solutions.

MacX.400 comes in two flavors, a low-cost ($3,000) single-domain version, which can connect only to a single X.400 MTA, and a more expensive ($5,000) multiple-domain version, which can connect to more than one MTA. MacX.400 does not require a dedicated Macintosh. Depending on the traffic load, you could run MacX.400 on the same Macintosh that is already acting as the e-mail post office and gateway. MacX.400 also supports both ISO and TCP/IP transports (in the recently released version 1.1), for a wider range of connection options.

MacX.400 is not a full partner in the X.400 backbone. For example, MacX.400 will not act as a pass-through gateway, routing e-mail messages from one MTA to another. The multiple-domain version will route outgoing messages to multiple adjacent MTAs, though, based on any O/R name attribute.

By itself, MacX.400 doesn't do anything. To make it useful in an e-mail network, third-party gateways and UAs

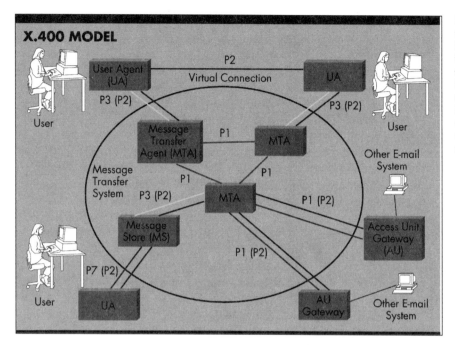

Figure 3: A user gains access to an X.400 mail system via the User Agent, which is responsible for helping users compose, send, and receive mail. The Message Transfer System, which delivers the mail, is made up of Message Transfer Agents (MTAs) and Message Stores (MSs). Access Units (AUs) are gateways to systems such as fax or Telex.

are required. InterCon Systems (Herndon, VA) and Star-Nine Technologies (Berkeley, CA) have applications to link QuickMail and Microsoft Mail networks to X.400 via the MacX.400 server.

InterCon's Dispatcher/MacX.400 for QuickMail ($995) installs on the QuickMail server and routes QuickMail messages into and out of the X.400 environment. Star-Nine's Mail*Link for MacX.400/MS ($595 for up to 10 users) runs on the MacX.400 server and works with Microsoft's MS Mail Gateway (included with Microsoft Mail). StarNine also offers a QuickMail version of its Mail*Link software.

MAKING THE CHOICE

The task of linking Macintosh e-mail users to an X.400 network has many potential solutions. With all this flexibility, how can you decide which product to select? If your goal is connectivity, you should ask four key questions in comparing different solutions.

How does it handle addresses? Extended e-mail systems of any type have a serious directory problem. Users at one end of the system want to be able to send messages to someone at the other end without worries about incorrect addresses and without having to make a telephone

call ahead of time to figure out the address at the other end. Directory services based on X.500 can help.

X.400-based systems, such as TeamLinks and PathWay Messaging, have built-in support for large directory services. However, X.500 doesn't easily penetrate the veil of an X.400-to-proprietary mail gateway. If your network is large, pay attention to how different gateways propagate addressing information. Is it done manually? Is it easy to update? Are there rules-based or table-based translations?

Addresses aren't limited to single users. Distribution lists have become an important tool in the e-mail user's tool box. X.400 supports many kinds of distribution lists and distribution-list attributes. But will distribution lists on one side of a gateway be available to users on the other side?

How does it handle attachments? The age of the simple text e-mail message has passed. People now use e-mail to pass more than just text messages. Word processor files with text attributes, graphics files of all sorts, multimedia sound and video clips, and executable programs are all considered fair game for e-mail. The Macintosh, with its strange file format, remains a perennial problem for e-mail systems. Apple Single and Apple Double file-transfer formats are a way to handle this problem, but not every package handles either or both. Before considering any solution, make sure Macintosh users can send documents across the backbone and have them arrive intact.

X.400 defines a binary message part, and industry and national standards exist for platform-specific message parts, such as MacBinary. These standards transfer nontext information. Can the different gateways work with the backbone to make sure that standard and nonstandard message parts don't get garbled? How conversion of parts when transferring from Macintosh to MS-DOS, Unix, and OpenVMS users occur?

Is everyone compatible? X.400 is a large set of standards, and the release of 1984 and 1988 versions hasn't helped matters. Most X.400 MTA vendors have undergone specific compatibility testing to make sure they work with each other. Because X.400 networks are often multivendor monstrosities, you should keep a list of what software is running to check for compatibility and configuration issues. Have you selected TCP/IP while your vendor supports only ISO?

Even if everything is compatible on paper, X.400 is still a new ball game. It's all *supposed* to work together, but tweaks, shims, tuning, and adjustments are often necessary. Is your vendor committed to making the software work in your environment? Is he or she asking the right questions? Do you have complete answers?

Can it be managed? One e-mail system isn't hard to manage; 100 e-mail systems are. When selecting a connection, consider how you're going to manage the whole world of X.400. What may be cost-effective for one far, dark corner of the network may end up costing in the long run because it can't be managed from afar.

Section 3
The Internet and Other Remote Services

The 1990s will be remembered as the decade when the Internet rose to the center of public attention. With endless talk and speculation about the emerging information superhighway, the Internet has also been in the spotlight as the example of how millions of people worldwide can–and already do–share information via thousands of separate networks.

Putting users on the Internet is a two-fold process. First, you have to establish the actual connections, addresses, and protocols; and secondly, you have to implement the right navigational tools and expertise to make the connection worthwhile. Two stories, "Network of Networks" and "Internet Integration" address each of these areas and offer some insights into the idiosyncrasies of using the world's largest network.

But the Internet isn't the only way to communicate with distant strangers, as the last two stories in this section will prove. With groupware software, the branch office can be electronically linked to the main office, allowing employees to participate in virtual meetings. And at a lower level, software vendors are blending fax technology and computers into a symbiotic relationship, opening up new channels of communication. "Reach Out and Fax Someone" explains how network fax software allows users from their desktop computers to forward information to people anywhere in the world.

Network of Networks

STRETCHING ACROSS NORTH AMERICA, INTO EUROPE AND ASIA, IT PASSES 3 TERABYTES OF TRAFFIC PER MONTH; WHAT IS THE INTERNET, AND WHAT CAN IT DO FOR YOU?

BY JOEL SNYDER

A Hitchhiker's Guide to the Galaxy describes space as ". . . big. Really big. You just won't believe how vastly hugely mind-bogglingly big it is." These thoughts apply to the Internet, too. How big is the Internet? It's big enough that no one can definitively answer that question. The last time someone checked, they figured about 20 million people using a million different computers. To put it less abstractly, this figure is equivalent to the combined populations of Belgium, Benin, Bermuda, Bhutan, Bolivia, Botswana, and the British Virgin Islands–all able to communicate.

Likewise, the Internet itself defies a precise definition. It's not a single entity; instead, the Internet is a network of networks. Internet gurus disagree on exactly where the core stops and where the unfashionable backwaters begin. All agree, however, that the center is the 45Mbps TCP/IP backbone that stretches lacross North America into Europe and Asia. This backbone links the main service providers–organizations that connect your network to the Internet. Of the 7,000 networks linked directly to the backbone, about 5,000 are in the U.S. The backbone passes roughly 3 terabytes of traffic per month among Internet users.

The service providers and their customers link many other networks and protocols: Many of the 60,000 active nodes that participate in the Usenet network use the Unix UUCP protocol; Bitnet's 3,500 nodes run IBM's RSCS; Fidonet's 20,000 nodes use their own protocol; and the 50,000 nodes in SPAN use Digital Equipment's DECnet. Some links to the Internet hide the internal structure of the connecting network. When you send mail to one of CompuServe's 1,200,000 subscribers, you don't need to know which computer they're on because CompuServe takes care of routing the message for you.

The resources you can glean from the Internet are truly amazing. Once you're connected, almost all of them are free. Use this article's list of resources to convince yourself, or your boss, of the value of the Internet.

THE POSTMAN RINGS TWICE

E-mail constitutes one quarter of all Internet traffic. It is the lowest common denominator of the Internet–the one thing that links every single user. Need to get in touch with a cement supplier in St. Petersburg, FL? Want to discuss a problem with an engineer at Novell or at any major computer or software manufacturer? If you can figure out their e-mail address, you can communicate with them. Internet gateways pass e-mail from suppliers like MCIMail and CompuServe back and forth. With Telex and fax gateways, the possibilities are almost limitless.

If you're managing or using a LAN, you already know how useful e-mail within the organization can be. E-mail can help transcend barriers of time, space, and availability. To remain competitive, you have to have e-mail between organizations. A supplier who isn't available to clients via e-mail can't provide the same level of service as one who is. E-mail is no longer a curiosity; it is becoming an expectation.

Another important part of e-mail on the Internet is mailing lists. Mailing lists bring together small groups of users all over the world to discuss specific topics. There are about a thousand well-known lists. If a mailing list has at least a hundred readers, it may get turned into a Usenet news group.

ALL THE NEWS THAT'S FIT TO PRINT

One of the richest assets of the Internet is the Usenet news service. Again, people argue over names and boundaries, but what most folks call Usenet is a distributed bulletin board/conferencing system with more than 4,000 separate conferences (called "newsgroups") on every imaginable topic, from alien visitors and alcoholism to molecular biology, cold fusion, and neural networks. Usenet originally ran exclusively over the Unix UUCP protocols and was one of the prime motivations for the UUCP network. Now, Usenet news is passed over a variety of networks using many different protocols.

The most popular of these newsgroups are read by 200,000 people a day–for example, the group named misc.jobs.offered. At the 100,000-user level are such groups as comp.windows.x, which addresses X Window, and comp.lang.c, which addresses the C programming language. Something more esoteric, such as current research directions in Japan, garners a mere 15,000 readers.

While a good portion of the Usenet is devoted to recreational and nonprofessional issues, the availability of information on computing systems and applications is unmatched. The level of discussion and quality of advice is substantially better than on local bulletin boards, and the access to technical expertise for problem solving is unmatched.

The 340 "comp" groups, aimed at computer professionals and hobbyists, cover every major and minor application package, networking technology, and topic of interest to system managers and users. If you are a PC aficionado– or an otherwise inquiring mind–who wants to find out the latest before picking up *PC Week*, or if you want to get in touch directly with users and programmers the world over, you will want to explore the 31 different groups that distribute advice for DOS and Windows users and programmers, freeware and shareware. Have a question about your Oracle database? Check the group name comp.databases.oracle.

Working on a particularly knotty PostScript problem? Comp.lang.postscript. Want to know about the latest developments in massively parallel systems? Comp .parallel. Have to check a rumor about security problems in Novell? Comp.sys.novell.

A particularly interesting part of Usenet is ClariNet, which operates on a monthly subscription-cost basis, like newspapers. ClariNet brings machine-readable news of the world to your computer and can be a powerful tool.

FTP ME ABOARD, SCOTTY

Need some software? Patches and bug fixes from your applications and operating system vendors? The latest security alerts? Papers on electromagnetic engineering? Back issues of the *Biosphere* newsletter? Half of the traffic on the Internet is file transfer, people and machines busily moving information around. If Usenet is the dynamic part of the Internet, then file transfer archives are the static half. Almost everything that goes into Usenet is archived somewhere, and that's only a small percentage of what's available.

What is available? You name it–it's there. Interested in downloading the entire source code of the X Window System? It's there. Want a high quality C (or C++) compiler for every machine in your shop? Need documentation on U.S. Supreme Court decisions? How about a copy of the CIA's database on every country in the world? Or a complete set of digital maps? State Department Travel Advisories? *Roget's Thesaurus*? The list goes on and on.

You can perform file transfer via "anonymous FTP." FTP is the File Transfer Protocol, a TCP/IP utility that lets you move files from one system to another. The user name *anonymous* means you don't need to arrange your access ahead of time and you don't need a password; with it, you have access to whatever the system administrator has made available. Most anonymous FTP sites request you enter your e-mail address as the password anyway, and they can get this information even if you don't offer it, so be sure to realize that you aren't anonymous.

Like much of the Internet, no one knows how many sites are willing to let anyone log in via the "anonymous" user name and download interesting software. McGill University's Archie program tries: It indexes 1,000 sites with more than 2 million files, but that number is limited to sites that have requested to participate in the program.

THE REST OF IT

E-mail, news service, and file transfer are only the three largest services available on the Internet. Used as a wide area network, the Internet offers remote terminal access (usually called *telnet* and *rlogin)* from host to host. Telnet lets you log in to any of the time-sharing systems connected to the Internet–if you have a user name and password, of course.

The Internet is also the home to hundreds of smaller, special-purpose information services. Of course, you couldn't possibly know about all of them. *Krol's Whole Internet User's Guide and Catalog* contains several hundred resources in 120 different categories. These resources range from small databases of very local information, such as the campuswide information system at Arizona State University, to extremely sophisticated collections, such as NASA's data on nuclear decay and radiation. Many of these databases are now available using protocols based on the ANSI Z39.50 information retrieval standard, using a product called WAIS, the Wide Area Information Service, originally developed by supercomputer maker Thinking Machines (Cambridge, MA).

Almost everyone who has ever tried to find something on the Internet ends up being frustrated by the massive quantities of information and poor indexing. To help solve this problem, Internet users are working on tools for navigating through the Internet. The Internet Gopher, which originated at University of Minnesota, and the World-Wide Web (WWW), first developed at CERN, the European particle physics lab in Geneva, are two tools that build an interface on top of the Internet. Gopher is similar to a card catalog: It lets you find and retrieve resources by topic. WWW provides a trendy hypertext interface to the Internet, letting users follow links and find resources–if they're part of the "web."

Some of the resources are extremely valuable. If you're worried about security issues, the Internet is the fastest method for disseminating information about problems and fixes. The security incident reporting and management teams are all connected to the Internet, and their bulletins about problems and fixes for software and operating systems are available. Manufacturers such as Digital Equipment and Sun are also connected, and you can download the latest information and patches to their Unix operating systems from the Internet.

HOW TO CONNECT

Connecting to the Internet means finding a service provider. Providers will walk you through software and hardware installation, including phone-line installation, and will be your point of contact into the Internet. Before you find a provider, though, you have to decide what kind of service you want. For most organizations, the decision is largely a financial one, guided by the question "How much service will my current budget buy?" Naturally, the more money you have to throw at the problem, the easier the answer and the better the service.

Your choice of service provider has another important effect: It determines to which side of the Internet you get connected. Because large parts of the Internet are funded by the U.S. government, some commercial activity is regulated. As stated in the Internet policy statement, if you are connecting "in support of research or education," you can hop on pretty much anywhere. If you want to use the Internet for purely commercial purposes, you need to choose a service provider attached to the commercial side of the Internet. Your choice of service provider won't necessarily change who you can communicate with; it just ensures that commercial traffic doesn't use the federally-funded research backbone. (Any differences arising from connecting to one side of the Internet or the other are subtle ones. For example, direct TCP/IP traffic to Russia doesn't pass into the U.S. research network because it's blocked at the backbone for political reasons. U.S. educational institutions must route e-mail to Russia over a low-speed UUCP connection through Finland.)

The second half of getting connected is bringing the Internet into your organization. If you're already running TCP/IP internally, you're all set. But if you're working with a simple disk/printer operating system like NetWare or AppleShare, you'll have some work ahead of you. Most MS-DOS and Macintosh-based e-mail systems have SMTP gateways available. SMTP is the protocol used to transfer mail in the Internet; if you want to receive Internet mail in Novell's MHS, you'll have to install one of these gateways.

Bringing TCP/IP access to personal computers for network news, file transfer, remote terminal, and other services (such as Gopher, WAIS, Archie, and the WWW) means adding software.

Most medium- to large-size companies will want to have a dedicated gateway system that serves as the portal to their Internet connection. Gateway systems running either VAX/VMS or Unix are more flexible than their MS-DOS and Macintosh counterparts; they give the network manager greater control over issues such as security, mail forwarding and gateway service, access, and network management.

The gateway system doesn't necessarily have to be a large system; in fact, many organizations find that older and slower hardware is an especially cost-effective network server.

WILD SUCCESS

Getting on the Internet is relatively inexpensive. If you're on a shoestring budget, UUNet may be a good place to start. UUNet Communications was formed as an experiment by Rick Adams and Mike O'Dell in 1987 to increase the quality of service for the UUCP network. Before UUNet, several corporations and government agencies shouldered most of the burden of passing UUCP traffic around North America, a contribution they were beginning to regret as network growth exploded. UUNet was wildly successful, mostly because Adams brought the experience of running seismo, one of the major backbone UUCP sites, to UUNet with him. UUNet is now the largest provider of commercial Internet services to end users.

While UUNet provides all different types of Internet access, the low-end service they provide is one of the most popular: UUCP. The UUCP protocol family is available as freeware for every major operating system: MS-DOS, OS/2, Macintosh, Unix, VAX/VMS, and even IBM's VM. UUCP is a dial-up, store-and-forward protocol. This means that the only services you get are e-mail and network news. UUCP's primary advantage is that it's cheap: For $25 a month, you get three hours of connect time. If you use the latest modem technology, that gives you about 10MB of data a month–enough to get started with low-volume e-mail and a small set of newsgroups.

Through a provider such as UUNet (there are others), UUCP service pretty much requires a VAX/VMS or Unix system to handle the gateway function. A workstation on a company LAN probably has more than enough horsepower to handle the low volume a UUCP connection requires.

SLIP ME ANOTHER

The next step up in organizational connection hierarchy is to almost-dedicated access. The Serial Line Internet Protocol (SLIP) and the Point-to-Point Protocol (PPP) use standard voice-grade telephone lines and off-the-shelf modems to bring a "real" Internet connection to a LAN. The difference between SLIP/PPP and UUCP is important: When the SLIP or PPP circuit is up, users on the LAN can use all of the Internet services previously described.

With SLIP and PPP, you only have to bring the circuit up when you need access. If your network provider is a long distance telephone call away, you'll probably be bringing the line up and down. On the other hand, if you live in a city without usage-based telephone service, SLIP can be even cheaper than standard communications lines. Two telephone lines (one for each end) usually cost around $50 to $75 per month; a dedicated data circuit normally starts at around $100 per month and goes up from there. Moreover, new modem technologies such as V.32bis with V.42bis mean voice-grade phone lines give higher speeds and better throughput than ordinary data lines.

SLIP and PPP are excellent transition technologies. They get you up and running quickly with minimum overhead and few ongoing costs. You don't have to deal with the phone company, and you can change network providers very quickly. The down side, however, is that SLIP and PPP are slow; the best throughput you can manage over voice-grade lines is around 15Kbps. That's great for a company with a half-dozen users, but just won't cut it if you anticipate heavy usage.

SLIP and PPP may cost more than a UUCP link, depending on your traffic volume. If you're in a major city, you probably can get a SLIP link for as little as $100 a month.

DEDICATED TO THE NET

For medium- and large-size organizations, a dedicated link provides a good answer. Most companies start out with a 56Kbps Direct Digital Service circuit; the really ambitious begin with a T-1 line–1,544Kbps. Some network providers will let you connect using a T-1 line but will limit overall throughput to 56Kbps. This setup gives good response time during peak usage but keeps the total cost down. Depending on the distance, these lines start at around $250 a month and go up from there. Add the fees your service provider charges to get your total monthly bill.

When you install a dedicated line, the service provider will want to connect to a dedicated network router. If you're already running a TCP/IP network, you may already have a TCP/IP router with an extra port that you can use for an Internet connection. If you're not currently using a router, your service provider will either lease or sell you one.

Naturally, the faster service costs more than SLIP; you can plan on spending around $10,000 a year for your connection. That may sound expensive, but it's not for the services and access you get. If you're connected to the commercial side of the Internet you can even use it as your company's wide area network.

If you can find a small group of companies in your area, you can probably share the cost of an Internet link. Most providers don't limit the number of systems you put on your end of a link. In fact, many of the smaller companies offering Internet access are doing just that–trying to leverage their investment by sharing the cost among several organizations.

CURL UP IN FRONT OF A BLAZING FIRE AND...

Read About the Internet

Here are some resources to find out more about the Internet.

The User's Directory of Computer Networks, Tracy LaQuey; Digital Press, 1990

LaQuey's 600+-page directory gives lists of systems on some of the larger networks that are part of the Internet. Primarily for network managers, the organization-to-network index in the back helps readers locate which of the connected networks links a particular organization. Call (800) 344-4825 for information.

The Matrix: Computer Networks and Conferencing Systems Worldwide, John Quarterman; Digital Press, 1990

A must-read for anyone interested in the growing world of networks and the Internet. Quarterman sought out and described networks in every country on the globe. Quarterman's obsession with networks spills over into his Matrix News, a monthly newsletter about cross-network issues. Call (512) 451-7602 for a sample issue.

Exploring the Internet, Carl Malamud; Prentice Hall, 1992

In this reference, Carl flies around the world a great deal, eats an enormous amount of ethnic food, expresses

many opinions, and still manages to keep his trim figure.. Call (201) 767-5937 for a catalog.

Internetworking with TCP/IP, Volume I (2nd edition), Douglas Comer; Prentice Hall, 1991

Comer is the first and only author to provide a readable and understandable discussion of TCP/IP. If you intend to connect to the Internet using TCP/IP, you must have a copy of Comer's first book, or wallow in ignorance and confusion. For the dedicated, Volumes II and III are just as valuable, with discussions on the internals of TCP/IP software and applications. Call (201) 767-5937 for a catalog.

Internet Message, Marshall Rose; Prentice Hall, 1993

This book handles e-mail protocols and gateways in greater detail. Call (201) 767-5937 and ask for a copy of the "Prentice Hall Communications/PTR 1993" catalog.

The Whole Internet User's Guide and Catalog, Ed Krol; O'Reilly and Associates, 1992

In this book for Internet explorers, Krol gives a strong explanation of the history, technology, and politics of the Internet; discusses the servers and services available; and ends with a 50-page catalog of Internet resources, from agriculture and aviation through standards, travel, weather, and zymurgy. Call (800) 998-9938 for a catalog.

TCP/IP Network Administration, Craig Hunt; O'Reilly and Associates, 1992

A complete guide for attaching a Unix system to the Internet. Call (800) 998-9938 for a catalog.

!%@:: A Directory of E-Mail Addressing and Networks, Donnalyn Frey; O'Reilly and Associates, 1992

This guide shows how to address e-mail on 130 different networks worldwide. Call (800) 998-9938 for a catalog.

Zen and the Art of the Internet Brendan Kehoe; Prentice Hall, 1993

Like Krol's book, but less expensive and a quarter the length. In this case, shorter isn't better. Call (201) 767-5937 for a catalog.

NAVIGATING THE INTERNET

Usenet Groups

Here are some of the main groupings of Usenet along with some sample topics. Remember, the complete list is more than 4,000 lines long.

comp: More than 300 groups. Covers computer science, software, and hardware and distributes freeware and shareware for every operating system.

sci: More than 50 groups. Covers science research and questions and answers about topics such as astronomy, cryptography, economics and electronics, medicine, and space.

misc: More than 30 groups on topics not easily classified, such as: buying and selling of computer systems, employment, investing and taxes, and legal issues.

soc and talk: Groups primarily addressing social issues and socializing, cultures round the world; debates and discussion fill these 100 groups.

rec: This set of about 225 groups is oriented toward hobbies and recreational activities, including antiques, science fiction, television, audio, sports, cooking, games, and music.

alt: This collection of newsgroups takes the anarchy of Usenet to its limit. There are no restrictions on alt groups, and more than 400 of them exist. Some are cutting-edge topics too new to have a home under the other categories.

biz: Twenty-five newsgroups that are carried and propagated by sites interested in the world of business products around them—in particular, computer products and services. It includes product announcements, announcements of fixes and enhancements, product reviews, and postings of demo software.

ClariNet: ClariNet is the commercial side of Usenet. Each site pays to receive Clarinet postings, which include stock quotes and reports, news from the major wire services, local news in the U.S. and Canada, and other news information.

(Source: Gene Spafford, Purdue University, IN)

WHO YA GONNA CALL?

Here's a partial list of Internet service providers who cover large parts of the U.S. You can probably get a connection from a local provider as well–call the NSF Network Service Center at (617) 873-3400 for a list of regional and international providers.

Advanced Network and Services, (800) 456-8267

JVNCnet, (800) 358-4437

UUNet/Alternet, (800) 488-6383

Merit Network, (313) 764-9430

CERFnet, (800) 876-2373

PSInet, (800) 827-7482

International Connections Manager , (703) 904-2156

SprintLink, (703) 904-2156

Internet Integration

ESTABLISHING AN INTERNET LINK IS HIGH ON THE CORPORATE WISH LIST. HERE'S WHAT YOU NEED TO KNOW TO CONNECT YOUR COMPANY TO THE WORLD'S LARGEST WAN.

BY JOEL SNYDER

Only if you've been sequestered in Mongolia could you have missed all the hoopla over the Internet. The 1990s will be remembered as the decade that the Internet rose–and possibly fell–to the center of public attention. Newspapers from Tijuana to Bangor, ME, have been full of goggle-eyed reporters stumbling over the massive complexity of the Internet.

If your company has decided to join the headlong gold rush to connection nirvana, you may be feeling a little lost right now. You've got a line to the Internet; you've got a router; you've got some TCP/IP addresses. All the pieces are in place. But that's not good enough. You want your company, not just your network, to be connected to the Internet. Here's what to do after the phone installer's gone home. (If your company has even connected yet, get a copy of *Connecting to the Internet,* by Susan Estrada, published by O'Reilly and Associates; it will tell you everything you need to know to get started).

LOCK THE DOORS

The first concern for anyone who has just connected to the Internet is security. Notice the word "concern." Security should not be an obsession. Before you make the final connection between your corporate network and the Internet, you need to decide the level of risk you're willing to take and contrast that with the inconvenience to both corporate and external users. At one end of the spectrum, your Internet-connected computers are completely disconnected from the corporate networks. The "air gap" style of security is sure to please paranoid security managers but will also annoy and inconvenience everyone who wishes to join the Internet community.

At the other end of the security space is a complete merging of your corporate network and the Internet. Unless you've got security tightly wrapped up on every single system on the corporate wires, this approach is equally inadvisable. Besides, there's little or no reason why every PC in your company needs to have peer-to-peer communications directly with the Internet.

A better approach to security would include multiple tools combined with a common-sense policy. Packet filters are a good start. Packet filtering is a capability in well-designed TCP/IP routers that lets you specify conditions for filtering out packets to and from the Internet. Make sure the router between your network and the Internet has them. To use packet filters effectively, you'll need to characterize Internet communications based on TCP/IP address and traffic type.

For example, if you anticipate that your only connection to the Internet will be for e-mail, then you can use packet filters to allow only Simple Mail Transport Protocol (SMTP) TCP traffic to enter and leave your network. Similarly, you may want to allow management traffic to enter your network, but only from your Internet network provider. In this case, you'd filter out all Simple Network Management Protocol (SNMP) UDP traffic except that coming from known addresses at your provider. If you plan to have a *gopher* server, you will want only incoming connects to TCP port 70 (the *gopher* port) to be allowed to that particular server.

The key to secure use of packet filters is to start with the most restrictive case and work your way out. Don't ignore a port just because there is no assigned service. You never know what future bugs will bring.

Packet filters make your router the weak link in the entire security scheme, so protecting it from intrusion or manipulation is especially crucial. If at all possible, have your Internet provider apply filters on your incoming connection to block any and all attempts to talk directly to your router.

Some Internet service providers consider the router which connects your network to theirs part of their management domain and will either refuse to give you the configuration passwords or will insist on sharing them. In this situation, you should consider adding a second router–which only you control–to minimize risks.

A larger network or a particularly security-sensitive organization may want to build an electronic fire wall between the Internet and internal networks. Many different configurations are possible, but a typical fire wall would include a routing system with a tightly configured set of packet and address filters.

The next step beyond packet filtering, connection filtering, is a common fire wall service. In connection filtering, TCP connections are allowed only in certain directions. For example, an interactive terminal session, *telnet,* might be allowed only if it originated from within the corporate network. An attempt to enter the corporate network via a telnet session from the Internet would be denied by the fire wall.

Fire walls can be built from dedicated routers or can be part of a gateway computer which forms the bridge between the Internet and corporate networks. A gateway computer offers services to the Internet and has a limited capability to connect to the corporate network. These gateway systems, kept separate from other corporate information assets, can be used as e-mail, file transfer, and information servers for linking corporate users and public information to the Internet.

No matter how much confidence you have in the security of your Internet connection, you should still plan for a compromise in security. Take advantage of the configuration capabilities of your minicomputer networking software by activating its own port-filtering capabilities. For example, if your organization uses a small set of Class B or Class C IP network numbers, configure your minicomputers to allow only TCP connects from those network numbers. Although not as comprehensive as those offered by fire wall routers, any good minicomputer TCP/IP package

will allow broad restrictions on access. Publish a set of guidelines to help minicomputer and mainframe managers add this extra ounce of prevention.

For microcomputer users, education is your primary tool. Any microcomputer with an *ftp* server is a potential opening into your corporate LAN-based data. Make sure the default TCP/IP configuration is distributed with *ftp* service disabled and passwords enabled.

TRAINING WHEELS

You can't just dump your network users into the world of the Internet and expect them to make effective use of the resources. Your organization is paying for the connection, the hardware, and the people to support it. The company therefore has a right to expect some return on its investment. Plan from the start to have a wide variety of training services available to internal users.

Short courses of two to four hours for beginners should be a basic part of your training package. Plan for a snowball effect. What looks like little interest and small turnout will turn into overwhelming demand for training when word gets out about your new connection and the services it brings. Many training companies are now offering Internet training courses. Your network provider probably can help find good teachers nearby. If you can afford it, have a trainer familiar with your organization give several on-site classes. Internal end users will relate better to training when it is given in the context of their own responsibilities and interests.

Classroom lecture training should be supplemented with generous doses of information, both on-line and in hard-copy format. Several "how-to" books on the Internet are being distributed free of charge, including the well-written (and poorly titled) *Big Dummy's Guide to the Internet* (available for anonymous ftp from ftp.eff.org, in pub/Net_info/Big_Dummy).

Commercial publishers have dumped more than two dozen intro-to-Internet books on the market in the last two years. Many are poorly written and researched or are simply formatted printouts of major on-line listings (such as the list of news groups or list of mailing lists). This particular style of "value-subtracted" publishing should be avoided. Not only are the lists out of date within minutes, but they can't be searched or effectively browsed.

Some of the best of the current crop of Internet books

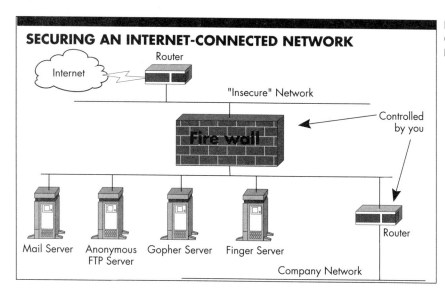

Figure 1: To secure an Internet-connected company network, use multiple tools, such as routers and firewalls.

are listed on page 99. These books are platform-independent and assume a general interface to the Internet. PC and Macintosh users may want to browse some PC- and Mac-specific titles.

MAIL FOR EVERYONE

Most organizations have a variety of internal e-mail systems that reflect a combination of history, hierarchy, and politics. Avoid spreading the internal chaos of your e-mail systems to the Internet. Many organizations joining the Internet are using an e-mail gateway system to accept e-mail from the Internet and translate it into the appropriate internal formats. At the same time, an e-mail gateway can provide a uniform addressing scheme to simplify connections between your organization and the rest of the world.

As an example, consider the consultancy firm Opus One, which has PC, minicomputer, and mainframe e-mail systems. Rather than ask outsiders to remember and try and recreate addresses like "snydjo%venus.mis%mhs@opus1.com," which might work to actually route the e-mail, Opus One's Internet e-mail gateway allows a much simpler format: joel_snyder@opus1.com.

A well-configured gateway will both accept this aliased e-mail and properly generate aliases for outgoing mail. Thus, mail sent by "snydjo" will appear to come from "joel_snyder." This setup ensures that random and confusing addresses don't get propagated into the Internet.

The exact format of the e-mail addresses you use isn't important, as long as you enforce a consistent approach.

Gateways can have other features. By requiring that all e-mail pass through a gateway, a network manager has access to a single choke point in case of problems. A gateway can also reject or reroute e-mail that needs special handling. Some e-mail gateways include heuristics to try to deliver misaddressed e-mail by matching a partial or ambiguous address. For example, e-mail sent to "snyder@opus1.com" would be delivered if there were only one Snyder or would be returned with a list of all the Snyders if there were more than one.

SEND OUT FOR HELP

The *sendmail* package, part of most standard Unix systems, is a commonly used software package for managing an e-mail gateway. Unfortunately, it's also one of the worst choices. *Sendmail* is difficult to configure, has cryptic and misleading error messages, and usually leaves few traces when a problem needs to be tracked down. Its price (free) and wide availability are the main reasons for its popularity. If *sendmail* is your only choice, make sure to get Bryan Costales' 830-page book, *Sendmail*, (O'Reilly and Associates) which makes a valiant attempt at decoding the mysteries of *sendmail*.

Commercial vendors have played to *sendmail*'s weakness by introducing a variety of enterprise e-mail gateways. Retix (Santa Monica, CA) and SoftSwitch (Wayne, PA) are two popular, if comparatively expensive, solutions that can run on Unix platforms. SoftSwitch's roots lie in the mainframe IBM world, bringing together enterprise e-mail systems with thousands of users. Retix has approached the market from the other direction by being first with ISO standards-based networking and e-mail products, such as ITU-T X.400 e-mail. Other Unix-based vendors include The Wollongong Group (Palo Alto, CA), Isocor (Los Angeles), and Worldtalk (Los Gatos, CA).

For a combination of economy, performance, and strength under load, the OpenVMS platform from Digital Equipment is difficult to beat, particularly on the new Alpha hardware. An organization interested in a truly robust e-mail gateway should consider packages such as PMDF running on OpenVMS from Innosoft International (West Covina, CA). For a hardware and software investment of less than $15,000, you can assemble a gateway which will transfer messages between popular PC e-mail systems, along with Internet (SMTP) mail and ITU-T X.400 e-mail. Wingra Technologies (Madison, WI) offers Missive, a similar e-mail gateway product which runs on OpenVMS. And Digital has its own messaging backbone product line, called Mailbus.

ELECTRONIC 411

Hand-in-hand with e-mail services go automated directory systems. The absolute best way to discover someone's e-mail address is through what datageeks call "out-of-band a priori knowledge," or "calling them on the phone." But Internet correspondents have a curious reluctance to use this tried-and-true approach. Instead, they seek out on-line directory information. The hope, I conjecture, is to get the electronic jump on their quarry, the equivalent of showing up, uninvited and unannounced, at the home of a high-school sweetheart simply to see the look on his or her face.

Toward this end, a number of redundant directory-services technologies have been used by Internet-connected organizations. They include the simple *finger* and *whois* commands, with their simple syntax and limited capabilities, up through packages and experiments such as the Computing Services Office of the University of Illinois at Urbana-Champaign *ph* (phone book) protocol, Packet Switching Interface (PSI) White Pages, *whois++*, and the long-awaited ITU-T X.500-based directory databases.

Even if you have a full-featured internal electronic directory, you should probably not make that corporate database fully available on the Internet. Information that employees and other users consider reasonable to divulge to their coworkers, such as home addresses and phone numbers, may not be reasonable to publish to the entire network community.

Pick a common technology, such as the *finger* or *whois* command, and use that as a primary directory tool. Other less-common directory channels should be activated but should return only information about how to use the real directory. For example, if you chose to use *finger* as the interface from the Internet into your electronic directory, someone attempting a *whois* would get a polite message to try *finger* instead.

As X.500-based servers and, more importantly, clients become more widely deployed in the Internet, you will probably want to change to an X.500-based directory server.

A *finger* or *whois* directory server does not easily provide the capability to search based on personal attributes, something the newer directory services (such as CSO's *ph* or X.500) do with ease. Expressing a request for "the e-mail address or phone number of anyone in Accounts Payable in Chicago" through the simple *finger* protocol would be difficult.

Searches based on more common criteria, such as last or first name, are quite easy. For most organizations, though, the additional flexibility that X.500 brings does not justify the risk and difficulty of being an early adopter. Even with the relatively stupid *finger* and *whois* protocols, more specialized information can also be distributed with only a little ingenuity. For example, the California State Legislature has installed a *finger* server that, when given a California ZIP code, returns the county in which the ZIP code lies, the names, addresses, and phone numbers of the representatives who are responsible for the area, and the legislative committees to which they belong.

MAKING CONTACT

Organizations in the computer business should use their Internet connection as an opportunity to make better contact with their customers. One prime technique is through a Usenet news group dealing with your products and services. A news group can provide a forum for users of your products to discuss issues, problems, rumors, and solutions. Eavesdropping on these discussions is a valuable form of market research. Of even greater value is participation: actively responding to questions and problems, giving information about features and product changes, and keeping in touch with your most loquacious users.

Proper participation in a Usenet news group does not require huge investments of either engineering or support staff. However, your participation will be a valuable marketing edge when those customers make their repurchase decisions. Companies are finding good reputations "on the net" more and more valuable.

If a news group seems like too large a step, mailing lists are a good way to get your electronic feet wet (without a huge shock). Some corporations, such as Digital Equipment and Sun Microsystems (Mountain View, CA), have created mailing lists that are used solely to broadcast corporate information and press releases. Other companies have used mailing lists as part of a two-way communication between vendor and customer.

Mailing lists will usually require an automated list-management system. Such a system lets end users subscribe (and stop subscribing) from mailing lists without human intervention, usually by sending an e-mail message in a specific format to a specific address. High-quality, public-domain mailing list-management software is available for your e-mail gateway system, whether it runs on Unix, OpenVMS, or IBM's VM.

NAMELESS AND FACELESS

Any organization linking to the Internet should expect potential customers to come knocking at its electronic door in search of marketing information. While blatant advertising on the net is considered poor "netiquette," having a comprehensive set of information about products and services available over the wires is praiseworthy. Organizations with other information to share, such as locally developed public-domain software, databases, or random musings from the company president, will also want to establish an anonymous *ftp* area.

Anonymous *ftp* should be limited to a small number of (perhaps even as few as one) well-known computers. Internal network users must consider any bit of data on the anonymous *ftp* system as freely available, even if it isn't in common anonymous *ftp* directories. Similarly, the anony-

mous *ftp* computers should not have any access to organizational data stored on the network. For example, if there are network file system (NFS) disks shared between corporate computers, the anonymous *ftp* system should not have these disks mounted (or even accessible). Other disk-sharing systems, including PC network systems such as NetWare or LANtastic, should have similar restrictions to their access from the anonymous *ftp* server.

Anonymous *ftp* goes hand-in-hand with an organizational policy regarding what kinds of information can be made publicly available, how files will move from internal systems to the anonymous *ftp* system, and who will be responsible for updating the data.

Other information-based services, such as *gopher* servers, World Wide Web (WWW) servers, and Wide Area Information Service (WAIS) servers, are all admirable goals for organizations seeking to take part in the Internet's current information obesity. As long as they are well-maintained, they also help to convey a favorable impression of their sponsoring organization. On the other hand, nothing looks sloppier than a *gopher* server where most of the links jump off to electronic never-never land. Before embarking on an information publishing expedition, make sure you have management support to keep things current–or be prepared to pull them off at any time.

Some companies try to cover themselves by declaring each and every service a temporary one. This lack of commitment gets old fast; one service I use has been calling itself "experimental" since 1990.

CONTROL THE THING

When setting up these services, use some good sense about how people are going to come hunting for you. Putting your *gopher* service on a computer called Boombox is not nearly as useful as putting it on Gopher. Remember, too, that the domain name system (DNS) allows a single system to have an unlimited number of names. Even if everything is packed onto a single computer, you are better off telling people to access *gopher* on "gopher.bogus.com," *ftp* on "ftp.bogus.com," and WWW on "www.bogus.com." This setup gives you flexibility to move things around as needs and capacities change, without confusing the world at large.

The only exception to this strategy is in the area of e-mail. Although making everyone send mail to "mail.bogus.com" is perfectly acceptable, those extra five characters will simply frustrate frequent correspondents and clutter already overburdened business cards. (You were planning to have everyone's e-mail address on their business card, weren't you?)

As long as you're fiddling with your DNS servers, consider having two views of your DNS namespace, an internal one and an external one. The internal name servers would have full knowledge of your corporate TCP/IP DNS tree and would be used by internal systems as part of day-to-day TCP/IP operations. This approach is what most organizations use now. When connecting to the Internet, you may want to create a new DNS server that contains only information about the externally available systems from your corporate network. This new "external" server would be used by systems on the Internet, while the "internal" servers would continue to serve local users.

This bipartisan view of your TCP/IP network can increase network security by hiding names of systems that no one should ever connect to from the Internet. This configuration can also be used to split the load between internal and external messaging systems. For example, to the Internet, "opus1.com" might be one system used to funnel all e-mail into the corporate network. Within Opus One, "opus1.com" might be an entirely different system that has a similar function. This separation is easily accomplished with multiple DNS servers.

NOTHING IS FREE

When planning your Internet e-mail gateway, be sure to plan for the additional time needed to manage the resource and respond to random queries from the world at large. The Internet junta highly recommends that every e-mail destination have a user postmaster responsible for smooth operation and troubleshooting. The omnipresent postmaster often turns into a corporate communications officer. Every Internet postmaster has stories of random questions and demands that float in over the wires.

For example, I recently received a message from someone in India asking about a friend of his who lives in Arizona and likes to play tennis. Why was I targeted? Our corporate name server, usually known by the relatively anonymous opus1.com, had its internal name of "tennis.opus1.com" listed in an obscure database somewhere. Many novice network researchers have taken to mass-mailing surveys and announcements to every domain they can discover, usually to the attention of the poor postmaster.

Despite the interruptions that unsolicited e-mail causes, conscientious gateway managers should create a wide range of e-mail destinations to help hapless citizens in search of a contact. Good starting points, in addition to "postmaster," would include "root," "system," "operator," "hostmaster," and customer-oriented addresses such as "sales," "support," "service," "info," and, of course, "complaints." Missives don't have to necessarily flow directly from the Internet to the heart of the organization. Having someone listening should anyone knock at your electronic door is simply a good idea.

Keeping track of problems and questions should be an integral part of your postmaster's job. When outsiders make contact with an organization, they expect that their communications will be taken at least as seriously as a letter–even if you think of them as casually as a telephone call. A system to track incoming messages that ensures timely replies is a good idea. You don't want anything to fall through the cracks.

Postmasters also need to have the right attitude about handling incoming queries. Many correspondents will be confused or are beginners at the e-mail game and may need some special hand-holding. Some system managers, while technically supportive, may not have the people skills to properly represent your organization to the outside world. In the world of e-mail, where most of our normal communications cues are missing, even an innocuous message can be interpreted as hostile or insulting. If your network and system managers don't have diplomatic writing skills, you should find someone who would make a good spokesperson to read and respond to mail sent to the corporate postmaster.

FEAR NO EVIL

Linking corporate cultures to the anarchy of the Internet isn't difficult. All you need is a little discipline, a little planning, and the willingness to adapt your attitudes to the world around you. Go forth and be informative.

Mac Groupware: A Collaborative Effort

BEYOND A MACINTOSH ON EVERY DESK: NOW GROUPS OF MAC USERS CAN COLLABORATE WHETHER THEY ARE IN THE SAME ROOM OR IN A BRANCH OFFICE.

BY JOEL SNYDER

If computers are here to serve us, why aren't they doing a better job at helping us do our jobs?

Now that there's a computer on every desk, and a network in every company, perhaps they can. After years of hype, a new breed of software is here. Designed to help groups of people work together, "groupware" is finally mature enough to use and depend on.

This family of software products goes by many names. Groupware is easy to say and remember, but researchers in the field have lots of alternatives: Computer Supported Cooperative Work (CSCW); collaboration tools; coordination technology; electronic meeting systems; and group decision-support systems.

The names are confusing because no one can agree on a definition. Is e-mail groupware? Maybe. What about an airline reservation system? Probably not. A multiuser sales and inventory database? If you insist. A real-time conferencing package? Almost certainly. The debate continues.

This special report digs into groupware on the Macintosh. I start by looking at groupware's origins and trying to give you a little meat to add to the steady diet of buzzwords and vaporware. Then, I take a hard look at what groupware products are available. I poke under the hood and take a few test drives. I also spend some time with Apple's new vision for a networked world, the Apple Open Collaboration Environment (AOCE).

WHERE DID IT ALL COME FROM?

The roots of groupware lie in the late 1960s work of Peter Drucker, one of the first to notice that the United States was changing from a nation of farmers and manufacturers to a nation of "knowledge workers." Soon people such as Douglas Engelbart started trying to figure out how to make these knowledge workers more efficient. (Remember Doug Engelbart? He helped invent the mouse, the workstation, graphical user interfaces, and remote procedure calls.) From there, making *groups* of knowledge workers more efficient was just a small step away.

While the researchers and experimenters began to flesh out the idea of groupware, ARPAnet, the Internet's great granddaddy, began to spread its network tendrils into universities and think tanks across the United States. The ARPAnet was initially justified as a way to share expensive resources: big CPUs, disks, and other special-purpose hardware. Once people got onto the ARPAnet, though, they found other applications: e-mail and conferencing, sometimes called bulletin boards. The first groupware applications had arrived.

The explosive growth of electronic mail and conferencing wasn't a result just of the ARPAnet. Many technologies, including interactive time sharing, inexpensive computers, local and wide area networks, along with a good dose of government funding, combined to make the first groupware applications a roaring and continuing success.

The obvious benefits of groupware for businesses have led to a massive amount of hype. Vendors have renamed their products "groupware" simply to catch attention. And vaporware is ever-present. A recent IDG study listed 17 different Macintosh groupware applications. When *LAN Magazine* went looking for demonstrations, five turned out to be unavailable.

Meanwhile, the real innovators in the groupware world have begun to bring mature products to the playing field. Researchers at universities and corporate R&D centers are slowly trying to cash in on the fruits of their labors through both large software publishing houses (such as Lotus Development) and tiny start-up firms.

I'VE BEEN FRAMED!

Once you dive into the wild world of groupware, you'll find a perplexing pile of products and pronouncements. To make sense of it all, I put together a framework for grouping groupware. In this special report, I concentrate on products for the Macintosh. I found it helpful to divide the field along three axes: time, place, and structure.

In this model, the *time* axis is defined by whether the several users work simultaneously or individual users work at various times. Groupware that I classify as *same time* is ideal for people who work on projects simultaneously. For example, screen-sharing applications, such as Farallon's (Alameda, CA) Timbuktu, are same-time groupware because they let multiple users view the same screen at the same time. *Any-time* groupware is suited to situations in which users work one at a time. For example, one user will generally send an e-mail message to another and the recipient can go into e-mail and retrieve the message later.

The *place* axis is defined by where the group works. A meeting in a single conference room is a same-place meeting. Groupware for that kind of meeting is *same-place* groupware. A package that helps a group vote anonymously on items in a meeting is same-time, same-place groupware. However, most groupware applications are *any-place* applications. They don't care whether you're at your desk or on the road–as long as you can dial in. Bulletin board systems and conferencing packages are good examples of any-place groupware.

Structure divides applications based on how they view information. A *low-structure* application, such as a group text editor, doesn't care what kind of information you put in it. Group text editors let multiple people write text into the same document at exactly the same time. The only structure they impose is one to keep the group from stomping all over itself by group editing the same paragraph, line, or even word.

High-structure applications, such as project management systems, work in exactly the opposite way. This kind of software usually has origins in a particular management theory or work idea that predicts the most efficient or effective way in which a group can work. Sometimes called "fascistware" by its users, high-structure groupware leads a group down a particular path. It manages what kind of information goes in and exactly what it means. For example, e-mail packages that require users to respond to a message using a specific form would be considered high structure.

Of course, this model isn't perfect. Not every application fits into one neat little box. But because virtually any software that two people use at the same time gets labeled "groupware," it's important to divide up the products so they make sense.

HARD SOFTWARE

Good groupware is hard to write. Most software tries to automate a single operation. Consider a word processor or a spreadsheet. These programs are designed to imitate very simple tools: typewriters, calculators, graph paper. Groupware automates something much more complex: the interactions of a group of people. If the groupware doesn't successfully mimic human interactions, people may not accept it, something groupware developers learned the hard way. Build a poor graphical user interface, and the product will flop. On the other hand, some groupware, such as e-mail, is so valuable that people will use it even if it looks like it was designed by a 12-year-old.

Choosing good groupware sounds pretty easy. If it fits your group's view of the world, it's good groupware. If it can be adapted to your group's schedule and workflows, it's good groupware. If it's available on all the platforms your group needs, it's good groupware. If it handles the group's pace without choking or collapsing, it's good groupware.

Unfortunately, you can't answer any of these questions until you bring groupware into a real group and try using it. Evaluating groupware isn't like evaluating a database. To determine whether groupware will work, a group has to try it. Nothing less will do.

Many products that look great in a technical evaluation fail miserably when used by some groups. The reason? Group interactions are so complex that users are unwilling to compromise for the sake of automation.

If the software can't emulate the subtle, behind-the-scenes negotiations involved in setting up a meeting, people just won't use it.

LEARNING MORE

Because much of groupware has academic roots, several good books are available on the topic. If you're interested in a good overview, *Shared Minds* by Michael Schrage (Random House, 1990) discusses a wide variety of workgroup issues. Schrage spent a year at MIT's Media Lab and has written a very approachable book.

Irene Greif, who now works for Lotus Development (Cambridge, MA), assembled *Computer-Supported Cooperative Work: A Book of Readings* (Morgan Kaufman, 1988), recommended reading for anyone trying to do groupware on a medium or large scale. Although her selection of material is somewhat idiosyncratic, you can find enough good advice and experience among the 28 papers to make reading this book worth your while.

More recently, Ronald Baecker has assembled a newer and larger set of 73 articles in *Readings in Groupware and Computer-Supported Cooperative Work* (Morgan Kaufman, 1993). Baecker's selection easily forms the basis for a college course on groupware and will be valuable to anyone interested in the latest results from research labs around the world

---

ATTACHING THE "GROUPWARE" LABEL TO SOFTWARE YIELDS HIGH RETURNS. BUT WHAT PRODUCTS ARE REALLY AVAILABLE, AND HOW CAN THEY HELP MAC USERS COLLABORATE?

Touring the Marketplace

To help you sort through the myriad products called "groupware," the introduction to this special report divides products into four categories based on how they work over time and in terms of place and structure. To meet the demands of workgroups, developers have brought many different groupware products to market. In this section, I separate out the software from the vaporware.

ANY TIME, SAME PLACE: REINVENTING THE MAINFRAME

Mainframes are bad. Everyone knows that. We have it drilled into us by every publication we read. Rightsizing. Shattering the glass house. Reengineering. A lot of action and rhetoric is putting the mainframe manufacturers out of business. When a mainframe application can be replaced by a single accountant running a spreadsheet, getting rid of the mainframe is obviously a good idea. Groups, however, have a special affinity with mainframes. A group of people can coordinate their work much more easily when all the data and computing is done on a central resource. Distributed systems sound good, but they're genuinely hard to develop and deploy. An intermediate step between mainframes and fully distributed systems exists: client-server computing. A lot of client-server applications are being billed as groupware.

The connection isn't that hard to make. Groups of people all run the same application. They look at the same data in different ways. The server-based databases help to coordinate their actions. That sounds like groupware, and the "groupware" label brings prime returns in the marketplace.

This new family of client-server application developers has reinvented the mainframe. They've created a virtual mainframe, sharing some of the best attributes of the behemoths users worked so hard to obviate. Fortunately, client-server groupware is politically correct.

A LOOK AT SPECIFICS

Vantive System (from Vantive, Mountain View, CA) is a good example of this new family of client-server applications. Vantive System is a family of five customer-support applications. Together, these applications combine all aspects of the support relationship between a business and its customers: customer support, help desks, sales, quality assurance, and distribution of product information.

When a business selects Vantive System as its customer-support tool, it's accepting both the software Vantive sells and the style of business the product reflects. Vantive System centralizes all information for all applications in a single integrated database. That setup creates implicit coordination: People work better as a group because they're sharing the same view of the world.

Vantive System sits on the Macintosh as a client only. Vantive's server runs on Unix minicomputers. Client software is also available for MS-DOS PCs running Windows and for X Window system terminals and workstations.

Vantive and other client-server groupware application authors have recreated the shared space of the mainframe. Users get the power of a shared database without having to give up the friendliness of their desktop microcomputer.

In the client-server groupware business, the single dominant player is Lotus Notes. Lotus is the company that brought the term "groupware" to everyone's lips. With half a million Lotus Notes licenses out there, Notes has become the standard against which client-server applications are measured.

When Lotus introduced Release 3 of Notes in early 1993, it jumped with both feet into the Macintosh groupware business. Well, maybe one foot: It took Lotus until 1994 to come up with a version of the Macintosh Notes client that worked with most existing Notes servers. Lotus also plans to begin shipping, this year, Unix and NetWare NLM Notes servers to complement the existing MS-DOS and OS/2 platforms.

Notes and applications built in it are organized along classic client-server lines. The Notes server (or servers) keeps all the shared data, handles security and database replication, runs management batch jobs, and processes database queries posed by clients. Notes clients are responsible for managing the user interface, the connection between the client microcomputer and the server, and handling any local databases (such as a personal phone book). Unlike most PC LAN database applications, a Notes database is truly client-server software.

Notes itself isn't a groupware application at all, in the same way that COBOL isn't a business data processing application. Notes is a platform for building groupware applications. Notes takes care of a lot of the hard stuff that groupware developers need to handle.

For the groupware end user, Notes is almost completely useless out of the box. For a groupware developer, Notes can form the operating system, database, communications subsystem, and programming language, all from one package. This makes developers very happy. Most Notes users are running custom-written applications, which translates into dollars for the corps of Notes consultants and VARs that have sprung up. For a list of Notes developers and third-party applications, call Lotus at (800) 828-7086 and ask for a copy of *The Lotus Notes Guide.*

Andy Jeffrey, president of Quality Decision Management (North Andover, MA) is enthusiastic about his success as a Notes application developer: "People love our Notes applications. They're not sure what [Notes] is, but they know they like it." Jeffrey credits Notes for cutting his development time, saying "Notes is the cheapest way I can create public space."

Although a few Notes applications can be purchased off-the-shelf for immediate use, the great majority of Notes installations are heavily customized. Notes customizations don't necessarily tie you to a single software vendor, though. Notes' architecture encourages applications and users to communicate–and makes it easy to do so.

The ideas behind Notes applications will be familiar to Macintosh users: Make every application look the same; bring functions such as e-mail to every single application; have each application use the same conventions when communicating with the user; and make sure that details of management are taken care of automatically by the system, rather than burdening end users or network managers.

Like the Macintosh itself, Notes is based on the idea that if you learn one Notes application, you can easily apply your knowledge to others, even ones that haven't been written yet. Good Notes applications will work together without causing anxiety to developers or, more importantly, end users.

Although other companies have released groupware applications and compared them to Notes, no one has developed a functional equivalent. Notes stands alone in the world of groupware development platforms.

SAME TIME, SAME PLACE: WE MEET AGAIN

People spend an awful lot of time in meetings. In many organizations, the job of manager means going from one meeting to the next, all day long. Demand is high for some sort of groupware to ease the pain of continually attending meetings.

Unfortunately, electronic meeting systems developers haven't selected the Macintosh as a platform. Products such as Ventana's (Tucson, AZ) PC-based GroupSystems, which brings 16 different meeting management and support tools into the meeting room itself, don't have commercial Macintosh-based brethren. Instead, Macintosh developers have concentrated on another aspect of meetings: scheduling them.

The acknowledged king of multiuser scheduling programs is Meeting Maker XP from ON Technology (Cambridge, MA). The XP stands for "cross platform." Meeting Maker support both Macintosh and Windows clients. To handle the network issues of connecting both Macs and Windows systems to the same server, ON Technology includes an IPX (NetWare) protocol stack. Meeting Maker co-

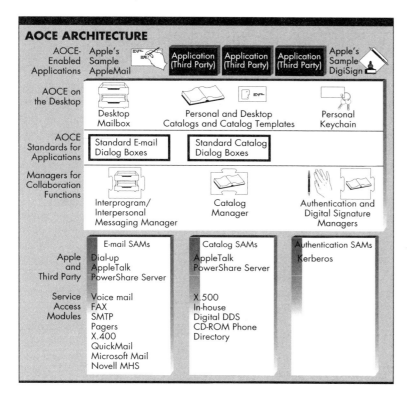

Figure 1: The AOCE architecture includes a core provided by Apple on which third-party developers can build.

ordinates calendars, handling the scheduling of meetings, conference rooms, and resources (such as a slide projector).

Using Meeting Maker, you can propose a meeting with a series of attendees ("guests" in Meeting Maker's terminology). Meeting Maker helps users find an appropriate free time slot by comparing all the calendars and sends out invitations along with any agenda. Guests receive notifications of the proposed meeting and can agree or refuse (or put off making a decision) to attend the meeting.

Meeting Maker's calendars can also be used for other activities, such as private appointments. Any entry on your calendar can also have an associated reminder to help keep you on schedule. Meeting Maker also supports both private and group to-do lists, handled in much the same way as the calendars.

Meeting Maker doesn't have all the bells and whistles of its mainframe precursors, but it makes up for such shortcomings in its ease of use. Meeting Maker doesn't require training, and it uses the visual representation of a calendar in a very natural way. Handling your calendar is simple and intuitive.

ON Technology has also thought about people who move around a lot. Meeting Maker doesn't require you to sit at your own workstation to check your calendar, and it doesn't require you to be in contact with the server. This setup is ideal for PowerBook users. Sign on to Meeting Maker at least once before you leave the office. It'll automatically grab a copy of your calendar, and you can hit the road. While you're out of touch, you can propose and respond to meetings. These actions are queued up until you next connect to the server. Then, Meeting Maker synchronizes your calendar and sends and receives all pending actions–all without any special thought on your part.

Group scheduling is such an obvious application that Meeting Maker has lots of competition from Milum's (Austin, TX) Office Tracker Pro, Now Software's (Portland, OR) Now Up To Date, Microsoft Schedule+, and WordPerfect's (Orem, UT) WordPerfect Office.

Milum's Office Tracker Pro takes a slightly different approach. Office Tracker Pro evolved from an automated "In/Out" board package. With Office Tracker Pro, for example, you could ask to be notified via an Apple Open Collaboration Environment (AOCE) message whenever a particular user indicates they are in. The connection with AOCE is unique: Office Tracker Pro is the first scheduling package to include support for AOCE mail. Office Tracker Pro is designed for a different kind of office environment, one in which the scheduling of meetings is not quite so contentious.

Now Up To Date takes the portable features available in Meeting Maker XP one step further: calendar and scheduling information can be exported to a variety of personal schedulers, including the popular Sharp Wizard. At the time of this writing, none of the group scheduling software includes support for the Newton PDAs, but that's sure to come very soon.

Microsoft and WordPerfect both provide group scheduling as part of their larger office-automation packages. Schedule+, from Microsoft, works only as part of a Microsoft Mail network. Schedule+ uses Microsoft Mail messages as a way of scheduling meetings: A request for a meeting comes to you as a mail message. WordPerfect Office works in the same way. Calendars and meeting scheduling are handled as an integrated part of the whole Word-Perfect Office system, which also includes e-mail, reminders, phone messages, group notices, and to-do lists.

Deciding between these contenders is not as hard as it might seem. Each one takes a slightly different view of the process of scheduling meetings and agreeing on task lists. For the workgroup looking for an integrated e-mail and calendaring package, Microsoft Mail and WordPerfect Office are candidates. Any standalone installation should consider both Meeting Maker XP and Office Tracker Pro. These products have very different organizational philosophies. With luck and perhaps a little customization, one of the two will fit your philosophy.

SAME TIME, ANY PLACE: BRINGING GROUPS TOGETHER

Virtual meetings take place in some cybernetic ether. A virtual meeting has real people talking to each other in real time across a computer network. Groupware, sometimes combined with multimedia hardware, pulls these virtual meetings together.

The company that has been in the Macintosh virtual meeting business the longest is Farallon Computing (Alameda, CA). Farallon's Timbuktu package was origi-

nally designed as a way for two Macintosh users to share a single screen and became widely accepted as a way to manage AppleShare servers remotely. Since then, Farallon has extended Timbuktu to create a build-it-yourself virtual meeting environment.

With Timbuktu, multiple networked Macintosh (or Windows) users can all view each other's screens. Timbuktu distinguishes between observers, who can only see what's happening, and controllers, who can drive the remote Macintosh as if it were local. A shared screen is called a *host*; observers and controllers together are called *guests*.

Using Timbuktu, members of a networked workgroup can all edit a word processing document, draw in a drawing package, chart data from a spreadsheet, and pull out information from a corporate database. Because Timbuktu is logically independent of the application on the shared screen, users can continue working with the tools they find most comfortable.

Timbuktu has no way for participants to synchronize their work, however. To be truly effective for meetings, Timbuktu would have to be combined with an audio teleconference. Farallon understands the value of having a groupware application but hasn't spent much time working on adding virtual meeting features to Timbuktu. For example, Timbuktu users cannot easily pass control of a shared screen amongst themselves.

Timbuktu is extensible to reasonably complex environments. As long as you don't try to build an infinite loop (remember the effect when two mirrors face each other), Timbuktu lets you link hosts, observers, and controllers in any topology and combination. Even though Timbuktu allows for complex configurations, simple ones are easy to put together. Timbuktu's well-designed user interface and shrink-wrap packaging have made it a popular application.

Aspects, from Group Logic (formerly Group Technologies, Arlington, VA) is virtual meeting software with lots of groupware support built in. With Aspects, up to 16 Macintoshes can be linked together in a virtual meeting that supports shared editing, painting, and drawing programs. Aspects' shared tools are part of the Aspects product, so you can't use your usual word processor in a shared environment.

However, because Aspects shares at the application

level, instead of at Timbuktu's screen level, conference members don't all have to view the same part of the same documents at the same time. Aspects' shared documents (both text and graphics) can be tightly linked into "what you see is what I see" (WYSIWIS, pronounced wizzy-wiz) views, or participants can look at and edit different parts of the same document at the same time.

Aspects supports different types of mediation, the process of choosing who will draw or write next. With Aspects, the conference manager can choose to open a document as a free-for-all where multiple participants can write at the same time or can restrict things so that only one person can edit at a time. In its one-at-a-time mode, Aspects enforces a round-robin style of editing. To edit something, you electronically raise your hand. If no one is editing at that time, you get editing control. If someone else is editing, you'll be put into a queue. When one editor releases control, the first participant to raise her hand gets edit control of the document.

Aspects includes a Chat box, which participants use to exchange short messages about the conference. Although Aspects recommends that its virtual meeting capabilities be augmented with a conference all, some workgroups might be able to operate using only the Chat box for synchronization and discussion. Aspects' pointer lets you point to a specific part of a document or drawing during a group discussion, a feature that came in very handy during out testing.

Both Aspects and Timbuktu are slickly produced and documented groupware tools. At the other end of the spectrum is RTZ Software's (Cupertino, CA) The Virtual Meeting. RTZ has put together a suite of applications that can be built-in to a multisite, multiuser meeting environment. The Virtual Meeting users will select from RTZ's menu of custom software to generate the meeting tools they need.

The core of The Virtual Meeting is a conference server that passes Apple Events (real-time, application-to-application messages) and other messages from the program between conference gateway applications located on each participant's machine. The Virtual Meeting's server is unusually flexible. Conferences can be built using serial connections, AppleTalk, TCP/IP, X.25, or even using the shared chat capacity on a bulletin board or on-line service, such as CompuServe.

Using Apple Events, The Virtual Meeting multicasts ac-

tions from one participant to the rest of the meeting. These events can be used to launch The Virtual Meeting applications or, for that matter, any other Macintosh application that supports Apple Events.

The Virtual Meeting's WhiteBoard application is a shared drawing tool that lets every conference participant see sketches being prepared by a single member. Only one member can draw on a single WhiteBoard sketch at a time, but the capability to draw can be passed around among multiple members. Mediation in The Virtual Meeting is similar to the same feature in Aspect. People raise their hands and can then be recognized by a moderator. The Virtual Meeting includes a message window that lets participants type short messages for shared display.

The Virtual Meeting also includes a capability for simultaneous control of multimedia displays using Apple QuickTime movies. Using the SimulView application, one meeting participant can show multimedia presentations on everyone else's Macintosh. The disadvantage? Movies and other multimedia materials must be distributed ahead of time to each participant. RTZ has also built The Virtual Meeting tools to give tests and quizzes and to support live auctions, with bidding and auctioneers.

MAKING A CHOICE

Choosing between Aspects, Timbuktu, and The Virtual Meeting is pretty simple. All three are designed to supplement, not supplant, existing teleconferences. The Virtual Meeting is a set of tools that can be used to build custom conferencing environments. That undertaking can be expensive, but it may be the best way to handle very special needs. For most organizations, starting with Aspects or Timbuktu is better. Going that route can help you get the flavor of groupware and decide whether a custom system will pay off.

A big difference between Aspects and Timbuktu is how each uses the network. Because Timbuktu thinks in terms of screens, sharing large screens or color screens can use a lot of network bandwidth. For someone trying to join a conference using a dial-up modem, Timbuktu will probably be intolerably slow. Because Aspects works with documents, not screens, it needs less bandwidth to update participants, making remote use via modem a lot more practical.

Timbuktu is a general-purpose screen-sharing application. That attribute makes it a good choice for environments in which small groups may want to share all sorts of different applications in a very impromptu way. Aspects has much more structure and a good set of meeting-specific tools. It will fit better into environments where drawing, painting, and editing are typical group tasks.

ANY TIME, ANY PLACE: REACH OUT AND GROUP SOMEONE

By far the most popular category of groupware is anytime, anywhere products, also known as asynchronous groupware. Almost any software can fit in the any-time, any-place category. E-mail, for example, is the original groupware–and the most successful.

Not every e-mail package immediately deserves the lofty label "groupware." A system that does little more than send and receive messages is pushing the definition quite a bit. More sophisticated packages, such as Microsoft's Mail, CE Software's (West Des Moines, IA) QuickMail, or Lotus' cc:Mail, add considerably to the basic e-mail functions. Microsoft, for example, integrates Schedule+, its scheduling and calendaring package, with e-mail. Quick-Mail includes "Quick Conference," a real-time conferencing utility, and QM Forms, which lets users and administrators create forms for e-mail, such as vacation requests, time sheets, or repair orders.

At the high end of the groupware/e-mail line are products such as WordPerfect Office and Digital Equipment's TeamLinks. WordPerfect Office integrates e-mail, calendar, and time-management functions; group scheduling; simple project management; and reminders into one package.

TeamLinks is an office-automation product that combines many groupware products into a single package. Digital's entry is an attempt to move its existing OpenVMS users off its terminals and onto a user-friendly PC interface. For that reason, TeamLinks still depends on server software running on minicomputers–software that's not very easy for a new installation to get up and running.

Nevertheless, TeamLinks is one of the few packages that really attempts to be an enterprise solution. Ask CE Software about putting 5,000 people on QuickMail, and you'll be met with a simple answer: CE Software doesn't do that. TeamLinks, however, really comes into its own in environments with many users. TeamLinks combines e-mail, shared document libraries (*group memory* in group-

ware terms), conferencing/bulletin board software, and document routing into a single package. TeamLinks works with multiple clients, including OpenVMS, Ultrix (Digital's Unix), and OSF/1 terminal and workstation users, as well as with Macintosh and Microsoft Windows users.

Most TeamLinks applications are pretty standard. The exception is TeamLinks Routing, which simplifies the process of routing forms and documents in organizations. It allows you to create a form, route it to a list of people who can update, approve, and sign it electronically. With TeamLinks Routing, you always know where a document is. No more losing things on crowded desks; TeamLinks Routing lets you lose them in crowded e-mail directories.

Installing TeamLinks on the client is easy, once the server has been set up. TeamLinks servers, though, are another story. I had to add five different packages to my OpenVMS server to build a complete TeamLinks system. What took 30 minutes for cc:Mail or QuickMail took a whole morning for TeamLinks.

Nevertheless, TeamLinks–once you get it going–is a pretty slick package. To get all the features of TeamLinks with other software, you'd have to install four different packages on each client.

If you've got 1,000 users on Mac, Windows, OpenVMS, and Unix platforms, TeamLinks is a very efficient way to put a lot of form and function onto the desktop. TeamLinks does not have the extremely tight integration that WordPerfect Office does. When you use TeamLinks, you still feel as if you're running four separate applications. But the four applications look similar enough to reduce training costs, even across such disparate platforms as OpenVMS terminals and Macintosh desktops.

While integrated packages, such as TeamLinks, and e-mail are the most common any-time, any-place groupware, others are out there. Smaller applications for specific purposes have found enthusiastic supporters. For example, The ForeFront Group's (Austin, TX) Virtual Notebook system helps workgroups maintain a single, integrated group memory (information that group members want to share with each other). That sounds simple, but it isn't. Using Virtual Notebook, clients on Macintosh, Microsoft Windows, and X Window system workstations can all share information in a "notebook." Notebook pages have combinations of text and graphics on them. A set of notebooks can comprise the shared knowledge of a workgroup or a work-in-progress, as Virtual Notebook allows for simultaneous updating of pages. Virtual Notebook pages can be linked in a hypertext-like web of information, presenting different views of the same data to different users.

ON Technology's Instant Update occupies an even smaller niche. All it does is manage the process of group editing. That doesn't sound like much, but when a geographically dispersed team has to work together on a single document, Instant Update can be a life saver. Imagine an artist in San Francisco trying to change a drawing for a Boston client in real time without repeatedly sending faxes back and forth.

CAN WE TALK?

The groupware community likes to draw lines between the pedestrian and oh-so-common bulletin boards and sophisticated collaborative conferencing systems. Both are based on the same premise: Users engaging in group discussion, spread across time and space. Whether a particular package is a bulletin board or a conferencing system isn't really important. As with any groupware, the most important questions are "How well will my group accept and use this product?" and "How does this software meet the needs of my group?" With the tremendous popularity of Internet news groups, CompuServe forums, and PC bulletin board systems all over the world, conferencing has become a national sport.

Most conferencing has been the domain of minicomputers and mainframes, but Macintosh alternatives do exist. Digital's TeamLinks Conferencing joins several older competitors in the Macintosh conferencing arena. ResNova Software's (Huntington Beach, CA) NovaLink is the most professional of the Macintosh-based BBSs. NovaLink brings together a host of bulletin board features in a single "information server." NovaLink is a client-server application. End users connect over AppleTalk, TCP/IP, or X.25 networks or over low-speed dial-up lines. The information server supports e-mail, file libraries, conference discussion groups, voting, real-time conferencing, and links to the Internet. NovaLink clients run one of ResNova's two Macintosh user interfaces or, for clients without Macintoshes, a terminal-based user interface. SoftArc's (Scarborough, Ont., Canada) First Class BBS has a similar set of features.

PacerForum, from Pacer Software (La Jolla, CA), is a conferencing system that is aimed directly at small work-groups. A PacerForum system is divided into bulletin boards that contain various discussion topics. PacerForum users post messages into discussion topics using the full spectrum of Macintosh capabilities. A message can have attached documents from any of the other Macintosh applications, including spreadsheets, graphics, charts, and even sounds. PacerForum lets users indicate their level of interest in each bulletin board. For boards with high interest, PacerForum will send a notification every time a new response is posted.

PacerForum is best used by workgroups who are constantly collaborating. We found its superior user interface intuitive, easy to learn, and powerful. Setting up a Pacer-Forum server is also simple. With Pacer's well-written documentation, our setup took less than 30 minutes.

NovaLink could also fit within a workgroup's collaboration plans, but its considerable power may be a better match for other environments. Setting up and managing NovaLink is a longer-term investment. With NovaLink's menu of choices, you have to think about what kind of information services you want to bring to a group. PacerForum and Digital's TeamLinks Conferencing are more limited in their functions, with straightforward designs that let groups get into conferencing very quickly.

If what you need is Macintosh workgroup conferencing, PacerForum will feel most comfortable. TeamLinks Conferencing requires a VAX server and doesn't support special Macintosh documents, such as graphics files. Team-Links also links Windows, Macintosh, terminal, and workstation user interfaces. For less-intimate environs where a single bulletin board with more than just discussion sections is needed, NovaLink is a better choice.

APPLE'S NEW STANDARD FOR COLLABORATION PROVIDES A SET OF UNIFIED SERVICES.

AOCE: A Familiar Face

Macintosh software packages have one fundamental difference from their MS-DOS or Windows cousins: They all look about the same. That's a design goal. For example, every well-designed Macintosh application lets you leave the application–Quit in Macintosh terms–by either hitting Command-Q or by selecting the last entry from the File menu. In turn, the File menu is always the left-most application menu on the screen.

One key idea behind Apple's Macintosh system software and the Macintosh ROMs is to make software uniform enough from package to package that users don't have to remember different commands to do the same thing. Apple has helped this similarity along by providing guidelines, tools, and routines to direct the interactions between users, applications, and the Macintosh operating system.

Every few years, Apple's designers carve out another piece of technology, standardize it, and document it in a series called "Inside Macintosh." A few years ago, the technology was communications, and Apple introduced the Communications Toolbox. This year, collaboration is all the rage, and the architecture is called Apple Open Collaboration Environment (AOCE).

The brain behind the plan is Gursharan Sidhu, the same fellow who designed the original AppleTalk. Sidhu brought together families of products into a unified architecture that can be used by collaborative applications and users. AOCE isn't the answer to every applications writer's dreams, but it does provide a wide range of services that are common to lots of collaborative applications.

FIRST OUT OF THE CHUTE

The first AOCE software to be released is PowerTalk, available as part of Apple's System 7 Pro product. PowerTalk brings the functions of the AOCE environment to your desktop Macintosh, and it includes some basic client pieces that ease the interaction between you and any AOCE application.

Along with PowerTalk, Apple has announced an intention to ship two products under the PowerShare name: a PowerShare mail and message server and a PowerShare catalog and authentication server. PowerShare is to AOCE as AppleShare is to files; both act as centralized servers for information. PowerShare servers, when they ship, will act as mail servers and information gateways and otherwise broker the AOCE information.

For now, the PowerTalk in System 7 Pro is all you get. System 7 Pro is essentially Apple's System 7 (version 7.1.1) along with the PowerTalk client software, support for AppleScript (Apple's scripting language), and a new version of QuickTime (Apple's multimedia file format). Apple is aiming System 7 Pro at business and professional communities; standard System 7 (which comes with every new Macintosh) is targeted for personal and home use.

Apple's Sidhu selected five different capabilities he believed collaborative applications would need. Not surprisingly, two of the capabilities are communications-based: interapplication messages and interuser e-mail. A way for applications to talk to each other using store-and-forward technology rather than direct communications, messages are a further refinement of the Apple Events technology introduced with System 7.

The AOCE view of e-mail is also a logical extension of existing technology. With AOCE's e-mail, users send documents to each other without a care as to network topology, addressing, or document format. AOCE still doesn't solve the problem of sending a Lotus spreadsheet to an Excel user, but it will let the Lotus user send the spreadsheet while working in Lotus, rather than by invoking a separate e-mail application.

Third, AOCE provides a uniform way of representing network resources–as entries in a catalog. Almost anything can go in a catalog. E-mail addresses could obviously be listed as entries in a catalog, as could other resources, such as AppleShare servers. AOCE also lets applications developers build gateways between the AOCE catalog and other directories, such as an X.500 directory or a real phone book on a CD-ROM. Catalogs are represented as hierarchical sets of people, places, and things. All AOCE users share a single global catalog and may have their own private catalogs in which frequently accessed objects are stored. For example, you might keep e-mail address entries for people you correspond with frequently in a private catalog. That setup saves the effort of browsing through the global catalog every time you send a message.

Security capabilities round out AOCE's plate. Authentication and privacy capabilities can be used to enhance security at the same time they make security less intrusive. The first visible manifestation of such capabilities is the Apple key chain. A *key chain* is a place where you put keys, also called passwords. Then you lock the key chain with yet another password. The passwords on the key chain are encrypted and protected.

When you unlock the key chain by giving its password, all the "keys" you stored there are available for AOCE to use in accessing resources. If you have to log on to three different AppleShare servers with three different passwords, you'll appreciate this capability: You won't have to type those passwords any more. AOCE will store the server name and your password on the key chain and use it automagically thereafter.

Of course, if you change your password on the server, you'll have to manually change the password on the key chain. And if someone discovers the password to your key chain, they have access to all the resources you have added to it.

A final AOCE security capability is digital signatures. Digital signatures can be applied to a document offering two guarantees. First, authenticating a digital signature confirms that you are the person who signed the document, and no one else could have (without you giving away your password). Second, digital signatures guarantee that any changes to the document can be detected as part of the analysis of the signature.

The PowerTalk digital signature is based on RSA Data Security's (Redwood City, CA) public-key cryptosystem algorithms. To get your digital *signer* (a data tool for creating the signature), you go through a goofy but fun procedure. First, you run a Mac application that generates a form on your laser writer.

Then, you take that form along with three pieces of identification to your friendly notary public. The notary verifies that you are who you say you are and then RSA registers your digital signature. The intent here is that your digital signature becomes as legal as your written signature. Someone can bring a digital signature to RSA and verify that you are, indeed, who you says you are (or at least who your IDs say you are). Apple includes a certificate for a free signer with each copy of the PowerTalk software.

Of course, you can go ahead and use digital signatures without going through RSA. The point of their getting involved is to build a digital signature that is useful for businesses and organizations doing business that require a real signature.

AOCE'S FIVE-LAYER MODEL

The AOCE model is made up of five layers. (Figure 1 shows Apple's architecture for AOCE.) At the very top are applications that use the services. Apple includes only a couple of sample applications with AOCE: a very, very simple mail system and a simple digital signature application. Even though Apple is providing the architecture, it expects third parties to provide the applications. To prove its

commitment, Apple lined up 36 different companies on AOCE announcement day, all of which promised to ship products. Amazingly enough, some products were actually ready. And more are beginning to ship every day.

Below the application layer sits the desktop layer. This layer includes simple interfaces to the catalog of network resources, the mailbox, and your PowerTalk key chain. The Catalog does for AOCE resources what the Macintosh Finder does for files and applications. You can pick things up, move them around, and look at them, more or less, but applications will do most of the interesting work. The mailbox and key chain are also Finder-like interfaces, but they have little power in the AOCE world. AOCE-savvy applications will do most of the work.

NOT VICTORIA'S SECRET

Because PowerShare servers aren't yet available, our test PowerTalk Catalog doesn't contain many entries. Apple does include one access manager for linking AppleTalk networks into PowerTalk catalogs. The AppleTalk catalog access manager gathers all the AppleShare file servers on an AppleTalk network and enters them in a hierarchy in the AppleTalk portion of the catalog. Using the catalog to access file servers is about as easy as using the Chooser, with the added benefits of the key chain: You have only to type a password for each AppleShare server once.

In this first version of the PowerTalk software, the AppleTalk catalog has another type of entry: users running the PowerTalk software. Apple's goal with the catalog comes clear: one interface to any object on the network–person, file server, printer. Instead of having a file system here, an e-mail directory there, and file servers on the Chooser, Apple has tried to standardize the interface for all network resources.

These beginning entries are just a starting point for AOCE. When PowerShare mail servers are available, the network topology will no longer require partitioning of users into artificial AppleTalk zones. When third-party applications begin to put network volumes, e-mail addresses, and user names into AOCE catalogs, using network resources should get even easier.

In addition to the global catalog, each user can have a personal catalog of entries–favorite file servers, e-mail correspondents–copied from the global catalog.

The desktop-layer mailbox interface allows users to see

incoming and outgoing mail and to do some basic mail sorting. It doesn't actually allow you to read, receive, or reply to e-mail. It simply shows the mailbox contents that some AOCE-enabled mail application will manipulate. The desktop mailbox is so basic that Apple included AppleMail, a mail package that adds a minimum of functions to the basic AOCE mail. AppleMail is just a demonstration e-mail program; Apple is leaving the market open for third-party packages.

Similarly, the PowerTalk key chain does little more than let you look at the keys you've stored on the key chain. Applications, such as the Catalog, are responsible for actually putting keys on the chain. For example, when you double click on an AppleShare file server in the Catalog, you get an extra dialogue box after you enter your file server password. The dialogue box asks if you want to put a new key (to unlock that server) on your key chain (see Figure 1). Once you do, you won't have to type your password on that server again unless you change it.

AN EASIER TIME OF IT.

The dialogue box in Figure 1 is a part of the next layer of the AOCE architecture, standards for applications. At this package layer Apple provides a set of higher-layer functions commonly used by collaborative applications. Application standards make the developer's job easier and, more importantly, they make applications easier to learn, because all AOCE applications perform the same function using the same user interface.

This standardization is an extension of the basic Macintosh philosophy: Do the same thing the same way every-

where, and you only have to learn it once. This layer provides standard dialogue boxes and other user-interface elements to "allow users to select addresses, add attachments, and approve documents in a consistent, intuitive way from within any application," according to Apple.

AOCE managers for collaboration sit below the application standards layer. These managers present services to AOCE applications above them: catalogs, messages, and security operations. Developers add services by calling the AOCE managers through an Apple-defined API. The common API shields users and developers from having to use different interfaces for every technology. The AOCE managers are linked to a series of access modules (the lowest layers in the AOCE architecture), which implement the services.

Let's consider the example of an AOCE e-mail user who wants to find someone's address. He uses e-mail to call the catalog manager. The catalog manager on our hypothetical system has links to an AOCE-defined service access module (SAM) for QuickMail, an X.500 SAM, and a SAM that reads a CD-ROM with the city telephone directory.

All these different addresses appear to the user in a uniform format because the application uses the same dialogue and selection boxes and because the application uses the catalog manager API to get the information. The directory databases may look very different, but the different SAMs present the information to the catalog manager in the same format.

Reach Out and Fax Someone

FROM IMPROVED INBOUND ROUTING TO FAX ON DEMAND SYSTEMS TO BINARY FILE TRANSFER, FAX TECHNOLOGY IS EXTENDING ITS REACH INTO A VARIETY OF FIELDS.

BY MICHELLE RAE McLEAN

No longer confined to simply sending digitized text messages, facsimile technology has unfurled its arms into a surprising number of new fields. Computer-based faxing, in particular, is making its presence felt in areas once devoid of fax technology.

The installed base of fax servers is growing exponentially. A study conducted by BIS Strategic Decisions (Norwell, MA) estimates that at least 28,000 fax servers will be in place by the end of 1994, and by 1996 that figure will grow to 175,000 units. Judy Pirani, director of Image Communication Systems Market Advisory Service for BIS, says a study currently underway indicates these figures are on the conservative side. "With an 80 percent compound annual growth rate, the LAN fax market is really poised to take off," Pirani says.

In addition to becoming more widespread, computer-based faxing is also making many technological advances. Manufacturers are exploring numerous techniques for inbound routing, including the use of extensions and optical character recognition (OCR). Similarly, new applications for outbound faxing, such as fax on demand, offer improvements in customer service and productivity.

But the hottest trend is integration; vendors are incorporating fax capabilities directly into other applications, so you can fax from your e-mail program or right out of Lotus Notes. Voice integration and binary file transfer are other technologies soon to arrive.

OLDER AND WISER

"The fax server industry is coming of age," declares Boris Elpiner, director of product marketing for fax-server manufacturer Castelle (Santa Clara, CA). In the past "fax-

ing was a novelty. It was more of an exotic toy. The technology is a lot more mature now. The fax machine is becoming the water cooler of the 1990s," he quips, referring to a fax machine's role as a gathering place for people while they wait to use it. And waiting in line is precisely what computer-based faxing can help eliminate.

The advantages of computer-based faxing increase in a network environment. Network fax servers offer one-time installation and centralized management. As opposed to putting a fax modem in each user's PC, installing a network fax server requires just one PC and one modem, with each network user having access to its services.

"When your traffic is focused, you can do incremental investments in higher-speed boards," notes John Taylor, vice president of engineering at GammaLink (Sunnyvale, CA).

WHICH ROUTE TO TAKE?

Fax servers offer another advantage over standalone machines: routing. Vendors can implement inbound routing in a number of ways.

The simplest method is manual routing, in which an operator views incoming faxes–often he or she can see just the first page–and routes them to the appropriate person or people. While somewhat time-consuming, this method is in use in many companies. Microsoft (Redmond, WA), for example, has two people dedicated to viewing and forwarding the faxes received on the company's 800 number. A more common implementation, though, is for a company to have faxes come in to a console near a receptionist, who, in between other tasks, scans the in-box and forwards faxes.

"Manual routing is probably the best option," says John

Faig, senior research analyst with The Meta Group (West-port, CT). He explains that a company may have a mailbox full of faxes, and the fax operator "hits a button, looks at the cover sheet for maybe 15 seconds, and routes it. That's four faxes a minute. If you want more forwarded than that, get more people."

But others see manual routing as backward. "Manual routing is a dinosaur," asserts Howard Anderson, president of The Yankee Group, a research firm based in Boston. To avoid setting aside special resources for manual routing, companies are looking to a number of automatic inbound routing techniques.

ON THE AUTO ROUTE

One much-discussed method is Direct Inward Dialing (DID). DID requires end user companies to order a trunk line that supports multiple virtual numbers on a single line from the telephone company. Users are assigned their own fax number, which can be linked to their e-mail ad-dresses. Users are notified of an incoming fax similarly to how they are notified of e-mail, and they pick up the fax from their e-mail in-box.

The routing technique is transparent to users, but one of DID's drawbacks is its expense. In addition to the spe-cial phone line, users also need a special DID interface to convert the DID line into a regular line. "Basically, the phone company's doing the routing for you," says analyst Faig. James Rafferty, president of consulting firm Human Communications (Danbury, CT) points out another prob-lem with DID: "Typically these lines are receive only. If you want to send out, you need another line."

Another method, called dual-tone multifrequency (DTMF), uses a vendor-defined extension that a user dials after the fax-to-fax connection completes. This method re-quires some training because it uses a tone-assisted prompting, and it cannot be used to fax from a fax server since the extra extension has to be dialed after the con-nection is made. Furthermore, not all fax machines are ca-pable of accepting the extra extension after the fax num-ber has been dialed.

READ IT AND WEEP

Another inbound routing method uses optical-charac-ter recognition technology. Some fax servers use OCR to read the addressing name on the cover sheet of a fax. Its low accuracy rate, however, keeps this technology from be-ing widely implemented as a routing method. "If you try to fax something that someone else has faxed to you, OCR falls off a cliff," says analyst Faig.

Some companies use channel-based routing to distrib-ute faxes to their users. With channel-based routing, ad-ministrators assign phone numbers by department. These lines are not virtual DID lines, but rather are actual sepa-rate phone lines dedicated to a single department. An en-tire fax card, then, is assigned to a department, and all faxes coming in to that card are automatically routed to that department.

Another method is called Source ID routing, which routes faxes based on where the fax originated. The sys-tem reads the number from which a fax is sent and, ac-cording to a predefined table, forwards it to the person designated to get faxes from that number.

EVEN BETTER

Perhaps the most talk in the area of inbound routing surrounds a method called subaddressing. A standards committee of the International Computer Facsimile Asso-ciation (ICFA), a coalition of 42 computer fax hardware and software manufacturers, has been studying the issue of inbound routing. The standards body recently recom-mended subaddressing to the Telecommunications Indus-try Association (TIA), the authorizing standards body for fax technology in the United States.

With subaddressing, fax numbers include a unique ex-tension for each person. A sample fax number might be (415) 123-6789**1234. In contrast to DTMF, which requires a user to enter the extension after the connection is made, subaddressing works transparently. "You do nothing after dialing," explains Richard Holder, product marketing man-ager for WordPerfect (Orem, UT). "The receiving fax server reads the extension, looks in a table for 1234, finds the per-son, and routes the fax."

Implementing subaddressing requires changing the software that drives modems, but Holder doesn't see this need for a technological update as insurmountable. "It's re-liable, it's easy to implement, and the user doesn't have to be retrained." The 1992 version of Group 3, the most wide-spread fax protocol, includes subaddressing, so "as people upgrade their machines, they'll get this feature built-in," says consultant Rafferty.

The biggest problem with inbound routing is that no single standard has been approved. Tom Dolan, vice president of sales for Westcon, a training company based in Eastchester, NY, says "Most faxes are still coming in on standard machines and are being delivered internally. You really have to be a large company to implement some of these methods."

But despite the impediments, The Yankee Group's Anderson thinks automatic inbound routing will materialize. The lack of a standard problem "will solve itself with volume, and the volume is going to be enormous," he says.

ON YOUR WAY OUT

Most benefits for sending faxes out via fax servers are obvious. The most often cited savings consist of collecting outgoing faxes in batch jobs and sending them out after hours when the phone rates are cheaper.

When fax servers first became popular, many companies took advantage of the servers' broadcast fax ability. People complained about receiving numerous copies of faxes they didn't want in the first place. In large part, the number of companies using that blanket outpouring of faxes has declined, and companies are looking at fax on demand as a better way of distributing information particular to a customer's request.

Fax-on-demand-systems allow customers to respond to questions via a touch-tone phone. In response to one of the questions, customers input their fax number, and about 15 minutes later they receive a fax of the information they requested. For instance, people can receive faxes of product information or documents offering technical support. Companies are able to save money not only by not printing too many document updates but also by reducing costs incurred for storage space of numerous product specification sheets. Furthermore, the immediate response time helps increase the productivity of companies' sales forces.

"I call it demand printing BYOP–bring your own paper," jokes Jack Powers, director of the Graphic Research Library based in New York.

LOG THIS

Management features are another area in which computer-based faxing offers an advantage over standalone machines. The systems include logs for tracking inbound and outbound faxes. The logs provide current as well as long-term status of outbound faxes, helping users track their faxes and also helping administrators monitor usage. Information includes which faxes have gone through, when they were sent, how many pages went through, and if the transmission failed after a user-defined number of retries.

Usually a fax server maintains a general phone book or group of phone books listing recipients and their fax numbers. Users can select an entire group or can designate certain individuals to receive a fax.

One possibly unsettling feature for users of fax servers is the inability to see pages feed through a fax machine. With a traditional standalone machine, users know that when the transmission is complete, the document exists in full at the other end. "Psychologically, it's very important for a user to watch a fax go through," notes Steve McBride, vice president of sales and marketing for Alcom (Mountain View, CA).

Real-time access to the status of outgoing faxes can be an important feature. Senders also like to know that their recipients have the fax in hand the moment the transaction is complete. With issues of inbound routing still unresolved, senders to fax servers can't always be sure the recipient will get the fax immediately.

ONE POINT OF VIEW

Having a central point for outgoing faxes offers businesses a complete view of fax traffic. The consolidation also eases management of incoming faxes. In addition, upgrading a board or series of boards on a single machine is easier than replacing them on every user's machine.

But these advantages over standalone fax machines look minor in comparison to some of the other advances in network faxing technology. Many technological improvements, here or on the way, permit direct integration of fax capabilities into other network applications.

The majority of this integration is happening with e-mail applications. "If you're thinking about automating e-mail, you might as well automate both [fax and e-mail]. The person responsible for implementing e-mail will be the same person doing the fax," says Max Schroeder, president of Optus (Somerset, NJ). A lot of companies are choosing to write software for Novell's Message Handling System (MHS) protocol because so many e-mail vendors support it, and it's easier to write to than X.400.

One benefit of integrating fax with e-mail is that users can maintain a single distribution list. Some of the names on that list may be fax recipients while others will be local or remote e-mail addresses. This integration is happening in private as well as public e-mail products.

A REMOTE CHANCE

E-mail integration products can have far-reaching benefits. Let's say, for example, you want to send a fax from the road. You've entered the phone numbers in your fax server phone book in the format necessary for sending from your office. For instance, if you need to dial 9 to reach an outside line, all the numbers in your fax phone book will start with a 9. But those kinds of parameters change on the road. If you are in a foreign country, none of your faxes sent to the United States from your portable will arrive because all the numbers, as they are entered in your directory, lack a country code. "You have to change all your numbers to be able to fax. That's a pain," says Optus' Schroeder.

But if your e-mail and fax systems are integrated, you can write your documents, dial in to your company's e-mail system, and all the faxes will go out through your e-mail hub, with that office computer doing the dialing. An added benefit of this integration is that you've picked up all your e-mail during the same connection, making this solution cost-efficient.

Companies have combined other applications with faxing capabilities. The training company Westcon has written its training course reservation program to the cc:Mail API set. Westcon's customers call into the company's toll-free number to sign up for classes at any of 14 different sites. Westcon employees enter the booking information into the company's reservation program, and a fax of that information automatically goes to the attendee 15 or 20 minutes later.

Also, the company works in conjunction with other training companies in different locations across the country. When people want to attend courses in those companies' areas, Westcon books them. If the other company also has cc:Mail, the system sets up a direct connection. If that direct connection isn't possible, Westcon's reservation program automatically sends a fax of the booking to that company as well as to the attendee.

"We're saving a lot of time, and we're saving a lot of money. Faxes cost 12 or 15 cents–there's no envelope, no stamp," says Dolan.

Hugh Mackworth, principal at Adelphi Consulting (Portland, OR), points to other extensions of fax as a communications technology. Companies are developing agent-based software, which furthers the integration process. Users of Lotus Notes, for example, with a fax gateway, can fax information collected within Notes to people directly from the program.

MORE THAN A FAX

All these examples and improvements still result in traditional fax output. However, another application of fax technology wouldn't rely on this type of output. In fact, having the output not become digital at all is its main benefit. The technology is called binary file transfer.

Proposed in 1988 and approved in 1992, the standard only specifies the capability of binary file transfer; how a company would actually choose to send a file across still has to be established.

Binary file transfer uses today's fax modem technology. "You need a fax server, not a fax machine. A fax server has a good idea of what a file is. Your fax machine, sitting there with a plant on top of it, isn't gonna know what a file is," says The Meta Group's Faig.

If both fax servers in a transaction are capable of binary file transfer, the sending computer will transmit the document in its original format, rather than convert it to digital output. So a spreadsheet will stay a spreadsheet, for example. The receiving computer gets an editable file rather than a series of digitized dots, but users can implement necessary security, designating a file as read-only, for instance.

The Telecommunications Standardization Sector (TSS), a standards body, is working on incorporating a means for binary file transfer into Group 3, the most widely used fax technology standard. The TSS has also included the routing method of subaddressing in the standard. Specifying routing techniques represents a change on the part of the TSS. "Previously, routing has been external to the protocol," says Taylor.

Industry watchers point to ease of use as an impetus for the acceptance of binary file transfer. "The reason fax is so successful is that you don't have to know anything. All the interesting stuff is hidden by the computer fax devices," explains Adelphi's Mackworth. "Right now, you can use a modem to send a file, but you have to do it. You have to do every step. With binary file transfer, sending files can be done transparently–the modems are sitting there already. The protocols and everything is negotiated by the devices."

Microsoft has incorporated binary file transfer technology into Microsoft at Work, the company's specification for making office equipment more intelligent. "We're looking to connect office devices with the PC world," explains Suzan Fine, product marketing manager, digital office systems, Microsoft. "We've established a protocol that supports binary file transfer. Users can think of faxing as just another type of messaging."

Because no standard for binary file transfer yet exists, Microsoft has designed its protocol to be downward compatible. If a receiving machine is not capable of binary file transfer, then the document will be output as a traditional fax. "We want to send rich information around, such as binary files or high-resolution files. But we work with specifications that already exist," says Fine.

Fine says Windows for Workgroups will include Microsoft at Work technology. Other companies have jumped on the Microsoft bandwagon. Castelle, for example, is one of the 50 partners building to this specification, with a Microsoft at Work server on the market, according to Elpiner.

Many people tout the benefits of binary file transfer. "Fax is the one piece of technology that every company has up and running all the time," explains Powers of the Graphic Research Library.

But not everyone agrees. "I just don't see it," says Dolan. He thinks people will send files via e-mail. "What's the advantage of using fax technology? So many more people are connected to the Internet. That's where you're going to send them a file."

The Meta Group's Faig says, "It's an addressing issue. With faxing, you use a phone number. People understand phone numbers. People don't necessarily understand X.400 addressing."

But even when addressing becomes simpler, faxing will maintain one advantage over an e-mail transfer system, and that is fax's capability to transmit images. With e-mail, "if you want to send an image, you have to fax that image into the system somehow," Faig points out.

GROW, GROW, GROW

In addition to integration with existing applications, other trends are driving change in the fax industry. "Fax

machines will come below $200. By 1995, 30 percent of all houses will have a fax machine," says Powers.

With prices coming down and more and more people buying fax machines, businesses will have to accommodate not only sending but also receiving correspondence via fax. "In three to five years, we'll see more input from fax machines than from U.S. mail," continues Powers.

Along with e-mail and other applications being integrated with fax, some people discuss the possibility of integrating voice, as well. John Walley, product manager for LAN products at SofNet (Atlanta), claims the industry will see the integration of e-mail with voice mail on the network. "Fax modems now come with voice chips. You'll get a voice call or a fax call, and the system will route it appropriately. We'll receive voice, fax, and e-mail all in one mailbox."

Faxes in our homes, faxes in our e-mail boxes–soon it may be impossible to avoid them.

THE TOP 10 MOST REQUESTED
FAX SERVER FEATURES
What am I Looking For?

With so many variations and advancements in the fax industry, how does a fax server buyer know what to look for? Fortunately, vendors and analysts alike agree on a number of important features.

1. Integration with many applications. Not surprisingly, topping the list is the hottest trend in the industry.

2. A good user interface. Look for a powerful but easy-to-use interface.

3. Compatibility with your NOS. Look for a product written for your operating system.

4. Scalability. The ability to add boards to increase accessibility is important to protect your investment.

5. Routing features. Despite a lack of standards, many vendors still encourage getting this feature.

6. Ability to support more than one fax board from more than one vendor. Analysts warn against getting stuck with a "monolithic," single-vendor approach.

7. Support for multichannel fax boards. This feature is important in securing a scalable product.

8. Ease of use in Windows. Since fax standards emerged from the DOS side, make sure the product ports well to Windows.

9. Management and sophisticated tracking abilities. Logs and usage tracking help control costs.

10. Ease of use. Users who don't understand a product won't use it.

MAYBE IT'S NOT INTEL INSIDE

CAS Takes On FaxBios

The dominant API in fax server technology is CAS, the Communication Application Specification written by Intel (Hillsboro, OR) and introduced in 1987. All fax server technology to date uses CAS, which Intel designed for the DOS environment.

A few years ago, some manufacturers wanted to make cross-platform support part of the fax API. "CAS is a good standard. But it was a standalone design, and it's six years old. Intel has refused to advance it, and we need a new standard," says Max Schroeder, president of Optus (Somerset, NJ).

Everex (Fremont, CA), now out of the fax industry, started the ball rolling on FaxBios, designed to be more portable to other operating systems. The association responsible for writing FaxBios delivered the API in October 1990.

That association has since disbanded, but WordPerfect has taken responsibility for sponsoring and maintaining the standard. According to Richard Holder, product marketing manager for WordPerfect, the company is working on a 1.1 version of the API. "We have a long-term interest in promoting it," he says. "More than 80 percent of the documents faxed are generated from a word processor. That's a huge market." To date, however, few vendors include support for FaxBios in their products.

Intel also sees the need for a cross-platform API, but "our position is that the right next step is to go to a CCITT-based standard rather than another de facto standard," says Dan Wagner, fax modem product manager for Intel. "We're ready to support T.611 as soon as there is sufficient market demand," he explains. T.611 is a CCITT-approved standard for a cross-platform fax API, but it doesn't currently have any market support in the United States.

But the CAS-FaxBios debate may end up becoming moot because "e-mail APIs will allow users to send a fax. The whole question of FaxBios or CAS doesn't mean a lot," explains James Rafferty, president of Human Communications, a consulting firm based in Danbury, CT.

Section 4
Wireless Networking

The only way to experience true mobile computing is to cut the cords–literally–but yet somehow maintain the network connection. Wireless technology lets you do just that.

The current choices in wireless network technology allow mobile users to work in a variety of ways. Users can wander around in an office building with a laptop and maintain active network connections; "Networks Unplugged" explains the latest technology that facilitates this type of wireless roaming. Or a single user might prefer to sit quietly on a beach with a Personal Digital Assistant and check electronic mail. This can be done using a very innovative transmission method, Cellular Digital Packet Data (CDPD). Working in conjunction with the analog cellular system, CDPD can use the cell sites, transmission towers, and some radio-frequency equipment of existing voice cellular networks. "Cellular Hero" unveils the details of this emerging technology.

Private companies as well as the federal government have taken a keen interest in the future of mobile computing. The Federal Communications Commission (FCC) is in the process of redistributing precious frequency for Personal Communications Services (PCS) equipment, which could be a boon to companies interested in developing inexpensive portable network devices that can link wirelessly to enterprise networks. "Personal Space" looks at what is happening in PCS development in the United States, while "Wireless Lands" takes a more global view of mobile computing worldwide.

Cellular Hero

CDPD WILL ALLOW YOUR APPLICATION TO SEND DATA OVER THE VOICE CELLULAR NETWORK, ENGENDERING A SLEW OF NEW APPLICATIONS FOR FIXED AND MOBILE USES.

BY PATRICIA SCHNAIDT

If you've ever tried to get a Coke from a vending machine and found that only orange soda is left, a new technology may be right for you. If you've ever tried to use your notebook computer to send a message from a hotel room but found that the telephone didn't have a modular jack, a new technology may be right for you. If you've ever waited for a taxi in the rain, a new technology may be right for you.

Oddly enough, the same technology is potentially viable for these applications and many more. Cellular Digital Packet Data (CDPD) is a nascent technology that will help keep vending machines stocked with comestibles people want, help people send messages from their notebook computers or personal digital assistants, and help them call for cabs more easily.

CDPD works in conjunction with the analog cellular system, allowing users to send data packets in between voice calls. CDPD can use the cell sites, transmission towers, and some radio-frequency (RF) equipment of the existing voice cellular networks. Many of the analog cellular carriers are in the midst of building and testing their CDPD networks, and service should begin to be available by the end of 1994.

COMPETING WITH RAM AND ARDIS

CDPD competes with other wireless packet networks, primarily RAM Mobile Network (New York) and Ardis (Schaumburg, IL), but CDPD has a couple of advantages. For one, CDPD has industry support. It was developed by eight major carriers in North America: Ameritech Cellular (Chicago), Bell Atlantic Mobile Systems (Bedminster, NJ), Contel Cellular (now part of GTE Mobilnet), GTE Mobilnet (Atlanta), McCaw Cellular Communications (Kirkland, WA), Nynex Mobile Communications (Orangeburg, NY), Pacific Telesis Cellular (San Ramon, CA), and Southwestern Bell Mobile Systems (Dallas). From the start, these carriers have worked together to ensure that their individual CDPD networks will operate as one nationwide network.

Proponents contend that the CDPD network will provide greater bandwidth with lower latency, increased geographic coverage, and lower costs than other wireless packet networks.

CDPD provides a 19.2Kbps wireless link between the user's device and the CDPD base station, although multiple users share that link. RAM Mobile Data supports an 8,000bps data rate. Ardis supports 9,600bps and will be extended to support 19.2Kbps in 1995. Transmissions over Ardis and RAM can suffer from several-second delays, which makes them unsuitable for two-way interactive communications. In contrast, CDPD promises only subsecond delays, although the exact latency will be determined by the design and implementation of each CDPD carrier's network.

When fully built, the CDPD network stands to have the largest geographic coverage, since analog cellular provides nationwide coverage from approximately 10,000 cell sites, all of which could have CDPD equipment added. RAM has about 800 base stations serving about 100 metropolitan areas. Ardis has about 1,300 base stations serving approximately 400 metropolitan areas.

One important side effect of broader geographic coverage is increased power consumption. Transmitting within a small cell site requires less power than transmitting in a large one, since the receiver is closer. Power consumption is vital for battery-powered devices, as mobile devices will be. Ardis and RAM have larger cell sites than analog cellular, and each requires two-watt transmitters. CDPD will require 600 milliwatts, 1.2 watts, or 3.0 watts, depending on the device and application.

Although pricing has yet to be set for CDPD, it is expected to cost less than sending data over RAM, Ardis, or circuit-switched cellular networks.

WHERE CDPD WILL BE USEFUL

Although CDPD proponents engage in one-upmanship with RAM and Ardis over which network has the greatest bandwidth, the stark reality is that CDPD provides a 19.2Kbps wireless link that's shared among all users in a particular cell. In an era when network users are crying out for more bandwidth on the LAN, an era when users routinely have 14.4Kbps wire-line modems and still complain about the slowness, 19.2Kbps isn't much bandwidth, especially since wireless is a much less-effective transmission medium than wire.

The upshot: CDPD is particularly suited to sending small messages and transactions. CDPD won't be appropriate for sending multimegabyte files; you'll need circuit-switched cellular, which is another burgeoning service, to send large files or faxes. However, if you wish to send short messages, CDPD may be a technology for you.

Although cellular phones quickly became a status symbol with corporate executives, CDPD is likely to be deployed as a top-down effort as companies try to make a key application more efficient. The mission-critical application may be for executives or salespeople on the road dialing in to the corporate network, but more commonly CDPD will be used for delivering packages, managing field service engineers, dispatching taxis, or monitoring the status of vending machines. CDPD is likely to be used first in these vertical-market applications rather than in horizontal applications (see Figure 1).

The early applications will be sales-force automation, field service, fleet management, and telemetry, says Charles Parrish, general manager of mobile data at GTE Personal Communications Services. "Over a longer term, you'll see the horizontal applications emerge. These are less structured, where you have the individual worker who wants access to corporate e-mail and databases. In the long run, this application is going to be the biggest," says Parrish.

McCaw Cellular, the leader in CDPD, outlines four classes of applications that are suitable for CDPD:
- transaction applications,
- location services,
- broadcast applications, and
- multicast applications.

Transaction applications provide limited communication between two users. Transactions typically consist of one message to request an operation and another to acknowledge the success or failure of that operation, although in some cases, multiple messages must be exchanged. CDPD can be used for transaction-oriented applications, such as credit card verification; point-of-sale; taxi, truck, and job dispatch; package pickup, delivery, and tracking; inventory control; emergency dispatch services; message services; and notification of voice mail or e-mail.

CDPD can be used to locate people and devices, particularly if used in conjunction with a global positioning satellite. In this vein, CDPD can be used for location services such as managing fleets of vehicles or recovering stolen vehicles.

Fixed telemetry is an important application. CDPD can be used to deliver the status of vending machines, engines, or vehicles. It can also be used to deliver instrument measurements, such as for reading gas, electric, and water meters or the flow through pumps and valves.

Broadcast and multicast services, along with messaging services, are more likely to be deployed across a variety of industries. In a broadcast service, messages may be delivered to a single cell or group of cells. Since broadcasts are not acknowledged by the receiver, the messages may have to be sent several times to increase the probability of reception. General information, such as news, weather advisories, traffic advisories, movie guides, television guides, and restaurant guides, can be delivered to mobile users.

Both broadcast and multicast services are one-way, unacknowledged messages, except multicast messages are sent to a specific group. Multicasts are useful for information services and private corporate bulletins.

HOW CDPD WORKS

CDPD is deployed alongside the existing analog cellular system, which makes it less expensive for the cellular carriers to build than a system that carries only data. How

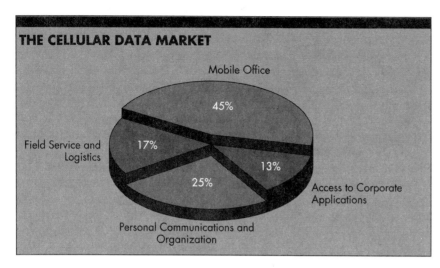

Figure 1. Corporations are likely to deploy Cellular Digital Packet Data (CDPD) as part of their business reengineering process. In the short term, CDPD is likely to be used in vertical-market applications, but over the long term, CDPD is likely to be a key component in horizontal applications.

are data packets sent along with voice calls? It's all in the architecture.

CDPD runs in conjunction with any cellular system that's Analog MultiPoint Service (AMPS) or AMPS-compatible, which is the predominately installed analog cellular system in the United States. The analog cellular system has additional bandwidth which allows it to support data and voice calls.

In analog cellular, the channel must remain idle for a set period between each voice call. CDPD uses channel hopping to move data packets through these interstices across different frequencies. Voice calls take precedence over data, so cellular phone users shouldn't experience any delays. Since data is not a time-sensitive service as is voice, data can be packetized and reassembled at the receiving end.

The eight originators of the CDPD specification intended to create a system that could be deployed rapidly, economically, and with technology that was generally available in the marketplace. It had several other objectives, including:
• compatibility with existing data networks;
• support for multiple protocols;
• minimal impact on end systems, so existing applications operate without change;
• interoperability between service providers, without compromising the service provider's ability to differentiate its offering based on features and service;
• subscriber roaming between serving areas;

• protection against casual eavesdropping; and
• protection against fraudulent use of the CDPD network.

The CDPD Group released version 1.0 of its specification in July 1993. It included definitions for the necessary components and communications protocols to support its outlined objectives. Figure 2 shows the components of a CDPD network.

The *mobile-end system* (M-ES) is the subscriber's device. As the physical location of the user with an M-ES changes, the M-ES remains in continuous contact with the CDPD network. Because the CDPD Group's intent was to work with existing applications, CDPD does not require any changes to protocols above the OSI Network layer. IP and OSI's Connectionless Network Protocol (CLNP) are currently supported. Although OSI protocols are not popular in the United States, the CDPD system uses OSI messaging, directory service, and network management protocols for network management. Also, support for OSI is essential for building CDPD networks in Europe and the Pacific Rim.

The M-ESs communicate with the *mobile-data base system* (MDBS) over a 19.2Kbps wireless link. The MDBS provides the link between the cellular radio and the wired CDPD network. From the MDBS, data is transported over the CDPD carrier's wired network to the destination's MDBS, and then to a fixed-end system, such as a file server, a mobile-end system, or another user.

Mobile-data intermediate systems (MD-ISs), or routers,

are responsible for the transportation. Internally, the carriers use frame relay, T-1, or X.25 networks to carry the traffic.

All M-ESs in the same sector of a cell use the same channel. Access to this shared frequency is governed by a protocol called *Digital Sense Multiple Access* (DSMA). Unlike Collision Sense Multiple Access (CSMA), which allows Ethernet stations to act as peers to gain access to the cable, in DSMA the MDBS referees the M-ES's access to the bandwidth. Otherwise, DSMA's operation is similar to CSMA's.

How many users can share this 19.2Kbps wireless link? "It depends on how the application is architected and what traffic it sends or receives," says Rob Mechaley, senior vice president of McCaw Communications and general manager of the company's Wireless Data Division.

GTE's Parrish says, "Based on our analysis, a cell will support hundreds of users. In a market like San Francisco, you literally have hundreds of cells. The bottom line, even with single data stream per cell, is that we have the capacity to absorb the entire market in the early years."

As corporations buy and use CDPD service, if a 19.2Kbps wireless link becomes heavily loaded, the carrier can subdivide the cell, making additional transmission frequencies available and effectively doubling the number of users it can support.

ROAM AS FREE AS THE DATA

The users see and use the M-ESs; the MDBSs and MD-ISs are transparent to them. The three components play a critical role in allowing the user to roam from one cell to another even amid a data transmission.

Each M-ES has a permanent address that identifies its home router or MD-IS. When a user travels from cell to cell, the M-ES identifies itself to the new serving MD-IS. The serving MD-IS registers the user, authenticates the user's identity, and verifies the user's access rights and billing status. A subscriber device must register with the serving MD-IS every time it is powered on or it moves to a new serving MD-IS.

Data sent to an M-ES is always sent through the subscriber's home MD-IS, since the home MD-IS maintains a database of location information so it can always discover in real time where its M-ESs are located. Sending data through the home router ensures that data can reach a subscriber no matter where he or she is located, even if the subscriber is mobile.

Users can roam from one carrier's network to another while maintaining the connection. Much of the handoff is procedural. When moving from one carrier's region to another's area, the second carrier will ask the first carrier if the user has access rights. If so, the user is transferred. The user's identity, the type of service, and the rates are not visible to the second carrier, thereby creating a service that's beneficial for the user without the carrier having to expose competitive information.

Even the billing procedures were designed for intercarrier service. "We built the accounting functions into the stack so the accounting records are generated automatically and forwarded automatically to the right carrier," says Mechaley.

Anyone who's eavesdropped on a cellular phone knows security and privacy are major faults with analog cellular. The CDPD specification calls for stringent user-authentication procedures and encrypts data. For authentication, CDPD uses RSA Data Security's (Redwood City, CA) electronic-key exchange. For encryption, CDPD employs RSA's RC4 symmetric string cipher encoding. Both schemes are highly regarded for verifying users' identities and preventing casual eavesdropping.

LOOK, A CDPD APPLICATION

CDPD carriers contend that existing applications can run over the CDPD network with little or no modification. In November 1993, McCaw demonstrated its CDPD service in Las Vegas by running American Airlines' Sabre reservation system. "The American Airlines' reservations person said she thought it was just a little bit faster than the system she usually uses," says Mechaley.

While applications will probably run over CDPD with little or no modification to the Transport layer, the Application layer may need more changes. "Making an application wireless requires more than just hooking up an adapter and sending it out over the airwaves," says Glenn Kaufman, business development manager of Lotus Development's Mobile Computing Group (Cambridge, MA). Lotus has a version of cc:Mail for RAM and is working with McCaw to ready its mobile applications for CDPD service.

The wireless environment is different than wired. Applications may time out because of the network's low bandwidth and high and variable latency, unless the protocol's timers are set very carefully. The actual latency will

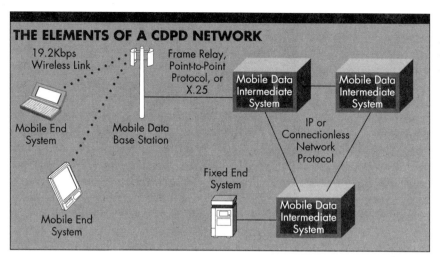

THE ELEMENTS OF A CDPD NETWORK

19.2Kbps Wireless Link

Mobile End System

Frame Relay, Point-to-Point Protocol, or X.25

Mobile Data Base Station

Mobile Data Intermediate System

Mobile Data Intermediate System

IP or Connectionless Network Protocol

Mobile End System

Fixed End System

Mobile Data Intermediate System

Figure 2. From the 19.2Kbps wireless link, a mobile-data base station receives the data transmission and forwards it to the Cellular Digital Packet Data (CDPD) carrier's wired network. Mobile-data intermediate systems then route the packets to their destinations, which could be other mobile-end systems or fixed-end systems.

depend on where the sending station is located in relation to the receiving station. If there are 10 routers between the two devices, the latency will be greater than if there are two.

"For the past couple of years, we've spent so much time talking about ATM and other high-speed networking technologies. Bandwidth is certainly not free when it comes to wireless," says John Reidy, director of new business development at Retix (Santa Monica, CA). Retix is providing its RX 7000 MD-IS routers to McCaw and PacTel Cellular for their CDPD networks.

Some applications can be changed with relatively little effort; some will require a greater undertaking. "There are existing applications that can be easily modified. 'Easily' means four or five people can work for a few months," says Andy Papademetriou, business manager for wireless data products at Motorola (Schaumberg, IL). "The excitement will be in '95 when many more people will see the light of what wireless can do. New applications will be invented."

Applications, whether modified or brand new, need to understand how to operate in a world of precious bandwidth. Existing applications, particularly messaging, will be optimized for wireless. Using filters to select what information users wish to receive on the road is an important first step. Agent software, such as General Magic's (Mountain View, CA) TeleScript, will enable software to act on the user's behalf.

"The goal is to reduce the amount of information over

a narrow pipeline. We are facing these challenges right now," says Kaufman. How do those applications have to change? Kaufman won't say exactly, but he comments, "The Application-layer protocol has to be designed so that it's not chatty. Over a LAN, a protocol sends data, gets a response, sends data, gets a response. You can't do that over a wireless network."

Client-server applications will tend to be more suitable for CDPD. The more data that has to be transmitted between the client and server, the slower the response time.

"It's hard to express how useful wireless is until you're in the middle of a meeting," says Kaufman. "You can't pull out a cellular telephone because it's considered rude, so you open up your HP 100LX and compose the message, 'The meeting is running late. Meet me at the restaurant.' "

FOLLOWING PROTOCOL

The CDPD network currently supports IP and CLNP as transport protocols, although others can be added. Since CLNP is not widely supported in applications, IP is the key protocol for corporate applications. If you are not using an IP application, CDPD also supports the AT modem command set.

Novell's IPX is not supported. IPX's origin as a LAN protocol becomes obvious in a wired WAN; it's doubly clear in a wireless WAN. One twist that may help is Novell's IPX WAN, which reduces the broadcast burst. "IPX Wide Area would work and could be instantiated very easily on a CDPD network. The question is whether it's worth the effort," says McCaw's Mechaley. "It looks to me like Novell is moving toward supporting IP as the wide-area protocol as opposed to native IPX."

If you have a Macintosh-based application, get familiar with MacIP. AppleTalk protocols are particularly unsuitable for wireless networks.

CLNP may play a large role in vertical-market applications. IP is running out of addressing space. "In parcel services or taxi dispatching, thousands of devices have to be accommodated. The kind of application that says 'I need six cases of Coke, two cases of Pepsi, and a case of a ginger ale' is machine-readable, and the machine doesn't have any embedded bigotry as to what the correct protocol should be," say Retix's Reidy.

CDPD FOR REAL

CDPD is in its earliest stages. In January 1994, aggressive carriers were building their networks in limited geographic areas. The number of CDPD users can be counted on one hand, and you'd be hard-pressed to find a paying customer. Interoperability testing among the different CDPD carriers is just beginning. Pricing hasn't been set, and CDPD carriers mostly negotiate a custom contract.

"CDPD is starting to form a picture," says Jim Wilson, Southwestern Bell Mobile Systems' director of network development. "It's like when they take the prebirth pictures of babies. Everyone 'oohs' and 'aahs' over them, but all I ever see is a blur. I see the blur with CDPD, and I want to see it more crisply."

McCaw is the most aggressive CDPD carrier, and it deployed its AirData CDPD networks, or at least parts of them, in New York, Dallas, Miami, Seattle, San Francisco, and Las Vegas at the end of February.

Bell Atlantic Mobile Systems is also pushing CDPD. In January 1994, it tested 10 cell sites in Baltimore, and it expects to offer the service commercially in April, according to Russ Brankley, product manager. It was also installing nine cell sites in Pittsburgh in January. "By the end of the year, we'll have CDPD in all of our markets in 15 states, which range from Massachusetts to the Carolinas, although not contiguous, and in parts of Arizona, New Mexico, and in El Paso, Texas," says Brankley.

At the end of January 1994, PacTel Cellular was ready to go into beta testing with its San Francisco CDPD network, which it built with McCaw. A beta test for its own network in San Diego was scheduled on the heels of the San Francisco test. "We're committed to begin deployment immediately," says Susan Rotella, director of marketing. "From San Diego, we'll roll into other markets: Atlanta, Sacramento [CA], and Los Angeles."

GTE, too, was building its networks in San Francisco and in Houston in January. "We're still in the network test process. We're not in field trial applications yet. During the winter and into the spring, we'll move from the testing of technology to the testing of applications," says Parrish.

Nynex Mobile Communications conducted two CDPD trials. "We haven't committed to a commercial deployment. We're looking at mid-'94. We're looking to get CDPD out as early as we can," says Jim Dukay, director of wireless data.

Of the members of the CDPD consortium, Southwestern Bell is the most conservative. "We won't see a substantial volume of subscriber units or applications before the third quarter. We need to be in a position in early '95 to turn up our CDPD networks. That time frame will be behind the other guys, but it's hard to gauge what we lose or give up. It's not much," says Wilson.

Southwestern Bell ran trials of digital cellular service but decided not to be a CDPD front-runner. "We've decided to let the market drive our technology. Our customers will tell us when it's time [to enter the market]. Everyone says CDPD is neat, but I'm not getting my door knocked down by people saying I want it and here's how much I'm willing to spend," Wilson continues.

Pricing is foggy, and the carriers uniformly say their offerings will be "cost-effective." Although GTE hasn't announced pricing, Parrish says, "What we're doing and what I think you'll see throughout the industry is that we're looking at a packet-oriented pricing structure rather than a distance-sensitive or time-oriented structure. The price structures will be developed with basic monthly amounts that look like your application, and perhaps the meter only runs after a large amount of traffic."

The real test of CDPD is yet to come: Users, whether vending machines or executives on the road, will determine its merits. Whether CDPD becomes a cellular hero or a celluloid flash can only be divined in 1995.

POWER, EMISSIONS, SIZE, AND HEAT
CDPD in the Palm of Your Hand

Once the carriers offer commercial Cellular Digital

Packet Data (CDPD) service, subscribers will need a way to access it. CDPD is designed to work with the AT command set used by Hayes-compatible modems, although using IP or Connectionless Network Protocol applications will be much more efficient.

Issues of the CDPD devices' power consumption, radiofrequency (RF) emissions, size, and heat dissipation will arise, although they will be more pointed in mobile applications than in fixed telemetry applications. A vending machine doesn't move and doesn't complain about the weight of a CDPD modem; executives, salespeople, field service personnel, and package-delivery people do.

"You can't put RF inside of a device that wasn't designed to understand how it works. Microprocessors generate a tremendous amount of RF noise, so the receiver section of your device will be overwhelmed by what it's hearing from the microprocessor. There may not be a way to effectively shield the receiver. So you have a conundrum, which generally says put stuff outside," says Rob Mechaley, general manager of McCaw Cellular's Wireless Data Division (Kirkland, WA). He also points out that the RF transmitters will interfere with the LCD screen.

Cincinnati Microwave designed the MC-Dart 100 CDPD modem for fixed and mobile telemetry. "It's reasonably small, at 6.3 inches by 3.4 inches by one inch," says Greg Blair, vice president of Cincinnati Microwave's OEM

Division. One three-watt, half-duplex radio costs $495. Cincinnati Microwave plans to bring out the MC-Dart 200 for mobile applications by year-end. This modem will be full-duplex, with a 600-milliwatt transmit power (which is the voltage cellular phones use) and will include circuswitched cellular for fax and large file transfers.

Blair says, "We don't get to the PCMCIA form factor until version 3, and that's Extended PCMCIA. There are some significant technical challenges to make a Type 2 or Extended Type 2. When you put the radio inside, it's a challenge."

Power consumption is another issue for the CDPD user on the go. CDPD modems can use 600-milliwatt to three-watt batteries. The denser the cells in a CDPD carrier's network, the less power is required to transmit. Look for CDPD modems that "go to sleep" when not transmitting. CDPD modems will require external batteries over the near term. Down the road, notebooks and PDAs will understand that they contain a CDPD modem, and the power-management functions will be integrated.

Heat dissipation out of the transmitter must be tackled. "The smaller the device, the greater the heat. When you try to transmit at 600 milliwatts, heat will be a problem," says Blair. The notebook and PDA manufacturers will have to work with the makers of CDPD subscriber equipment to resolve these issues.

Personal Space

WITH STANDARDS ON THE HORIZON AND THE HOPE OF A NEW UNLICENSED PERSONAL COMMUNICATIONS SERVICES BAND, WIRELESS NETWORKS MAY FINALLY BE UNLEASHED.

BY MELANIE McMULLEN

Radio networks of all varieties suffer from an ongoing wave of problems. For example, anyone who has ever tuned in to late-night AM radio has experienced the frequent frustration of frequency fade-outs. Halfway through a commercial-free broadcast of Meat Loaf Live, in chimes some station operating in turbo-transmission mode from Omaha that overpowers the Loaf with some rappin' 2 Live Crew.

Unfortunately, this type of transmission crowding isn't confined to your AM/FM radio dial. The electromagnetic spectrum is currently the carrier of millions of disparate wireless services. And the radio portion of the spectrum, a scarce and finite resource, has a seemingly infinite number of users and potential users. This creates one basic problem–airwave overpopulation.

Some recent contributors to this ongoing frequency crowding include a slew of companies sprinkling the market with spread spectrum-based networking devices. While years ago the number of vendors in the market was negligible, the laundry list of wireless radio network companies now includes AT&T's Global Information Solutions (owners of NCR, Dayton, OH), Motorola's Wireless Data Group (Schaumburg, IL), Windata (Northboro, MA), Proxim (Mountain View, CA), Digital Equipment Corp. (DEC, Littleton, MA), Symbol Technologies (Bohemia, NY), Metricom (Los Gatos, CA), and Solectek (San Diego), to name a few.

The big guns of hardware, such as IBM, Apple Computer, and Compaq (Houston), are also tentatively slated to release radio-based products sometime in 1994. The newcomer list from 1993 alone contains several formidable forces of networking: Xircom (Calabasas, CA), National Semiconductor (Santa Clara, CA), Digital Ocean (Overland Park, KS), Aerocomm (Lenexa, KS), and Aironet Wireless Communications (Akron, OH), a merger of Telesystems, Telxon Radio Frequency Group, and Software Engineering.

While lack of new competition and technology is no longer an impediment to the wireless network market, growth has ushered in a new set of obstacles. Two problems currently cloud the future of wireless networking: an absence of frequency dedicated specifically to wireless data communications and a lack of any IEEE standards.

But don't give up on this market, not yet at least. Help is on the way in both areas, with airwave relief coming in the form of a new spectrum allotment for wireless Personal Communications Services (PCS) and standards help coming via the IEEE 802.11, which promises to offer up a preliminary draft of its first wireless standard by November 1994.

CROWDS AND CRIMPS

To understand why a dedicated frequency is needed for wireless data networks, take a look at the crimps in the shared areas of transmission. Debates are raging as to which currently available frequency band can provide optimum transmission for spread spectrum-based networking. Many of the first devices on the market were designed to work in the extremely crowded 902MHz to 928MHz unlicensed Industrial, Scientific, and Medical (ISM) band. In 1993, the trend shifted up, with many companies starting to eke out their space in the other two high-range ISM bands, the 2.400GHz to 2.4835GHz and the 5.850GHz to 5.725GHz bands (see figure).

Note that the ISM bands were originally earmarked in

1985 for use by factory radio devices, such as the machine that seals the plastic over a TV dinner. These bands are now used for cruise missile testing, baby monitors, cordless phones, and car tracking devices, as well as wireless networking. "ISM is the kitchen sink of the radio spectrum," says Bennett Kobb, a wireless communications consultant based in Arlington, VA. "And over a period of time, the bands have simply become too crowded."

And a crowd, whether sharing space in the bleachers at a soccer match or in the airwaves of a network spectrum, can wreak havoc. "An immense amount of redundancy and error correction is needed to operate in a crowded band," says Bob Rosenbaum, vice president of product marketing at Windata.

The two higher microwave ISM bands, which are a little less crowded than the 902MHz space, do offer network users less interference. But they come complete with other drawbacks. "The higher the frequency, the more the components cost. Making components for the 2.4GHz band is the upper limit of cost that the market can bear," Rosenbaum adds.

SOMEONE'S IN THE KITCHEN

The higher microwave bands also have inherent sharing problems; other devices in that air space are cooking up all sorts of trouble for wireless networks. Wireless networks operating in that frequency could likely suffer a performance burn if located near the kitchen, or more specifically, near a microwave oven. Essentially, the network packet has to share the air with the bursty energy needed to heat up a coworker's Lean Cuisine.

While nobody is sure of the amount of interference a microwave oven could cause to a wireless office network, the effects have been noted in early demonstrations. Jeff Alholm, the president of Digital Ocean, makers of the Macintosh-based Grouper, tells of such an incident at a recent IEEE 802.11 meeting. During a demonstration of a 2.4GHz product, he explains, "A funny thing happened around noon. The radio started working significantly worse." He says the best explanation anybody could come up with was that the building had several microwaves humming along in the kitchen.

In addition to oven-based interference, the microwave bands have other drawbacks—power and performance. Power requirements in these two areas are more stringent,

which can put a strain on portable devices. Throughput, as well as distance, in the 2.4GHz band is also questionable. "You have limited coverage in the 2.4 band," explains Cees Links, director of product marketing for NCR's Wireless Communications and Networking division in Utrecht, the Netherlands. "You get the coverage of a telephone booth in that band."

Despite these drawbacks, NCR is developing a version of its WaveLAN product that will operate in the 2.4GHz band. Why? Here's the upside to microwave LANs. The 2.4GHz band affords a worldwide opportunity. This frequency is about to become available internationally, specifically in most of Europe and in Japan. The European Telecommunication Standards Institute (ETSI) will vote in March to allocate a 2.4GHz band as well as a high-performance band in the 5.2GHz range. Radio products designed for that space can operate—and be sold into—an international market.

"Demand in the international market for wireless networks is as strong or stronger than in the United States," says Links. He adds that offices in countries such as India and China are not wired during construction as most U.S. buildings are, making wireless networks a viable and even affordable option.

SEND HELP

While the crowded ISM bands are currently the only unlicensed bands available for data networking, help is coming—maybe. The Federal Communications Commission (FCC) is the master of the spectrum domain, deciding through a lengthy petition process who can legally use which parts of the spectrum, including both the licensed and unlicensed portions. Several years ago, the FCC entered a proposal for rulemaking to reallocate spectrum in the 1.85GHz to 2.2GHz range for use by what the government dubbed "emerging technologies."

These technologies have now emerged under the popular name of PCS. The technologies and devices vying for spectrum space in the PCS area will run the gamut from pagers, phones, Personal Digital Assistants (PDAs), and a variety of pocket-size, low-power communications devices. Devices in the PCS area will operate at a more intelligent level than those in the ISM band, with the ability to sense each other's presence and share the frequency more efficiently.

In 1993, the FCC further divided the PCS bands into licensed and unlicensed areas, then had to determine how much to allot for each area. After intense lobbying from Apple and the Wireless Information Networks Forum (WINForum, Washington, D.C.), the Commission earmarked 40MHz for unlicensed use.

Concerning the licensed PCS portions, the FCC divvied up a 120MHz bank of frequencies into seven trading areas consisting of a variety of allotment sizes ranging from 10MHz to 30MHz. These areas will be up for grabs, or rather for sale, as early as June 1994. The government intends to raise $10 billion in revenue from the reallocation of these frequencies, according to Becky Diercks, program manager for wireless research services at Business Research Group (BRG, Newton, MA). While these frequencies can be used for both voice and data, the cellular providers will most likely provide the more profitable voice services first, Diercks adds.

PCS services in the licensed spectrums will operate over a network of base stations and operating areas, called microcells. PCS will function much like the cellular network, allowing users to roam from one cell to the next. However, PCS devices will operate with lower power, meaning the microcells in the network will be smaller and necessarily more numerous within a given area. PCS will use a digital voice transmission, unlike cellular, which uses analog. The strongest competitor to licensed PCS services will be the emerging Cellular Digital Packet Data, or CDPD, network.

THE FREE BAND

While the licensed portion of the PCS spectrum appears to be moving forward, the unlicensed area, which falls in the 1.890GHz to 1.930GHz range, is a hotbed of controversy. The area was originally targeted by companies interested in developing the market for wireless, roving, low-power computing devices, such as PDAs. Specifically, Apple was interested in obtaining the area as part of Sculley-vision–a world of spontaneous networks comprised of millions of nomadic users. While developing the vision was easy enough, the efforts needed to obtain the necessary spectrum were a little more difficult, as Apple quickly discovered.

The first step Apple took in its attempt to accrue spectrum began in 1991 when it organized a lobby group,

WINForum, made up of those companies interested in garnering an unlicensed PCS band. While thousands of lobbyists in Washington protect those who have, "Organizing a lobby group for people who don't have something is a formidable task," says Kobb, who was president of WINForum until 1994. "Pulling this group together was as hard as forming a group for people who don't have a driver's license."

As WINForum developed and grew closer to achieving its goals, more companies became interested in this free band, including the powerful–and very wealthy–telecommunications companies such as Northern Telecom (Ottawa, Canada) and AT&T (Basking Ridge, NJ). "The movement for more spectrum for unlicensed use started with the data companies, but then the phone companies got involved. The two factions had tremendous disagreements," explains Kobb. The politically savvy phone companies managed to do what they do best in Washington–exercise clout. "The FCC wasn't as interested in the computer companies with the telephone people breathing down its neck," says Kobb.

Over the past year, the voice forces also began to dominate WINForum itself, and Apple and a handful of other data companies dropped their membership and financial support of the organization. "A lot of cantankerous things have happened at WINForum," says Nancy Bukar, a Washington, D.C., attorney who is serving as project coordinator of the group. "Billions of dollars are at stake, so really everyone is upset."

THE BETTER HALF

All the squabbling between the voice and data factions eventually pushed the FCC into going halvsies with the band. In the fall of 1993, the Commission decided to split unlicensed PCS into two distinct areas: a 20MHz area from 1.900GHz to 1.920GHz dedicated to asynchronous communication, and two 10MHz bands, located at 1.890GHZ to 1.900GHz and 1.920GHz to 1.930GHz, earmarked for isochronous communication, or voice-based networking.

The split, while harmless at first glance, contains a costly loophole. The FCC requires that the manufacturers interested in using these frequencies pay to relocate the incumbents that currently operate in this area of the spectrum. And to make the relocation fair, or rather miserable,

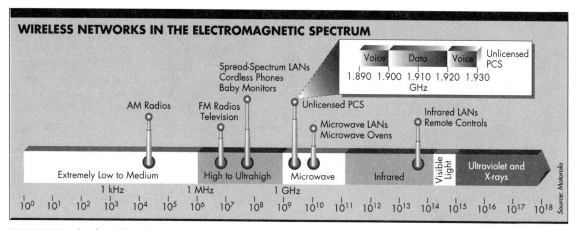

WIRELESS NETWORKS IN THE ELECTROMAGNETIC SPECTRUM

Spread-Spectrum LANs
Cordless Phones
Baby Monitors

AM Radios

FM Radios
Television

Unlicensed PCS

Microwave LANs
Microwave Ovens

Infrared LANs
Remote Controls

Voice | Data | Voice | Unlicensed PCS
1.890 1.900 1.910 1.920 1.930
GHz

Extremely Low to Medium | High to Ultrahigh | Microwave | Infrared | Visible Light | Ultraviolet and X-rays

1 kHz   1 MHz   1 GHz

10^0 10^1 10^2 10^3 10^4 10^5 10^6 10^7 10^8 10^9 10^{10} 10^{11} 10^{12} 10^{13} 10^{14} 10^{15} 10^{16} 10^{17} 10^{18}

Source: Motorola

SHARE THE AIR:. The unlicensed Personal Communications Services (PCS) band falls in the microwave area of the electromagnetic spectrum. According to current FCC allocations, a 20MHz data portion of the PCS band will be encased by two 10 MHz voice areas.

for both sides, the FCC split the 40MHz so that each group, voice and data, has one portion that is not heavily laden with incumbents and one portion that is.

"The FCC believes in inequality and unfairness for everybody," says Dave Murashige, director of product marketing and U.S. PCS marketing at Northern Telecom's Richardson, TX, branch.

Keep in mind that moving just one incumbent can be colossally expensive, costing as much as $250 million to move just one pair of transmission towers. And the total number of incumbents in the unlicensed band is somewhere around 100, according to Kobb. The cost of moving incumbents would eventually have to trickle down into the retail price of the products to be used in the PCS area, creating a mark-up that most wireless manufacturers cannot afford to tag on to their already expensive radio portables.

"When the voice guys and the incumbents in the unlicensed band reared their ugly heads, the promises of PCS got really bleak," says Greg Hopkins, chairman of Windata. "Most of the data companies have backed away from it."

Other wireless company leaders interested in the PCS band have also expressed disappointment. "With the cost of relocation borne by the makers of the new products, the notion of moving people out of the band is a big challenge that is too costly and complex," says David King, president and CEO of Proxim. "If a manufacturer has a million users and only sells a $50 product, then this action will kill the market before it starts."

LOBBY TILL YOU DROP

Even though the first promise of a clear, unlicensed PCS band looks dim, hope is not dead. The PCS band would allow devices to operate at low power levels at a high data rate with little interference, an offer too good to refuse.

In addition, the FCC intends to adopt a type of spectrum etiquette, parts of which were developed by WINForum, for this band which would regulate how products can communicate. This move would keep out any ham radio operators or other hobbyists that might produce interference and thereby hinder device throughput and performance.

Apple has already sent several petitions for reconsideration to the FCC. Other computer industry powers, including Compaq and Microsoft, have also sent detailed letters pleading for reconsideration. The Compaq letter dubbed the current allotment of unlicensed PCS "a black hole," saying it would be a complete flop for the computer industry. Microsoft offered the FCC a detailed list of the types of products that could operate in the band–if the frequency situation is remedied.

"The FCC is looking things over and will have to decide what to do," says Kobb. "Reconsiderations can take a year or longer. It will be a political dogfight over who is most persuasive." NCR's Link estimates that moving the incumbents and clearing the way for PCS products in the unlicensed area won't happen until at least 1996.

MOVERS AND SHAKERS

To get the moving process going, the FCC has sanctioned an Unlicensed Transition and Management (UTAM) committee to come up with two proposals: an acceptable financial plan of incumbent relocation and the relocation plan itself that specifies a new location for each incumbent.

The UTAM committee is comprised of officials from Northern Telecom, AT&T, Motorola, and Sony, among others. Northern Telecom's Murashige notes that conspicuously absent from the lineup are any data-only companies. He blames this absence on a lack of political organization among the data ranks. "There is less of a consensus among data people for working with the FCC," he says. "The voice people have been doing this for years."

Windata's Hopkins sums up the battle for bandwidth this way. "Unlicensed PCS, with its high data rates, was once wonderful and altruistic. Then the voice people got greedy, and the incumbents got greedy. Greed is what did us poor LAN guys in."

WIRELESS STANDARDS ALMOST A REALITY

The Real Missing Link

After three years of debating and politicking, the IEEE 802.11 wireless group finally has a focus. If all goes as planned, the committee may have a long-awaited draft of the first wireless network standard by November of 1994, with final approval coming in 1995.

While IEEE standards meetings traditionally are not fast-moving proceedings, 802.11, encumbered by more than 200 members, has been particularly slow to come to a consensus. "When the group first started, our original focus, or lack of focus, was to cover everything that had to do with wireless," says Bob Rosenbaum, vice president of product marketing at Windata (Northboro, MA). "Now we're focused on addressing the portable, mobile marketplace and making sure that laptops and handheld devices can all play together in the same area."

To make the devices play, the group adopted a Media Access Control (MAC) protocol, dubbed the foundation protocol, jointly developed by NCR (Dayton, OH), Symbol Technologies (Bohemia, NY), and Xircom (Calabasas, CA).

The basic access method of the protocol is distributed, based on Carrier Sense Multiple Access (CSMA) with collision avoidance. The protocol can support two types of peer-to-peer wireless LANs: ad hoc LANs and infrastructure LANs interconnected via access points to a wired network. The foundation protocol supports asynchronous data service and time-bounded services.

While the one-size-fits-all MAC foundation is close to being set, the physical layer (PHY) side of the standard will take more work. The 802.11 committee intends to develop PHY standards for three different methods of wireless transmission: direct sequence, frequency hopping, and infrared.

In direct sequence, signals are spread over a continuous band of frequencies. Each bit of information is replicated many times and transmitted as smaller pieces. The receiver, using a unique code, then reassembles the package into the original bit. Products such as NCR's WaveLAN use this method.

Frequency hopping does what its name implies–it switches signals from one frequency to another. Multiple bits are transmitted on a specific sequence of frequencies, where each frequency is used only for a short duration. Xircom's Netwave uses frequency hopping. Infrared uses infrared light to transfer signals. It is cheaper to implement than the other two radio-based wireless methods. Photonics (San Jose, CA) uses infrared in its Collaborative and Cooperative product lines.

The direct sequence and frequency hopping PHY groups are each looking into developing a dual-mode 1Mbps standard and a 2Mbps standard. The frequency of interest is the 2.4GHz ISM band. The speed issue has led to some heated debates, although most members seem to agree that two levels are necessary. "Having only a slow standard would be like standardizing only Arcnet," says David King, president and CEO of Proxim (Mountain View, CA).

As far as future progress is concerned, the committee members are optimistic. "We still have a few religious issues to get over," says Rick Heller, president and CEO of Aironet Wireless Communications (Akron, OH). "But with a lot of players, everyone eventually has to line up and support something."

Wireless Lands

WITH MANY COUNTRIES LACKING A RELIABLE INFRASTRUCTURE, CORPORATIONS AROUND THE GLOBE ARE TURNING TO WIRELESS NETWORKS TO BRIDGE THE GAPS.

BY MELANIE McMULLEN

Snippets of authentic Americana can be spotted in virtually every country in the world. Some American goods, such as Levi's and Coke, are commodities Europeans crave and even covet. Other U.S. treasures–EuroDisney, for example–are just too goofy for the European culture and are not held in high esteem. The trickiest part of thrusting American products into Europe is determining where the needs exist, followed by gaining trust and product acceptance from foreigners leery of American entrepreneurial engineering.

While peddling pop and jeans overseas requires only money and marketing, selling network products is a bit more complex. The international market poses a vast opportunity for technological development by American networking companies as well as European and Asian computing corporations. When it comes to the implementation of most networking technologies–with the exception of ISDN–Europe trails behind the states, for three reasons. First, the most basic element of networking, the local and wide-area wiring infrastructure, is still not in place in many countries. Anyone who has ever made a phone call in Italy knows that even voice communication isn't something to be taken for granted.

Second, Asian and European buildings and architectures pose a structural hindrance to networking. While most U.S. cities are a jungle of precabled glass and steel offices, the European skyline is much more dated, rife with ancient, historical buildings that offer no inner-wall spaces or wiring closets.

Third, standards in Europe and Asia for LAN and MAN transmission have been slow in coming. The governments, or specifically the government-owned postal, telephone, and telegraph administrations (PTTs) are the dominating bureaucratic forces of the European and Asian communications climate, and establishing committees to debate data network standards is not at the top of their lengthy priority lists.

BREAKING DOWN THE WALL

To overcome these and other obstacles, a handful of American network companies yearning for the yen and other international monies are counting on wireless networks, both spread-spectrum radio frequency (RF) and infrared, to provide the missing links. "Wireless data networking has significant potential in Europe," says Gail Kirby, group manager of Mobile Communications Services for BIS Strategic Decisions' international division in London. BIS estimates that by 1998, 15 percent of all network connections in Europe will be wireless. Currently wireless connections there account for less than 1 percent of the total number of connections.

Similarly, Dataquest (San Jose, CA) estimates that the international wireless network market will grow from $42 million this year to a whopping $750 million by 1997. Dataquest is predicting high growth percentages for wireless products in Europe as well as Asia, South America, and some currently underdeveloped countries such as Malaysia.

Analysts at Dataquest and BIS agree that the lure of wireless networking around the globe revolves around a few factors not present in the United States. Kirby cites the physical constraints inside many of the old offices in Europe and other areas as one of the prime motivators for companies to consider wireless alternatives. "The architecture in Europe is very different. We are proud of our heritage here and don't want to disrupt it," she says.

Older European buildings also have architectural and wiring blocks outside their doors, making short-distance, building-to-building radio networks attractive. "Governments in Europe have worked hard to prevent users from bypassing the phone company, yet the phone connections have not been reliable," explains Ira Brodsky, president of Datacomm Research in Wilmette, IL. "Users there are turning to wireless LAN technology, even infrared, for building-to-building connections."

Network integrators confirm that building-to-building solutions are currently the hottest market for wireless networks, especially in Eastern Europe. "In Western Europe, the PTTs can install a link in two or three weeks. But in Eastern Europe, this process is not so easy," explains Tony Formoso, a consultant for Gesto Computer located in Prague in the Czechoslovakia Republic. Gesto is a reseller of Aironet Wireless Communications (Akron, OH) products.

Formoso notes that in Czechoslovakia, "communications are difficult due to a lack of investment." This lack of development has led companies to integrators such as Gesto to establish connectivity any way possible. "We've put wireless devices in unattended and difficult-to-reach locations. We've even had to custom-build cabinets and put devices and antennas in roof space," says Formoso. He estimates that 90 percent of Gesto's wireless installations are for communications between buildings.

Competing with Aironet in the international market are several other American wireless vendors. Windata (Northboro, MA) is honing in on the short-distance wireless market with its AirPort building-to-building LAN that began shipping in February. AirPort offers 16Mbps outdoor transmission that can span 1.8 miles. With this product, Windata is targeting companies in southeast Asia and other areas looking for a way around unreliable phone systems.

Windata has been hesitant to dive wholeheartedly into the European market. "Europe is one incredible political football manipulated by the phone companies and other forces, such as Olivetti," says Bob Rosenbaum, vice president of product marketing at Windata. "Most countries use a digital cellular phone system, and they're trying to adapt it to data. But voice and data are not intended to be mixed. They're two different beasts," says Rosenbaum.

Solectek (San Diego) is also targeting the international market for floor-to-floor and building-to-building wireless networking. It currently sells its AirLAN line in Latin America, South America, and Mexico, and is targeting Germany, France, England, and Italy for future distribution. "Telephone lines in South America are terrible and inconsistent, and companies can wait six months to a year for installation of T-1 services," says Jim DeBello, president and CEO of Solectek.

The strongest Europe-based contender in both the indoor and outdoor radio-based wireless market is Olivetti. Based near Milan, Italy, Olivetti announced an upgraded release of its Net3 wireless network at CeBIT in March. Net3 is a spread-spectrum radio network that offers a 1.2Mbps transmission rate and operates in the 1.8GHz range. Olivetti intends to integrate Net3 with wireless PBXs.

Two of the most active American players in the European wireless market are AT&T and Digital Equipment Corp. (DEC). IBM, while deeply rooted in global computing, has been slow to enter the risky wireless radio market. Meanwhile, the AT&T Global Information Solutions division (formerly NCR Wireless Communications and Networking) in Utrecht, the Netherlands, is gunning for regulatory approvals for its 2.4GHz version of WaveLAN in many countries, including Holland, Germany, Belgium, and the United Kingdom.

DEC, which maintains 60 percent of its network business outside of North America, predicts that its wireless installations will follow that same tradition. "Wireless networking will build quickly in Europe," says Lois Levick, marketing manager for DEC's Emerging Network Technologies division in Littleton, MA.

ON THE MOVE

Levick and others are predicting that the worldwide interest in mobile computing and telecommuting–or "teleworkers" in Eurospeak–will add additional fuel for the growth of the untethered networking market. According to BIS figures, 20 percent of all computer shipments in Europe in 1993 were portables. While portables are not synonymous with wireless, sales in one area lead to boosts in the other. Trends shown by U.S. buyers demonstrate that mobile computers are most useful when they can connect to a network without being physically constrained, mak-

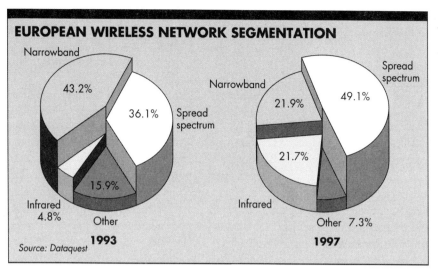

EUROPEAN WIRELESS NETWORK SEGMENTATION

Narrowband
43.2%

36.1% Spread spectrum

15.9%

Infrared
4.8%   Other

1993

Source: Dataquest

Narrowband

21.9%

Spread spectrum
49.1%

21.7%

Infrared

Other 7.3%

1997

Figure 1. Spread-spectrum networks will dominate the European wireless scene by 1997. Infrared connections, which require no government licensing, will also be on the rise.

ing docking stations, infrared eyes, and desktop radio adapters an attractive commodity to the user on the move.

Levick says that while the needs of the mobile worker in Europe are consistent with those in America, the controlling forces of technology development are very different. Europe is controlled by the large telecommunications carriers, many of whom are just now starting to respond to their roaming and hard-to-reach users. France Telecom, for instance, is looking at some of Digital's mobile wireless products to offer to its subscriber base as an enticement to use its network services. "The company came to DEC wanting to develop communication for people working in the vineyards," says Levick.

American companies that cater to the wireless mobile worker, such as Proxim (Mountain View, CA), are anticipating substantial future sales from the international market. David King, president and CEO of Proxim, predicts that within a few years, at least half of all wireless sales will be worldwide. "Growth in that market will be fast and furious," he adds.

THE INSTITUTE

DEC and others interested in the RF network market are awaiting the regulatory ruling scheduled to arrive this year from the European Telecommunications Standards Institute (ETSI). The European Radio Commission (ERC) is responsible for allocating wavelengths for its 32 member countries, and the ETSI sets telecommunications systems

standards for these allocated wavebands. In 1991, the ERC designated frequencies for wireless LANs in the 2.4GHz and 5.8GHz Industrial, Scientific, and Medical (ISM) bands as well as the 17.1GHz, 24GHz, and 60.1GHz ISM bands. ETSI then began work on developing the appropriate standards.

ETSI is now close to ratification of its RES.2 standards for medium speed (1Mbps to 20Mbps), 100 milliwatt wireless LANs in the 2.4GHz band. Once RES.2 is ratified, the 2.4GHz band will be available for wireless LANs in most countries throughout Europe, with the exception of a few holdouts, such as France, where the French military still occupy the 2.4GHz band.

ETSI is also working on standards for high-performance wireless LANs, or HIPERLAN. Under the RES.10 standard for HIPERLAN, products can operate in the microwave bands, 5.7GHz and 18GHz, at a speed of up to 20Mbps. Transmission in this area could also support video. HIPERLAN's first technical standards are expected to be released by the end of 1994, with final approvals coming in 1995 or 1996.

One other regulatory body of influence in Europe is the Digital European Cordless Telecommunications (DECT). Started in 1991, DECT is an ad hoc group set up within ETSI to establish a European standard for cordless applications, including telepoint and office applications such as wireless PBXs. Wireless LANs also fall loosely into this category. DECT has been allotted 20MHz of spectrum between 1.88GHz and 1.9GHz. DECT is intended for voice telephony, and it uses a cellular structure that operates on different radio channels.

The DECT standards and the ETSI standards have somewhat different subsets of supporters. For instance, Olivetti's Net3 product operates in the DECT range. Italy, the home of Olivetti, has certified the DECT bandwidth for wireless LANs, and the country's regulatory group has shown only moderate support in offering any official certifications in the ETSI 2.4GHz band.

RED ALERT

As the bandwidth debates rage on, many Europeans are turning to "the other" wireless network mode, infrared. Infrared transmission is not subject to all the regulatory, licensing, and approval delays, giving it instant appeal to the I-need-it-now wireless users of the world. Dataquest predicts infrared will garner a 21.7 percent share of all wireless network transmission in Europe by 1997 (see Figure 1).

The Infrared Data Association (IrDA) announced at CeBIT in 1994 the first draft of a proposed worldwide infrared connectivity standard for data devices, including Personal Digital Assistants (PDAs), laptops, telephones, and fax machines. This standard offers low power consumption and a transfer rate of 115.2Kbps. The standard's physical and protocol levels–Serial Infrared (SIR), Infrared Link Access Protocol (IRLAP), and Link Management Protocol–will likely be officially adopted at the IrDA meeting at the end of April., 1995 The IrDA was formed in July, 1993, and it now has more than 60 members worldwide, including Apple Computer, British Telecom, AT&T, Compaq, Hewlett-Packard, Microsoft, Olivetti, and Siemens.

In addition to worldwide compatibility, infrared has other benefits over radio, including smaller–and less-expensive–components. "Infrared is a mature technology, and it costs about $1.50 to $4.50 a unit to build it into mobile devices," says Datacomm's Brodsky.

Companies with products already in the international infrared scene include Photonics (San Jose, CA) and, most recently, IBM Microelectronics (Toronto). Hewlett-Packard (HP, Palo Alto, CA) and Apple Computer (Cupertino, CA) offer built-in infrared eyes on some of their mobile computers, including the OmniBook and the Newton, respectively.

Photonics offers the Cooperative family of adapters and access points that operate with the Macintosh, Powerbook, and Newton, and the Collaborate infrared family for the PC and laptop market. Photonics has six distributors in Japan and other parts of Asia.

In July 1993, Photonics signed a licensing agreement with IBM, giving it the rights to develop products using Photonics' diffuse infrared technology. IBM is now selling a line of 1Mbps infrared adapters and plans to announce a 4Mbps infrared product this fall, says Jacek Maryan, senior associate engineer at IBM Canada.

BETTER THAN NOTHING?

Whether infrared or radio, the worldwide market is being lured by the benefits of wireless computing. While the 1Mbps and 2Mbps throughputs of wireless networking make it somewhat unattractive to U.S. power users, the never-before networked have few complaints concerning the speed limitations of wireless. (Remember this is how Arcnet grew to an installed base in the millions.) "Wireless networks don't have the perception problem internationally that they do in the United States," says Richard Heller, president of Aironet.

In areas such as Czechoslovakia, wireless technology often surfaces as an all-or-nothing solution. "Wireless works when there are no other possibilities," adds installer Formoso. "Some companies here can have a wireless link or no link at all."

SEEING RED

Japan No Longer Stands Alone

Although the Japanese are known worldwide for their advanced manufacturing, electronics, and engineering, their country still remains a third-rate power in the adoption of network technology. With slow-moving technocrats in government and a powerful, very bureaucratic Ministry of Posts and Telecommunications (MPT) in charge of the country's communications, Japan is stuck in a world of standalone NEC PCs.

While 40 percent of the offices in the United States are wired for networks, only 5 percent of Japanese buildings are network-ready, according to research done by Photonics (San Jose, CA). This lack of wiring, coupled with years of tight import and commerce restrictions, renders Japanese businesses fertile areas of development for network companies that can work around a few physical and cultural roadblocks.

One such company is Photonics, a wireless network supplier that now has many Japanese firms operating in the red, or more specifically, in infrared. "In America, wireless is mostly an enabler to portables. In Japan, it's an enabler as well as a piece of the infrastructure," says Gary Hughes, CEO at Photonics. Hughes explains how the working environments in Japan are predominantly divided into small, open cubicles within older buildings, making infrared transmission a viable network option.

Photonics, which sells its infrared products under the name Space-LAN in Japan (since "Cooperative" doesn't translate well), has garnered a lot of interest in its Apple-compatible adapters. Apple computers have a 12 percent market share in Japan, a number which is growing "in leaps and bounds" according to Hughes. The Japanese are particularly fond of Apple's Kanji interface, he adds.

SAY NO TO RADIO

Radio-based wireless networking is not quite as easy a sell in Japan. The MPT keeps a tight grip on frequency allotments and power requirements, confining RF networks to tiny bandwidths of operational space and limiting power for wireless products to 100 milliwatts, one-tenth the level allowed in the United States.

Japan also suffers from a "not built here" attitude in electronics, according to Richard Heller, president of Aironet Wireless Communications (Akron, OH). "The balance of trade there is awful. The only U.S. companies with inroads are those that operate subsidiaries within Japan."

Japan also has a few cultural roadblocks to wireless computing. The mobile wireless manufacturers point out that Japan has a very stationary workforce. "When workers need to put in a few extra hours, they just stay at work," explains Mark Freitas, vice president of development at Microcom (Norwood, MA). "Most Japanese look puzzled at the word telecommuting. The concept just doesn't exist."

Networks Unplugged

ONCE ONLY A FANTASY, WIRELESS NETWORKS ARE ON THEIR WAY TO REPLACING EXISTING TECHNOLOGY AS VENDORS TACKLE THE ISSUES OF SPEED AND PRICE.

BY MARTHA STRIZICH

Remember the tiny "communicator" Captain Kirk used to stay in touch with his crew back on the Starship Enterprise? Or the clunky telephone that blundering secret agent Maxwell Smart kept hidden in the bottom of his shoe?

In the late 1960s, communicators that plugged into thin air and shoe phones without wires were all part of an evening's fantastical TV entertainment. But today, descendants of those devices–only imagined by Hollywood screenwriters two decade ago–are showing up in the real world in the form of cellular phones, palmtop computers, and other wireless devices we now take for granted.

Does this mean TV's futuristic version of an untethered world is close at hand? In a few short years, will the majority of computer users wander freely through the workplace, logging off and on their corporate LANs using nothing but the airwaves?

Probably not. Today, wireless networks account for a very small percentage of total LAN installations. Industry pundits predict the shift from a wired paradigm to a predominantly wireless one is still a long way off.

WHAT A DIFFERENCE A YEAR MAKES

Critics of wireless networking technology cite the higher costs of wireless solutions, the slower performance of wireless compared to wired LANs, and the instability of the technology itself as reasons for the sluggish deployment of wireless networks. Lack of wireless standards and concerns about security are also high on the list of reasons for wireless LANs slowly gaining momentum among corporate users.

But by making wireless equipment cheaper, smaller, and much faster, wireless vendors have started tackling some issues that have so far confined them to niche markets. One wireless vendor, NCR (Dayton, OH), recently dropped the price on its WaveLAN network interface card from $799 to $695. Telesystems SLW (Don Mills, Ontario, Canada), followed suit, reducing its ARLAN (Advanced Radio LAN) 600 NIC nearly $400, to $895.

This year, three wireless vendors–InfraLAN Technologies (Acton, MA), Motorola (Arlington Heights, IL), and Proxim (Mountain View, CA)–announced significant increases in the claimed data rates for their wireless LANs. InfraLAN says it cranked up the speed of its infrared Token Ring wireless LAN from 4Mbps to a whopping 16Mbps; Motorola boosted the throughput for its Altair, its narrowband wireless system, from 3.2Mbps to 5.7Mbps; and Proxim pushed up its claimed rates for the spread spectrum RangeLAN from only 256Kbps to 1.6Mbps.

Other vendors, including Photonics (San Jose, CA), Spectrix (Evanston, IL), and Xircom (Calabasas, CA), have announced a slew of new wireless products they hope will attract the growing number of users with notebook, palmtop, and pen-based computers who are starting to look for easier ways to connect to their corporate LANs.

Users are apparently starting to notice. "In the last year, we've seen greater market acceptance of wireless LAN technology," says Greg Hopkins, CEO of Windata (Northboro, MA), whose company makes the FreePort wireless LAN. "We've gone from hearing a customer response of 'What's wireless?' to 'Can I use wireless for this (particular) application?'"

The numbers show users' interest is piquing. According to market research firm Dataquest (San Jose, CA), wireless network connections installed in businesses across the country have jumped from 44,000 in 1992 to 184,800 in 1993–more than a fourfold increase. Dataquest predicts that 3.2 million wireless connections will be in place throughout the United States by 1997–a compound annual growth rate of 101 percent per year for the next five years.

Until then, wireless LANs will most likely remain a niche market. Today, most early adopters decide to go wireless because implementing their application with a traditional cabled solution would be impractical or even impossible.

Typical wireless LAN pioneers include hospitals, where point-of-care systems provide doctors and nurses with un-tethered access to a patient's medical records; airlines, where roaming personnel need to check on flight informa-tion and passengers' records from on the ground or in the air; and factories or warehouses, where workers perform-ing portable tasks need to update a database on remote LANs or where the construction of a building makes wiring difficult. Other likely candidates for wireless in-clude businesses that may move or reorganize frequently and companies that need to set up temporary networks.

WHERE NO LAN HAS GONE BEFORE

One early adopter of wireless networking is the Gen-eral Motors North American Operations Prototype Center in Detroit, a research and engineering site responsible for developing advanced automobile technologies. Faced with the problem of how to connect several PCs on its shop floor with GM's existing Ethernet network located in an-other building, Tom DeSimone, senior systems engineer at the Prototype Center, decided to give wireless a try.

Conditions in the factory–a solid, reinforced concrete slab floor with no basement, an overhead crane that runs through the shop, and heavy metal carts that are pushed across the shop floor all day long–made conventional ca-bling almost out of the question.

"Wireless seemed like it would be a slick solution," DeSimone says. "It meant we wouldn't have to worry about where our PCs were located or how to lay out the wiring to get to them."

DeSimone tried wireless LANs from several vendors before installing Windata's spread spectrum wireless FreePort system. He chose FreePort, with a throughput of 5.7Mbps, because it has the range to cover the entire shop

floor and is transparent to the protocols that the General Motors network uses. "FreePort solved our problem of get-ting Ethernet services to these devices," he says.

DeSimone plans to put four more wireless PCs out on the shop floor soon and has identified two other applica-tions he thinks are well-suited to wireless solutions.

One application is an exhibition, put on by the engi-neering staff each year to demonstrate the new technolo-gies under development at the Center. Before it can set up the equipment it needs for the show, DeSimone's staff has to lay thin-Ethernet cable in the garage where the exhibi-tion is held. "If I use wireless technology instead, all I'll have to do is throw one of our Windata hubs on top of an office wall and we won't have to worry about pulling any wires at all," DeSimone says.

He also wants to use wireless technology to set up ad hoc LANs in several conference rooms being temporarily used as customer-training rooms. "There is no way to get the number of network connections that we need into the conference rooms using regular wiring. The flexibility and portability of wireless makes it a perfect solution for this application."

DeSimone is pleased with the performance of his wire-less LAN but has a wish list for future releases of FreePort. Not surprisingly, it includes cheaper prices, small-size equipment, and the ability to achieve longer distances.

A PORTABLE PARADIGM

In spite of some of the drawbacks of today's wireless desktop LANs, the suitability of wireless solutions for users like those at the GM Prototype Center is apparent. But many analysts are saying it will be the explosive growth of portable computing, not the proliferation of wireless desktop LANs, that will finally push wireless net-working into the mainstream.

One analyst, Richard Siber with BIS Strategic Deci-sions (Norwell, MA), suggests that the largest potential for the wireless LAN market may well rest with the emerging population of roaming users who are buying laptops, palmtops, and personal digital assistants in larger num-bers every year. He predicts the wireless market will gather critical mass when the number of portable units sold reaches significant proportions and users start de-manding easier connectivity to their company's existing cabled LAN. A BIS study forecasts such demand may hit as soon as 1995, when the installed base of portable users is expected to reach 14 million.

Jennifer Pigg, program manager, data communications research and consulting at the Yankee Group (Boston), agrees. In a recent report, Pigg estimates that wireless LAN revenues will reach $237 million by 1996; 70 percent of those revenues will come from sales of wireless communication solutions for laptops, she says.

Betting that burgeoning sales of portable devices will have a positive impact on the sale of wireless systems, a half-dozen vendors this year announced products for mobile users. Some are adding new portable computing products to their existing line of desktop wireless LAN products. Others are entering the wireless arena for the first time with full product lines built from scratch to meet the needs of the mobile computing market.

HOW ROAMING WORKS

Wireless networks designed specifically for roaming users are configured differently from wireless networks that have been engineered for use with desktop PCs.

Wireless desktop systems, such as those from Motorola or Windata, are constructed around the concept of a single control module, or hub, and one or more user modules. The hub, which is hard wired to a server of a LAN backbone, routes data packets wirelessly between user modules as well as to and from the server or LAN backbone. Each user module typically supports between six and eight users and is connected to a user's desktop computer with a cable or wire.

Wireless LANs targeted at nomadic users are actually "more wireless" than their desktop counterparts. Instead of plugging into a wall socket and connecting to a hub with wires as many desktop wireless units do, wireless LANs designed with portables in mind give users untethered access to their LAN using a combination of cordless LAN adapters and wireless access points.

Cordless LAN adapter cards consist of a network interface card, a wireless transceiver, and an antenna, either in a single small unit or in two small units attached with a wire.

Some are external devices that plug into the parallel port of a notebook computer or the serial port of a handheld computer. Others are internal units the size of credit cards. These cards are compatible with specifications defined by the Personal Computer Memory Card International Association and easily fit inside the growing number of devices with PCMCIA slots. Both internal and external LAN adapter cards usually draw power form the battery of the portable device to which they attach, so users do not need an external power supply.

Access points, on the other side of the wireless portable equation, serve to integrate the wireless LAN into the wired LAN by making all the existing traditional LAN's services and resources available to wireless users within range of the access point. They also act as "traffic cops," directing packets sent by roaming users to other wireless users or to the wired LAN.

A single access point, sometimes called a *wireless hub,* has a range from 150 feet to 1,000 feet, depending on its manufacturer and whether it is operating in an open environment, such as a factory or warehouse, or in a densely furnished one, such as an indoor office divided into cubicles.

By installing multiple access points in strategic locations throughout their facilities, companies can extend the service area of their network throughout the enterprise. In such a scenario, access points serve as wireless repeaters, transparently "handing off" roaming users from one access point to another so they stay seamlessly connected to the LAN as they move around the facility. Some vendors' access points require dedicated PCs with adapter cards; others are book-size devices with external omnidirectional antennas that can be mounted on a desk, wall, or ceiling.

The configuration of different vendors' wireless roaming solutions can vary considerably. The transmission range of access points, the cost of additional software needed to implement roaming, and the power consumption of an adapter card are factors that affect the cost and performance of a wireless implementation.

A GOOD BET

NCR is one of several vendors, so far, placing its bet on the growth of portable users. Earlier this year, the company added roaming capabilities to its WaveLAN wireless LAN, which has been shipping since 1991. The roaming capability consists of an access point called WavePoint, software called WaveNet, and a release 2.0-compliant Type II PCMCIA card.

"WavePoint, WaveNet, and our PCMCIA card are a way

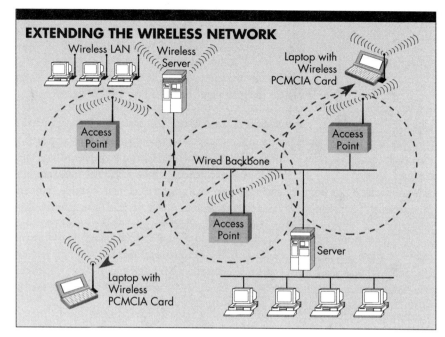

EXTENDING THE WIRELESS NETWORK

Wireless LAN · Wireless Server

Laptop with Wireless PCMCIA Card

Access Point

Wired Backbone

Access Point

Access Point

Server

Laptop with Wireless PCMCIA Card

FREEDOM TO ROAM: With "roaming," mobile computing, users can access all the resources on their corporate LAN, and they can also contact each other. Signals from laptop, palmtop, and pen-based computers outfitted with wireless PCMCIA cards are transmitted to the nearest wireless access point. Multiple access points connected into the wired backbone serve as wireless repeaters, seamlessly handing off nomads' signals from one access point to another.

to provide mobile users an infrastructure for wireless connectivity," says Darryl Maddox, NCR's senior product manager, network products division.

NCR sees two markets for its new products. "There's a tremendous market for people who are working away from their desks and who need access to information, such as point-of-care, point-of-sale, and inventory management," Maddox says.

The other big market will be organizations that decide to downsize desktop computers to portables but still need connectivity to their corporate LAN. "We think our main market in the next year will be Fortune 1,000 companies that see the strategic importance of having portable units and start buying them in large numbers," he says.

Another vendor betting on user interest in mobile computing is Spectrix, which has developed a new wireless LAN targeted at users of hand-held, pen-based computing devices, such as the Epson EHT30 and the Panasonic JT785.

The system, called SpectrixLite, uses infrared antennas connected to existing wiring to turn individual rooms within a building into "cells" of wireless coverage. An external transceiver the size of a cigarette pack, which plugs into the serial port of the hand-held unit, gives mobile

users the same access to LAN resources that users tied to their desks receive.

"SpectrixLite is targeted at applications-specific users who need to use hand-held computers, such as financial institutions, hospitals, and manufacturing facilities," says Tom Baumgartner, marketing director at Spectrix.

Earlier this year, traders at the New York Stock Exchange, the Chicago Board of Trade, and the Chicago Mercantile Association tested SpectrixLite. The system is scheduled to ship in December 1993; a PCMCIA card will be available in mid-1994, the company says.

The latest vendor jockeying for position in the portable wireless market is Xircom. This summer, Xircom announced Netwave wireless LAN technology designed exclusively for portable computing users. The Netwave product family can be used to set up wireless subnets on existing wired LANs or to establish ad hoc, self-contained networks so nomadic users can communicate in a peer-to-peer or server/workstation configuration without connecting to a cabled LAN.

Xircom's CreditCard Netwave Adapter boasts the smallest form factor of any product on the market. It is made up of a PCMCIA card, a radio transceiver, and an integrated antenna, in one single internal unit. A Pocket Netwave

Adapter, which attaches to a parallel port, is also available for notebooks that do not have PCMCIA slots. Several vendors are shipping products that let portable computing users "roam" through the workplace and still remain connected to the network.

RX FOR HEALTH CARE

Wireless roaming is in its infancy, and reports from pioneering users are just coming in. One such user is Maine Medical Center (Portland, ME), which has been testing the roaming capabilities of several vendors for more than six months to determine the viability of this new technology in two areas of its hospital–its emergency room and its point-of-care operations.

The emergency room staff signed on with Proxim to test the roaming capabilities of its RangeLAN wireless LAN. Two Proxim access points mounted on the ceiling and pen-based computers outfitted with Proxim's PCMCIA adapter cards and roaming software give medical personnel untethered access to Medi-Mouse, an emergency room application housed on the hospital's NetWare LAN.

Several nursing stations in the hospital are also trying out wireless technology. Nurses use pen-based devices mounted on portable stands to collect data at a patient's bedside and transmit it, without wires, to a TDS Healthcare patient-care system on the hospital's IBM mainframe.

Brian Wall, manager of telecommunications at Maine Medical Center, says wireless technology will help the hospital provide state-of-the-art health care services. He envisions the eventual installation of wireless capabilities throughout the hospital so that doctors, physical therapists, respiratory therapists, and other roaming users can access computing resources from anywhere in the medical facility.

But first, Wall needs to iron out some of the problems he has encountered in his wireless trials. A Proxim RangeLAN system worked fine with DOS applications but gives users a dismal response time of 20 seconds with their new Windows version of Medi-Mouse. (Response time should improve dramatically with the latest release of RangeLAN2).

The ARLAN 600 wireless LAN delivered a respectable data rate of 1.2Mbps but is incompatible with the pen-based computers the hospital uses until the vendor, Telesystems, finishes developing its PCMCIA card. For some reason, an HP Omnibook wouldn't boot with a Proxim PCMCIA card. And the battery life of its GridPad pen-based computers was so short–two or three hours– that Wall started using an external 12-volt battery about the size of a software box to power the units. "We call this the bleeding edge," he says.

NOT TO STANDARD

A nagging issue for adopters of new technology, such as Maine Medical Center, is the lack of standards for wireless LANs. Wall and others like him who are installing non-standard wireless products may find themselves locked into a single vendor's solution when standards are in place.

Most industry observers agree that standards won't be established any time soon. Despite several years of work by the 802.11 Working Group of the Institute of Electrical and Electronics Engineers (IEEE), the group responsible for setting standards for the emerging wireless market, standards for wireless LANs are nowhere in sight.

When they are set, separate standards will exist for infrared and for spread spectrum technologies. The majority of wireless LANs on the market today use spread spectrum technology, a transmission method developed by the U.S. military during World War II that resists interference and can coexist with other users in the same spectrum.

Spread spectrum wireless LANs currently operate in one of three frequency bands (902MHz to 928MHz; 2,400MHz to 2,483.5MHz; or 5,725MHz to 5,875MHz) that the FCC allocated in 1985 for unlicensed use by low-power radio devices. Wireless LANs share these frequencies, also known as the Industrial, Scientific, and Medical bands, with other low-power devices such as microwave ovens, government radar, and industrial gluing and heating machines.

Wireless LANs built on infrared technology, which use high-frequency light energy to send signals through the air, account for about 20 percent of wireless LAN connections today. Infrared allows for much higher data rates than spread spectrum but must operate within fixed locations or line-of-sight and cannot penetrate office partitions or walls.

Work by 802.11 on physical-layer specifications for both infrared and spread spectrum wireless networks is well underway, according to Wayne Moyers, chief technology officer at Wise Communications (Los Gatos, CA) and a member of the 802.11 Working Group. By the end of 1993, a draft version of the physical-layer (PHY) specification for spread spectrum wireless LANs operating at speeds less than 1Mbps will be completed; a draft specification for infrared should follow in early 1994, Moyers predicts. Work on the media access control (MAC) layer standard will take longer, with a MAC-layer standard in place by mid-1994 or later, he says.

802.11 is also working on standard methods of implementing roaming management standards for wireless LANs, and methods of eliminating interference among different vendors' products.

According to a recent survey by the Yankee Group of corporate communications managers from Fortune 1,000 companies, more than 55 percent of users who plan to implement wireless LANs consider the industry's lack of standards a major issue.

But once wireless standards are set, look out: The shift to wireless may be just around the corner. According to wireless advocates such as Moyers, "that's when the need for data access by nomadic users will make the wireless market take off through the ceiling."

Section 5
Personal Digital Assistants

Gone are the days of bulky, hard-to-carry hardware that forces users to remain tethered to the desktop. The newest network client is a portable device not much larger than a remote control–the Personal Digital Assistant (PDA). Ranging in form from flat, clipboard-shaped computers to very versatile hand-held devices, PDAs offer users an innovative way of communicating and sharing information.

With built-in electronic mail capabilities, fax software, and infrared links, PDAs allow people to keep in touch no matter where they are via easy-to-use links to the home network, to the Internet, or to the dozens of emerging on-line services.

Starting with the release of the Apple Newton MessagePad in 1993, PDAs have features that other mobile devices, such as laptops, can't provide. Some of the latest PDA models come with a relatively low price tag, integrated and sophisticated wide area network communications capabilities, and alluring network application suites that can interoperate, or at least swap data, with a user's desktop machine. Analysts predict that PDAs which offer all of these features will be something that both consumer and business users can't refuse; sales of the Newton are expected to hit 700,000 by 1995.

The stories in this section look at how PDAs can function as network clients, evaluating their connectivity options, strengths, and limitations.

Waiting for PDA Magic

WITH FEW BUSINESS APPLICATIONS AND WEAK NETWORK
CONNECTIVITY, PERSONAL DIGITAL ASSISTANTS ARE JUST WAYFARING
WANDERERS. BUT HELP IS ON THE WAY.

BY MELANIE McMULLEN

If you're in the market to buy a few Personal Digital Assistants (PDAs) for the mobile users on your network, you might be in for a few surprises. For instance, if you dial the main business number at EO, the AT&T subsidiary in Mountain View, CA, that makes the EO Communicator, nobody answers. If you call Compaq Computer in Houston to inquire about ship dates for the mobile companion that was once slated for delivery this year, most likely you won't find anyone who will discuss the topic. And if you want that PDA now, you can cross Hewlett-Packard (HP, Palo Alto, CA) and IBM off your list. Both companies are developing new PDAs, but neither will have a product ready to go until late this year or early 1995.

But don't despair, because PDAs do indeed exist. You could buy a few Apple Newton MessagePads, if you think your users will be satisfied with a $600 electronic daytimer that–only with great difficulty–can connect to their Macintosh or Windows desktop computers. Or you could zoom over to the nearest Radio Shack, and for a bit more than $500, pick up a few Zoomers, a low-end PDA developed by Japan-based Casio and Tandy (Ft. Worth, TX). As you can see, the options in electronic assistants, for now at least, don't appear very promising.

TOUCH IT

So with this weak and dismal first impression, are PDAs already doomed to extinction? Maybe not–maybe the electronic pen pals just need a magic touch, or more specifically, the General Magic software touch. General Magic, (Mountain View, CA), a four-year-old company funded originally by computing bigwigs Apple Computer, Sony Motorola (Schaumburg, IL), and AT&T (Parsippany,

NJ), will ship its long-awaited Magic Cap operating system and its accompanying Telescript communications technology this summer. The Magic Cap OS will be the brains behind Motorola's first PDA, the Envoy personal wireless communicator, also slated for a summer arrival.

Joining General Magic in the attempt to rescue the beleaguered PDA will be a pair of powerful headliners in the OS and NOS market–Microsoft and Novell. Microsoft intends to bring its Windows magic down a hardware notch with the release of its WinPad operating system. The WinPad OS, based on the Microsoft at Work architecture, will be resident on a handful of mobile companion platforms, including hardware from Toshiba, Motorola, Sharp, NEC, and Zenith Data Systems. WinPad will offer links to the Windows desktop and will run on Intel 386 and 486 chipsets.

Novell is also jumping on the PDA OS bandwagon. The company, along with HP, has made equity investments in Geoworks (Alameda, CA), makers of the GEOS object-oriented operating system that powers, among other devices, the Zoomer. In addition, Novell's Extended Networks Division in Monterey, CA, is developing a software toolkit scheduled for delivery this summer that will allow PDA OS-makers to embed networking code directly into the operating system, rendering PDAs into instant, network-ready clients.

LEARN FROM THE MISTAKES

These PDA software newbies as well as the PDA hardware manufacturers are all quick to point out the lessons they've learned from the pioneers in the field, EO and Apple. Those lessons revolve around three basic points: PDAs have to be affordable, costing less than laptops; the devices *must* have integrated and sophisticated wide-area network communications capabilities right from the start; and, like any new hardware platform, PDAs must offer alluring network applications that can interoperate–or at a minimum swap data–with a user's desktop application suite.

First, look at what happens when PDAs are too pricey. The EO Communicator 440 and 880 models came to market in early 1993 with a sticker price that started at $2,000. EO took the high-end approach and developed the jaguar of portable communicators that provided fax services, wireless e-mail, word processing, voice-annotation, and even a cellular telephone. It hummed along using the Pen-Point operating system developed by another AT&T subsidiary, Go, located in Foster City, CA.

While the hardware and software got rave reviews, the high cost didn't. As sales slumped, AT&T in August, 1993, merged EO and Go and laid off half the workforce. In January, AT&T pulled the plug again on the portables, laying off more employees and ousting Alain Rossman, EO's CEO and president. At that time, the company had sold fewer than 3,000 units, according to a former Go employee.

Several months later, the next entrants into the market, Apple and Tandy, both came in with a PDA that was much more affordable; the first Newton MessagePad cost less than $600 at discount computer shops. Although this price was much more appealing than the tag on the EO Communicator, the devices lacked in the computing basics: applications and communications.

"The PDA market needs to come up with some compelling applications other than crossword puzzles and 800-number directories," says Pieter Hartsook, editor of *The Hartsook Letter,* a Macintosh newsletter and research service based in Alameda, CA. Hartsook says the success of the Newton is predicated on development of "killer apps," which will likely come from vertical markets, such as health care, sales, and other untapped mobile markets.

Besides being weak in the area of business applications, the Newton, which Hartsook describes as "almost out of the beta phase," still experiences great voids in local- and wide-area communications. "The two-way wireless paging and cellular connections, as well as the connections to the desktop, are only half there," Hartsook continues. He predicts that critical mass in wide-area communications and desktop networking will be achieved by

the end of the summer. That boost, coupled with a bit of vertical market success, will keep the Newton ticking along until the market matures (see Figure 1).

STAYING ALIVE

In the meantime, Apple is doing its part to increase Newton-lust, both from a technical and an image standpoint. On the technical side, it released in March a much-improved version of its desktop connectivity software, Newton Connection Kit 2.0 for the Macintosh. Apple plans to release an upgraded Newton Connection Kit 2.0 for Windows, according to Christi Olson, product marketing manager, communications products, at Apple's Personal Interactive Electronics (PIE) Division.

The current 1.3 versions of these products have been described by users and analysts as nonfunctional and cumbersome. On the Mac side, Newton Connection uses Apple Events to allow Macintosh applications to talk to Newton. Sounds easy enough, but users on the Newton Forum in CompuServe have complained that version 1.3 frequently hangs both the desktop machine and the Newton, forcing users to reboot and start the synchronization processes over again. The difficulty stems for the fact that the object-oriented Newton operating system is quite different from the System 7 OS that powers the Mac. "The connection between a Newton and a desktop is as if two people were connected on the phone, and one speaks French and the other speaks Russian," says Hartsook.

The Newton Connection Kit for Windows, codeveloped by Traveling Software (Bothell, WA), faces an even greater cross-platform challenge and, not surprisingly, has also received it share of criticism from unhappy Newton users. The Windows Connection Kit attempts to link data and synchronize applications using Dynamic Data Exchange (DDE).

Despite the criticisms, Apple is optimistic about the product upgrades. The new versions of the Connection Kits, which are priced at $99, will have better data import and export capabilities as well as improved file transfer, according to Olson.

NEWT GETS A PHYSICAL

On the physical side, Apple intends to focus its efforts on establishing greater Newton connectivity to the network via wired and wireless connections to the desktop and also to the server, says Olson. Currently, the Newton can connect to the desktop via a serial connection using LocalTalk, and fellow Newton users can beam each other messages using the devices' 19.2Kbps point-to-point infrared capabilities. Apple will switch from the Sharp set of infrared communication protocols that the Newton currently uses to the new Infrared Data Association (IrDA, Walnut Creek, CA) specifications when the group finalizes its standard. Apple will also add infrared devices to the next generation of the PowerBook, Olson adds.

In addition to quick-and-dirty desktop connectivity, Apple intends for the Newton to be a full-fledged network citizen; it will have the infrastructure and options in place to do that by the end of 1994. "We're looking at enterprise connectivity solutions, including Ethernet connections," says Olson. "Now we understand what we need to have in the Newton to do that." Apple plans to add TCP/IP protocols to the Newton, although no exact time has been announced. The company is also considering IPX-based connectivity options as well as Cellular Digital Packet Data (CDPD)-based connections for wide-area links.

Apple also made some changes on the hardware front, releasing an upgraded Newton MessagePad 110 in March, 1994. The 100 offers longer battery life, more memory, and a faster recharge than the first model. It sells for $599.

THE WINDOWS ASSISTANT

As Apple struggles along trying to link its Newton to the billions of Windows desktops of the world, Microsoft is busy putting the final touches on its new PDA operating system, code-named WinPad. While Apple and others are waffling as to whether PDAs are really optimized for consumers or business users, Microsoft has a single focus for WinPad. "WinPad will provide links to existing Windows-based business applications," says David Britton, product manager at Microsoft's Handheld Systems Division. "We've put the emphasis on developing a way for mobile users to interact with existing business information, which typically lives now on the desktop and on servers."

WinPad, which is scheduled for release at the end of 1994, will include synchronization capabilities that will automatically update shared information between mobile companions and desktop applications. "The WinPad operating system will span the gap between the handheld computer and the PC, giving the mobile user an intimate relationship to the desktop," Britton adds.

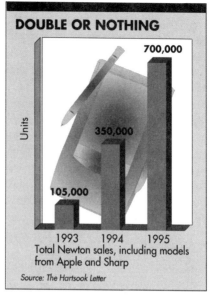

Figure 1: As the Newton hits critical mass in wide-area communications and desktop networking functionality in the next year, sales are predicted to skyrocket.

In addition to perfecting Windows desktop symbiosis, Microsoft is adding messaging and other communications protocols into the WinPad operating system. To do so, it is soliciting help from other divisions of Microsoft as well as from third-party companies.

Microsoft's Workgroup Division is developing software that will allow mobile companions to connect remotely to servers running Microsoft Mail. With this software, users will be able to preview mail headers, to download messages, and to read and create messages off-line. The WinPad OS will also support other network communications services, such as faxing and paging. Since WinPad is based on the Microsoft At Work operating platform, it will link to other At Work-compliant office machines, according to Britton.

In the applications world, Microsoft has lured software developers from the general business side as well as vertical market developers to develop WinPad applications. The company claims to have more than 100 developers working on applications that run the gamut from communications to navigation.

For example, AT&T EasyLink Services and SkyTel (Washington, D.C.) are both committed to developing WinPad versions of their communications products. And for the user who can't discern east from west, Navigation Technologies (NavTech, Sunnyvale, CA) is developing software that will enable WinPad users to access the NavTech DriverGuide on-line. This service gives users turn-by-turn driving instructions from any address in the database. It also pinpoints the nearest available spot of interest, such as gas stations, hotels, ATM cash machines, or even restaurants or wineries.

To overcome deficiencies in handwriting recognition technology, WinPad will support plug-in keyboards as well as on-screen keyboards in addition to pen support. The user interface will only slightly resemble Windows. "WinPad has to be much easier to use than a desktop operating system," explains Britton. "It won't have multiple menus, but it will offer more efficient navigation through screen layouts optimized for hand-held devices."

THE NOVELLIAN APPROACH

As Microsoft zealously pursues Windows-to-WinPad connectivity, Novell is seeking out ways for PDAs running various operating systems to become NetWare clients. The company's Extended Networks Division will release this summer its first Novell Embedded Services Technology (NEST) product. This release, which will be a software toolkit, will allow OS makers to embed a condensed version of NetWare client code in the operating system.

Aimed first at PDAs, the NEST technology could be expanded into any number of devices, including television set-top boxes, printers, and fax machines. "NEST is the network client for anything other than the standard desktop," explains Chris Sontag, director of product development at Novell's Extended Networks Division. Sontag describes NEST as "fast, tight code" that makes PDAs instantly into network clients that can use all NetWare services, including file sharing and printing. "This technology takes the network down to the next set of computing devices," he adds.

NEST technology works via a Portable Operating Systems Extension (POSE) that is processor-independent. The POSE adds an extra layer to the OS. Since the network software is embedded into the OS, one of the greatest benefits NEST offers to the PDA network client is speed. "Right now, the thinking process between the PDA and the desktop is slow and unresponsive. PDAs lack any sort of ubiquitous network connectivity," says Sontag.

Novell's interest in PDAs doesn't stop with NEST. Last year Novell and Geoworks announced an agreement in which Geoworks would license NetWare Universal Client software, giving GEOS-based PDAs access to NetWare networks. Geoworks is also on the move on the business side, with plans to become a public company this summer.

The agreement between Novell and Geoworks is a potentially lucrative one for both companies. By adding NetWare connections to GEOS software, Geoworks can pursue the business user as well as the consumer via the inexpensive Zoomer PDA sold by Tandy, Casio, and AST Research (Irvine, CA). "A Zoomer priced at $500 with built-in NetWare client capabilities makes a real compelling business solution," says Tony Requist, vice president of engineering at Geoworks. "Eventually there will be as many PDAs on a business network as there are PCs."

Requist points out that the business user is an easier buyer to target for these types of devices than the average consumer. "Consumers have to worry about whether they need to buy a washer and dryer or a PDA. Business money is spent very differently."

MOTORING ALONG

Also honing in on the mobile business user is a newcomer to the world of PDAs, Motorola. The company plans to release the Envoy personal wireless communicator this summer. The Envoy comes souped up with a jambalaya of wired and wireless communications services, including AT&T PersonaLink, RadioMail, America Online, and ARDIS.

Motorola didn't scrimp on the hardware side, either. The Envoy contains two PCMCIA Type II slots, a wireless data modem, a fax modem, and an infrared eye.

While Envoy will be in the pricey $1,499 range, Motorola is counting on the integrated communications, as well as the functionality and ease of use of General Magic's Magic Cap operating system, to lure the PDA-leery buyer into spending the big bucks.

"With our hardware and services and the Magic Cap operating system, a user can connect to the world from this one little device," says Ron Scheiderer, senior business manager for the Envoy product line in Motorola's Wireless Data Group. "It works like an enterprise LAN, but in a much grander scale."

THE REAL MAGIC

Envoy will be the first PDA to use the Magic Cap oper-

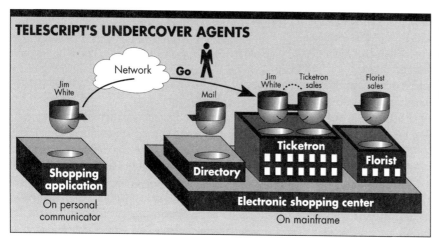

TELESCRIPT'S UNDERCOVER AGENTS

Figure 2: General Magic's Telescript technology uses object-based programs, or agents, to perform tasks across a wide area network. Agents can be instructed by PDA users to do anything from purchasing concert tickets to buying a dozen roses.

ating system, although other PDA makers have made licensing arrangements with General Magic as well as major equity investments. France Telecom, which runs the expansive Minitel network, announced in late April that it is taking an equity stake in General Magic. Company officials are so optimistic about their Magic Cap technology that they are taking the company public before the actual product ships, a rarity in the investment world.

Why all the fuss over an operating system? The magic is in the action going on behind the OS, according to Scheiderer. Magic Cap uses the Telescript language, in which object-based programs, called agents, are sent across a wide area network with a specific task to accomplish. Agents carry data as well as programs and security clearances. When the agent locates the proper receiving computer and executes the task, the agent reports the results back to the sender (see Figure 2).

Because agents are remote programs, users need to stay connected only long enough to launch their agent onto the network. This makes wireless connections from low-power portables much more practical, since users don't have to maintain expensive wide-area on-line connections. "Most dial-up services are session-based, whereas Magic Cap is transaction-based. As a busy person, a Magic Cap user could ask a question and get an answer without waiting on-line," says Scheiderer.

Agents can perform all different kinds of tasks, from electronic shopping to financial reporting, in places on Telescript-enabled networks. The agent program can also contain contingency plans, if it is unable to do the task as

first specified. For example, the user might send an agent to the on-line florist to buy a dozen roses, as long as the buds cost less than $75. If the shop only has roses by the $80 dozen, then the agent would order whatever the user's contingency plan called for, such as a bouquet of daffodils. Or the user could tell the agent to opt for chocolates if flower prices came in over the limit. Then it would consult the network directory for the nearest on-line chocolate store and go to work again.

THESE THREE SCREENS

Magic Cap software offers three navigational screens for users to explore, including a desktop view, a hallway for third-party applications, and a downtown screen for electronic commerce. To circumvent any pen-based problems, the user moves from screen to screen via tapping vs. text-based commands.

The desktop view includes mail and messaging services, a datebook, a clock, a Rolodex, and a calculator, among other icons. In the hallway scene, users can click into the library and check out books that offer help on Magic Cap operations and communications. Or they can tap into the store room, link to the desktop, and do system back-ups between their PDA and PC or to the on-board PCMCIA memory card. Data about the PDA, such as power settings, security, and the touch sensitivity of the screen is contained in the control panel in the hallway. The downtown screen is the Magic Cap mall, containing all the stores and services that users can reach via the agents.

The Magic Cap interface, while very lifelike, may be

just a bit too cute for the business user that Envoy is trying to lure. "Magic Cap users will give the same reaction to the interface as the first Mac users did. They'll say, 'I've spent this much money for a business device, and it looks like an adventure game?'" says Jeff Henning, senior industry analyst at BIS Strategic Decisions (Norwell, MA).

Henning also points out that General Magic may have including one too many floating icons, referring specifically to the desktop feline that wanders around the screen. "Magic Cap has a cat. I'm not so sure any operating system really needs a cat."

FARMLAND LANS BREAK NEW GROUND

The Newton Takes Root

When Apple first suggested that its Newton MessagePad would be good for field workers, Monsanto chemical company took the advice literally and began developing an application that would put the Newtons out to pasture. Software developers at Monsanto, the St. Louis-based manufacturer of agricultural chemicals, pharmaceuticals, and Ortho garden products, decided the Newton could be just the tool needed for the roving farmer to more efficiently track and monitor the harvest. All Monsanto had to do was develop the application and give the Newton a bit of a boost on the desktop connectivity front.

Now, after a year and a half of cultivation, Monsanto is releasing its first Newton application, Infielder. With the initial release aimed at the corn and soybean farmer in the Midwest, Infielder is essentially a portable database application that allows a Newton-toting farmer to track all varieties of planting and growing information. Using Infielder, farmers can store and monitor 450 different farming variables, including soil data, water conditions, fertilizer strengths, and harvesting schedules.

Infielder runs on the Newton and on a PC or a Macintosh, and it contains its own synchronization scheme between platforms. This arrangement allows the farmer to do the crop and harvest planning on the desktop, and then take all the information out into the field. "By developing a tandem Newton and PC application, we can use the real powers of each platform," says Marc Vanacht, a member of the innovation team at Monsanto that developed the application.

PROBLEMS CROP UP

Although Apple has released its own versions of Newton-to-Mac and Newton-to-Windows software in the form of the Newton Connection Kit, Monsanto wanted sure-fire synchronization for the Infielder, so it developed its own connectivity protocol suite.

Ensuring that the desktop data matches the information collected in the field is an essential part of Infielder, since a mistake could result in crop loss or incorrect harvesting schedules. "A farmer can plan the season's work comfortably on the big screen of the PC in the winter, and then carry his portable and his plans out into the field in the busy spring and summer seasons," says Vanacht. He points out that the average crop farmer usually has 15 or more operations that have to be done for each field at different times in the growing cycle; if a farmer has 50 fields, then he has to remember 750 things. "The farmer needs the Newton to get through the working crunch period," he adds.

With Infielder, the farmer can check off operations on the Newton as he completes them and then synchronize the data with the master plan software running on the desktop computer. "The farmer can come in at night, plug the Newton into the PC's serial port, and before he finishes his first can of Bud, the data is updated," says Vanacht.

Monsanto also has some wide-area objectives for Infielder, including electronic commerce. For instance, farmers running Infielder could link via modem to a database server at Monsanto headquarters, which could contain the recommended fertilizer strengths and dilution ratios based on that farmer's field information. Monsanto could then ship the premixed fertilizer directly to the farmer as needed.

These types of critical applications will sustain the Newton, according to analysts. "People think of a PDA as a yuppie upscale business too, but the real users of these devices are going out on a tractor," says Pieter Hartsook, editor of *The Hartsook Letter,* a Macintosh newsletter and research service based in Alameda, CA. "A farmer could save thousands of dollars by using the right fertilizer. The Newton in this setting has real financial value."

Toys of the Trade

USING PCMCIA CARDS AND WIRELESS CONNECTIVITY, PDAS MAY BECOME HANDY MOBILE CLIENTS THAT GIVE USERS ON THE RUN UNLIMITED ACCESS TO THE NETWORK.

BY MELANIE McMULLEN

Vanna White, Al Gore, Ed McMahon, Igor, the Newton MessagePad. Each of these will be remembered in history for their starring roles as The Assistant. Some will fare better in the books than others. Vanna, for instance, has one up on the Newton; she can easily recognize the letters of the alphabet. But the MessagePad, with its ballyhooed Newton Intelligence, probably ranks highest in the brains department among all assistants, especially inept Igor.

Despite their perceived shortcomings, each of these assistants has a certain value. Because no matter what type of activity and interaction a job requires, most people need some variety of lovely assistant to polish off the nagging, mostly mundane details of a job. Whether that assistant is vital to business or merely provides entertainment and diversion in those wasted moments waiting for trains or planes, everyone would agree that an assistant of some sort is great to have.

But in the world of mobile computing companions, or more specifically personal digital assistants (PDAs), the agreements end right there. The first point of dissension is who, besides the early technology gadgeteers, will really want, and subsequently buy, these expensive toys of the trade. This question is followed closely by *how* the aforementioned group will use these devices, specifically in terms of work vs. pleasure.

While buyers will most likely not pay $700 for a Game-Boy that can also store their addresses and appointments, they might shell out the bucks if the device can also serve as a mobile access point for communications, that is, if it offers network connectivity. If it doesn't, then PDAs may be doomed to failure as illiterate, Pretty Dumb Assistants that will forever be trapped in a small niche. "PDAs with-out network connectivity are good doorstops and book-ends," says Geoff Goodfellow, founder and chairman of RadioMail in San Mateo, CA.

But buried within the hype of PDAs is hope. While the application developers hash out the uses, PDA makers and other mobile mavens fortunately all agree that networking and PDAs should be one and the same. Tossing in a variety of connectivity options could move PDAs up exponential notches on potential buyers' "I want it" lists.

THE DETACHABLES

The first network assistants have mutated to market in all shapes and form factors, ranging from the basic palm-tops, such as the Hewlett-Packard (Palo Alto, CA) 95LX and 100LX, to the pen-based devices, such as EO's (Mountain View, CA) Personal Communicators and Apple's firstborn in the Newton family, the MessagePad. Sharp, which manufactures the Newton for Apple, in 1993 shipped its own version of the product, the ExpertPad.

Another PDA that came to market in 1993 is the Zoomer, a product codeveloped by Tandy (Ft. Worth, TX) and Japan-based Casio, who along with AST Research (Irvine, CA) market the product.

Two other mobile devices shipped in 1994, one low-end PDA, the Amstrad PLC PenPad, and one high-end device designed for vertical markets, the TelePad SL. The PenPad, manufactured by Amstrad, an Essex, England, consumer-electronics company, has already been a hit in Europe, with buyers scooping up more than 30,000 in its first months on the market. It sports a battery life of 40 hours, runs off three separate 8-bit chips, and costs $499. Scottsdale Technologies in Arizona distributes the PenPad in the United States.

The TelePad SL, made by TelePad Corporation (Reston, VA), is a true hybrid PC and PDA. Manufactured by IBM, the TelePad was originally only sold to government field work forces, such as the U.S. Air Force. The company decided to make it commercially available in September, 1993. The TelePad is equipped with an Intel 386 processor, and although it's pen based, it has a detachable keyboard and even a plug-in camera for multimedia applications. The TelePad is armed with Proxim's (Mountain View, CA) RangeLAN wireless technology. It costs $2,500 to $3,500.

In a relatively short period of time on the market, these first PDAs have already started to make a reputation for themselves as the detachable add-ons to the desktop, forging a new layer of networking: client client-server computing. Future PDAs will have a variety of options, ranging from sending and receiving e-mail and fax messages to actually running scaled-down versions of desktop applications. PDAs with third-party e-mail connections are already being successfully put to use.

"The most compelling aspect of PDAs is using them on the network," says Jeffrey Henning, senior industry analyst at BIS Strategic Decisions, a market research firm based in Norwell, MA. "People have to be able to easily access the network with these devices. That will sell the products."

But Henning points out that since network capabilities are limited in the early PDA renditions, potential buyershave been focusing on other aspects of the devices, which unfortunately for the makers is the less-than-perfect pen-computing capabilities. Predicted sales of PDAs over the next year will remain on the conservative side, with only 215,000 units in use in 1994, according to BIS forecasts).

But despite the poor pen performance of PDAs, analysts aren't totally writing them off. As connectivity options and availability increase, PDA sales will skyrocket, hitting annual sales of more than 4 million units in six years, according to BIS. This figure represents faster growth than any other advanced technology product, including cellular phones.

THE MISSING LINKS

As Apple seeds the market–it claims to have sold more than 50,000 Newtons in the first month after its September, 1993, launch–PDA-to-network connectivity is becoming a hotbed of commotion among optimistic PDA makers and numerous third-party developers.

Connectivity from PDA to the desktop, PDA to PDA, or PDA to other services such as the Internet currently comes in a variety of forms, ranging from wired and wireless local connections to wide-area solutions that use phone lines or existing cellular links. The high-end devices such as the EO Communicator have the components necessary for communications built-in, while Apple offers connectivity for the MessagePad as add-ons.

And, of course, wherever the PDA hardware manufacturer leaves off, someone else is there to make the connection or add value. "PDAs will realize their full potential when they have integrated communications," explains Roberta Wiggins, research director for wireless mobile communications at The Yankee Group (Boston). Wiggins says the door is open for other companies to provide the missing links.

Whether the network link is integrated or provided by an add-on product, one concept is vital to understanding the basics of PDA connectivity: A mobile user with a hand-held device will almost always be sending and receiving only small bits of information. The power and internal storage on a PDA, right now at least, is limited, and although automatic data compression is included in most of them, these mobile data appendages are targeted for information use, not information creation. "A Newton is not a computer at all," says Apple's Wirt. "If you want to create documents, a computer is the right thing. If you want a mobile personal device that can access information, the Newton is the right thing."

Other developers agree with this assessment. "The PDA user will mostly pull data from other sources," says David Larson, vice president of marketing at Notable Technologies (Foster City, CA), a firm that develops communications software for mobile computing devices. "Data is a huge asset that needs to be moved around and accessed on demand. The new mobile platform should allow you to leverage small pieces of existing information on host-based systems and networks." Notable announced its flagship product in August, 1993, dubbed Mobile Access Personal. This software links a PDA running Go's (Foster City, CA) PenPoint OS to public and private host-based systems, such as CompuServe.

OFF THE WIRE

Since PDAs will transfer data in small, byte-size pieces,

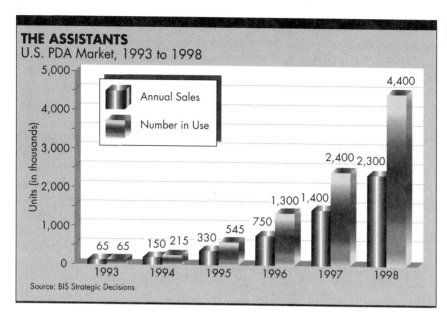

THE ASSISTANTS
U.S. PDA Market, 1993 to 1998

Annual Sales
Number in Use

Source: BIS Strategic Decisions

Commuter Computers: PDA sales will rise slowly, hitting the $4 million mark by 1998..

all varieties of information transportation come into play. On the wireless side, spread-spectrum radio and infrared transmission are already available for PDAs, as well as paging and cellular services. Almost 70 percent of new PDAs sold in 1999 will have wired or wireless communications capability, according to analyst Henning. "With PDAs, wireless communication is the holy grail," he adds.

In addition, the Cellular Digital Packet Data (CDPD) group, spurred forward quickly by the AT&T takeover of McCaw Cellular Communications, has already released the 1.0 specification. This spec outlines details of the CDPD architecture, including airlink, external network interfaces, and network support and applications services.

CDPD technology, ideally suited for applications that require short bursts of data, could quickly become a boon for PDA connectivity. CDPD-enabled mobile devices can be constantly connected, allowing them to function much like a live, connected node, sending and receiving e-mail and faxes with no user intervention.

PADDING THE INFORMATION

Priced from $699 to $949, the Newton MessagePad offers faxing capabilities, wireless messaging, and alphanumeric paging via MobileComm's local, regional, or national services; e-mail via the NewtonMail service and a

modem; infrared Newton-to-Newton beaming; and both local and network printing functions. Newton has an RS-442 serial port, one PCMCIA slot, and a 19.2Kbps infrared transceiver.

While all these features sound impressive, remember that Apple was anxious to get the Newton to market, shipping the device several months before the communications basics, such as faxing, paging, and desktop connection software, were ready. "Newton was squeezed out the door," says Larson of Notable Technologies.

Larson adds that his developers, who are working on a cross-platform product called Shared Whiteboard that will allow various PDAs to communicate graphically with one another, are finding Newton's operating system difficult to work with. Even Apple has struggled with the OS, shipping four revisions to it in the first month after its release.

Other companies interested in offering platform support for the Newton are in more of a wait-and-see mode. "Communication is one of the least-developed aspects of the Newton," says Dan Schwinn, president, CEO, and chairman of Shiva (Burlington, MA). He intends to offer support for PDAs as a dial-in client to all his remote access products by the end of next year. But he adds that right now, "the Newton is just unbelievably slick but not quite useful."

plies–a personal device–and has to be customized to be appreciated. "If I took my shoes off and asked 12 people on the street to try them on, and I asked them, 'hey, are these comfortable?' they would probably say, 'no.' Newton is the same way. You learn it, you train it, and then it fits your needs," Wirt adds.

But Newton does indeed seem to be the shoe that fits, according to a sample of some of its first users on the street. "At least two-thirds of the people I know who use the Newton are happy with it," says Steve Costa, executive director of the Berkeley Macintosh User Group (BMUG) in Berkeley, CA. The group there and the Apple user group in Boston are both forming special interest groups (SIGs) for users of the PDA, appropriately dubbed SIG Newton.

MAKING THE CONNECTION

The SIG Newtons may soon have more to play with, as Apple offered two pieces of desktop connectivity software, Newton Connection kit for the Macintosh and Newton Connection kit for Windows. Apple sells the software kits for approximately $150 each.

On the Mac side, Newton Connection will use Apple Events to allow Macintosh applications to talk to Newton. Since the object-oriented Newton operating system is quite unlike that on the Macintosh, "Newton Connection will serve as the main gate to the Newton from a Mac," says Rick Kapur, product manager for Newton Connection.

The Mac desktop running Newton Connection will have an application set equivalent to the Newton, allowing users to plug the Newton into the desktop via a serial or LocalTalk port and automatically synchronize data. In addition to supporting Newton's built-in applications, Newton Connection will support data transfer with three or four applications in other categories, such as databases or spreadsheets, says Kapur.

Newton Connection for Windows is codeveloped by Traveling Software (Bothell, WA). The Newton has Traveling Software's universal communications object embedded in ROM. The first version of the Newton-to-Windows software will use Dynamic Data Exchange (DDE) to transfer data, while the next version will use Object Linking and Embedding (OLE), according to Mark Eppley, CEO of Traveling Software.

He says one of the key elements of linking PDAs with networks is keeping the applications on the desktop and the portable Newton in synch, not an easy task when platforms differ. "This product is the first automatic synchronization software between different platforms," adds Eppley.

THE TRAVELING LAN

Keeping automatic data synchronization in mind, Traveling Software codeveloped with National Semiconductor (Santa Clara, CA) a wireless portable-to-desktop product. The connection kit contains two National Semiconductor Airshare spread-spectrum transceivers, the necessary antennas, and LapLink Remote Access and synchronization software for both the desktop and the portable.

By plugging a transceiver into the portable and the desktop, the product maintains a wireless, 1Mbps link between a DOS or Windows portable and the desktop machine, automatically updating data anytime the portable device comes within 30 feet of the desktop. The product will sell for less than $200. The next form factor for this product will be a PCMCIA version that will have drivers for PDAs and other portables, according to Eppley.

Eppley's product fits into the slot of choice for PDA connectivity, the PCMCIA slot. This I/O hole may become the one unifying element between desktops, laptops, and PDAs. "The market for PCMCIA cards will take off with PDAs," says Andy Prophet, president of AP Research (Cupertino, CA). Prophet predicts that the PCMCIA LAN card market will top 2.6 million by 1997.

Prophet says that since PDAs may have only one slot, makers of PCMCIA cards may start to bundle functions, such as fax/modem and LAN interfaces, on the same PCMCIA card, which will make them very functional but also more expensive. "PDAs fall under the razor-blade theory of hardware, where 40 percent to 50 percent of the revenue from the product comes from add-ons. In the case of PDAs, these will be PCMCIA cards," he says.

Apple is developing some PCMCIA cards of its own for the Newton, with the first one, a Type II modem card, according to Kapur.

OTHER TWISTS

Connecting the PDA directly to the network via a PCMCIA card is the first order of business for New Media (Irvine, CA), a new start-up. The company is currently working on a Newton LAN card and some wireless LAN connectivity cards.

Once modem PCMCIA cards become available, Newton users can go on-line via Ex Machina's (New York) PocketCall, terminal emulation software that allows Newton users to view incoming information or queries from host systems. It costs $99. The company is also developing Notify! for PowerTalk, a wireless messaging add-in for Apple's Open Collaboration Environment. Notify! will cost $149.

If Newton users don't want to tie up the PCMCIA slot, they could physically connect the PDA to the network by the old-fashioned, cable-based LocalTalk port methods. Apple has combined serial port and LocalTalk port functions into one slot, calling it the Communication port. Existing LocalTalk connectors, such as Farallon Computing's (Alameda, CA) PhoneNet Connector and StarConnector products, work in this port.

In addition, Farallon has plans to release the EtherWave family of daisy-chain 10BaseT connectivity products by year's end. EtherWave allows users to chain up to eight connections in an Ethernet link, creating a desktop landing pad for the mobile Newton and other LocalTalk devices. The EtherWave Newton adapter sells for $379.

MOBILE COMPUTING: IS IT FOR THE BIRDS?

One in the Hand

Dragging a hand-held portable computer out into the wilderness may at first seem like a birdbrained idea. After all, the machine is one more thing that can fill up the already packed backpack, and it adds a few extra pounds to be hauled over that next hill. But to bird-buffs Chip Haven and Jane Becker-Haven, portable computing has engendered new possibilities in seeking the endangered.

The Havens, who reside in Palo Alto, CA, are avid bird-watchers and have been faithfully pursuing their hobby for 15 years. Since that time, their bird-watching expedi-tions have led them near and far in pursuit of possible sightings of rare birds, including a two-mile hike up a 2,000 ft. mountain in Big Bend, TX, to catch a glimpse of the Colima Warbler, a Mexican species that has been spotted in that one location.

To map out their searches for fine feathered friends, the Havens regularly swoop on-line to the Internet's Birdchat forum. Birdchat is a service hatched by the University of Arizona that now has more than 400 subscribers who electronically discuss sightings of rare birds all across the U.S. "Birdchat is a very active, ongoing way of letting others know when an unusual bird arrives in a certain vicinity," says Haven

ON THE FLY

In the fall of 1993, Haven, a network consultant at Stanford University, heard from a coworker about RadioMail, a service based in San Mateo, CA, that allows mobile computer users to send wireless e-mail messages to and from the Internet. The company set him up with the necessary software and some portable gear, including a Hewlett-Packard 95LX palmtop and an Ericsson cellular modem, and he headed for the hills.

After his first outing with the gear, he quickly discovered that portable computing, with a wireless link to Birdchat, could be a birdwatcher's bonanza. "People fly miles and miles just to spot rare birds," says Haven. He explains that people on the Internet already give excellent directions as to where birds are, such as under this bush or that tree, but the information quickly becomes dated as birds dart hither and yon, never to be seen again.

Mobile computing could change the way bird-watchers watch, says Haven, allowing birders to report and update sightings on the spot. "Instant access is desirable in this kind of work," he adds.

Portable Apples: Young and Restless

AT THE BEACH, AT THE OFFICE, OR ON THE PLANE–POWERBOOKS AND PERSONAL DIGITAL ASSISTANTS CREATE A MOBILE LINK TO YOUR NETWORK INFORMATION.

BY MELANIE McMULLEN

He spotted her from across the plane. Sitting a mere two rows ahead, she was the ultimate woman of his dreams. She had flowing blond hair, gorgeous, well-tanned skin, a pearly white smile, and, most importantly, she had the quintessential travel essential–a Macintosh. With her PowerBook 180 perched on her tray-table, he watched in marvel as her mango-tinted fingernails floated gracefully across the keyboard, creating a masterful spreadsheet. She had treated herself with this high-end model of the Power-Book, he thought, splurging for more power, the high-res display, and the math coprocessor. He began to sweat.

Throughout the flight, he dreamed of them spending time together on The Island, fishing, swimming, dancing, spending the evenings talking only of LocalTalk (or did she prefer EtherTalk?) while sharing some fresh, grilled Mahi-Mahi on the beach as the orange Hawaiian sun set over the cresting waves of the horizon.

He couldn't stand it any longer. Only one hour until Honolulu. He really wanted to see her After Dark, and he didn't have much time. For once in his life, he was thankful for Bill Gates–Microsoft Mail could make his dreams come true. He spotted her infrared adapter, flickering like warm embers above her screen. He fired up his own infrared; eager anticipation now had to be transformed into some serious messaging. With his Chooser, he could choose her, and the rest would be history. Maybe.

Out goes the message, direct and to the point: *Hello, gorgeous 17D. This is 19A. Let's share some RAM over some rum. How about it?*

After anxious seconds that lasted for hours, back comes the response. *Drop dead.*

If only getting a date were as simple as impromptu PowerBook networking. Sharing files Mac to Mac is as easy as booting up, which explains why more than 65 percent of all Macs are networked, according to Pieter Hartsook, editor of the *Hartsook Letter*, a Macintosh market-research newsletter and service in Alameda, CA. And mobile Macs, high in functionality but low on storage and processing, are even more likely to want connectivity to the home LAN, dropping in and out of the network like planes at an airport.

While the PC world is quietly shifting from desktop to laptop machines, Apple Computer is forging the path of mobile computing with two separate extensions to the enterprise: the PowerBook and the Personal Digital Assistant (PDA). Both of these road warriors fulfill the vision of computing held by John Sculley, chairman and CEO of Apple, who says simply, "The obstacles of time and place must be overcome."

ANYWHERE, EVERYWHERE

First, the PowerBook. Not yet 3 years old, the Macintosh PowerBook has become one of the top sellers in portable computing. According to International Data Corp. (IDC, Framingham, MA), the worldwide PowerBook installed base topped 550,000 at the end of 1992. Figures from the first half of 1993 reveal a continued PowerBook buying frenzy, with Apple's second-quarter earnings statement showing a 70 percent increase in demand worldwide and a 100 percent increase in the United States.

Demand for the PowerBooks has been so high that parts shortages have restricted Apple's ability to keep up with shipments. "It's nice to know that you're loved," says Bruce Cooper, PowerBook product manager at Apple.

"We've been actively chasing the parts problem." Cooper says that Apple now has larger inventory balances and is currently running 24-hour shifts in manufacturing.

Modern economics dictates that high demand equals high sales. PowerBook sales have generated more than $1 billion in revenue for Apple, which couldn't have come at a better time. Recent price cuts and an industry price war forced Apple into some sacrificial margin cuts on its hardware, dropping the company's net income 18 percent in the second quarter of 1993. Apple was counting on the Newton and its workgroup servers announced in March, 1993, to boost fourth-quarter sales. In the meantime, the PowerBook was its cash cow.

"PowerBooks have gone from nowhere to capturing major market share," says analyst Hartsook. He estimates that Apple currently has a 25-percent to 30-percent share of the portable market. And note that the portable market isn't just a niche anymore. Dataquest (San Jose, CA) estimates that, at the end of 1993, more than 1.6 million notebooks were in use in the United States. Currently, 15 percent of all computers sold are portables, and Dataquest predicts that number will grow to 30 percent by 1995.

"Replacement machines will be mobile computers," says Jeff Leopold, director of integrated computing at the Yankee Group, a market-research firm based in Boston. "Unless desktop computers become dirt cheap, buyers will have no good reason to buy anything other than a portable." Leopold says the price of the PowerBook has entered into the attractive "buy me" zone. The low-end Power-Book 145, for example, sells for $2,149, much more attractive than Apple's first portables, which sold for $5,000 and, according to Leopold, were just too heavy. "The weight, the high-quality screen, and the price-performance ratio has brought Apple success in the mobile market," he adds.

Hartsook says the PowerBook lure is its sleek design and inherent networking capabilities. He attributes Apple's success to its understanding of the needs of the mobile user in all areas, ranging from such unrelated features as remote network access to trackball placement. "Apple offers intelligent human engineering better than anyone else around, " says Hartsook. "Other laptop makers just don't get it. They're unclear on the concepts of mobile computing."

MOBILE MANIACS

To be clear on the concepts, a vendor must first understand the mobile workforce and the computing needs of the roving users. The actual numbers of the mobile mob are staggering. The Yankee Group estimates that 25 million Americans work outside their offices. Another 13 million workers have jobs that require them to travel at least 20 percent of the time. And the last group, a large mass whose numbers simply can't be counted, are those corridor crawlers who have office-wandering syndrome, going from meeting to meeting or floor to floor, and could greatly benefit from impromptu networks.

These workers don't want to choose between being connected or mobile–they simply want to be both, and subsequently they use a variety of methods to maintain contact. According to Forrester Research, a Cambridge, MA-based market-research firm, mobile users access the LAN on average four times a week. In the Apple sphere, long-distance connectivity methods currently available include PowerBook modems that use either regular analog phone lines or cellular links, which require you to have a cellular-phone account.

On the receiving end, these users can make contact by remote control of a device on the LAN or by a client-server connection in which the mobile user dials into a router or communications server and becomes a peer on the network.

And, of course, Apple assists you with the connection. It offers a PowerBook Express Modem for $319 that includes fax capabilities. The Apple modem can transfer data at 14.4Kbps (or 57.6Kbps with data compression). This modem, combined with AppleTalk Remote Access, creates a relatively painless way to phone home.

LOCAL MOTION

Local network-connectivity options for the PowerBook vary depending on the model. For the person who can't decide between a desktop and a laptop, Apple offers its dynamic duo, the Macintosh Duo Dock and Duo MiniDock models that can provide a desktop home for the Power-Book Duo. The dock portion provides a full-fledged desktop machine, with a full-size screen, keyboard, and two NuBus slots. The pop-out PowerBook Duo sidekick measures a mere 1.5 inches thick and weighs in at 4 pounds.

The freestanding PowerBook models include two serial ports for LocalTalk networking and a speedier SCSI port that can facilitate multiple devices, including an Ethernet connection, which doesn't come standard on the Power-Book. A serial connection offers a maximum data-transfer rate of 57.6Kbps, but SCSI emulation can be much faster. Companies such as Farallon Computing (Alameda, CA), Compatible Systems (Boulder, CO), and Asanté Technologies (San Jose, CA) recently announced products that connect PowerBooks via a SCSI port to an Ethernet network.

"Connecting PowerBooks to Ethernet has become a problem," explains Wilson Wong, president and CEO of Asantœe. "We wanted to come up with something the size of a pack of cigarettes that the user could carry around." Asanté's Virginia Slim is the 6-ounce Mini EN/SC, which can link the PowerBook via the SCSI port to thin Ethernet and 10BaseT. It sells for $459. Wong says the PowerBook's built-in Lo-calTalk support is no longer enough. "The line between PCs and Apples is getting fuzzy. Mobile users just want the best possible machine, and then they have to integrate it with mixed networks on Ethernet," he says. "Having only Lo-calTalk would freeze you out."

In addition to SCSI connections, Farallon offers a more inexpensive, but slower, method of reaching Ethernet from a PowerBook. Using Farallon's PowerPath, the mobile computer is hooked up via LocalTalk to the host Ethernet Mac. Working much like a router, PowerPath uses Faral-lon's Forward Transfer Algorithm, making PowerBooks appear as a node on the primary LAN. PowerPath, which includes the necessary software, PhoneNet StarConnectors, and cable, costs $149.

In contrast to Asanté, Farallon is a LocalTalk believer. "LocalTalk is a simpler and much cheaper solution," says Larry Jones, product manager for networking at Farallon. "LocalTalk is easier to install, and it's not constrained by the distance requirements of 10BaseT."

He predicts that Apple's PDAs, which will have a Lo-calTalk connection, will be a boost for products such as PowerPath that can connect these devices to the network. "LocalTalk is dirt cheap for Apple to put into the Newton. It makes sense to go that route."

BABY SLOT

A final connectivity remedy, coming from the Power-Book's cohorts on the PC side, will be the Personal Computer Memory Card International Association (PCMCIA) slot. This tiny form factor will most likely first be seen in the Newton, with an eventual migration to the Power-Book.

"PCMCIA is a good multipurpose slot that addresses the customer issue of adding a modem, expansion, and a network link" to a PowerBook, says Apple's Cooper. Apple hasn't announced a specific time frame for development of PCMCIA slots.

According to other vendors, Apple was initially hesitant to jump on the PCMCIA bandwagon because of a few technical problems. "PCMCIA was designed around an Intel processor, leaving it with a few software problems for the Apple environment," explains Farallon's Jones. "PCMCIA is just a different beast for the Macintosh." Jones says that despite these problems, "PCMCIA is still an obvious solution."

Even though Apple hasn't publicly disclosed its PCM-CIA path, Asanté is already developing PCMCIA cards for the Mac. "PCMCIA is where everyone is headed," says Wong. "Apple will have to support it. PCMCIA is becoming a significant bus standard, more important than the AT bus. PCMCIA is becoming almost universal." He points out that PCMCIA cards could fit into a desktop Mac, Power-Book, or Newton, making the cards the form factor of choice for the buyer.

DON'T FENCE ME IN

Note one important contradiction with all these cable-based network options: You just took a mobile device and hooked a wire to it. That's a mobility don't. Apple and others are not sitting on their hands in this area, either. Apple is interested in two very different forms of wireless transmission: spread-spectrum radio transmission and infrared. Each offers specific benefits to the user.

"Wireless networking is hot and exciting," says Apple's Cooper. "But integrating it into a PowerBook requires the cooperation of software, hardware, and communications companies. This is no slam dunk."

Apple has already begun passing the ball in the spread-spectrum game. In 1991, Apple petitioned the FCC to allocate a 40MHz frequency band to an area it dubbed Data Personal Communications Services (Data-PCS), targeting this area for unlicensed use by buyers of its PDAs and other wireless devices. Apple then helped form a lobby group, dubbed Wireless Information Networks Forum (WINForum), based in Washington, D.C., to help politick its wishes to fruition. In response to Apple's request, a nonenthusiastic FCC divvied out a small 20MHz slice of bandwidth, that is still currently in the petition stage, to an area it dubbed User-PCS.

WINForum is still pushing for more bandwidth. "In the world of mobile computing and portable devices, adequate bandwidth in the user premises is vital," says Benn Kobb, executive director of WINForum. He explains that Apple and others need the new band, with adequate bandwidth, to allow the devices to transmit at low power without having to "shout" over interference–such as baby monitors, cruise missiles, and antitheft devices–that currently transmit in the unlicensed band.

The new PDAs will be "highly intelligent devices that can detect each other's presence," says Kobb. WINForum is coming up with a set of rules, or spectrum etiquette, that would outline to vendors a method in which one device would not overpower another device sharing the spectrum. Essentially, the device would monitor the frequency before transmitting and not lock out other devices.

Users could also realize other benefits in this bandwidth. Apple's requested space, in the 1910MHz to 1930MHz range, is also adjacent to carrier-based frequencies, which would allow for synergy and interaction between licensed and unlicensed devices, facilitating long-distance messaging and other services.

And keep in mind that Apple and Motorola have multiple development agreements, so jumping from the unlicensed user band with the PDA to a carrier-based messaging band could be more than a remote possibility.

The FCC could reach a bandwidth decision as early as this summer, according to Kobb. The Clinton/ Gore protechnology administration has "pushed the accelerator even more," says Kobb. WINForum has to battle powerful government and railroad lobbies fighting to keep Apple and others from legally stealing their bandwidth.

But the wireless industry is optimistic about Apple's politicking power. "Apple will be successful in acquiring bandwidth," says David Frankland, vice president of Digital Ocean (Overland Park, KS). "Look who was sitting next to Hillary Clinton on inauguration day." (That would be John Sculley, for those who are television impaired). "The entire bandwidth will probably be redistributed."

IN THE SWIM

Digital Ocean does have a vested interest in this redis-

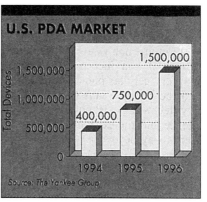

Figure 1. Analysts predict the PDA market will take off, going from zero to 1.5 million units in the next three years.

tribution. It is one among a school of new wireless third-party products for the PowerBook, including Photonics' (San Jose, CA) Collaborative Mac infrared adapters. Digital Ocean Grouper is a spread-spectrum product designed specifically for the PowerBook.

Photonics, owned 17 percent by Apple, will have a Collaborative Mac adapter, a user-installed infrared device for Mac desktops and PowerBooks. It will allow users to create an instant network, in an office, classroom, or plane.

PowerBook users who feel fenced in by infrared's inability to penetrate walls might prefer to network with radio devices, such as the Grouper. Then they could network without having to look at one another, which is a coup in some office environments.

The Grouper, with a wedge-shaped design, can be attached to any PowerBook model or be used freestanding with desktop Macs. The Grouper provides wireless network access within a 250-foot radius in an average office. Groupers network by joining a group called–you guessed it–a "school," which includes up to 15 Groupers. Groupers also can connect directly to wired LocalTalk networks, with one centrally located Grouper in each school directly attached to the network and acting as a hub.

IT KEEPS GOING, AND GOING . . .

Now that the Grouper is shipping, Frankland says, Digital Ocean will look to Apple for possible technology integration. "Apple doesn't have the not-invented-here syndrome anymore," he says. Specifically, Frankland says the Grouper's low power consumption may be most interesting to Apple. The Grouper, with its patented power technology, lessens the power required to network using chatty

AppleTalk, which can swiftly drain an already quick-to-die portable battery. "We use one-sixtieth the power of other wireless products out there," says Frankland. "This will be one of the secrets to our success."

Power is a critical problem among all laptops, and PowerBooks are no exception. Forrester Research estimates that if wireless connections drain the portable battery more than 25 percent, they won't be feasible.

"You just don't have a big enough battery if you incorporate wireless adapters, cellular phones, and pagers into the laptop," says Cooper. "Battery technology is now a rampant science, but the expectation from the user is way beyond what science can now provide."

PC MUTANTS

Science (and Apple) in 1993 provided a new device, though, that could exceed user expectations–PDAs. These small, hand-held devices, sitting somewhere in the computing food chain between calculators and laptops, are called everything from PC mutants by analysts to network appliances, organizers, personal information managers, and miniature mobile offices. They could provide messaging, sports scores, stock reports, weather, traffic, and even standard office functions, such as e-mail, faxing, and enterprise connectivity. As Jay Leno quipped, be careful when you put one in your pocket–the paper cutter could slice your finger when you try to get it out.

While PDAs fit into the bevy of products that no one knew they needed until they had one (for example, portable CD players), analysts already foresee a growing market (see Figure 1). BIS Strategic Decisions (Norwell, MA) says the personal digital-device market will hit $396.9 million by 1995, with 81 percent of them networked (see Figure 2).

Apple's first PDA, the Newton, is marketed toward individual business users, according to the company. Priced under $1,000, the Newton will run on its own operating-system software and use pen technology, both print and cursive, along with a keypad limited to symbols and icons. The Newton is based on a RISC processor from Advanced RISC Machines Ltd, a British firm.

Apple describes the Newton as the third layer of a network, sort of a detachable extension for the road. "On a client-server network, this is a client to your desktop client," says Larry Tesler, vice president of development in Apple's Personal Interactive Electronics (PIE) division.

He says the Newton will have built-in intelligence that "completes your thought." For example, if you note in the Newton that you have a lunch date with mom on Thursday, you won't have to exit your current program and enter your calendar; your Newton will do it for you.

Tesler says the Newton will initially use paging technology for wide-area communications. On the local front, it will have a few LAN-connect options. Apple confirms it will have network connectivity via AppleTalk on first shipment, but details have not been disclosed. "You can assume the Newton will have a serial port with a LocalTalk connection," says analyst Hartsook. He says the device will also have point-to-point infrared connectivity.

Apple will sprout a whole family of Newtons. The second device will be slate-size, have a faster processor, and most likely have a PCMCIA slot. Apple's future PDA plans include devices sophisticated enough to support multimedia.

ANYTHING, EVERYTHING

Portable devices must contain everything the user needs, according to John Sculley. "There is no space for add-on boards in a briefcase," he says. Vendors are speculating that the Newton will have built-in e-mail along with the messaging functions.

BIS Strategic Decisions found, in a survey of 200 prospective PDA buyers, that remote database access via an e-mail link was one of the most desired applications for PDAs. Another typical application was the ability to remotely update appointment schedules for staff in the field.

As with any new technology, the Newton will have its share of problems coming out of the barrel, the first one being cost. Rolling all these applications and functions into one small device dictates a high price tag. "Cost is a barrier. Would you pay $1,000 to be able to read your e-mail on the bus? Probably not," says Yankee Group's Leopold.

And like the PowerBook, another Newton problem could be battery based. These devices need to last at least a day without a recharge, according to the Yankee Group.

In addition, the Newton could have a literacy problem. Pen-based computing is still unproven, leaving people unconvinced of its accuracy. "Initially, the handwriting technology is just not there," says Hartsook. "You wouldn't want to take notes with the Newton." This shortcoming puts the Newton in the forms-based, vertical markets–UPS and Federal Express–that Grid and other companies are aiming at.

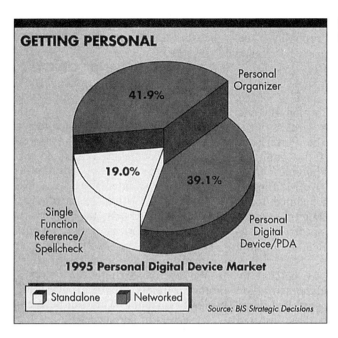

Figure 2. Although designed strictly for mobility, most personal digital devices will have built-in network-connectivity options.

But eventually the Newton will be able to read the handwriting on its wall, and, as Hartsook says, then "people will actually use these things." In the meantime, Apple will try to sell the Newton as the greatest thing for mobile communication since, well, the PowerBook. As Hartsook puts it, "There's always a group of people who just have to have the latest toy. They'll buy a Newton."

USING APPLETALK REMOTE ACCESS
Cruisin' with the PowerBook

The black Volvo comes cruising into the rounded driveway of the white Southern mansion, and the tuxedoed man and his shimmering mate flow out the door. Or should a red Volvo come careening to the beachfront, with the top of the surfboard jutting out of the sunroof? These are the kinds of crucial decisions that ad agency producers and executives at Messner, Vetere, Berger, McNamee, and Schmetterer have to make on a daily basis.

And needless to say, they don't have time to fly from commercial shoots in Los Angeles back to agency headquarters in New York to discuss the latest outtake. Instead, their scripting takes place using Apple Remote Access via their PowerBooks, which allows the ad execs to keep in touch with both the home base and, through an e-mail link, with Volvo, one of the agency's largest clients.

"AppleTalk Remote Access is amazing. It's as easy as plugging into a phone jack," says Tripp McCune, network manager for the firm. And although another one of the agency's largest clients is MCI, McCune boldly says, "It's the next best thing to being there."

Connectivity is fairly straightforward with AppleTalk Remote Access. You first establish the connection with the remote Mac running System 7, then log on to the services you want. If you call the same connection frequently, you can set up an alias. Clicking on that icon will start a series of events: It activates AppleTalk Remote Access, dials the remote number, establishes a network connection, and mounts the remote disk of your choice on your laptop's desktop.

McCune's users access the network through Shiva (Cambridge, MA) LanRover/L, which connects to the LocalTalk workgroups.

To accommodate a flood of users, the company also has the multiport LanRover/E, which can handle simultaneous connections to the Ethernet mail and file servers. The agency's 260 users use CE Software (West Des Moines, IA) QuickMail.

"AppleTalk Remote Access is simple and very reliable," adds McCune. "People don't even realize that they're getting e-mails from someone in Hong Kong. It's that transparent."

Section 6
Case Studies

Remote access and mobile computing are just meaningless networking theories until proven that they can actually work. Whether working at home, on the beach, or in an airplane, mobile users have certain communications requirements that need to be satisfied before they feel comfortable being on their own.

Although based on relatively new technology, remote access has already been put to the working test and will most certainly continue to evolve. Hundreds of corporations and government agencies have mobile workers that need to be out and about just to get their jobs done; a police force is a good example. "Computer Chips" describes how the California Highway Patrol uses a networked dispatching service to get help to those in need quickly and efficiently. Other professionals, such as those in medicine, count on remote access to save people's lives. See "Modern Medicine" and "Saving Children's Lives" for a few down-to-earth examples of how well-designed mobile computing and networking makes a difference.

Modern Medicine

TELEMEDICINE ENABLES DOCTORS AT URBAN HOSPITALS TO CARE FOR PATIENTS IN RURAL AREAS.

BY SHERI HOSTETLER

Residents of the tiny town of Alpine, TX, used to drive more than five hours to visit the doctor. Although primary-care physicians practice in Alpine, the nearest medical specialist was 300 miles away in Lubbock. Some Alpine residents couldn't afford to make the drive, which often meant missing two days or more of work. And when anybody needed emergency medical treatment from a specialist, they were simply out of luck.

Now the same people have immediate access to high-quality, specialty health care thanks to telemedicine, a technology that marries telecommunications, videoconferencing, and medical technologies to deliver health care from a distance. Using medical scopes attached to the videoconferencing system, a specialist in Lubbock can look into the ear of a patient in Alpine. Diagnostic images such as X-rays are transmitted over dedicated T-1 lines and interpreted by experts at Texas Tech University's Health Sciences Center.

In the past three years, more than 25 projects like the one in Alpine have sprung up across the United States,; most of these projects connect urban medical centers with small rural hospitals. Boston's Massachusetts General Hospital has just started what is possibly the first international telemedicine network. Hospitals from around the world have round-the-clock access to Mass General physicians in all major medical subspecialties. Health care professionals can access continuing medical education programs offered by Mass General and Harvard Medical School.

Telemedicine advocates contend that the technology not only increases access to health care but also saves money. A 1992 study concluded that the use of videoconferencing for remote consultations could slash $132 mil-lion from annual U.S. health care costs. Another $103 million could be saved by using videoconferencing for medical education and professional development, according to a study called "Telecommunications: Can It Help Solve America's Health Care Problems?" by Arthur D. Little, a consulting firm based in Cambridge, MA.

More importantly, telemedicine saves lives, say physicians. The first time the telemedicine system in Alpine was used, it saved the life of a 2-hour-old newborn with respiratory problems. The Alpine doctor who delivered the baby conferred with a neonatologist at Texas Tech University's hospital using the system. The specialist, who also remotely viewed the baby's lab report and X-rays, was able to correctly diagnosis the problem and suggest an appropriate treatment plan.

Cases such as this one lead telemedicine's true believers to tout telecommunications as the next revolution in health care. "There is no doubt that within 10 to 15 years telemedicine systems will be as common as today's fax machine," says Dr. Jay Sanders, director of telemedicine at the Medical College of Georgia in Augusta.

Many agree that health care reform will spur the growth of telemedicine. President Clinton's health care proposal emphasizes the role of telecommunications in improving medical care in rural and underserved areas. And key Washington insiders–from members of Congress to former Surgeon General C. Everett Koop–have publicly advocated telemedicine as a means of improving health care access and decreasing costs.

A SLOW START

Although the bulk of telemedicine activity has occurred

in the past several years, one of the first uses of the technology was in 1967, when a doctor at Massachusetts General Hospital grew tired of sitting in traffic jams en route to Boston's Logan Airport medical center. He and Sanders, then a resident at Mass General, improvised a telemedicine system between the airport and the hospital using a television monitor and microwave unit.

But the high cost of communications and a lack of inexpensive, commercially available equipment kept telemedicine systems from being widely implemented, Sanders says. The country's growing health care crisis, however, made health care professionals reconsider telemedicine. "While we very clearly identified health care access as a problem in the 1970s, in the 1990s it became an emergency," Sanders says. "That was a definite stimulus for telemedicine's growth."

At the same time as the health care crisis escalated, researchers made breakthroughs in the ability to compress digital image data thanks to advances in digital electronics, information theory (a branch of mathematics devoted to representing and transmitting information), digital communications and networking, and the study of how the human eye and brain process visual information. Those technological leaps drove down the cost of videoconferencing equipment and made it possible to send much more information over phone lines, greatly lowering communications costs.

For instance, an uncompressed analog video signal, once digitized, must be transmitted at 90Mbps to achieve real-time video–a bandwidth equal to about 4,500 standard phone lines. Before compression, the only communications modalities capable of transmitting such signals were satellite or microwave, both prohibitively expensive technologies for health care. Most videoconferencing manufacturers now offer systems that effectively squeeze that 90Mbps signal through a 128Kbps pipeline. AT&T's videophone compresses the signal all the way down to 11.2Kbps.

The price of the codec–the device that converts and compresses the analog signal to digital form and then back again–fell as compression ratios soared. In 1982, codecs could compress a picture to 1/300th of its original size while still delivering a good video image, according to Jim Sauerhaft, project manager for multimedia and personal video at Compression Labs (San Jose, CA). Those

codecs were the size of refrigerators, however, and cost a quarter of a million dollars. They now sell for less than one-tenth that price, are the size of a computer CPU (or smaller), and can produce even higher-quality video with a signal 1/800th the original size.

In the wake of these technological advances, videoconferencing system costs plummeted. Customized teleconferencing sites that cost up to $500,000 per room a decade ago have been replaced by cabinet systems requiring no customization and running less than $100,000 for a two-site system. In the past year and a half, most of the major videoconferencing companies have introduced roll-about units that cost less than $20,000.

The next evolution in videoconferencing–desktop systems–promises to bring down the price much further. PictureTel (Danvers, MA) introduced a system last summer that turns a personal computer into a videophone. Priced at $6,000, the PCS 100 transmits at 56Kbps to 128Kbps and operates at full common intermediate format (CIF), a video standard specifying a resolution of 288 lines by 352 pixels at 30 frames per second. Compression Labs sells a Cameo personal video system that runs on a Macintosh for $3,000. Computer companies such as Sun Microsystems (Mountain View, CA), Silicon Graphics (Mountain View), and IBM are also marketing videoconferencing software for their workstations and PCs.

Equipment standardization has also opened up the videoconferencing market. Most major vendors' equipment now conforms to International Telecommunications Union (ITU-T) recommendation H.320, an umbrella standard covering narrowband visual telephone systems and terminal equipment that allows systems from different videoconferencing manufacturers to talk to each other. Unfortunately, doctors have found that images produced by videoconferencing equipment complying with the standard were of such poor quality they couldn't be used for diagnosis or diagnostic consultations.

That situation is mitigated somewhat by the fact that most vendors manufacture codecs containing both their own proprietary compression algorithms, which produce a higher-quality image, and the H.320-compliant algorithm. A user can easily flick a switch and change from one standard to the other. Still, many health care professionals believe that telemedicine networks using two different makes of videoconferencing equipment will be impossible to implement until the quality of the H.320 standard improves.

TELECOMMUNICATIONS

Perhaps the major barrier to widespread telemedicine implementation is the lack of an adequate, inexpensive telecommunications infrastructure–especially in rural areas, where telemedicine is most needed. "The infrastructure development in rural areas is about 20 years behind the times," says Jim Reid, the project director of the Eastern Montana Telemedicine Project in Billings.

Reid faced a discouraging slate of choices when he began planning his telemedicine project two years ago: a dedicated T-1 network from the regional Bell operating company or a dedicated T-3 network from a regional telephone cooperative. Both were costly, and both gave him more bandwidth than he needed for his VTEL (Austin, TX) videoconferencing system, which uses only 384Kbps of a T-1. He decided on the T-1 lines and now pays about $8,000 a month for a 320-mile network that connects six different health care sites in Montana.

More fortunate telemedicine projects have been able to tap into statewide networks built initially for government use. A telemedicine project in Kansas leases T-1 lines from the state at the attractive rate of $35 an hour during the day and $10 per hour during evenings and weekends. In Iowa, the state hospital association has proposed legislation that would enable its hospitals to use a fiber optic network owned by the state government. Such state networks are rare, however, and telemedicine advocates say that telecom companies must offer some type of fractional T-1 bandwidth on demand if the technology is to take off.

Despite its reputation as a technology whose time has come and gone, Integrated Services Digital Network (ISDN) tops just about every telemedicine advocate's telecommunications wish list, Reid says. Three ISDN lines multiplexed together would give sufficient bandwidth for videoconferencing at a fraction of the cost of leased T-1 lines. IDSN service is still fairly rare in rural areas, however. Almost half of the lines belonging to five of the seven regional Bell operating companies are ISDN-capable, but the bulk of these lines are concentrated in urban areas.

As for everyone's dream technology–fiber optics–it will be at least 10 years to 20 years before rural locations have access to it, predicts Bill Jolitz, a telecommunications consultant in Oakland, CA. "The whole fiber infrastructure is going through a lot of changes right now. Until the economics of it grounds out a little more, fiber will be unpredictable enough that rural service providers will be somewhat hesitant to provide it," Jolitz says. If providers do offer fiber, it is more likely to be point-to-point rather than switched service.

One of the best options for users waiting for ISDN to arrive may be Switched 56 service, which can interoperate with ISDN. Although usually more costly and slower than ISDN, Switched 56 service is almost universally available.

Cable also appears promising. Technology recently developed by Digital Equipment Corp. (DEC, Maynard, MA) allows ordinary cable television lines to be used for high-speed multimedia data networking. Running the Ethernet protocol, the technology uses existing coax cable channels to connect sites up to 70 miles apart. While cable can carry about six times the traffic of T-1 lines, cable operators are expected to charge less than $500 per month for their lines, at least $200 less than the cost of T-1 lines.

DEC is targeting hospitals as one of the major users of the new technology. In fact, one of the first tests of the technology's capabilities was a telemedicine application. The cable company Scripps-Howard of Northwest Georgia used the technology to allow physicians at three different sites in the state to view magnetic resonance images while discussing the patient's case over a live, full-motion video link.

Some telecommunications experts contend that Asynchronous Transfer Mode (ATM) will make all these delivery technologies obsolete. But ATM is in its infancy, and if it moves at the pace of other telecommunications technologies, it won't hit rural areas for years, according to Richard Brennan, technology manager for AT&T Network Systems in San Ramon, CA.

ATM technology is rapidly becoming available in urban areas, however, and large teaching and research hospitals that want to transfer high-resolution diagnostic images are already demanding it, says Diane Brown, Sprint's national marketing manager for health care. "For a small rural hospital, fractional T-1 is all they're going to need for the immediate future," she says. "At the next level, though, I think you're going to see ATM widely deployed, perhaps before we see ISDN, because we're moving so fast with ATM."

Dr. Bernie Huang is one physician who believes ATM can benefit his medical center right now. Huang, vice chairman of radiology at the University of California at San Francisco (UCSF), says he needs network speeds up to 600Mbps to establish a teleradiology link that can transmit mammography, neuroradiology, and real-time magnetic resonance and computed tomography dynamic studies. UCSF is working with Pacific Bell and Sprint on establishing an ATM network between its medical center and an affiliate hospital a few miles away.

ATM switches are also being used in an ongoing telemedicine test project at the University of North Carolina at Chapel Hill. Running at 622Mbps over a fiber optic network, the project's network connects a Cray Y-MP 8/432 supercomputer, an image processing system, and a medical workstation. The supercomputer is used for dynamic radiation therapy planning, a cutting-edge method for developing radiation treatment plans for certain types of cancer.

INTO THE HOME

Not content with connecting health care facilities to one another, many telemedicine advocates insist that the technology must eventually reach into the home if it is to fulfill its promise of optimal health care access.

The nation's new health care system will focus on wellness, preventive medicine, and consumer access to self-help information, says Mary Gardiner Jones, president of the Consumer Interest Research Institute in Washington, D.C. In addition, having patients convalesce at home instead of in hospitals will present additional cost savings. Telemedicine will play an essential role in this new system by providing health care information to the home and by allowing physicians to monitor patients remotely. "The home will once again become the center of health care," Jones says. "In the past, we had the black bag coming into the home. In the future, it will be the black box."

The "black box" refers to the computer that many futurists say may soon be connected to every television. This computer will allow interactive multimedia information, including the much-ballyhooed "video on demand," to be brought into the home. The entertainment industry will probably subsidize the costs of delivering broadband, interactive networks to the home, and the technology can then be used for telemedical purposes, says Danny Cohen,

a computer scientist with the Rand Corp. in Santa Monica, CA.

The Medical College of Georgia is already working toward this goal of providing home health care via telemedicine. Along with the health maintenance organization Cigna Healthcare, the Medical College of Georgia has submitted a proposal for federal grant monies to set up a home monitoring system that would target patients who need frequent hospitalizations or emergency room visits. By monitoring these patients at home, the medical college will be able to identify their illness at the earliest stage and begin preventive care to keep them out of the emergency room or hospital, Sanders says.

An array of remote monitoring devices already exists, including a product called an MDphone that uses a portable defibrillator to restart a heart by remote control over a standard or cellular phone line. Other devices allow doctors to remotely monitor heart rate, blood pressure, and temperature.

Eventually, visionaries hope to set up "telehealth" networks. These networks would not only connect health care providers to patients but also tie in any organization connected to the health care process within a given community, says Barbara Kerlin of Mitre, a systems engineering company in McLean, VA. "We're moving rapidly toward community telehealth networks, which would combine LANs, MANs, and WANs to provide networking within health care facilities and to link those facilities to each other, insurance carriers, pharmacies, and academic research centers," Kerlin says.

TELEMEDICINE HELPS GEORGIA PREVENT HOSPITAL CLOSINGS.

Open for Business

Of the more than 800 hospitals that have closed in the United States since 1980, nearly 75 percent have been rural facilities. Such closures jeopardize the lives of rural residents, who may have to drive hours more to get to an emergency room. Hospital closings also threaten the overall health of rural communities, which stagnate and often die after local health care facilities shut down.

In response to this decline in the availability of health care to rural Americans, the Medical College of Georgia (MCG) launched a project in 1991 to determine if telemedicine could stem the trend of hospital closings. A 130-mile telecommunications link was set up between the medical center in Augusta and Dodge County Hospital in the small town of Eastman. A VTEL (Austin, TX) codec was used to transmit videoconferencing and diagnostic images over half a dedicated T-1 line.

Several diagnostic cameras at the Eastman site enhance the examining capability of the system. The main diagnostic camera is a three-chip charge-coupled color camera with 16-power zoom that allows the doctor in Augusta to pan the entire examining room or to zoom in on a hair coming out of a skin pore, says Dr. Jay Sanders, director of telemedicine at MCG. An Elmo (New Hyde Park, NY) camera captures still images of diagnostic images and other documents and a miniature camera, which can be fully zoomed and focused, is attached to a variety of medical scopes.

Collectively, the equipment allows a physical examination performed in Eastman to be simultaneously viewed by a specialist in Augusta. "Our ear, nose, and throat specialist says he can see the nose and ears better over this system than he can in his office," Sanders says.

The only aspect of a typical medical exam not able to be performed via telecommunications is palpating (touching) the patient. Even this may be possible within the next several years by using a virtual reality glove being developed by an MCG physician.

By all accounts the system has been an unqualified success, Sanders says. To date, 83 percent of patients previously transferred to a larger medical center are now kept in rural hospitals. Retaining patients–and, thus, revenue–is critical to keeping rural facilities open.

Physicians in Eastman also reported that conferring with specialists via the telemedical system reduced their sense of professional isolation. Some rural hospital administrators believe that having a telemedicine system will enable them to more successfully recruit physicians and retain the ones they have.

Sanders emphasizes that all these benefits are obtained using relatively inexpensive, off-the-shelf technology. One of his goals is to demystify telemedicine technology so that physicians, who are notoriously technophobic, will be more willing to take advantage of it. "We watch Tom Brokaw talking to a correspondent interactively live in Somalia and don't think anything of it," he says. "Why can't we take that same technology and apply it to health care?"

A Client-Server Success

CLIENT-SERVER MAY BE DIFFICULT TO MANAGE, BUT IT'S HELPED ONE PUBLISHING GIANT STAY ON TOP.

BY LENNY LIEBMANN

Lately the fashion is to trash client-server computing as expensive and difficult to manage. But such a focus on administrative costs and implementation pitfalls misses the key value of distributed technology: It solves business problems better than centralized systems. A recent development effort by The Reader's Digest Association (Pleasantville, NY) demonstrates that client-server applications can be rolled out on time and within budget.

The association's first client-server application combined SQL database design, graphical user interfaces, and e-mail to save the company time and money. While this setup cannot contradict the fact that managing LANs is a daunting challenge, it does show that a valid reason exists for corporate America to shoulder the burden of client-server architecture. And it offers some important instructions about to how to be a first-time winner.

MAIL MANIA

Most people disparagingly refer to it as "junk." This year, each of us will get an average of 1,000 pieces of it. And few people think of it as a high-tech communications medium. But when executed properly, direct mail solicitation is one of the most powerful and effective forms of advertising.

Like other forms of communications, direct mail requires a special mix of science and art. Content, presentation, distribution, and production must all be properly executed to make the mailing a success. The fact that the recipients give direct mail pieces only a few seconds of attention only increases the amount of time, effort, and ingenuity the advertiser must put into its creation.

Reader's Digest is one of the country's largest and most successful direct mailers. One of Reader's Digest's major corporate assets is its database of more than 100 million households worldwide, including half the households in the United States. Half of those in the database have made at least one purchase from the company in the last two years. In addition to the sheer volume these figures represent, Reader's Digest has also developed expertise in selectively targeting potential customers for its promotions. This targeted approach reduces promotional costs and increases return on investment.

Another important aspect of maximizing profitability as a direct mailer is minimizing production costs. Savings of even a fraction of a cent can be significant when hundreds of thousands to millions of pieces are involved. Multiply the number of recipients by the approximately 7,500 individual mailing components that Reader's Digest produces each year and the impact on the corporate bottom line of even small per-mailer savings is obvious.

In addition to keeping the cost per individual component low, the company would like to reap the potential savings of combining the production costs of separate mailings. But since the dozens of different buyers have their hands full just managing their own projects, such opportunities have been difficult to pinpoint and exploit.

So in May of 1992, Reader's Digest's IS managers began to look for ways to enhance the procurement process. They wanted to give buyers the tools they needed to expedite their individual projects while at the same time giving the procurement managers the ability to more effectively monitor the process as a whole.

With its PC-based network environment already in place, a client-server application architecture was a natural choice for Reader's Digest. And, although this attempt was the IS department's first rollout of a distributed (and mail-enabled) application, the resulting Promotion Quotation Management System (PQMS), which was implemented in January of 1993, stands as a telling example of how client-server computing can be successfully implemented, even by organizations without previous experience in the technology.

THE QUOTATION PROCESS

At first glance, the workflow required to put a job out to bid seems simple enough. When the marketing department develops a mailer, it fills out a specification sheet, which is then passed on to the buyers. The buyers distribute these specs to vendors for bids and await a response. When the responses come in, they choose the best price and pass along the winning bids to the purchasing department.

But anyone familiar with the printing business knows just how complex this process can actually become. Components are interdependent; for example some fliers must be inserted by machines inside envelopes of a specific size, or the total weight of all pieces is not to exceed a designated limit. With today's advanced imprinting technologies, several factors affect how pieces fold and where imprints are to be located. And sometimes a slight change in dimensions may yield substantial cost savings. The design team may not always take all these factors into account. The designers may also leave out some specifications, either through oversight or because the specs are not critical to the design. And then there are always the inevitable last-minute changes. Ultimately the company's buyers must pin down these details before putting the job out for bid.

Added to these internal communications issues are the complexities of interfacing with the bidding vendors. With up to 12 components in a given mailing and up to 10 suppliers bidding on each component, the buyer may be managing as many as 120 interactions per project. Bidders may have questions on the specifications or may have suggestions on how to run the component more efficiently. As the deadline approaches, buyers may want to check with vendors on the status of their bids and, when a final decision has been made, inform them whether (and why) they have won or lost the job. Buyers may also want to review bid-ding histories periodically to evaluate vendor performance.

With the thousands of information transactions involved in a single project, a buyer's job is extremely time-consuming. The particulars of Reader's Digest's promotion bidding process can easily be abstracted to apply to a wide variety of manufacturing and distribution situations. Most businesses face the same productivity issues: boosting purchasing efficiency, coping with changing or incomplete data, reducing internal and external communications cycles, and streamlining team tasks.

BEFORE AND AFTER

Before the PQMS application was deployed, much of the bidding process was handled manually. Buyers transcribed information from the marketing department's spec sheets onto their own bidding forms. "There were documents flying all over the building," says Mark Zimmerman, an IS manager who spearheaded the development of PQMS. This manual transcription opened the possibility for human error and added to the overall project delivery time.

The discrete handling of each project also afforded the company little or no chance of spotting opportunities to "gang up" mailing components. "Unless somebody happened to notice a similar requirement on somebody else's project, we wouldn't put the two together," says Zimmerman. Evaluating the bids also involved manually consolidating each vendor's quotation into a single spreadsheet. Then, after choosing a supplier, several additional manual steps were required to cut the purchase order.

The manual nature of the process also prevented Reader's Digest from building a good database of vendor bidding histories. The information available on promotion pricing was limited to winning bids, and it resided on a mainframe. Without user-friendly querying tools, even this data was not easily accessible to the buying team for ad hoc analysis.

Zimmerman and his staff decided to build their new application around a SQL database and a Windows-based front end built using the SQLWindows development environment from Gupta (Menlo Park, CA). The 35 promotion buyers were already among the more than 2,000 NetWare users connected over Reader's Digest's 12 Token Ring networks.

The company also had Lotus Development's (Cambridge, MA) cc:Mail in place and was a subscriber to the General Electric Information Service (GEIS), which has a high level of acceptance in the graphic arts community and serves as a communications gateway to suppliers of printing and production services.

Production specs are initially uploaded to the mainframe from the network-based desktop publishing department using Attachmate (Bellevue, WA) APIs. A mainframe application then runs a series of back-end validation routines that enforce certain rules, such as mailing-weight requirements. The validated specifications are subsequently downloaded onto the PQMS application's OS/2 Microsoft SQL server.

The buyers can then easily access this data from a graphical interface to create their bidding documents and to automatically populate them with the appropriate data. The buyers transmit these electronic bidding documents to the appropriate suppliers via cc:Mail to GEIS, where the suppliers can pick them up and process them internally (see Figure 1).

This is not Electronic Data Interchange (EDI) in the strictest sense of the term, since the suppliers do not automatically download the bidding data into their own in-house applications. But because GEIS presents the suppliers with an electronic form, the end result is essentially the same: The supplier's bids are returned in a uniform manner, and any variances or missing fields are immediately evident. A once-laborious process, requiring buyers to manually enter each vendor's bid into a spreadsheet and to cope with different quotation formats, has been drastically simplified. With the fully formatted responses, Reader's Digest's buyers can sit at their PCs the day after bids are due and have their "decision spreadsheets" ready for evaluation. The PQMS-cc:Mail-GEIS connection also lets them send out automatic reminders to vendors as deadlines approach and simplifies the process of letting participating vendors know whether they got the job.

After the buyer evaluates bids and makes a decision, a click of the mouse triggers PQMS' automatic review using a set of qualifying rules applied to all winning bids before the contract is awarded. The bidding information along with the initial vendor selection is sent to the team's manager for review. Once the manager signs off on the decision, the winning vendor's quote is automatically forwarded to the purchasing department. The data from the quote automatically populates Reader's Digest's purchase order application, and the process is complete.

MAKING THE SYSTEM RESPOND

Besides providing relational database support for Windows clients on the network, the Sybase (Emeryville, CA) DBMS provides additional benefits for the PQMS application. Using an exception-based reporting tool, changes in specifications can be flagged as they occur. Buyers thereby receive immediate and automatic notification of revisions. Buyers can also easily augment the specifications as required by production constraints. And, by selecting key parameters such as size, stock, and required time of delivery, the system can quickly scan all active projects for potential production combinations.

A denormalized copy of the database is used for ad hoc querying. (*Normalization* is a database management technique for reducing duplicate information and maintaining data integrity. These queries allow buyers to create useful reports for analyzing trends. They can easily determine which vendors are consistently high or low bidders. Buyers can look for changes in vendor pricing and zero in on their respective strengths and weaknesses. They can quickly see how much business is currently or historically being given to any particular supplier. All these reports can be generated at the buyer's discretion using Gupta's flexible Quest querying tool.

PQMS demonstrates the key benefits of client-server application architecture. Client users are given easy access to data as well as the ability to use that data to execute their appointed tasks quickly and effectively. At the same time, the server data repository provides a centralized point of control for managing the bidding process and for integrating the process with the activities of other departments in the enterprise.

Most important, according to Zimmerman, is that client-server enables IS managers to choose the individual components of the overall solution. "It used to be that if you decided to go with a certain company's products, you were locked in," says Zimmerman. "Client-server technology has allowed us to take the server we want, use the development environment we want, and integrate it with the other pieces we already have on the LAN."

By building PQMS and other client-server applications

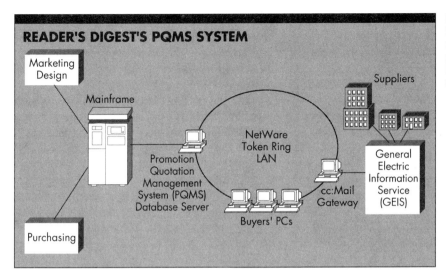

READER'S DIGEST'S PQMS SYSTEM

- Marketing Design
- Mainframe
- Promotion Quotation Management System (PQMS) Database Server
- Purchasing
- NetWare Token Ring LAN
- Buyers' PCs
- cc:Mail Gateway
- Suppliers
- General Electric Information Service (GEIS)

Figure 1. The Reader's Digest PQMS information makes its way from the networked desktop publishing department through the mainframe to provide buyers with decision spreadsheets, simplifying the bidding process.

using an optimum combination of existing resources and best-of-class additions, Reader's Digest has reduced bid processing time by 50 percent with PQMS. "Our overall client-server effort has saved Reader's Digest millions," Zimmerman says.

A RAD APPROACH

How was Reader's Digest able to roll out its first client-server application so quickly? Zimmerman points to several factors. One was his department's decision to apply Rapid Application Development (RAD) techniques to the project.

"With RAD, you take what we call a 'straw man' approach," says Zimmerman. "You put together a prototype as quickly as you can and get it in front of your users so they can go ahead and critique it."

By getting the prototype reviewed early, as opposed to waiting until something as bulletproof as possible could be built and then presenting it for review, the team was able to get better user input and get it sooner. "Users can't always tell you what they want," says Zimmerman. "By showing them an interface and some features right away, you create better communication between the development team and the department."

Decreasing the amount of time between user review sessions and increasing the number of prototyping iterations puts an added strain on programmers, giving them tighter deadlines and more frequent changes to the devel-

opment spec (see Figure 2). But Zimmerman says, "I'd rather find out that what we're working on is wrong halfway through the process than when we're in the home stretch."

The emphasis on user involvement is also characteristic of Joint Application Development (JAD) techniques. "We received tremendous support from the business area," says Zimmerman. The briefings and brainstorming sessions helped Zimmerman make sure his team was addressing the issues that most concerned the buyers. Suppliers were also brought into the process. By increasing the participation of the department managers and end users, the IS staff was better able to boost acceptance of the application.

Zimmerman says Gupta's development tools are well-suited for the fast turnarounds and frequent revisions the RAD/JAD approach demands. "SQLWindows gives you the tools to demonstrate your direction in a compressed time frame," says Zimmerman. "And it's flexible enough to let you build from there."

CLIENT-SERVER SUPPORT

Reader's Digest was assisted in its development effort by InterAccess (Totowa, NJ), one of Gupta's authorized integrators. Jim Cinquegrana, senior applications analyst at Reader's Digest, interviewed numerous consultants before deciding which outside support would be brought in.

"On one end, we had the groups who could send us one or two developers. But the people they sent were indepe-

Figure 2. In Reader's Digest's RAD approach to development, prototypes—rather than bulletproof final programs—are sent out for early review by users. While the cycle may require many iterations of the product, problems become obvious earlier on.

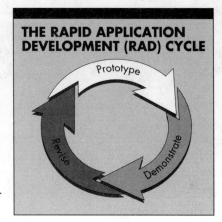

THE RAPID APPLICATION DEVELOPMENT (RAD) CYCLE

Prototype

Demonstrate

Revise

dent consultants, rather than true employees with real accountability to the company we were dealing with," says Cinquegrana. "On the other end, we could go to a major consulting firm. But we decided to keep our costs down." Cinquegrana chose InterAccess because of its familiarity with SQLWindows and because of the reputation of the company's president, Robert Coven.

InterAccess provided training for the Reader's Digest programming staff and placed several additional staff developers on-site. These developers came in handy for other tasks besides the SQLWindows portion of the PQMS project. In the summer of 1992, when the PQMS team wanted to set up its interface to the company's cc:Mail system, Lotus had still not published the specifications for its Vendor-Independent Messaging (VIM) APIs which were to provide the necessary e-mail links. So Cinquegrana and an Inter-Access developer arranged a meeting at Lotus' Cambridge headquarters with a member of the VIM development team for an intensive day-long briefing. InterAccess was then able to use its C programming expertise to quickly write its own Dynamic-Link Libraries (DLLs) and APIs. "With the time frame we were operating under, I was glad to have someone offload these tasks," says Cinquegrana.

Coven, whose company has been involved with a broad range of client-server application development efforts, points out how the example of Reader's Digest illustrates the changing role of the systems integrator. "In the past, you could count on your systems vendor to supply the support you required, because they were most familiar with the products you were using," says Coven.

"In today's typical scenario, the workstation environ-

ment, development tools, network operating system, and back-end DBMS all come from different suppliers. So customers require a new breed of vendor-independent support provider who understands the various individual components and how they interact."

Coven also sees "support" as involving a broader set of services, including development time, training, testing, project management, and other consulting services, as well as the technical 'hot line' service.

SUCCESS BREEDS SUCCESS

The success of the PQMS rollout has opened the door for IS to bring client-server technology to other Reader's Digest departments.

While the company does not usually divulge its development plans in advance, one likely candidate is Reader's Digest's extensive corporate art collection. More than 8,000 pieces, including works by Van Gogh, Monet, Renoir, and Picasso, as well as important contemporary artists such as Rauschenberg and Warhol, adorn Reader's Digest's domestic and international offices.

Tracking each piece's historical data, appraised value, current location, and other information, as well as creating the ability to make ad hoc inquiries to the database, will make the collection much easier to manage and improve. This application would also be likely to exploit SQLWindows' advanced image-handling capabilities.

While horror stories about first-time client-server projects abound, autocratic IS departments, overambitious managers, or short-sighted budgeting are often to blame. But with a clear focus and a team-oriented approach, there's no reason why every company's initial experience with client-server computing shouldn't be as positive as Reader's Digest's.

SOME CONSIDERATIONS FOR CLIENT-SERVER IMPLEMENTATION

Learn from Reader's Digest

Beyond Reader's Digest's immediate successes, the success of the PQMS application also illustrates some general points to consider when engineering a new information systems project:

• **Clearly define goals.** Zimmerman and his staff did not set out to completely reengineer the bidding process. They focused on automating the current procedures and providing the tools for better information access and manipulation.

• **Include users**. The development staff enlisted the support of the buyers and made them part of the team, as opposed to "customers" of the IS department. Users viewed the application as a result of their own efforts as well as those of "the computer people."

• **Leverage existing resources**. Reader's Digest strengthened the cost justification of the project by eliminating unnecessary investments. No additional end-user or network capacity or staffing was required.

• **Get outside help**. Reader's Digest didn't wait until its project was bogged down and behind schedule to get outside assistance. The IS department proactively sought out the most cost-effective support they could find and used it strategically where it was needed most.

• **Invest in training**. Reader's Digest took advantage of available training resources for both developers and end users. Again, rather than waiting for a problem to arise and then trying to fix it, Reader's Digest took a proactive approach.

Computer CHiPs

THE CHP INSTALLS A DUAL ETHERNET COMPUTER-AIDED DISPATCHING SYSTEM TO IMPROVE RESPONSE TIME.

BY MICHELLE RAE McLEAN

You're driving along Highway 101 in the San Francisco Bay Area. Suddenly the traffic slows. Inching around a recent two-car accident, you see only one driver. Is the other driver OK? Does he or she need help? Just in case, you dial 911.

You tell the operator where the accident is and as many details as you can. Help is on the way. Once again, you're glad you bought that cellular phone. But where did your call actually go? How does the California Highway Patrol (CHP) dispatch the closest patrol car or emergency vehicle?

Unbeknownst to you, your call to the CHP has entered a networked dispatching service. Thanks to a complex, fully redundant Ethernet network, with WAN links to other law enforcement databases and agencies, the CHP can respond quickly and efficiently. But the process wasn't always so speedy.

THE WAY THINGS WERE

Under the old system, operators, or call takers, wrote incident information on cards formatted for dispatching. They then placed the cards in the correct track to be moved along a conveyor belt to the appropriate dispatcher.

This system presented numerous problems. It was slow, subject to jams, noisy, and space consuming. A greater potential for human error was also inherent in the belt system; operators could put an incident card in the incorrect track, which would consequently drop it off at the wrong dispatcher.

And how could a conveyor belt system deal with urgent calls? "Oh we had a system for emergency calls. When one came in, the operator stood up and shouted to a dispatcher," recounts Frank Bowers, systems software specialist for the CHP.

Automation was in order. The CHP's Golden Gate Communications Center, located in Vallejo and serving the nine Bay Area counties, decided to install a computer-aided dispatching system. In August 1988, the CHP began the bidding process for such a statewide system. The CHP narrowed the bids down to those from three companies, but each bid significantly deviated from the original request for proposal (RFP). Such differences could have affected the cost of the project or caused the proposal to fall short of the RFP's requirements.

ROUND TWO

A second round of bidding began in May 1989, with similar results: the same three vendors were finalists, but again they failed to meet the necessary criteria. In October 1989, after a third round of bidding, a vendor won the contract. However, more than a year later the state declared the company in default for failing to deliver within the specified time.

In June 1991, the CHP awarded the contract to Andersen Consulting (Chicago), the primary contractor, which provided project management. Level II (Mercer Island, WA), the subcontractor to Andersen, specializes in law enforcement systems and wrote the computer-aided dispatching software.

The contract specified installation of the statewide computer-aided dispatching system at eight sites at a cost of $8.7 million. The Golden Gate site was the first, with plans for a new site to go on-line every four months to six months.

NEWER AND BETTER

By the time Andersen Consulting got the contract, the

Golden Gate site had gone so long without a computer-aided dispatching system that the CHP issued an emergency order to get one installed.

"The CHP wanted the system soon, so we had 90 days to get Vallejo operations," recalls Lester McEvoy, president and cofounder of Level II. To expedite installation, Level II ported the interim computer-aided dispatching software system Level II had installed in the Los Angeles Communications Center in 1989 to a new hardware platform. Andersen got the system up and running within 90 days.

The CHP and Andersen agreed to a two-phase upgrade of the interim 90-day system to the final configuration specified in the RFP. The statewide, system, minus one feature called Geo-File, had to be ready within 160 days; a version including Geo-File was expected within 280 days. Geo-File is a geographical information database dispatchers use to verify that the location of an incident is within the dispatch center's area of responsibility. Dispatchers also use it to pinpoint the location of an incident.

Andersen Consulting and Level II successfully met the deadlines in the contract. In June 1992, the CHP accepted the final version of the system. The computer-aided dispatching system not only provides quicker response times but also simplifies search processes. With the old conveyor belt system, a search required dispatchers to look through multiple boxes for the card or cards pertaining to the incident in question. The process took at least a half hour.

Now incident logs are available on-line for 60 days. They are transferred daily to a write once, read many (WORM) disc. A record search takes less than a second, a big time savings since private citizens, attorneys, law enforcement agencies, and district attorney offices, for example, may request five to 10 searches per day.

THE NETWORK

Andersen and Level II chose Stratus (Marlboro, MA) XA/R300 RISC machines to host the computer-aided dispatching systems. Four CHP regional offices, including the one in Vallejo, run both the dispatching system and a statewide MIS message switching system, also developed by Level II. Some sites run just one system or the other.

In Vallejo, Andersen installed a fully redundant 10BaseT Ethernet network (see figure, page 187). For the dispatching software, Level II embedded FTP Software's (North Andover, MA) PC/TCP as the transport protocol.

The Stratus machines are fault-tolerant, with duplexed RISC processors, memory units, disk controllers, communications and I/O controllers, disk drives, system buses, and power supplies. Each host includes two SynOptics (Santa Clara, CA) LattisNet hubs and fully duplexed Ethernet lines. The hosts run Stratus' proprietary operating system, called VOS, or virtual operating system.

The dispatching terminals are 386 ISA bus machines with duplexed Ethernet cards. The dispatchers can switch among four window to track multiple incidents simultaneously. The CHP hopes to upgrade to workstations that can display the four incident windows simultaneously.

Active incidents are dynamically updated. If one dispatcher updates a log, changes appear automatically in the logs of other dispatchers tracking the same incident.

BIG SAVINGS

This new network reduced by 50 percent the time it takes for a call taker to relay an incident to a dispatcher. "The dispatching system improves the overall efficiency of the operation of the command center," says Kin Ho, communications supervisor at the Golden Gate Communications Center.

Ho admits the duplexed Ethernet system "is expensive, but cost is not the primary issue. We can't afford to lose the lifeline to the officers in the filed. Officer safety is one of our major concerns, as is the safety of the public we serve." Besides, he says, "in the long run, it saves us money because our downtime is minimal to nonexistent."

GET THE SUPPORT YOU NEED

The Stratus machines are networked to Stratus' customer service desk, and the CHP maintains a service contract with Stratus to keep the system up and running. The Stratus machines use comparative self-checking logic on each board so that if any part fails, Stratus can pinpoint the faulty component and send a replacement the next morning. The company also calls the site to inform personnel of the failed component. The CHP's three on-site computer system technicians update and correct the day-to-day information in the dispatching system.

Level II's software is built to run in a redundant Ethernet environment. To verify that both Ethernet lines to a workstation are active, the system alternates the path used for every transaction. If a workstation is quiet for more than a minute, the system sends a signal down both lines to check that they are operational.

DIAL 911

So how does you call make its way through the system? The Vallejo site receives all cellular 911 calls, calls from roadside call boxes, hot-line calls from allied police agencies, and calls from the general public. 911 calls from hard-line telephones go directly to local agencies, which can transfer callers to the CHP. Calls from call boxes located on bridges are handled by other agencies.

The CHP's telephone system routes these calls based on priority. The 911 and hot-line calls have the highest priority and are handled in the order received; calls from the general public seeking information receive the lowest priority. The phone system routes calls to open phone lines among the call takers signed on to the system.

Call takers type the incident information into the computer-aided dispatching system. They enter information such as the location of the incident, the type of incident, and the name of the caller. If other calls come in regarding the same incident, the dispatcher can add details to the first incident or create a new incident log. Duplicate incident logs can be cross-referenced.

Information such as the call taker's and dispatcher's identity, the date and time of day, and the workstation ID automatically become part of the incident log.

KNOW YOUR PLACE

Once Geo-File validates the location of an incident log, the dispatching system automatically routes incidents to the dispatcher responsible for that area. Often callers on cellular lines are just visiting the area and need help identifying their location. Call takers become familiar with landmarks throughout the Bay Area and ask questions to figure out the caller's location.

"If you're traveling on I-880, for example, the call taker might say, 'Have you passed the Breuner's sign yet?' Based on signs you've seen already, they can figure out where you are," explains Ho.

Calls from call boxes ring on a certain bank of phone lines. Call takers determine the call box's location by pressing a key that triggers a modem signal from the PC to the call box to learn its identity. When the call box is identified, the system accesses a database of call box information and displays it on the screen. Information includes allied agencies responsible for that area and items such as the closest hospital.

If the caller just needs information, the call taker can answer questions and the incident is over. If the caller needs assistance, the call taker presses another key to automatically create an incident log and forward it to the appropriate dispatcher.

FAST DELIVERY

When incidents arrive at a dispatcher's station, the workstation sounds an alarm. When an incident is so critical that it needs to be routed immediately, a call taker routes it with just the location and the incident type. The call taker then stays on the line and continues to enter data, which appears on the dispatcher's record.

Because the dispatching system is available to other agencies and contains confidential information, the system employs various security measures. Each employee needs an ID number to log in to the dispatching system. Every transaction a dispatcher performs, including searches, information additions, and incident creations, automatically logs the employee number.

IN TRAINING

When the computer-aided dispatching system was first installed, dispatchers accustomed to the handwritten card system had to learn the computer system. "The more veteran dispatchers had a harder time adjusting. There was some psychological resistance," recalls Ho. But most dispatchers had some familiarity with computers since they used them to access other CHP databases.

After the new system was up and running, dispatchers received two weeks of training. "They had one week in the classroom and one week of hands-on training on the system," explains Ho.

New dispatchers receive more extensive training because they need to learn not only the computer system but also the protocols and procedures of dispatching. They spend two weeks in a training facility which runs a system just like the one on the dispatch floor. The training system includes a database of incidents used for practice. After trainees learn the policies and procedures of the job, they spend a month on the actual system with a dispatcher to help in any crisis.

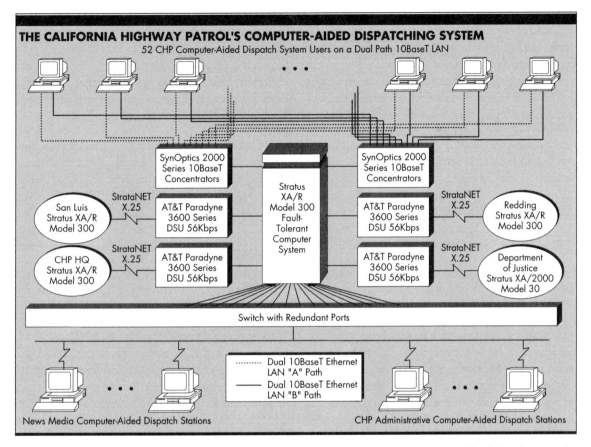

THE CALIFORNIA HIGHWAY PATROL'S COMPUTER-AIDED DISPATCHING SYSTEM
52 CHP Computer-Aided Dispatch System Users on a Dual Path 10BaseT LAN

SynOptics 2000 Series 10BaseT Concentrators

SynOptics 2000 Series 10BaseT Concentrators

San Luis Stratus XA/R Model 300

StrataNET X.25

AT&T Paradyne 3600 Series DSU 56Kbps

Stratus XA/R Model 300 Fault-Tolerant Computer System

AT&T Paradyne 3600 Series DSU 56Kbps

StrataNET X.25

Redding Stratus XA/R Model 300

CHP HQ Stratus XA/R Model 300

StrataNET X.25

AT&T Paradyne 3600 Series DSU 56Kbps

AT&T Paradyne 3600 Series DSU 56Kbps

StrataNET X.25

Department of Justice Stratus XA/2000 Model 30

Switch with Redundant Ports

.... Dual 10BaseT Ethernet LAN "A" Path
———— Dual 10BaseT Ethernet LAN "B" Path

News Media Computer-Aided Dispatch Stations

CHP Administrative Computer-Aided Dispatch Stations

It Takes Two: The computer-aided dispatching system at the Golden Gate Communications Center of the California Highway Patrol runs on a fully redundant Ethernet network.

LET ME IN

Outside agencies access the on-line information in the dispatching system. Local news media, for instance, have two options for accessing the system. They can pay for a dedicated line into the system for 24-hour access. The CHP also has two lines available for dial-up access. To ensure availability, the system disconnects calls after a set period of time.

Of the 150 possible incident types the dispatching system allows, the media see only the 30 or 35 traffic-related types. They have view-only rights to the information, so they cannot alter data or make any inquiries about law enforcement data.

Furthermore, certain information is automatically suppressed in the records the media see; the name and phone number of the person calling and any data regarding accident victims or incarcerated people is withheld. Dispatchers also have the option of blocking out other sensitive information.

CONSOLIDATING RESOURCES

Originally, the CHP maintained 27 dispatch centers, but the computer-aided systems have reduced the number of sites needed. The Golden Gate site, for instance, replaced four separate sites.

The computer systems provide a larger and more accurate database, so employees can work together at one site more effectively than they could at separate smaller sites.

Bowers offers the following example to illustrate the advantages of consolidation. A driver might have to travel three or four miles from the scene before he can pull over to a call box. The call ends up at the dispatcher responsible for the call box, but the incident actually falls within another dispatcher's territory.

When dispatchers for different areas worked in separate offices, such situations required yet another phone call and further routing of the incident to get it to the appropriate dispatcher. But with the dispatchers working in the same room, one dispatcher can simply turn around and explain the situation to another who will handle the incident.

"It's better to be at the same site than to have to make a long distance call," Bowers explains. "Plus, operators can learn larger areas and make better decisions. If you worked in Barstow, for example, and you got a call about an incident outside your jurisdiction, you would have to call another dispatch center to find out which emergency services are responsible for that area. That takes time. You've got a big delay there."

If consolidation continues, the CHP may need as few as nine sites, with some additional sites accessing the computer-aided dispatching system remotely. "Where it's economically feasible, we're putting remote in place rather than full-blown systems," explains Bowers. Users of remote dispatching terminals, which connect to Stratus machines via X.25 links, do not experience any degradation in performance. "They don't know if the computer is in the next room or if it's 400 miles away," explains Bowers.

IT'S PORTABLE

The CHP is also looking to expand a mobile digital computer project currently in place in the South Los Angeles area office. There, patrol cars have mobile digital computers communicating with the computer-aided dispatching system at the Los Angeles Communications Center. Officers can receive incident information and report their status and location on these 386 laptops running Windows, which connect via RAM Mobile Data's wireless network into the computer system.

Using these laptops, officers can substantially reduce radio frequency traffic. The mobile digital computers also let officers run license plate checks without using the radio or receiving help from a dispatcher.

Limiting traffic over the radio offers many advantages. Since dispatchers no longer have to deal with multiple officers talking on the same frequency, they have a much easier time tracking officer and incident status. "When you've got two or more units on the radio at the same time, it's impossible for a dispatcher to figure out what's going on," says Bowers. "If they have to wait for their turn, the officers don't get the service they require." But with limited radio traffic, more officers can be assigned to the same frequency.

The laptops also help in situations such as pursuits, where dispatchers have to clear the radio frequency to have constant contact with the officers pursuing a suspect. Using the laptops, other officers can continue to communicate with the dispatch system.

NOW AT A SITE NEAR YOU

As of this writing, six of the eight sites specified in the contract with Andersen Consulting and Level II are up and running. The original contract did not include installing a system at the Los Angeles site. Because Level II had just installed the interim system, the CHP decided to wait to install the statewide system. Installation at the Los Angeles site will be accomplished through a clause in the original contract with Andersen Consulting and Level II that permits the state to purchase additional computer-aided dispatching systems within three years after the original contract award.

Despite the improvements the computer-aided dispatching system provides, the CHP still has "an extensive list of enhancements we want," says Bowers. "But like any other industry, we're affected by the economy. We want a Cadillac, but we can only ask for a Chevy."

Saving Children's Lives

CENTER FOR MISSING CHILDREN DISTRIBUTES CASE INFORMATION THROUGH A VARIETY OF MEDIA.

BY LENNY LIEBMANN

Somewhere a parent's nightmare has come true. A child is missing. In the hours that follow, local law enforcement agencies do everything in their power to locate the child and apprehend the abductor. But as time passes, the case becomes more difficult to solve, and the possibility that the child has been taken to another state increases.

How is the information about this disappearance relayed to other law enforcement agencies? How do those photos of missing children get printed on the fliers and milk cartons you see every day? And how do phone tips from one part of the country get correlated to cases that originated elsewhere?

The answer is the National Center for Missing and Exploited Children (Arlington, VA). Founded in 1984 in association with the Adam Walsh Children's Fund, the Center operates under a contract with the Department of Justice and receives supplemental private funding. The Center acts as a clearinghouse for a variety of law enforcement and child welfare agencies throughout the country (see Figure 1). As such, the Center serves as the critical channel for the management of information that can save a child's life and a parent's dreams.

THE NETWORK

The Center's core network consists of a 92-node Arcnet LAN. Among the nodes are: PCs that serve the Center's more than 50 staff members, the in-house training facility, and six employees of an associated organization on the same site; four file servers; more than a dozen print, fax, and backup servers; and nine external communications links.

The file servers are an assortment of 386 and 486 ISA, EISA, and LocalBus machines. Applications are run on the machine most appropriate for their requirements, so all internal users have access to all servers. Cumulatively, the four servers give the Center approximately 1.4GB of on-line memory.

Most of the external communications links reside on a J&L Communications (Chatsworth, CA) Chatterbox that includes a multiline DigiBoard (Eden Prairie, MN) and an Intel (Hillsboro, OR) fax card running FACSys software from Optus (Somerset, NJ). These lines provide system access for remote users, as well as certain designated vendors, such as developers and accountants. They also give the Center access to the FBI National Crime Information Center (NCIC) mainframe and to on-line services, in particular CompuServe and Lexis.

THE ORGANIZATION

The Center's case-handling organization is divided into three main functional areas: the hotline and the case-management and case-analysis departments.

The hotline fields between 500 and 600 phone calls per day, and operates 24 hours a day, seven days a week. The calls include questions about cases, requests for literature, and other inquiries that do not relate to actual cases. Those that do relate to abductions are divided into two categories: new cases, referred to as "intakes," and information about possible victims and perpetrators, referred to as "leads."

Hotline operators use a customized data entry application called HMIS, or Hotline Management Information Service. If the call is about a new case, the information is labeled an intake, and several actions take place automatically:

• The intake is added to the case-management queue.

• Four copies are printed on the case-management printer.

• The appropriate state clearinghouse is notified.

• An abbreviated form of the intake is added to the Center's historical database of all cases.

These automated actions are indicative of how the Center has devised its own approach to workflow. By linking database events with other databases, departments, and outside agencies, the Center ensures quick communications and avoids missteps in the case-handling process.

When the call is about a lead, a window pops up showing the active cases. The operator can then determine if the lead can easily be correlated to an existing case. If so, the database captures the case number, and the assigned case manager is notified. If not, the lead is marked appropriately, put in the lead queue, and printed.

Intakes are assigned to the case-management staff. Staff members are primarily retired police officers with experience in juvenile cases. Their job is to work with parents, law enforcement agencies, and the case-analysis department to ensure every effort is made to locate missing children.

With six case managers sharing a typical active load of approximately 6,500 cases, automation is essential. The Center's case-management system is designed to relieve the case managers of as much administrative work as possible. "Ticklers" ensure that each case is reviewed at appropriate intervals. Macros cut the time it takes to fill in forms and generate reports. And the core suite of database applications gives the managers instant access to case information.

The first goal in handling a case is to make it *media ready*, which means that the vital information on the child's age, appearance, and the circumstances of his or her disappearance are collected and put together with the best, most recent photograph available. The Center refers to this combination of data and image as a *poster*. Most of us are familiar with these posters, ubiquitously present in our mail, on packaging, in publications, and on television.

Leads go to the case-analysis department. Here a variety of techniques correlate incoming information with specific disappearances. Case-analysis staff members use the Center's databases to search for common threads, such as an abductor's occupation or the circumstance of the abduction. Or they may use software such as MapInfo (from the eponymous Troy, NY company) to plot leads by loca-

tion. Using a combination of computing resources and the staff's analytical acumen, the Center has achieved a remarkable 80-percent resolution rate for its cases over the last three years.

POSTER CIRCULATION

The effective circulation of posters is critical to the Center's mission. The Center provides posters to 43 state clearinghouses and to companies in the private sector, such as direct-mail giant Advo, which regularly print and distribute the information as a public service. In addition, the Center must be able to quickly meet the ad hoc requests of various police departments, public agencies, media outlets, and other interested parties for specific posters.

The need to circulate posters quickly and on a large scale constitutes a unique technical challenge. Because the Center has no control over how these other agencies are equipped, it must be able to deliver posters in a variety of ways. "We basically have to address the lowest common denominator," says Bob Thomas, the Center's director of information systems.

The most basic means of distributing the posters is via hard copy. Originally, creating hard copy involved bringing a data printout and a photograph to an offset printer, who had to shoot a halftone image, lay out the poster, and then run 100 pieces at a time. "The printing process was costly and time-consuming," says Thomas. "And we would always wind up with a wasted inventory of posters on resolved cases."

Now, thanks to an application built free of charge by Steve Mann of Pegasus Imaging (Tampa, FL) and a Sony video printer, the Center can produce high-quality posters suitable for print reproduction on an as-needed basis.

The application allows linked data and images to be produced in a variety of standardized formats. These formats feature either a photograph of the child only, photographs of both the child and the abductor, or a photograph of the child accompanied by an age-progression image. The application also allows the Center to produce single-case posters or multiple-case formats for more efficient distribution.

LIFE-SAVING FAXES

Fax capability provides another critical link to the outside world. The universal presence of fax machines makes

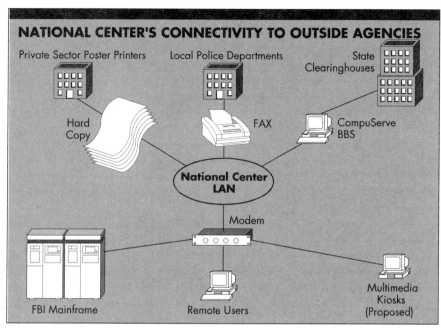

NATIONAL CENTER'S CONNECTIVITY TO OUTSIDE AGENCIES

Private Sector Poster Printers

Local Police Departments

State Clearinghouses

Hard Copy

FAX

CompuServe BBS

National Center LAN

Modem

FBI Mainframe

Remote Users

Multimedia Kiosks (Proposed)

Figure 1. The Center acts as a clearinghouse for state and national organizations and distributes its lifesaving information using faxes, BBS, and eventually, multimedia kiosks.

it the quickest and most reliable means of getting posters distributed on both a routine procedural and emergency basis. In addition, because the Center uses a fully integrated network fax server, fax transmissions are faster and cleaner than they would be with a conventional fax machine.

Thomas relates one case in which a fax resulted directly in the arrest of a perpetrator and the return of two children who had been missing for more than a year. An anonymous tip to a local police department prompted the town's sheriff to call the Center's hotline, which in turn relayed the call to case management.

When Ben Ermini, the Center's director of case management offered to immediately fax the case poster, which showed both the children and the abductor, the sheriff expressed a great deal of skepticism. He had received many faxed photographs and found them of little use in identifying suspects, since they usually came through as muddy, low-detail images.

"When he saw the quality of the halftone that appeared on his office machine, he couldn't believe it," says Ermini. Within half an hour, he was able to positively identify the children and arrest their abductor. The children were home the next day.

The Center has also made progress in its ability to distribute posters electronically. With grants and contribu-

tions from vendors (including IBM, Sony, and Codex), the Center has been able to provide the state clearinghouses with a consistent hardware and software configuration.

The configuration includes a 386SX PC with CD-ROM and a modem, along with essential software: WordPerfect, CompuServe Information Manager, PCAnywhere, and a component of the Center's own database application. The Center also tries to ensure uniformity among clearinghouses by providing initial training at its own facility.

Thus equipped, the clearinghouses are able to use a private CompuServe forum to help deliver the poster images as well as other important documents, such as relevant legislation. The CompuServe link provides an e-mail connection for simplified communications with the Center and between the clearinghouses themselves.

The Center does not yet have facilities for transmitting digital images to law enforcement agencies via modem. Although the Center can provide the dial-in link, distribution of the client software for viewing, printing, and cataloging posters is problematic at present. The use of computers by local law enforcement is still in its early stages, and many police departments lack even the most rudimentary communications resources.

The Center also has ambitious plans for a new, more public, information infrastructure. With the assistance of

IBM, the Center is developing its own network of remote multimedia kiosks for installation in airports, shopping centers, and other strategic locations.

These PS/2-based kiosks will provide full-motion video and sound displays of both active cases and informational programs on child safety. Using wide-area links, the Center will be able to instantly update and revise the programming at an individual kiosk or at a group of them.

Civic-minded companies sponsoring their own sites will probably underwrite the cost of the kiosks. By supplementing existing media outlets with its own network for disseminating data, the Center will significantly enhance its use of on-line data to locate children and save lives.

IMAGING CHALLENGES

The ability to share images across these various platforms–print, fax, LAN, modem, CompuServe BBS, and digital video–depends on a variety of file-conversion processes. The central application uses a modified JPEG file, which offers the right combination of compression and quality.

According to Pegasus Imaging's Mann, the Center is able to store complete poster data in less than 18K per case, which is approximately one-third the memory that the image alone would require stored as a TIFF file. This compression capability is important not only to keep the Center's storage needs to a minimum but also to permit the display of 16-color gray-scale images on low-end 286s with VGA monitors.

The JPEG images must also be transferred to the video printer which produces the Center's hard copy and converted for the video-based software that the Center's experts use to create the age-progression images helpful in solving long-term disappearances.

The system must convert these files to PCX format for them to be useable by the fax server. The PCX file must also be a well-defined halftone image. (*Halftoning* is the technique used to create the illusion of gray tones in a printed black-and-white image.)

The exceptional photographic quality of the Center's faxes is the result of a sophisticated approach to this conversion, which yields crisp halftone "dots" at a density of 200 lines per inch to match the resolution of the fax machine on the receiving end.

The CompuServe BBS requires yet another format:

GIF. This format is even more compressed, minimizes the burden on the relatively low-speed modem links, and provides common access to uploaded images. The Center found its method for converting JPEG to GIF in IBM's Audio Visual Connection, the platform selected for the multimedia kiosks.

Other formatting and conversion challenges continue to be addressed as the Center adds to its technology base. The use of desktop publishing applications may result in the need to share PostScript files electronically. The Center also plans to purchase higher-resolution laser printers, increasing their capability from 300 dots per inch (dpi) to 600 dpi.

The mechanics of the Center's poster production and distribution point up some key issues for interorganizational image-oriented applications. Primary among these issues is that of file formats. The lack of a common file format–or a universally accepted conversion medium–is a serious, though surmountable, challenge to widespread image distribution. This problem becomes especially challenging for such organizations as the Center which deals with a heterogeneous community of users, including some that are technically unsophisticated.

This lack of standard file formats directly affects the second issue, which is the selection of the most effective mode of communications. Remote access is complicated by the fact that users have not yet standardized on a method. And again, because of the client community's heterogeneity, traditional e-mail or advanced electronic data interchange (EDI) links are not practical. Instead, the Center is forced to use a pragmatic mix of hard copy, fax, and a secure BBS.

Format and communications issues will also be critical for the Center's projected move into digital video. In addition to the multimedia kiosks, the Center envisions a broader use of video as a supplement to the use of posters.

"Full-motion video and sound will provide an even better means of identification," says Jesse Bensen, the Center's IBM account representative. "And with the proliferation of home video recording, we will have a rich supply of material to draw from."

The Center plans to convert videotape provided by the family of the missing child to digital format and then provide edited sequences to local law enforcement agencies. For this scenario to become workable, a common standard will have to emerge for digital video. And the Center will have to establish much faster communications links to local law enforcement agencies.

DISTRIBUTION MANAGEMENT

A third issue is distribution management. Sharing posters with the outside world is not sufficient. To do its job effectively, the Center must also maintain security and accountability.

The Center must be accountable for its distribution of poster and other case information for a variety of reasons. Each case must receive its fair share of publicity. Resolved cases must be deactivated as quickly as possible so that distribution resources are not wasted. Concerned parents want to know what is being done to locate their child. The Center also tries to accommodate the conditions set by companies which distribute posters on a pro bono basis.

Hard copy is easy to track because the individual who sends it out can log his or her own activity. Fax activity is also simple to document through the capabilities of both the fax server and the applications that send files to the fax queue. The BBS is essentially self-documenting, leaving a trail of what activity has taken place; all active cases are posted and only the state clearinghouses have access to it.

The obvious personal and legal sensitivity of the matters it handles make security a primary concern for the Center. Because they don't involve direct access to any part of the Center's network, the current communications media–hard copy, fax, and BBS–all offer a high degree of protection from both unauthorized eavesdropping and malicious data modifications.

Any dial-in access to the Center would have to address these security and accountability issues. This necessity adds another level of complexity to the remote access method, above and beyond the questions of communications and file formats. The Center may therefore opt for an expansion of the BBS to service outside agencies rather than implement full remote access. Its staff is still reviewing the options.

EXPANDING INFLUENCE

The Center's success has made it an important resource for other public welfare agencies across the country and around the world. The hotline now dispatches reports to the National Runaway Hotline in Chicago since cases involving runaways do not fall under the Center's specific mission.

The FBI makes extensive use of the Center's research and analysis facilities. And the Center is initiating a new Safe Return operation for victims of Alzheimer's Disease who, because they are prone to becoming disoriented, require similar identification and location services.

The Center also offers consulting services for law enforcement agencies that want to implement computer technology. "One of our mandates is to provide technical instruction and assistance," says Ermini.

According to Ermini, some of the local police departments that call the Center for help are still tracking missing persons on 3-by-5 index cards. As a model developer of computerized case management, the Center freely shares its expertise and experience.

The Center has also been a trailblazer in building relationships with the private sector. "We've been very fortunate with the computer industry," says Ermini. "When we've looked for a solution to a technical problem, they've been right there to show us what their latest technology can do."

Because it has been able to work so effectively with high-tech companies as well as the businesses that assist it in the distribution of posters, the Center has been able to equip itself much better than it could under its budget alone. Such equipment allows it to boost its performance and to teach other agencies how to make the most of the charitable instincts of the business community.

The Center is a prime example of just how valuable the effective distribution of information can be. It shows how a relatively low-tech configuration of databases, imaging tools, and communications links can deliver outstanding results when properly applied to operational objectives. And the Center's success dramatizes how the computer industry, dedicated to boosting business productivity and profitability, can also have a powerful effect on human lives.

If you have a product or service that you believe could assist the Center in its mission, write or call: National Center for Missing and Exploited Children, 2101 Wilson Blvd., Suite 550, Arlington, VA 22201, (703) 235-3900; fax: (703) 235-4067.

The French Connection

US WEST IMPORTS FRANCE'S MINITEL–THE WORLD'S MOST POPULAR VIDEOTEX NETWORK–HOPING AMERICANS LIKE IT AS MUCH AS THEY DO BORDEAUX AND BRIE.

BY SUKETU MEHTA

If you to go France for any length of time, you'll notice that very few people use the yellow pages for anything. And, if you're in a hotel in Paris and you want to see what movies are playing on the Rue Champollion or check out the time of the next train to Lyons, your concierge won't look at the newspaper or pull out a printed timetable. He'll turn to a little terminal at his side, tap a few keys, and in a minute, you'll have the information you requested. What is this oracular terminal, you ask your concierge. "Ah, monsieur," he responds, his chest puffed up with justified national pride. "Eet eez ze Minitel."

Minitel is the "electronic workhorse" of France–the biggest on-line database in the world and the biggest server in France. In less than a decade, this videotex-based network has become an essential part of the life of the French. Through more than 6 million terminals, 40 percent of the French population has access to Minitel. In 1991, the information-hungry French placed a staggering 1.65 billion calls to the 18,000 services offered. So successful is the Minitel network in France that it has deterred PC-based database providers such as CompuServe and Prodigy from gaining a foothold in that country.

And now Minitel has arrived in America.

AN ELECTRONIC YELLOW PAGES

The Minitel success story started as an experiment in 1978. France Telecom, the state telephone monopoly, had a reputation for running the most antiquated phone system in Western Europe. So nobody paid much notice when the company decided to start a videotex information service. Videotex services in Europe are divided between those based on a TV set and those based on a dedicated termi-

nal. After lots of field trials, France Telecom decided to go with a terminal-based service, because it generated more traffic than a TV-based one.

The single biggest reason France Telecom launched Minitel was to give its users access to an electronic telephone directory. The paper directory is costly and difficult to update, whereas an electronic one can be updated instantly. France Telecom's electronic directory service was launched in parallel with the unveiling of the network, and, along with the directory of Minitel services and the Minicom user mailboxes, are the only information services provided directly by France Telecom. The remaining database services, more than 18,000 of them issuing forth from more than 4,000 host computers, are provided by some 8,000 independent information providers.

At the outset, France Telecom did something that won over reluctant users unaccustomed to anything that looked like a computer: It gave away the terminals free to anybody with a telephone line, making signing on to the network risk-free. Telephone subscribers were given the choice of receiving a paper telephone directory or a Minitel terminal.

"It was important to get the information providers to create services, so we had to distribute a large number of terminals," explains Catherine Rouet, a marketing strategist at France Telecom. The basic terminal is still free; users pay only for the services they consult and for more sophisticated terminals that come with an array of features, from a portable notebook to one with a voice/data answering machine.

THE TELETEL NETWORK

The videotex network behind the Minitel system is

called Teletel, which is the name of the presentation protocol it uses. The Teletel network works as follows. When the user, from her Minitel terminal or a PC equipped with emulation software, dials into the telephone network, she is connected to a videotex access point. The access point then routes the call via Transpac, the French public X.25 packet-switching network, to a host computer containing the database the user has requested (see Figure 1).

The videotex access points, of which there are 123 in France and more in overseas departments of the country such as Guadeloupe and Martinique, are built by Alcatel (Paris) and are essentially intelligent telephone switches. Each access point has an interface to the telephone network on one side and an X.25 interface to Transpac on the other side. Each contains a service provider file, which is a listing of X.25 addresses. When the user keys in the keyword of the service she wants, the access point looks up the full address of the service provider and routes the call accordingly. The access point also bills users through the telephone network.

Considering the immense amount of data on the system, how does the network sort through the queries? The system employs three methods of text search and retrieval. The first is a search through a hierarchical system, or a "tree" structure. Here, the user asks, for example, to see a listing of railway timetables. In her next query, she chooses a particular route and then orders the tickets.

The second method of sorting is a multicriterion search, where the user specifies at the beginning several different criteria that narrow down her search and make it faster. The third method is a natural language search, where the user says directly, "I want to rent a flat in Paris," and the system responds with a listing of rental agencies. The France Telecom electronic directory, for example, allows this kind of natural language search.

A recent innovation in the Minitel system is the LECAM smart-card reader. The reader is a small box that sits on top of a Minitel terminal and accepts cards conforming to the ISO IS7816 standard for data cards. With the reader, users actually pay for services right through their Minitel, without having to key in their credit-card numbers. SNCF, the French railway company, already accepts payment for tickets through LECAM. Users get the card through their bank, which debits their account directly for purchases. Another function of LECAM is to con-trol access to confidential databases. This security feature is useful in applications such as medical databases for which a simple password is not enough–the card provides an extra degree of verification.

For the future, Rouet says France Telecom is field-testing terminals capable of faster access, up from the 1,200bps used now to 9,600bps, and will decide this year if it will upgrade the entire system to 9,600bps. The faster access speed would, among other things, enable the transmission of still photos. A color Minitel will also be offered to niche markets. Already, guests at the Hotel New York at EuroDisney in Europe enjoy a color Minitel in each bedroom.

AN AMERICAN IN PARIS

After the success of Minitel in France, France Telecom started looking to expand the service overseas, and it contacted US West, one of the largest Baby Bells. One of the biggest problems standing in the way of US West offering an information service over telephone lines was cleared by a 1988 court decision to give the regional Bell operating companies (RBOCs) greater flexibility to operate in the data communications market. A number of the RBOCs took advantage of this regulatory change to open gateways through which users can make a single call to a local number to browse through and connect to the services available. The RBOCs were allowed for the first time to charge users on their telephone bills for on-line time. Previously, the only way users could pay for on-line time was through credit-card billing or by prepaying.

In 1989, US West and France Telecom decided to enter into a joint venture called Community Link Minitel (CLM) Associates, which started a Minitel-type network called Community Link. First test-marketed in Omaha, NE, the service came on-line in 1993 in Minneapolis/St. Paul and is now starting up in Seattle. Next to receive the glorious benefits of Community Link are other cities in the US West empire, such as Denver and Phoenix. The total time to launch the project is estimated to be four years, and the company expects 800,000 clients to be on-line in the next decade.

A PILLAR OF THE COMMUNITY

The Community Link service uses a mainframe architecture consisting of a gateway application processor

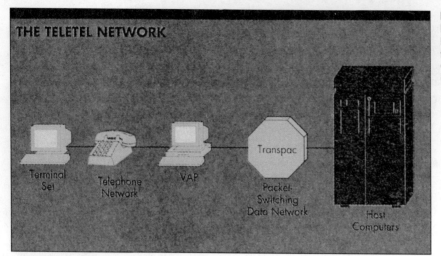

THE TELETEL NETWORK

Terminal Set · Telephone Network · VAP · Transpac · Packet-Switching Data Network · Host Computers

Figure 1. The Teletel network is the French videotex network behind Minitel. From a Minitel terminal, calls go through the telephone network to a videotex access point and are routed from there through Transpac.

(GAP), the overall management system, and a router that administers the network communications (see Figure 2). When a user wants a connection to a service, the GAP transports the call to the Information Service Provider (ISP) system. Once connected, the router links the user's terminal or computer to the ISP. A packet-switched network handles the switching among ISPs and users.

The GAP is connected to the Digipac X.25 packet-switched network. ISPs in the US West calling area use Digipac to connect directly to Community Link. ISPs beyond the calling area connect via a variety of value-added networks or an interexchange carrier's network. At present, the interexchange carriers that provide connections outside the Minneapolis LATA (Local Access and Transmission Area), for example, are Accunet, Sprintnet, Infonet, and BT North America.

Community Link is similar to Minitel in most respects, but it is also significantly different. For example, when a French user wants to look up a name in the telephone directory, her call does not have to go through the United States. But a user in Minneapolis who wants the same information must first take the electronic version of a stroll along the boulevards of Paris. Her call is actually routed to a host in Paris where the Minneapolis directory is stored. This routing takes place because the US West-France Telecom group that provides the Minneapolis electronic telephone directory is based in Paris. However, as far as the user is concerned, this process is transparent. Response time is a couple of seconds.

A TERMINAL CASE

Terminals offered by France Telecom and US West use ASCII (or ANSI X3.64, which is almost the same thing) and Teletel. ASCII is capable of displaying text only. The Teletel presentation protocol is the one the Minitel and Community Link terminals use to display text and graphics. The Teletel screen supports a display of 25 rows with 40 characters per row, or, in what is known as Teletel *mixed mode*, 24 rows of 80 characters per row, with the top row remaining at 40 characters. It supports color displays of up to eight foreground and eight background colors. The Teletel protocol also provides additional character sets not found in ASCII (such as accented European characters); allows forward and reverse scrolling; supports double-height and -width character sizes; and can feature flashing characters.

Presently, US West offers its customers two types of terminals: an M2B terminal manufactured by Phillips (Eindhoven, Netherlands) and an Exeltel II terminal by Alcatel. Both terminals support ANSI X3.64 and Teletel presentation protocols. The terminals have monochrome monitors and a built-in 1,200-baud modem. In addition to the standard keyboard, both terminals have a telephone keypad and the nine Teletel function keys, <Index>, <Cancel>, <Previous>, <Repeat>, <Guide>, <Correction>, <Line/Local>, <Send>, and<Next>. Both also have two user-programmable keys, <Phone> and<ID>., that store frequently used numbers and the user's Community Link account number.

In addition to these features, the Exeltel II terminal offers these enhancements:

• It has a telephone handset, which, when used with the keypad, allows the user to make voice calls.

• The keypad includes pause, hook flash, and redial keys.

• Other keys store up to 40 speed-dial numbers. Ten of these can be used for data calls to host computers.

• It has a port to connect the terminal to a printer. This connection allows the user to print information received from an information service.

• A Community Link function key allows the user to automate the call and sign-on procedures with a single keystroke.

For access to Community Link, the terminal must send a service-request signal that identifies the modem's speed and terminal parity. This signal allows Digipac to complete the terminal's connection to Community Link. The Exeltel II terminal automatically sends the service-request signal upon connection to Digipac, but the M2B requires the user to enter the service request signal manually.

In addition to terminals, the service can also be accessed through a PC equipped with emulation software and a modem. US West supplies the emulation software to its subscribers.

SERVICE PROVIDERS

Community Link presents a potential bonanza for ISPs who want to take advantage of US West's large installed base of telephone subscribers. ISPs need to have three features if they want to offer a service over Community Link:

1. Hardware and software that supports ANSI X3.64, Teletel, or both presentation protocols.

2. Hardware and software that supports an X.25 packet-switching connection to Digipac (or offers connection directly through a packet assembler/disassembler).

3. Analog or digital leased lines for connection to Digipac or a connection through an interexchange packet-switching network.

ISPs don't have to own and operate their own equipment. A number of service bureaus can handle all the hardware, software, and network connections. Some of the bureaus also help design the service to work well with the relevant protocols. What service bureaus can't tell an ISP is what kind of service to offer. But, if the French can serve as guides, the opportunities for U.S. ISPs are vast. Think of

an exotic group of fetishists, such as armpit worshippers, start a chat line exclusively for them (Pit Meet?), and you're in business. Or, offer all the information available in some arcane field, such as Home Arugula Growing, and start a database. Already, there exist ISPs selling everything from pediatric advice (All Pediatric Hints) to your personal horoscope (Astro Prediction–Delphi).

Meanwhile, users, even if they are not subscribers to Community Link, can access any of the 18,000 services on Minitel as transparently as if they were sitting in France. New York-based Minitel Services Co., a venture jointly owned by France Telecom and Infonet, has its own gateway to Minitel in France. The company has been providing individual users access to Teletel-based networks in other countries since 1987 and inaugurated its X.25 connection with Community Link last year.

When a Community Link subscriber wants to access any one of a package of French Minitel services, her call goes through Digipac, then via Infonet to the Minitel Services gateway in New York. This gateway consists of two Motorola (Arlington Heights, IL) minicomputers linked to an Ethernet and equipped with an X.25 interface. The gateway identifies the call, routes it to the correct service, and bills the user. Through the international Infonet network, the call goes out to service providers in France or elsewhere. "We use Infonet to operate in 23 countries," says Jean-Pierre Cacara, the company's director of technology.

Users who want to access French services log into the gateway through the public switched telephone network. All they need is an IBM PC or Macintosh and a modem; the company provides free software, and there are no sign-up charges. Sample rates are 25 cents per minute to access the French telephone directory and 45 cents per minute to exchange mail with users of Minicom, the Minitel mailbox service. The most popular service is the chat line Aline, operated by the French magazine *Nouvel Observateur*, where you can exchange salacious conversation with lonely Parisians.

MINITEL MA BELLE

US West will have to face the same problem France Telecom encountered in the early years of Minitel: What certain users really want from the service is a porno line. Paris is full of posters of scantily clad women with cryptic slogans such as "3615 LOLA." Lola and her cohorts on

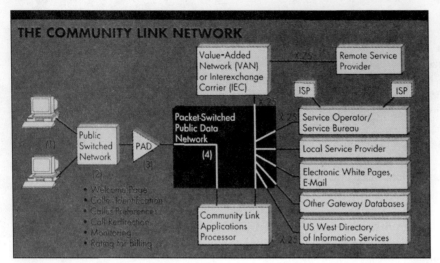

Figure 2. A call to the Community Link Gateway is passed through the public-switched telephone network (2) to an access point of an X.3 Packet Assembler/Disassembler (3). An X.25 session is established through the Digipac packet-switched network with the gateway application processor (4).

other pornographic chat lines are what rescued Minitel financially and still bring in enormous revenues both for their operators as well as France Telecom. US telephone companies are well acquainted with the cursed blessings of porno voice lines, and now a new dimension is about to enter the lives of lonely onanists all across the US West telephone territory.

So pervasive were the porno lines in France, that the authorities had to set up a special committee, the CCKTT (Consultative Committee for the Kiosk in Telephone and Telematics), to regulate the services on Minitel, deciding what is prohibited by French law (very little is). The pornographic services offer interactive dialogue with a seductive, skilled typist of your choice. Some of them provide the terminal-based equivalent of X-rated movies, transmitting to your Minitel a succession of screens displaying stick fig-

ures copulating in jerky movements reminiscent of the early silent films. Lines of dialogue flash across the bottom of the screen, in case you're not sure what's going on, which is often the case since the graphic resolution is so poor that your parents' prophecy will come horribly true and you will go blind.

An advantage to going directly via Minitel Services Co. (vs. going through Community Link) is that the package of French services offered through Community Link is censored. "US West was concerned with the porno services in France," says CeCe Drummond, marketing manager for Minitel Services Co. "When we package the services for Community Link, we have to take them out. A user on Community Link cannot reach any of them."

One way or another, France Telecom and US West are determined to bring Minitel Mania to the United States.

LANs in Transition

TRANSAMERICA LEASING RECENTLY COMPLETED A CORPORATE MOVE. THANKS TO GOOD PLANNING AND AN EXPERIENCED RELOCATION SERVICES VENDOR, ALL WENT WELL.

BY PAUL DONOHOE

It's Wednesday afternoon and you just finished putting out the last fire from Monday. Rumors have been circulating for months that your company will be moved (someplace close you hope) and you wonder if you need to plan accordingly.

The phone rings and from the caller ID you can tell it's the VP of Information Services calling. Uh oh.

"Hello, this is John."

"Hi John. I'm sure you have heard the rumors that the company is relocating. Well, they are true. Don't be worried, though, we are only moving to the next town, and into a real class-A building, too. The move is scheduled for four months from now and I'd like you to handle the IS part of the move. I've got time at 4:30 this afternoon. Why don't you bring any questions you have and rough out your thoughts about a plan, and we'll discuss it then. Oh, by the way, the formal announcement won't be made for another day or two, so keep this confidential, OK?"

"Sure."

"Fine, see you at 4:30 in my office."

What an opportunity to stand out. But since you're running mission-critical applications on the LANs, you could be in big trouble if the move doesn't go as scheduled. Also, how can you possibly prepare for the meeting with the VP in two and a half hours, without telling anyone else about the move?

Are you a candidate for corporate relocation? You might be. According to Dennis Donovan, senior managing director of The Wadley-Donovan Group, a corporate location consultant firm in Morristown, NJ, chances are increasing that your company will relocate in the next three to six years. Although corporate relocations in 1993 were expected to be down about 35 percent from their high point in 1988, they are expected to increase in the following years as the United States, Europe, and Japan come out of the recession. In addition, moves within the same county seem to be on the rise, driven by factors such as the continuing trend to downsize and reengineer, increased competition forcing companies to reduce all expenses including rents, and the depressed commercial real estate market in much of the country that is providing opportunities for successful companies to upgrade space at little or no extra cost.

MOVE IT AND LEASE IT

In the case of Transamerica Leasing, the motives included a need for more, usable space, an acknowledgment that the Transamerica Leasing "knowledge workers" required a different kind of space, and a desire to provide equal or better services for employees in a better quality building. Lawrence Kalish, the director of facility management who was responsible for the move, sums it up: "Our objective was to provide better, more usable space for everybody."

A subsidiary of Transamerica Corp., Transamerica Leasing leases containers and trailers to transportation companies around the world and has more than 800,000 20-foot containers in inventory. The Transamerica Leasing corporate headquarters move only took them five miles away from White Plains to Purchase in Westchester county, NY, but it involved 400 employees and 120,000 square feet of office space.

The distributed computing environment that had to be relocated included 196 PCs, five networks, and mainframe connectivity to an IBM ES9000 Model 620. Lease contract information is maintained on the mainframe. Users throughout the headquarters use the PCs to communicate to the mainframe and to perform mission-critical tasks in marketing, legal, and tax departments. The installed equipment includes:

- 27 IBM PCs and XTs;
- 12 IBM ATs;
- 102 various IBM PS/2s;
- 16 Compaq 286 and 386 machines;
- 31 Toshiba and Compaq portables and laptops;
- 8 miscellaneous clones; and
- 150 dot matrix and laser printers.

Fifty-five of the PCs had direct connections to the mainframe via emulation boards. The five existing LANs were:
- Information Services: 16 workstations on Ethernet using the NetWare 3.11 NOS;
- Marketing: 10 workstations on Ethernet and a Novell PCOX gateway to an IBM mainframe using NetWare 2.15;
- Tax: 10 workstations on a Token Ring using NetWare 3.11;
- Human Resources: three workstations on a Token Ring using NetWare 3.11; and
- Legal: three workstations on Ethernet using LANtastic.

For the organization to continue business in a normal manner after the move, it was essential that the networks and PCs be moved on schedule and be fully functional immediately after the move. Kalish says that the keys to a successful move like the one he engineered at Transamerica Leasing are planning, teamwork, communication, dedicated people, and the support and involvement of upper management.

Everything about the move was planned, down to the details such as determining who would have access to which elevators at what time. The target date of June 25 for the actual move date was set in February, and the date was met. (Kalish had a backup plan for two weeks later in case construction at the new site was delayed.) Kalish kept an overall project plan that was updated on a daily basis. Each department level or functional team was responsible for maintaining its own strategy and updating the master plan.

Teams did the planning and execution. Top management participated in Kalish's team and set the goals and standards. Kalish encouraged and required outside vendors to participate in team meetings and fostered a "we are all in this together" attitude. Representatives from the architectural consulting firm, construction managers, engineer-

ing consultants, and moving company participated in various teams.

Communication between the employee population and the teams became a top priority. A relocation liaison team, composed of representatives from each of the departments, was responsible for communicating the plans and progress reports to the departments and for bringing feedback to the team. Kalish says: "It was the function of the liaison team to focus on making people aware of what was happening. The personal communication and involvement made the process work."

In addition, the company published a special newsletter, "Movin' Up the Road," to provide another communication vehicle. The newsletter came out several times during the period between the announcement and the move, and the last page of the four-page newsletter was a form for asking confidential questions about the move. The forms went through the Human Resources department, and the newsletter published some of the answers. Teams communicated primarily during meetings held every five to 10 days.

When the announcement was made in February, Joseph Napolitano, Information Services vice-president, understood the critical nature of the move and chose Ron Palmieri, Quality Assurance manager for the PC Support Group, to direct the team responsible for the IS portion of the move. Palmieri immediately pulled together a team from IS and started to develop a strategy.

This process resulted in a 23-page plan that provided the details for the move. Initially, Palmieri planned to use only internal resources for the move, but various issues indicated that using an outside vendor for the removal and reinstallation of the workstations and networks might be a better choice. Since the team had upgrades and installations they wanted to do at the same time as the move, Palmieri considered they might need to use three different companies: one to reinstall the standalone PCs, one for the NetWare upgrades and LAN moves, and another familiar with converting a LANtastic network to NetWare Lite.

During the selection process Palmieri talked to a number of companies, but only PC Technical Services of Elmsford, NY, had the experience and capability to do all three parts of the project. PC Tech had been maintaining Transamerica Leasing's LANs for a few years, and Palmieri had confidence in their abilities. In addition, as a subsidiary of Gorham Clark, a network integration firm based in New

York City and a member of USConnect, PC Tech had additional resources available if necessary. Selecting PC Tech as the single vendor made communications easier within the PC Support Group team and meant there would only be one project manager to coordinate all the vendor activities.

With the vendor selected, the team proceeded to fill out the details of the plan. Although the support group had some idea of the equipment base, they took a complete physical inventory, including serial numbers of all components, descriptions, user name, location, and destination. This inventory proved extremely valuable during the actual move, when the movers delivered parts of systems to the wrong destinations.

Next, decisions had to be made about network upgrades and changes. Since the new building had been wired for Token Ring, the existing LANs in marketing, IS, and the legal department needed to be changed to Token Ring. The marketing file server needed additional memory and needed to be upgraded from NetWare 2.15 to 3.11. The Novell PCOX on the marketing LAN had to be converted to NetWare SAA since PCOX would not be supported by 3.11. Various marketing PCs needed to be upgraded to DOS 5.0, and Lotus 1-2-3 had to be installed on the network. The legal department's LAN had to be converted to NetWare Lite.

After team meetings with PC Tech, it was decided that the hardware upgrade to the marketing file server, the upgrading of the workstations to DOS 5.0, and the Lotus installation would be done before the move. The NetWare upgrade would be done during the move. Initially, the installation of the NetWare SAA was planned for before the move, but when the NetWare upgrade was postponed until the move, so was the SAA, since drivers were not available for 2.15. Those postponements meant the most critical part of the move would be the NetWare upgrade and SAA install.

Based on the inventory and outline of the upgrades and changes, the team began laying out the details of the physical move. Floor plans of both the old and new locations were color-coded to indicate locations of priority PCs, network nodes, and mainframe emulation workstations. A "tag and bag" system was developed to identify equipment during the move. Each individual piece of equipment was to be tagged with color-coded labels that matched the color codes used on the floor plans. All cables, mice, boot diskettes, and other small items were placed in large resealable plastic bags and the bag was labeled as part of the system.

While the team was managing its preparations using its own task list, PC Technical Services prepared a project plan using Suretrak project scheduler from Primavera Systems (Bala Cynwyd, PA). Cindy Connors, the project manager for PC Tech, thinks using the scheduler was one of the reasons the project succeeded. "We used the plan during project meetings to chart our progress. Critical unfinished tasks were obvious from the graphical presentation and we were able to redirect resources and attention to tasks needing them," she says.

The IS team took its job very seriously. Palmieri credits "the dedication and determination of the people to get the job done on time and with minimal loss of services to the users. They wanted the move to be perfect." The team had backups for every problem they could think of and even backups for situations that they could not have expected. For example, although PC Tech had installed NetWare SAA before and was familiar with the product, it took the precaution of opening a support call with Novell before the actual move date since it expected that the actual installation of the SAA would take place Friday night and Saturday when it would be difficult to get support from Novell if necessary. As an additional backup, PC Tech contacted two other USConnect partners and set up backup support for SAA for the weekend. Three days before the move date, PC Tech held an orientation meeting for all the people who would be involved in the move. Details of the move schedule, people schedule, and procedures for removal and reinstallation were reviewed in detail.

However, not all problems could be anticipated. A week before the move, when most of the heavy construction at the new site had been completed, Connors was finally able to do a site inspection. She found the information about the cabling terminations was inaccurate. New MAUs with the correct connections had to be ordered and tested.

The actual relocation of the networks began on Wednesday at 3 p.m. when PC Tech brought down and tagged four LANs for the movers. The Human Resources LAN was handled separately because of the confidential nature of the information stored on it. On Thursday at noon, the LANs were at the new location and the upgrades and reinstallation began. No Token Ring card failures occurred, although spares had been brought in case, and all the new MAUs and cable plant worked. The upgrade to NetWare 3.11 proceeded normally.

Problems started at 3 p.m. Thursday. The movers had planned to use two different building exits at the old site to load the 60 trucks it would take to complete the move. However, the building management would permit only one exit to be used at a time. This limitation delayed the receipt of the equipment at the new location on Friday and forced the reinstallation of the workstations to continue into Saturday. Connors said: "We had planned to complete the reinstallation by late Friday night, so that we would have Saturday to take care of problems. However, our backup plan included a full schedule for Saturday. We needed it."

In the meantime, trouble started with the SAA install. The SAA server could not find the router. With the help of Novell technical support, (provided on Saturday by the Novell technician who called from a phone booth in a park where a Novell picnic was being held), the IS team identified the problem and reconfigured the software with a new driver. At the same time, the LANtastic to NetWare Lite conversion proceeded without any difficulty.

By 7:30 p.m. Saturday, all the workstations had been reinstalled, tested and marked off on the floor plan. Also, communications with the mainframe had been established. During the three days, Palmieri and the IS team monitored the progress from a command post at the new site. All team members had beepers and check lists, but Palmieri remained the central point of contact.

The best testimony of the success of the move came from John Diehl, manager, Marketing Planning, when he said "When my people came to work on Monday morning, the fact that we had moved was totally transparent as far as their computer services were concerned. Everything they needed was there and working."

The success of the IS move is widely recognized throughout both Transamerica Leasing and PC Technical Services, but improvements can always be made. For one thing, the team should have made a listing of the details of each system at the time of the move and the contents of the bags. The bags should have been taped to the system units or monitors instead of being transported separately. Team members should have left an obvious visual indication that a relocated system had been installed and was working. (Perhaps a large "Completed" sign could be placed on the monitor). They should have kept extra power cords and parallel printer cables as backups when the originals were misplaced. Communications during the move might have

been better if they had had portable cellular phones in addition to the beepers, because it was sometimes difficult to find an available working phone.

In the end, the dedication and determination of the people involved in this project guaranteed its success. Connors summed up the move. "There is a tremendous sense of accomplishment over a job well done. Transamerica really made us feel part of the team, and the communication among all the team members was great. It was a challenge and a lot of work but also a lot of fun. It was just about as perfect as this kind of a project can be."

IF YOUR COMPANY IS PLANNING A MOVE
Make A List

If your company is planning a move, check for the following criteria while selecting a vendor for relocation services.

1. *Experience in computer relocation.* Has the vendor moved companies before? How many? What size? Are they familiar with the logistics of a move? Can they provide references of satisfied clients they have helped move?

2. *Reasonable price.* Is their total cost within budget? Are they providing services which increase the costs but may not add any value, for example extensive diagnostics before the move? Or conversely, are there services that have not been offered but which may be of interest?

3. *Availability of staff.* Is the company large enough to be able to provide the number of people to get the job done within the schedule? In the case of Transamerica Leasing, PC Technical Services provided up to eight people over a four day period.

4. *Organized approach.* Are they experienced in project management and team efforts? Who will be the vendor project manager? Do they use project-management tools? If so, what kind? Can they contribute ideas to make the move go smoothly?

5. *Flexibility and willingness to satisfy your needs.* No matter how many moves a vendor has done, differences make each one special. Does the vendor understand this particularity, and can it make your life easier?

6. *Network knowledge.* It's essential that the vendor understand networks if you are upgrading your networks or changing the topology at the same time that you move. But even if everything is staying the same, specific network experience in your environment is a must.

Contributors

EDITOR

Melanie McMullen is the editor-in-chief of LAN Magazine and Interoperability. She has been involved in the computer industry for six years and has written hundreds of articles on LAN and WAN technology. She specializes in the areas of portable computing and wireless networking. Her work has been published in MacWorld and Cadence magazine as well as in the Computer Security Institute newsletter.

STAFF CONTRIBUTORS

Dave Brambert is editor-in-chief of Stacks magazine and executive editor of LAN Magazine.

Becky Campbell is reviews editor for LAN Magazine.

Michelle McLean has served as copy editor of LAN Magazine.

Patricia Schnaidt has served as editor-in-chief of LAN Magazine.

OTHER CONTRIBUTORS

Nina Burns is president of Creative Networks, a Palo Alto, CA-based, consulting and research firm specializing in electronic messaging systems and applications including e-mail, directory services, workflow automation, and workgroup applications.

Tom Dolan is vice president of sales and marketing for Westcon, a distributor located in Eastchester, NY.

Paul Donohoe is the president of PC Technical Services, the chairman of Gorham Clark, and a founder of USConnect. All three companies provide integration services and support for distributed computing environments in metropolitan New York, Boston, and throughout North America.

Ned Freed is chief development officer at Innosoft International in West Covina, CA. He is also one of the coauthors of the MIME standard.

Sheri Hostetler is editor of the Telemedicine newsletter, a Miller Freeman publication based in San Francisco.

Gary Kessler is a senior member of the technical staff of Hill Associates, a data communications, education, and consulting firm in Colchester, VT.

Cheryl Krivda is a Philadelphia-based technical journalist specializing in data communications.

Lenny Liebmann is a consultant and writer based in Highlands, NJ, who specializes in computer networking.

Howard Marks is a principal of Networks Are Our Lives, a network consulting firm based in Scarsdale, NY. He conducts Windows and LAN training seminars.

Suketu Mehta is a technical writer based in Ridgewood, NJ, who writes about networking in Europe and the United States.

Joel Snyder is a senior analyst with Opus One in Tucson, AZ, a company that specializes in networks and international aspects of information technology.

Peter Stephenson has been an independent consultant in the network industry for 10 years.

Christine Strehlo is a freelance networking writer based in Palo Alto, CA.

Martha Strizich is a technical writer based in Pleasant Hill, CA, who covers the networking and telecommunications industries.

LAN Magazine Glossary of Terms

Professionals ostensibly use jargon to aid communication among peers, but the plethora of obscure terms, invented words, and acronyms serve often serve to confuse not only the uninitiated, but after awhile, confuse the initiated as well. Here is a glossary of networking terms meant to dispel the mystery of network argot.

3+. 3+ was 3Com's network operating system that implemented Microsoft MS-Net file sharing and Xerox's XNS transport protocols. 3Com no longer sells 3+.

3+Open. 3+Open was 3Com's network operating system based on Microsoft's OS/2 LAN Manager. 3Com no longer sells 3+Open.

1Base5. 1Base5 is the implementation of 1Mbps Starlan, which is wired in a star topology.

10Base2. 10Base2 is the implementation of the IEEE 802.3 Ethernet standard on thin coaxial cable. Thin Ethernet or thinnet, as its commonly called, runs at 10Mbps. Stations are daisy-chained and the maximum segment length is 200 meters.

10Base5. 10Base5 is the implementation of the IEEE 802.3 Ethernet standard on thick coaxial cable. Thick, or standard Ethernet, as its commonly called, runs at 10Mbps. It uses a bus topology and the maximum segment length is 500 meters.

10BaseF, 10BaseFO. This is the draft specification for running IEEE 802.3 Ethernet over fiber-optic cable. It specifies a point-to-point link.

10BaseT. 10BaseT is the implementation of the IEEE 802.3 Ethernet standard on unshielded twisted-pair wiring. It uses a star topology, with stations directly connected to a multi-port hub. It runs at 10Mbps, and it has a maximum segment length of 100 meters.

802.1. This is the IEEE standard for hardware-level network management. It includes the spanning tree algorithm for Ethernet MAC-layer bridges and the Heterogeneous LAN Management (HLM) specification for managing Ethernet and Token Ring wiring hubs.

802.2. This IEEE standard specifies Logical Link Control (LLC), which defines services for the transmission of data between two stations at the data-link layer of the OSI model.

802.3 This IEEE standard governs the Carrier Sense Multiple Access/Collision Detection (CSMA/CD) networks, which are more commonly called Ethernet. 802.3 networks operate at varying speeds and over different cable types. See 1Base5, 10Base2, 10Base5, 10BaseF, and 10BaseT.

802.4. This IEEE standard defines the use of the token bus network access method. Token bus networks are sometimes used in manufacturing networks, but are rarely used in office-automation networks.

802.5. This IEEE specification standard defines a logical ring network that uses a token passing access method. It is commonly called Token Ring. It comes in 4Mbps and 16Mbps speeds. It is physically wired in a star topology, with multistation access units, or hubs, as the center, to which workstations, servers, and other network devices are attached. Token Ring runs over shielded twisted-pair, unshielded twisted-pair, and fiber-optic cabling.

802.6. This IEEE specification standard defines metropolitan area networks (MANs). The MAN standard implements a distributed queue, dual-bus access method over a fiber-optic cable plant. Switched Multimegabit Data Services, an emerging high-speed WAN service, can run over a MAN physical network.

802.7. Defined by the IEEE, the 802.7 standard defines broadband LANs. They can carry video, data, and voice traffic. Broadband LANs are constructed of cable television-like components and use RF to transmit information in separate channels in a single cable. They are built using a tree topology. Broadband LANs are rarely used anymore. Do not confuse with Broadband ISDN or wideband networking, which is a term used to denote a wide-area network service with substantial bandwidth, usually in the hundreds of megabits per second.

802.9 The IEEE 802.9 standard defines integrated digital and video networking.

802.11 When finalized by the IEEE, the 802.11 standard will define wireless networking. The standard will encompass many different methods of wireless transmission, including infrared and spread spectrum radio. Many data communications, computer, and telephone vendors are involved in the wireless LAN committee.

A

access method. An access method is the set of rules by which the network arbitrates access among the nodes. Collision Sense Multiple Access Collision Detection and token passing are two access methods used in LANs.

address. An address is a unique identification code that is assigned to a network device, so it may independently send and receive messages.

Address Resolution Protocol (ARP). Within TCP/IP, ARP is the protocol that determines whether a packet's source and destination addresses are in the Data-Link Control (DLC) or Internet Protocol (IP) format. ARP is necessary for proper packet routing on a TCP/IP network.

Advanced Program-to-Program Communications (APPC). APPC is the protocol suite within IBM's Systems Application Architecture that provides peer-to-peer access, enabling PCs and midrange hosts to communicate directly with mainframes. APPC is key for distributed computing within an IBM environment. APPC can be used over an SNA, Token Ring, Ethernet, or X.25 network.

Advanced Peer-to-Peer Networking (APPN). APPN is the network architecture within IBM's Systems Application Architecture that provides for peer-to-peer access among computers. Under APPN, a mainframe host is not required. It also implements concepts such as dynamic network directories and routing in SNA.

American National Standards Institute (ANSI). ANSI is the principal group in the United States for defining standards. ANSI represents the U.S. in ISO, the international standards-making body. Fiber Distributed Data Interface, a 100Mbps network, is one network standard developed by ANSI.

AppleShare. Apple Computer's network operating system designed to run primarily with Macintoshes, but also accommodates DOS and Windows PCs. AppleShare Pro runs under A/UX, Apple's version of Unix, and is a high-performance version of the network operating system.

AppleTalk. AppleTalk is the name of Apple Computer's networking specification. AppleTalk includes specifications for the physical layer as LocalTalk, EtherTalk, and TokenTalk; network and transport functions as Datagram Delivery Protocol and AppleTalk Session Protocol; addressing as Name Binding Protocol; file sharing as AppleShare; and remote access as AppleTalk Remote Access.

application programming interface (API). An API is set of programming functions, calls, and interfaces that provide access to a particular network layer.

application layer. The seventh and uppermost layer of the OSI model, the application layer allows users to transfer files, send mail, and perform other functions where they interact with the network components and services. It is the only layer that users can communicate directly with.

Arcnet. Datapoint designed this 2.5Mbps token-passing, star-wired network in the 1970s. Its low cost and high reliability can make it attractive to those companies on a tight network budget, although it is not endorsed by any IEEE committee. ArcnetPlus is a proprietary product of Datapoint that runs at 20Mbps.

Asynchronous Transfer Mode (ATM). ATM is a method of data transmission used by Broadband ISDN. It is specified as 53-octet fixed length packets that are transmitted over a cell-switched network. Speeds up to 2.2 gigabits per second are possible, and it is capable of carrying voice, video, and data. ATM has been embraced by the LAN and WAN industries, who have proclaimed it as the solution to integrating disparate networks across a large geographic distance. It is also called cell relay.

asynchronous communication server (ACS). An asynchronous communication server is some combination of a computer motherboard, asynchronous modems, and software that enable multiple people to dial out of a LAN. ACSs also provide dial-in service, where users not in the office can use modems to call up their network services in the office. ACSs are also called dial-in/dial-out servers or modem servers.

attenuation. Attenuation is amount of power that is lost as the signal moves over the cable from the transmitter to the receiver. It is a measured in decibels (dBs).

B

backbone. A backbone is the main "spine" or segment of a campus network. Departmental networks are attached as "ribs" to the central backbone.

bandwidth. Bandwidth is the amount of data that can be transmitted over a channel, measured in bits per second. For example, Ethernet has a 10Mbps bandwidth and FDDI has a 100Mbps bandwidth. Actual throughput may be different than the theoretical bandwidth.

bandwidth on demand. A concept in wide area networking in which the user can dial up additional WAN bandwidth as the application warrants. It enables users to pay only for bandwidth that they use, when they use it. Implementing bandwidth on demand requires switched services, such as ISDN or Switched 56 lines.

Basic Rate ISDN (BRI). BRI is an ISDN service that offers two "bearer" channels (B) with a 64Kbps bandwidth that can be used for bulk data transfer plus a "data link" (D) 16Kbps channel for control and signalling information.

blackout. A blackout or power outage is an interruption or total loss of commercial electrical power. Uninterruptible power supplies provide battery-backed up power that will supply electricity during a blackout (while their batteries last).

bridge. A bridge connects two networks of the same access method, for example, Ethernet to Ethernet or Token Ring to Token Ring. A bridge works at the OSI's Media Access layer, and is transparent to upper-layer devices and protocols. Bridges operate by filtering packets according to their destination addresses. Most bridges automatically learn where these addresses are located, and thus are called learning bridges.

Broadband ISDN (B-ISDN). A class of emerging high speed data and voice services for the wide-area network. Switched Multimegabit Data Services and Asynchronous Transfer Mode are two emerging B-ISDN services that will provide megabits and gigabits of bandwidth across a wide-area network.

broadcast. A broadcast message is addressed to all stations on a network.

broadcast storm. In a broadcast storm, network congestion occurs because large numbers of frames are transmitted by many stations in response to a transmission by one station.

brownout. A brownout is an abnormally low voltage on commercial power distribution lines. Power utilities may intentionally produce a brownout when there is near overload demand for power, or natural conditions, such as storms, fires, or accidents, may cause a brownout.

brouter. A brouter is a device that can transparently bridge protocols as well as route them. It is a hybrid of a bridge and a router.

bus topology. A bus topology is a network architecture in which all of the nodes are connected to a single cable.

C

campus network. A campus network connects LANs from multiple departments within a single building or campus. Campus networks are local area networks, that is, they don't include wire-area network services, but they may span several miles.

campus wiring system. A campus wiring system is the part of a structured wiring system that connects multiple buildings to a centralized main distribution facility, local exchange carrier, or other point of demarcation. It is also referred to as a backbone.

Carrier Sense, Multiple Access with Collision Detection (CSMA/CD). Ethernet and 802.3 LANs use the CSMA/CD access method. In CSMA/CD, each network device waits for a time when the network is not busy before transmitting and it detects transmissions already on the wire that were put there by other stations.

cascaded star. A cascaded star topology is a network configuration in which multiple data centers or hubs are constructed for the purposes of redundancy. It is also called a tree topology.

Category 1. The Electronics Industry Association/Telecommunications Industry Association (EIA/TIA) specifies a five-level standard for commercial building telecommuncations wiring. Category 1 wiring is old-style unshielded twisted-pair telephone cable and it is not suitable for data transmission.

Category 2. The EIA/TIA 568 standard certifies Category 2 UTP for use up to 4Mbps. Category 2 UTP is similar to the IBM Cabling System Type 3 cable.

Category 3. The EIA/TIA 568 standard specifies Category 3 UTP for speeds up to 10Mbps, and it is the minimum cable required for 10BaseT. The wire pairs should have at least three twists per foot, but no two pairs should have the same twist pattern.

Category 4. The EIA/TIA 568 standard specifies Category 4 as the lowest grade UTP acceptable for 16Mbps Token Ring.

Category 5. The EIA/TIA 568 standard specifies Category 5 is certified for speeds up to 100Mbps but 155Mbps will be possible. It is suitable for FDDI and other high-speed networks.

cell. A fixed-length packet. For example, Asynchronous Transfer Mode (ATM) uses 53-octet cells.

cell relay. Cell relay is a form of packet transmission used by Broadband ISDN networks. Also called ATM, cell relay transmits 53-octet fixed-length packets over a packet-switched network. ATM is important because it makes it possible to use a single transmission scheme for voice, data, and video traffic on LANs and WANs.

client. A client is a computer that requests network or application services from a server. A client has only one user; a server is shared by many users.

coaxial cable. Coaxial cable has a inner conductor made of a solid wire that is surrounded by insulation and wrapped in metal screen. Its axis of curvature coincides with the inner conductors, hence the name coaxial. Ethernet and Arcnet can use coaxial cable. It is commonly called coax.

concentrator. A concentrator is a multiport repeater or hub that brings together the connections from multiple network nodes. Concentrators have moved past their origins as wire concentration centers, and often include bridging, routing, and management devices.

Connectionless Network Protocol (CLNP). Of the two OSI transport protocols–CLNP and Connection-Oriented Network Service (CONS)–CLNP is more efficient for LANs. Like TCP/IP, it uses datagrams to route network messages by including addressing information in each.

Connection-Oriented Network Service (CONS). Of the two OSI transport protocols–CLNP and CONS–CONS is more efficient for WANs. CONS allows the transport layer to bypass CLNP when a single logical X.25 network is used.

Consultative Committee for International Telegraphy and Telephony (CCITT). The CCITT defines international telecommunications and data communication standards. In March of 1993, the group changed its name to ITU-TS.

Controlled Access Unit (CAU). A CAU is a managed Multistation Access Unit (MAU), or a managed multiport wiring hub for Token Ring networks. Management features include turning ports on and off.

common carrier. A common carrier is a licensed, private utility company that provides data and voice communication services for a fee. For example, Sprint and MCI are common carriers.

Common Management Information Protocol (CMIP). CMIP is the OSI management information protocol for network management. It is not widely implemented.

compression. A technique to "squash" files, making them smaller as to optimize bandwidth utilization. Compression is important for WAN transmission and disk and tape storage.

D

Data Access Language (DAL). DAL is Apple's database query language that is based upon SQL, but it provides far greater functionality.

data dictionary. In a distributed database, a data dictionary keeps track of where the data is located and stores the necessary information for determining the best way to retrieve the data.

Data Encryption Standard (DES). DES is the United States government's standard for encryption, in which data is scrambled and security codes called keys are added, so data cannot be deciphered by unauthorized users.

data-link layer. The data-link layer is the second layer of the OSI model. It defines how data is packetized and transmitted to and from each network device. It is divided into two sublayers: medium access control and logical link control.

database server. A database server is a database application that follows the client-server model, dividing an application into a front end and a back end. The front end, running on the user's computer, displays the data and interacts with the user. The back end, running on a server, preserves data integrity and handles most of the processor-intensive work, such as data storage and manipulation.

DECnet. Digital Equipment Corporation's network system for networking personal computers and host computers. DECnet can use TCP/IP and OSI, as well as its proprietary protocols.

departmental LAN. A departmental LAN is a network that's used by a small group of people laboring toward a similar goal. Its primary goal is to share local resources, such as applications, data, and printers.

directory services. Directory services provide a white pages-like directory of the users and resources that are located on an enterprise network. Instead of having to know a device or user's specific network address, a directory service provides an English-like listing for a user. The OSI's X.500 and Banyan's StreetTalk are examples of directory services.

distributed computing. In a distributed computing architecture, portions of the applications and the data are broken up and distributed among the server and client computers. In the older model, all applications and data resided on the same computer.

distributed database. A database application where there are many clients as well as many servers. All databases at remote and local sites are treated as if they were one database. The data dictionary is crucial in mapping where all of the data resides.

Distributed Queue Dual Bus (DQDB). The medium access method of the IEEE 802.6 standard for metropolitan area networks.

downsizing. Downsizing or rightsizing is the process of porting mission-critical applications from a mainframe to a minicomputer or PC LAN or from a minicomputer to a PC LAN.

Dual-Attached Station (DAS). In FDDI, a DAS connects to both of the dual, counter-rotating rings. Concentrators, bridges, and routers often use DAS connections for fault tolerance. In contrast, a single-attached station is connected to only one ring.

dual homing. In FDDI, dual homing is a method of cabling concentrators and stations in a tree configuration that permits an alternate path to the FDDI network in case the primary connection fails.

Dynamic Data Exchange (DDE). DDE is Microsoft's specification for Windows that enables applications to communicate with each other without human intervention.

E

E-1. In Europe, E-1 is the basic telecommunications carrier, and it operates at 2.048Mbps. In the U.S., the basic carrier is T-1, which operates at 1.544Mbps.

electromagnetic interference/radio frequency interference (EMI/RFI). EMI and RFI are forms noise on data transmission lines that reduces data integrity. EMI is caused by motors, machines, and other generators of electromagnetic radiation. RFI is caused by radio waves.

Electronic Data Interchange (EDI). EDI is a method of electronically exchanging business documents, such as purchase orders, bills of lading, and invoices. Customers and their suppliers can set up EDI networks. EDI can be accomplished through OSI standards or through proprietary products.

electronic mail. E-mail is an application that enables users to send messages and files over their computer networks. E-mail can range from a simple text-based system to a messaging system that accommodates graphics, faxes, forms-processing, workflow, and more.

encapsulation. Encapsulation or tunnelling is the process of encasing one protocol into another protocol's format. For example, AppleTalk is often encapsulated into TCP/IP for transmission over a WAN because TCP/IP is more efficient over a WAN.

end system. In Internet terminology, an end system is a host computer.

End System To Intermediate System (ES-IS). ES-IS is an OSI routing protocol that provides the capabilities for hosts (or end systems) and routers (or intermediate systems) to find each other. ES-IS does not handle the router-to-router protocols; the Intermediate System to Intermediate System protocol does.

Enterprise Management Architecture (EMA). EMA is Digital Equipment Corp.'s umbrella architecture for managing enterprise networks. EMA is a distributed approach.

enterprise network. An enterprise network is one that connects every computer in every location of a company, and runs the company's mission-critical applications.

Ethernet. Ethernet is a 10Mbps CSMA/CD network that runs over thick coax, thin coax, twisted-pair, and fiber-optic cable. A thick coax Ethernet uses a bus topology. A thin coax Ethernet uses a daisy chain topology. Twisted-pair Ethernet uses a star topology. A fiber Ethernet is point-to-point. DIX or Blue Book Ethernet is the name of the Digital Equipment Corp., Intel, and Xerox specification; 802.3 is the IEEE's specification; 8802/3 is the ISO's specification.

EtherTalk. EtherTalk is Apple Computer's implementation of Ethernet.

F

fault management. Fault management, one of the five categories of network management defined by ISO, is the detection, isolation, and correction of network faults.

fault tolerance. Fault tolerance is the ability of a system to continue operating in the event of a fault. You can implement fault tolerance in many places in a network, including in file servers with Novell's NetWare SFT III, in disks with RAID, and in bridges with the spanning-tree algorithm.

fast packet. Fast packet is a technique for asynchronously transferring data across the network.

fiber-optic cable. Fiber-optic cable can be used to transmit signals in the form of light. Glass fiber is composed of an outer protective sheath, cladding, and the optical fiber. It comes in single mode and multimode varieties. Single-mode fiber is more often used in the public-switched telephone network; multimode fiber is more often used in local and metropolitan area networks. Single-mode fiber uses lasers to transmit the light; multimode uses light-emitting diodes.

Fiber Distributed Data Interface (FDDI). FDDI is the ANSI X3T9.5 specification for a 100Mbps network that is logically implemented as dual, counter-rotating rings. A fiber FDDI network can support up to 500 stations over 2 kilometers. FDDI, originally specified to run over fiber, can also operate over shielded and unshielded twisted-pair, although the distances are greatly shortened.

File Transfer, Access, and Management (FTAM). FTAM is the OSI protocol for transferring and remotely accessing files on other hosts also running FTAM.

File Transfer Protocol (FTP). FTP is the TCP/IP protocol for file transfer.

filtering. Filtering is the process by which particular source and destination addresses are prevented from crossing a bridge or router onto another portion of the subnetwork.

firewall. A firewall is an impermeable barrier through which broadcast or other types of packets cannot pass. Routers, not bridges, are used to set up firewalls.

flow control. A router controls the progress of data through the network in a process called flow control. It ensures that other routers are not being congested by a heavy traffic flow, and it will route around congestion points.

forwarding. Forwarding is the process by which a bridge copies a packet from one side of the subnetwork to the other after it has been filtered.

fractional T-1. Many telephone companies and service providers offer fractional T-1 service. In fractional T-1, the 1.544Mbps T-1 bandwidth is divided into 64Kbps increments. Users can order as many channels as they need, but they are not required to purchase the entire 1.544Mbps from the service provider.

fragmentation. Fragmentation is the process in which larger frames from one network are broken up into smaller frames–and into the frame size that is compatible with the network to which they'll be forwarded.

frame relay. Frame relay is the CCITT standard for a low-overhead packet-switching protocol that provides dynamic bandwidth allocation at speeds up to 2Mbps. Frame relay is in its early stages of deployment in the United States. It is considered a second generation X.25 in that it is more efficient.

front-end application. Users present, manipulate, and display data via front-end applications, which are client applications. These applications work with back-end applications, such as a mail or database engine.

G

gateway. In OSI terminology, a gateway is a hardware and software device that connects two dissimilar systems, such as a LAN and a mainframe. It operates at the fourth through the seventh layers of the OSI model. In Internet terminology, a gateway is another name for a router.

global network. A global network spans all departments, campuses, branch offices, and subsidiaries of a corporation. Global networks are international, and bring with them the problems of dealing with multiple languages, cultures, standards, and telephone companies.

Government OSI Profile (GOSIP). GOSIP is the U.S. government's specification for OSI conformance. Some level of GOSIP support is required for all bids made on government projects.

H

heterogeneous network. A heterogeneous network is made up of a multitude of workstations, operating systems, and applications of different types from different vendors. For example, a heterogeneous network may contain 3Com Ethernet adapter cards, Dell 486 PCs, Compaq SystemPros, Novell NetWare, FTP TCP/IP, and an HP 9000 Unix host.

Heterogeneous LAN Management (HLM). HLM is an IEEE 802.1 specification for jointly managing mixed Ethernet and Token Ring networks with the same objects.

High-level Data Link Control (HDLC). HDLC is an ISO standard for a bit-oriented, link-layer protocol that specifies how data is encapsulated on synchronous networks.

High Level Language API (HLLAPI). HLLAPI is a set of tools developed by IBM to help developers write applications that conform to its Systems Application Architecture.

High-Speed Serial Interface (HSSI). HSSI is a standard for a serial link up to 52Mbps in speed over WAN links.

homogeneous network. A homogeneous network is comprised of similar components–one type of workstation, server, network operating system, and only a few applications.

horizontal wiring subsystem. This part of a structured wiring system connects the users' computers in the departments. It is attached to the vertical wiring system. The horizontal wiring system is often copper cable, such as twisted-pair or coax.

hub. A concentrator is a multiport repeater or hub that brings together the connections from multiple network nodes. Concentrators have moved past their origins as wire concentration centers, and often house bridges, routers, and network-management devices.

I

impedance. Impedance is the resistance equivalent for AC, and it affects a network's propagation delay and attenuation. Each protocol and topology has its own impedance standards. For example, 10BaseT has an impedance of 100 ohms to 105 ohms, while 10Base2 has an impedance of 50 ohms.

infrared. Infrared electromagnetic waves are above that of microwaves but below the visible spectrum. Infrared is used for wireless LANs.

intermediate system. In Internet terminology, an intermediate system is a router.

Institute of Electronics and Electrical Engineers (IEEE). The IEEE is a professional society of electrical engineers. One of its functions is to coordinate, develop, and publish data communications standards for use in the United States.

Integrated Services Digital Network (ISDN). ISDN is the CCITT standard for carrying voice and data to the same destination. ISDN specifies 23 "B" 64Kbps channels plus one "D" 16Kbps channel. Although ISDN is not popular in the United States, it is a common method of wide area networking in Europe (especially in the U.K., Germany, and France) and in Japan.

Intermediate System-to-Intermediate System (IS-IS). IS-IS is an OSI routing protocol that provides dynamic routing between routers or intermediate systems.

International Standards Organization (ISO). ISO is a multinational standards-setting organization that formulates computer and communication standards, among others. ISO defined the OSI reference model, which divides computer communications into seven layers: physical, data-link, network, transport, session, presentation, and application.

Internet. The Internet is a collection of more than 2,000 packet-switched networks located principally in the United States, but also in other parts of the world, all linked using the TCP/IP protocol. It links many university, government, and research sites.

Internet Activities Board (IAB). The IAB is the coordinating committee for the design, engineering, and management of the Internet. The IAB has two main committees: the Internet Engineering Task Force (IETF) and the Internet Research Task Force (IRTF). The IETF specifies protocols and recommends Internet standards. The IRTF researches technologies and refers them to the IETF.

Internet Protocol (IP). IP is part of the TCP/IP suite. It is a session-layer protocol that governs packet forwarding.

internetwork. An internetwork is collection of several networks that are connected by bridges and routers, so all users and devices can communicate with each other, regardless of the network segment to which they are attached.

Internetwork Packet Exchange (IPX). IPX is the part of Novell's NetWare stack that governs packet forwarding. This transport protocol is based on Xerox Network System.

interoperability. Interoperability is the ability of one manufacturer's computer equipment to operate alongside, communicate with, and exchange information with another vendor's dissimilar computer equipment.

inverted backbone. An inverted backbone is a network architecture in which the wiring hub and routers become the center of the network, and all subnetworks connect to this hub. In a backbone network, the cable is the main venue of the network, to which many bridges and routers attach.

isochronous transmission. An isochronous service transmits asynchronous data over a synchronous data link. An isochronous service must be able to deliver bandwidth at specific, regular intervals. It is required when time-dependent data, such as video or voice, is to be transmitted. For example, Asynchronous Transfer Mode can provide isochronous service.

J

jitter. Jitter is a form of random signal distortion that interferes with the reception of signals.

L

LAN Manager. LAN Manager is Microsoft's network operating system based on OS/2. It uses NetBEUI or TCP/IP network protocols. LAN Manager supports DOS, Windows, OS/2, and Macintosh clients. Through LAN Manager for Unix, it offers connections to various Unix hosts.

LAN Server. LAN Server is IBM's network operating system that is based on the OS/2 operating system and the NetBIOS network protocol. LAN Server supports DOS, Windows, OS/2, and Macintosh clients.

LANtastic. LANtastic is Artisoft's peer-to-peer, NetBIOS-based network operating system. It supports DOS, Windows, Macintosh, and Unix clients.

leased line. A leased line is a transmission line reserved by a communications carrier for the private use of a customer. Examples of leased-line services are 56Kbps or T-1 lines.

line of sight. Laser, microwave, and infrared transmission systems require that no obstructions exist in the path between the transmitter and receiver. This direct path is called the line of sight.

local area network (LAN). A LAN is a group of computers, each equipped with the appropriate network adapter card and software and connected by cable, that share applications, data, and peripherals. All connections are made via cable or wireless media, but a LAN does not use telephone services. It typically spans a single building or campus.

Local Area Transport (LAT). LAT is Digital Equipment's protocol suite for connecting terminals to an Ethernet network. Because LAT lacks a network layer, it must be bridged in an enterprise network, not routed.

LocalTalk. LocalTalk is one of Apple's physical-layer standards. It transmits data at 230Kbps using Carrier Sense Multiple Action/Collision Detection (CSMA/CD) over unshielded twisted-pair wire.

Logical Link Control (LLC). OSI Layer 2, the data-link layer, is divided into the Logical Link Control and the Media Access Control sublayers. LLC, which is the upper portion, handles error control, flow control and framing of the transmission between two stations. The most widely implemented LLC protocol is the IEEE 802.2 standard.

Logical Unit (LU). IBM's LU suite of protocols govern session communication in an SNA network. LU1, LU2, and LU3 provide control of host sessions. LU4 supports host-to-device and peer-to-peer communication between peripheral nodes. LU6.2 is the peer-to-peer protocol of APPC. LU7 is similar to LU2.

M

mail-enabled applications. Mail-enabled applications are a class of software that incorporates e-mail's functionality, but provides additional services, such as workflow automation, intelligent mail handling, or contact management software.

main distribution facility. In a structured wiring system, the main distribution facility is the portion of the wiring that's located in the computer room. From the main distribution facility extends the campus wiring subsystem, which runs to each building.

management information base (MIB). A MIB is a repository or database of the characteristics and parameters that are managed in a device. Simple Network Management Protocol (SNMP) and Common Management Information Protocol (CMIP) use MIBs to contain the attributes of their managed systems.

Manufacturing Automation Protocol (MAP). MAP is an ISO protocol for communicating among different pieces of manufacturing equipment.

Media Access Control (MAC). The MAC is the lower sublayer of the data-link layer (Logical Link Control is the upper sublayer), and it governs access to the transmission media.

mesh topology. In a mesh network topology, any site can communicate directly with any other site.

Message Handling System (MHS). MHS is Novell's protocol for electronic mail management, storage, and exchange. MHS is the most widely installed e-mail protocol.

Message Handling Service (MHS). MHS is another name for ISO's X.400 protocols for store-and-forward messaging.

Message Transfer Agent (MTA). In ISO's X.400 electronic messaging protocols, the MTA is responsible for storing messages then forwarding them to their destinations. The MTA is commonly implemented as the mail server.

metropolitan area network (MAN). A MAN covers a limited geographic region, such as a city. The IEEE specifies a MAN standard, 802.6, which uses the Dual Queue, Dual Bus access method and transmits data at high speeds over distances up to 80 kilometers.

Microsoft API (MAPI). When using MAPI, application developers can add messaging to any Windows application and the program remains independent from the message storage, transport, and directory services.

mission-critical application. A mission-critical application is one that is crucial to a company's continued operation. As corporations downsize from mainframes, many mission-critical applications are moved to networks.

multicast. Multicast packets are single packets that are copied to a specific subset of network addresses. In contrast, broadcast packets are sent to all stations in a network.

multimedia. Multimedia is the incorporation of graphics, text, and sound into a single application.

multimode fiber. Multimode fiber-optic cable uses light-emitting diodes (LEDs) to generate the light to trans-

mit signals. Multimode fiber is prevalent in data transmission.

multiplexing. Multiplexing is putting multiple signals on a single channel.

Multipurpose Internet Mail Extension (MIME). MIME is an Internet specification for sending multiple part and multimedia messages. With a MIME-enabled e-mail application, users can send PostScript images, binary files, audio messages, and digital video over the Internet.

multistation access unit (MAU). A MAU is a multiport wiring hub for Token Ring networks. IBM calls MAUs that can be managed remotely Controlled Access Units, or CAUs.

N

Narrowband ISDN. Narrowband ISDN is another name for ISDN. Narrowband ISDN offers a smaller bandwidth than the Broadband ISDN services, such as Asynchronous Transfer Mode (ATM) and Switched Multimegabit Data Services (SMDS).

NetBIOS. NetBIOS is a protocol developed by IBM that governs data exchange and network access. Because NetBIOS lacks a network-layer, it cannot be routed in a network, which makes building large internetworks of NetBIOS-based networks difficult. Examples of NetBIOS-based NOSs include IBM LAN Server and Artisoft LANtastic.

NetBEUI. Microsoft's version of NetBIOS is called NetBEUI. It is a protocol that governs data exchange and network access. Because NetBEUI lacks a network-layer, it cannot be routed in a network, which makes building large internetworks of NetBEUI-based networks difficult.

NetWare. NetWare is Novell's network operating system. NetWare uses IPX/SPX, NetBIOS, or TCP/IP network protocols. It supports DOS, Windows, OS/2, Macintosh, and Unix clients. Through NetWare for Unix, users can gain access to various Unix hosts. NetWare versions 4.x and 3.x are 32-bit operating systems; NetWare 2.2 is a 16-bit operating system.

NetWare Loadable Module (NLM). An NLM is an application that resides in the NetWare server and coexists with the core NetWare operating system. NLMs provide better performance than applications that run outside the core.

network. A network is a system of computers, hardware, and software that is connected over which data, files, and messages can be transmitted and end users communicate. Networks may be local or wide area.

network layer. The third layer of the OSI model is the network layer, and it governs data routing. Examples of network-layer protocols are IP and IPX.

Network Driver Interface Specification (NDIS). NDIS is a specification for generic device drivers for adapter cards that is used by LAN Manager networks.

Network File System (NFS). NFS is Sun Microsystems' file-sharing protocol that works over TCP/IP.

network interface card (NIC). A network interface card is the adapter card that plugs into computers and includes the electronics and software so the station can communicate over the network.

network operating system (NOS). A network operating system is the software that runs on a file server that governs access to the files and resources of the network by multiple users. Examples of NOSs include Banyan's VINES, Novell's NetWare, and IBM's LAN Server.

network-aware application. A network-aware application knows that it is running on a network and has file- and record-locking features.

network-ignorant application. A network-ignorant application has no knowledge that it is running on a network. It lacks file and record locking, and cannot guarantee data integrity in a multiuser environment.

network-intrinsic application. A network-intrinsic application knows it is running on a network and takes advantage of a network's distributed intelligence. For example, a client-server database is a LAN-intrinsic application.

noise. Noise is sporadic, irregular or multifrequency electrical signals that are superimposed on the desired signal.

O

Object Linking and Embedding (OLE). OLE is Microsoft's specification for application-to-application exchange and communication. It is more powerful and easier to use than Microsoft's Dynamic Data Exchange (DDE) API, but it is not as widely implemented by independent software vendors.

Open Data-Link Interface (ODI). ODI is Novell's specification for generic network interface card device drivers. ODI enables you to simultaneously load multiple protocol stacks, such as IPX and IP.

Open Shortest Path First (OSPF). The OSPF routing protocol for TCP/IP routers takes into account network loading and bandwidth when moving packets from their sources to their destinations. OSPF improves on the Routing Information Protocol (RIP), but it is not as widely implemented.

open systems. In open systems, no single manufacturer controls the specifications for the architecture. The specifications are in the public domain, and developers can legally write to them. Open systems is crucial for interoperability.

Open Systems Interconnection (OSI). The OSI model is the seven-layer, modular protocol stack defined by ISO for data communications between computers. Its layers are: Physical, Data Link, Network, Transport, Session, Presentation, and Application.

optical drives. Optical drives use lasers to read and write information from their surface. Because of their slow access times, optical drives are used for archiving and other activities that are not as time-sensitive. Several types of optical drives are available. CD-ROMs, or compact disk read-only memory, can be remastered. Information can be written to WORM, or write once, read many, disks only once; they cannot be erased. Data can be written to and removed from erasable optical disks.

OS/2. OS/2 is IBM's 32-bit multithreaded, multitasking, single-user operating system that can run applications created for it, DOS, and Windows.

outsourcing. Outsourcing is the process of subcontracting network operations and support to an organization outside your company.

P

packet. A packet is a collection of bits comprising data and control information, which is sent from one node to another.

packet switching. In packet switching, data is segmented into packets and sent across a circuit shared by multiple subscribers. As the packet travels over the network, switches read the address and route the packet to its proper destination. X.25 and frame relay are examples of packet-switching services.

peer-to-peer. In a peer-to-peer architecture, two or more

nodes can directly initiate communication with each other; they do not need an intermediary. A device can be both the client and the server.

personal communications services (PCS). PCS is a category of applications that includes wireless local and personal area communications for portable and desktop computers, wireless notepad and messaging devices, and wireless office and home telephone systems. The FCC is in the process of allotting both licensed and unlicensed frequency ranges for PCS-based devices.

Physical Layer. The lowest layer of the OSI model is the Physical Layer, and it defines the signalling and interface used for transmission media.

point-to-point. A point-to-point link is a direct connection between two locations.

Point-to-Point Protocol (PPP). PPP provides router-to-router and host-to-network connections over asynchronous and synchronous connections. It is considered a second-generation Serial Line Internet Protocol (SLIP).

Presentation Layer. The sixth, or Presentation Layer, of the OSI model is responsible for data encoding and conversion.

Primary Rate ISDN (PRI). PRI ISDN is a T-1 service that supports 23 64Kbps B channels plus one 16Kbps D channel.

propagation delay. Propagation delay is the time it takes for one bit to travel across the network from its transmission point to its destination.

protocol. A protocol is a standardized set of rules that specify how a conversation is to take place, including the format, timing, sequencing and/or error checking.

proxy agent. A proxy agent is software that translates between an agent and a device that speaks a different management information protocol. The proxy agent communicates the data to the network manager.

public data network (PDN). A PDN is a network operated by a government or service provider that offers wide area services for a fee. Examples are networks from British Telecom and Infonet.

Q

query language. A query language enables users to retrieve information. Structured Query Language (SQL) is one example.

R

Redundant Array of Inexpensive Disks (RAID). RAID 1 is disk mirroring, in which all data is written to two drives. In RAID 2, bit-interleaved data is written across multiple disks; additional disks perform error detection. A RAID 3 disk drive has one parity drive plus an even number of data drives. Data is transferred one byte at a time, and reads and writes are performed in parallel. Like RAID 3, RAID 4 has a dedicated parity drive, but the data is written to the disks one sector at a time. Also reads and writes occur independently. In RAID 5, the controllers write data a segment at a time and interleave parity among them. A segment is a selectable number of blocks. RAID 5 does not use a dedicated parity desk. It offers good read performance, but suffers a write penalty. RAID 1, 3, and 5 are appropriate for networks.

remote MIB (rmon). Rmon defines the standard network monitoring functions and interfaces for communicating between SNMP-based management consoles and remote monitors, which are often called probes.

Remote Operations Service Element (ROSE). ROSE, an OSI Application-Layer protocol, supports interactive applications in a distributed open systems environment.

Remote Procedure Call (RPC). An RPC is a set of conventions that governs how an application activates a process on another node on the network and retrieves the results.

repeater. A repeater is a Physical Layer device that regenerates, retimes, and amplifies electrical signals.

requirements analysis. A requirements analysis is the process through which you define and evaluate the business needs of your network system.

request for proposal (RFP). An end-user company issues an RFP document that asks systems integrators and manufacturers to bid on their network designs and specifications.

request for information (RFI). An end-user company issues an RFI document to ask systems integrators and manufacturers to propose and design a system that will fulfill the corporation's business requirements.

Request For Comment (RFC). An RFC is the Internet's notation for draft, experimental, and final standards.

return on investment (ROI). Calculating an ROI enables MIS shops to gauge the network's success from a business profit-and-loss standpoint. Calculate a ROI by subtracting the total cost of the network from the total benefit.

ring topology. In a ring topology, the network nodes are connected in a closed loop. Information is passed sequentially between active stations, and each one examines or copies the data and finally returns it to the originating station, which removes it from the network.

risk analysis. A risk analysis is the process by which a company analyzes the business and technology risks of installing a new system.

RJ-11. An RJ-11 is a four-wire modular connector that is used by the telephone system.

RJ-45. An RJ-45 is an eight-wire modular connector that is used by 10BaseT Ethernet and some telephone systems.

roll back. A database application's ability to abort a transaction before it has been committed is called a roll back.

roll forward. A database's ability to recover from disasters is called a roll forward. The database reads the transaction log and re-executes all of the readable and complete transactions.

router. A router is a network-layer device that connects networks using the same Network-Layer protocol, for example TCP/IP or IPX. A router uses a standardized protocol, such as RIP, to move packets efficiently to their destination over an internetwork. A router provides greater control over paths and greater security than a bridge; however, it is more difficult to set up and maintain.

Routing Information Protocol (RIP). RIP is the routing protocol used by most TCP/IP routers. It is a distance-vector routing protocol, and it measures the shortest distance between the source and destination addresses by the lowest "hop" count.

S

sag. A sag is a short-term drop (up to 30 seconds) in power-line voltage that typically is in the region of 70 percent to 90 percent of the nominal line voltage.

server. A server is a computer that provides shared resources to network users. A server typically has greater CPU power, number of CPUs, memory, cache, disk storage, and power supplies than a computer that is used as a single-user workstation.

Serial Line Internet Protocol (SLIP). SLIP is used to run IP over serial lines, such as telephone lines.

Sequential Packet Exchange (SPX). SPX is Novell's protocol for the transmission of data in sequence.

session. A session is a communications connection between two nodes.

session layer. The fifth OSI layer, the Session Layer, defines the protocols governing communication between applications.

shielded twisted-pair (STP). STP is a pair of foil-encased copper wires that are twisted around each other and wrapped in a flexible metallic sheath to improves the cable's resistance to electromagnetic interference.

Simple Mail Transfer Protocol (SMTP). SMTP is TCP/IP's protocol for exchanging electronic mail.

Simple Network Management Protocol (SNMP). SNMP is a request-response type protocol that gathers management information from network devices. SNMP is a de facto standard protocol for network management. Two versions exist: SNMP 1 and 2. It provides a means to monitor and set configuration parameters.

single-attachment station (SAS). In FDDI, a single-attachment station is one that is connected to only one of the dual counter-rotating rings. Workstations and other non-critical devices are normally connected using SAS, which are less expensive than dual-attached stations.

single-mode fiber. Single-mode fiber uses lasers, not light-emitting diodes, to transmit signals over the cable. Because single-mode fiber can transmit signals over great distances, it is primarily used in the telephone network, and not for LANs.

SNA mainframe gateways. An SNA mainframe gateway is a hardware and software device that connects a LAN to an SNA mainframe. It translates between the different systems, making the PC look like a 3270 terminal to the SNA host, so the PC user can access mainframe applications, files, and printers.

source-explicit forwarding. Source-explicit forwarding is a feature of MAC-layer bridges that enables them to forward packets from only those source addresses specified by the administrator.

source routing. Source routing is normally used with Token Ring LANs. In source routing, the sending and receiving devices help determine the route the packet should traverse through the internetwork. The route is discovered via broadcast packets sent between these two points.

source-routing transparent (SRT). Source-routing transparent addresses the coexistence of Ethernet, Token Ring, and FDDI. A SRT bridge passes both source routing and transparently bridged data. The bridge uses source-routing to pass packets with the appropriate embedded routing information, and transparently bridge those packets that lack this information.

spanning-tree algorithm. The spanning-tree algorithm is an IEEE 802.1D technique for configuring parallel MAC-layer Ethernet bridges to increase redundancy. The spanning-tree algorithm manages the illegal loop created by the redundancy of having dual bridges.

star topology. In a star topology network, the nodes are connected in a hub and spoke configuration to a central device or location. The "hub" is a central point of failure.

standby power supply (SPS). A standby power supply is a backup power device that is designed to provide battery power to a computer during a power failure. A SPS experiences small interrupts during switch-over to battery operation.

Station Management (SMT). SMT is part of the FDDI specification, and it defines how to manage nodes on the FDDI.

StreetTalk. StreetTalk is Banyan's distributed global naming and directory service for its network operating system, VINES.

Structured Query Language (SQL). SQL is an IBM and ANSI standard query language for extracting information from relational databases.

structured wiring. Structured wiring is a planned cabling system which systematically lays out the wiring necessary for enterprise communications, including voice and data. IBM's Cabling System and AT&T Premises Distribution System are two such structured wiring designs. A structured wiring system is made up of horizontal, vertical, and campus subsystems.

A horizontal subsystem is the system between the wiring closets and the users' systems. A vertical subsystem or backbone includes the wiring and equipment from the wiring closets to the central equipment room. The campus subsystem interconnects the buildings to a central distribution facility, local exchange carrier, or other point of demarcation.

superserver. A superserver is a computer that is designed specifically to serve as a network server. It typically has several CPUs, error-correcting memory, large amounts of cache, large amounts of redundant disk storage, and redundant power supplies. It is designed to provide high speed, high capacities, and fault tolerance.

surge. A surge is a short term (up to 30 seconds) rise in power-line voltage level.

Switched 56. A Switched 56 service is a dial-up connection that uses bandwidth in 56Kbps increments. A user can order a maximum of 24 channels from the telephone service provider, for a maximum bandwidth of 1.5Mbps.

Switched Multi-Megabit Data Service (SMDS). SMDS is a high-speed metropolitan area network service for use over for T-1 and T-3 lines. SMDS' deployment is being stalled by the enthusiasm for Asynchronous Transfer Mode, although SMDS can run in conjunction with ATM.

Synchronous Data Link Control (SDLC). SLDC is IBM's bit-synchronous link-layer protocol. It is similar to HDLC.

Synchronous Optical Network (SONET). SONET will establish a digital hierarchical network throughout the world that will enable you to send data anywhere and be guaranteed that the message will be carried over a consistent transport scheme. The existing telephone infrastructure is digital but is designed for copper lines; SONET is digital and has been designed to take advantage of fiber. SONET offers speeds up to 2.5Gbps.

synchronous transmission. A transmission wherein the events occur with a precise clocking.

Systems Application Architecture (SAA). SAA is IBM's set of rules for computer communications and application development. SAA was designed to help create programs that will run on a wide variety of IBM computing equipment.

Systems Network Architecture (SNA). IBM's protocols for governing terminal-to-mainframe communications. It is IBM's older architecture.

systems integrator. A systems integrator is a company who is paid to combine disparate pieces of technology into a unified, working system for an end-user company.

T

T-1. The CCITT specifies a four-level, time-division multiplexing hierarchy for the telephone system in North

America. T-1 provides 24 channels of 64Kbps bandwidth, for a total bandwidth of 1.544Mbps. A T-1 circuit can transport voice, video, data, and fax. T-1 service sold in 64Kbps increments is called fractional T-1.

T-2. T-2 is the equivalent of four T-1s, and it offers 6.3Mbps of bandwidth. Each T-2 link can carry at least 96 64Kbps circuits. T-2 is not a commercially available service, but it is used within the telephone company's hierarchy.

T-3. A T-3 circuit carries in one multiplexed signal stream the equivalent of 28 T-1 circuits. It provides 44.736Mbps of bandwidth. T-3 is not widely used for LANs.

Technical Office Protocol (TOP). TOP is the OSI protocol stack for office automation; it is not widely implemented.

Telnet. Telnet is the TCP/IP protocol for terminal emulation.

terminal emulation. A terminal emulator makes a computer of a different type appear to a host as a node in the host environment.

time domain reflectometer (TDR). A TDR is a troubleshooting device that is capable of sending signals through a cable to check continuity, length, and other attributes.

token. A token is an electronic character sequence that mediates access on a Token Ring or Token Bus network.

token passing. Token passing is a network access method that requires nodes to possess the electronic token before transmitting their frames onto the shared network medium. Token Ring, Token Bus, and FDDI use token-passing schemes.

Token Ring. Token Ring is the IEEE 802.5 specification for a 4Mbps or 16Mbps network that uses a logical ring topology, a physical star topology, and a token-passing access method. It works with UTP, STP, and fiber optic cable. Each ring can have up to 256 stations.

transceiver. A transceiver is a device for transmitting and receiving packets between the computer and the wire. The transceiver is usually integrated directly onto the network adapter card.

Transmission Control Protocol/Internet Protocol (TCP/IP). TCP/IP is the protocol suite developed by the Advanced Research Projects Agency (ARPA), and is almost exclusively used on the Internet. It is also widely used in corporate internetworks, because of its superior design for

WANs. TCP governs how packets are sequenced for transmission on the network. IP provides a connectionless datagram service. The term "TCP/IP" is often used to generically refer to the entire suite of related protocols.

transparent bridging. Transparent bridging connects similar LANs and is usually used with Ethernet. In transparent bridging, when the station transmits a frame, that frame does not know what path it will take. Instead, the bridges determine the best path at the time the frame is sent. In contrast, in source routing, the path is determined at the start of the transmission, rather than frame by frame.

transport layer. The transport layer is the fourth layer of the OSI model, and it provides reliable end-to-end data transport, including error detection between two end user devices. Examples of transport protocols are the Internet Protocol (IP), Sequenced Packet Exchange (SPX), and Transport Protocol Class 0 (TP0).

Transport Protocol Class 0, Class 4 (TP0, TP4). These protocols are OSI transport protocols. Transport Protocol Class 0 is a connectionless transport protocol for use over reliable networks. Transport Protocol Class 4 is a connection-based transport.

Trivial File Transfer Protocol (TFTP). TFTP is a simplified version of FTP, or the TCP/IP file transfer protocol.

tunneling. The process of encasing one protocol in another's format is called tunneling. For example, AppleTalk packets are often enveloped in TCP/IP packet formats for transmission on an enterprise network. Tunneling is also called encapsulation.

twisted-pair. Twisted pair is type of copper wiring in which two wires are twisted around one another to reduce the amount of noise absorbed. The Electronics Industry Association/Telecommunications Industry Association (EIA/TIA) specifies a five-level standard for commercial building telecommunications wiring. Category 1 wiring is old-style unshielded twisted-pair telephone cable and is not suitable for data transmission. Category 2 is for use up to 4Mbps; it resembles IBM Cabling System Type 3 cable. Category 3 UTP is specified for speeds up to 10Mbps, and it is the minimum cable required for 10BaseT Ethernet. Category 4 is the lowest grade UTP acceptable for 16Mbps Token Ring. Category 5 is certified for speeds up to 100Mbps, but it can handle speeds of up to 155Mbps. Category 5 cable is suitable for FDDI and other high-speed networks.

two-phase commit protocol. In a distributed database, a two-phase commit protocol ensures data integrity by asking the multiple database engines for permission before committing each transaction.

Type 1. The IBM Cabling System specifies different types of wire. Type 1 is a dual-pair, 22 American Wire Gauge (AWG) cable with solid conductors and a braided shield. It is a type of shielded twisted-pair.

Type 2. Type 2 is the IBM Cabling System's specification for a six-pair, shielded, 22 AWG wire used for voice transmission. It is the same wire as Type 1, but has an additional four-pair wire.

Type 3. Type 3 is the IBM Cabling System's specification for a single-pair, 22 or 24 AWG, unshielded twisted-pair wire. It is common telephone wire.

Type 5. Type 5 is 100/140 micron fiber; IBM now recommends 125 micron fiber.

Type 6. Type 6 wire is two-pair, stranded 26 AWG wire used for patch cables.

Type 8. Type 8 wire is a two-pair, 26 AWG, shielded cable without any twists; it is commonly used under carpet.

U

undervoltage. In an undervoltage condition, a lower-than-usual power-line voltage lasts from several seconds to several hours.

uninterruptible power supply (UPS). A UPS is a power conditioning and supply system that affords protection against short-term power outages. A UPS rectifies the incoming AC line voltage to DC, which is then applied to batteries. An inverter, driven by DC power, supplies AC voltage for equipment that requires conditioned power. During outages, the converter is driven by battery power.

Unix. Unix is a 32-bit multitasking, multiuser operating system. Versions of Unix are available for nearly every type of computer platform. Unix was initially popular in universities and research labs, but it is now the basis of many corporate applications. Since its purchase of Unix Systems Labs, Novell owns the license to Unix.

unshielded twisted-pair (UTP). UTP is a pair of foil-encased copper wires, twisted around each other. UTP is classified into several levels of wire quality suitable for different transmission speeds (see "Category").

user agent (UA). In X.400 mail systems, the user agent is the client component that provides the X.400 envelope, headers, and addressing. The user agent sends the messages to the X.400 mail server, or Message Transfer Agent, which then routes the messages to their destinations.

User Datagram Protocol (UDP). UDP is the connectionless transport protocol within the TCP/IP suite. Because it does not add overhead, as the connection-oriented TCP does, UDP is typically used with network-management applications and SNMP.

V

value-added reseller (VAR). Also called an integrator, a VAR is an independent company that resells manufacturers' products and adds value by installing or customizing the system.

VAX. Digital Equipment's brand name for its line of minicomputer and workstation hardware is VAX.

vertical wiring subsystem. The vertical wiring subsystem is the part of the structured wiring system that connects the campus wiring system to the departmental wiring system. It runs in a building's risers.

VINES. Banyan's NOS based on a Unix core and TCP/IP protocols. VINES supports DOS, Windows, Mac, and OS/2 clients and is especially popular in large enterprise networks. Its crowning feature is StreetTalk, its distributed directory service.

virtual circuit. A virtual circuit is a shared communications link that appears to the customer as a dedicated circuit. A virtual circuit passes packets sequentially between devices.

Virtual Terminal (VT). VT is the OSI terminal-emulation protocol. A terminal-emulation application makes one computer appear to a host as a directly attached terminal.

virus. A virus has the ability to reproduce by modifying other programs to include a copy of itself. Several types of viruses exist. Bacteria or rabbits do not explicitly damage files but do reproduce and eat up disk or processor space. A logic bomb lies dormant in a piece of code or program until a predefined condition is met, at which time some undesirable effect occurs. A password catcher mimics the actions of a normal log on but catches user IDs and passwords for later use. A Trojan horse is a program that appears to function but also includes an unadvertised and malicious feature. A worm scans a system for available disk space in which to run, thereby tying up all available space.

V.21. V.21 is the modem standard for the trunk interface between a network access device and a packet network. It defines signalling data rates greater than 19.2Kbps.

V.22, V.22 bis. V.22 is a 1200-bps duplex modem for use in the public-switched telephone network and on leased circuits. V.22bis is a 2400-bit modem that uses frequency division multiplexing for use on the public telephone network and on point-to-point leased lines. (The CCITT uses "bis" to denote the second in a series of related standards and "ter" to denote the third in a family.)

V.32, V.32 bis. V.32 are two-wire duplex modems operating at rates up to 9600bps (with fallback to 4800bps) for use in the public telephone network and on leased lines. V.32 bis offers speeds in increments of 4800bps, 7200bps, 9600bps, 12,000bps, and 14,400bps.

V.42 error correction, V.42 bis data compression. The V.42 error-correction standard for modems specifies the use of both MNP4 and LAP-M protocols. V.22, V.22 bis, V.26 ter, and V.32 bis may be used with V.42. With V.42 bis compression, data is compressed at ratio of about 3.5 to 1, which can yield file-transfer speeds of up to 9600bps on a 2400-bps modem. Manufacturers can provide an option that will allow a V.42 bis modem to monitor its compression performance and adjust the ratio accordingly.

V.35. Prior to 1988, V.35 was a modem specification that provided data transmission speeds up to 48Kbps. V.35 was then deleted from the V-Series Recommendations.

VMS. VMS is Digital Equipment's proprietary operating system for the VAX.

vulnerability analysis. A vulnerability analysis is a type of risk analysis in which you calculate the effects of a project's success or failure on your overall business.

W

wide area network (WAN). A WAN consists of multiple LANs that are tied together via telephone services and/or fiber optic cabling. WANs may span a city, state, a country, or even the world.

Windows. Microsoft's popular 16-bit GUI that runs on top of DOS. Windows 4.0, code-named Chicago, will be a 32-bit OS that integrates DOS and Windows. Windows for Workgroups is Microsoft's peer-to-peer network that uses a Windows interface and NetBIOS communications.

Windows NT. Microsoft's "New Technology" is the company's 32-bit, multitasking operating system that includes peer-to-peer file sharing. Windows NT Advanced Server provides high-end networking services. Cairo is Microsoft's code name for its next generation Windows NT.

wireless LANs. A wireless LAN does not use cable to transmit signals, but rather uses radio or infrared to transmit packets through the air. Radio frequency (RF) and infrared are the most commonly used types of wireless transmission.

Spread spectrum is used to access the low-frequency RF in the Industrial, Scientific, and Medical (ISM) bands. Most wireless LANs use spread spectrum transmission. It offers limited bandwidth, usually under 1Mbps, and users share the bandwidth with other devices in the spectrum; however, users can operate a spread spectrum device without licensing from the Federal Communications Commission (FCC). High-frequency RF offers greater throughput, but it is used less often because it requires an FCC license for the right to transmit.

Infrared may also be used as a wireless medium, and has greatest applicability for mobile applications due to its low cost. Infrared allows for higher throughput–measured in several megabits per second–than spread spectrum, but it offers more limited distances. Infrared beams cannot pass through walls.

wiring closet. A wiring closet is a room or closet that is centrally located and contains operating data-communications and voice equipment, such as network hubs, routers, cross connects, and PBXs.

workflow software. Workflow software is a class of applications that help the information worker manage and route his or her work. It is also called groupware or workgroup software.

X

X Window System (X). X Window System, developed by MIT, is a graphical user system most often implemented on Unix systems. The Open Software Foundation's implementation of X Window is Motif. Sun and HP use a version called OpenLook.

X.25. X.25 is the CCITT and OSI standard for packet-switching networks that provide channels up to 64Kbps.

Public and private X.25 networks can be built. In the United States, common X.25 networks are British Telecom, AT&T, CompuServe, and Infonet.

X.400. X.400 is the OSI and CCITT standard for store-and-forward electronic messaging. It is used for large enterprise networks or for interconnecting heterogeneous e-mail systems. X.400 divides an electronic mail system into a client, called a User Agent, and a server, called a Message Transfer Agent. Message Stores provide a place to store messages, submit them, and retrieve them. Access Units provide communication with other device types, such as telex and fax. Distribution Lists are routing lists.

X.500. X.500 is the OSI and CCITT specification for directory services. For computer users, a directory service provides a function similar to the function the telephone company's white pages provides telephone users. Using a directory service, computer users can look up easily the location of resources and other users.

Xerox Network System (XNS). XNS is Xerox's data-communication protocol; it is the basis for the IPX/SPX network protocols used in NetWare.

Index